PERPLEXITY AND ULTIMACY

PERPLEXITY AND ULTIMACY

METAPHYSICAL THOUGHTS FROM THE MIDDLE

WILLIAM DESMOND

STATE UNIVERSITY OF NEW YORK PRESS

Published by
State University of New York Press, Albany

For information, address State University of New York
Press, State University Plaza, Albany, N.Y., 12246

Production by Diane Ganeles
Marketing by Theresa Abad Swierzowski

Library of Congress Cataloging-in-Publication Data

Desmond, William, 1951–
    Perplexity and ultimacy : metaphysical thoughts from the middle /
William Desmond.
        p.   cm.
    Includes index.
    ISBN 0-7914-2387-5 (alk. paper). — ISBN 0-7914-2388-3 (pbk. :
alk. paper)
    1. Metaphysics.   I. Title.
BD111.D44   1994   94-17003
110—dc20   CIP

10 9 8 7 6 5 4 3 2 1

This book is dedicated to
Maria, William Óg, Hugh, and Oisín

Between extremities
Man runs his course;
A brand, or flaming breath,
Comes to destroy
All these antinomies
Of day and night;
The body calls it death,
The heart remorse.
But if all these be right
What is joy?

No longer in Lethean foliage caught
Begin the preparation for your death
And from the fortieth winter by that thought
Test every work of intellect and faith,
And everything that your own hands have wrought,
And call those works extravagance of breath
That are not suited for such men as come
Proud, open-eyed and laughing to the tomb.

From W. B. Yeats, *Vacillation*

Contents

Preface   ix

Chapter 1.   Being Between: By Way of Introduction   1

Chapter 2.   Being at a Loss: On Philosophy and the Tragic   27

Chapter 3.   The Idiocy of Being   55

Chapter 4.   Agapeic Mind   103

Chapter 5.   Perplexity and Ultimacy   167

Chapter 6.   Agapeic Being   199

Index   259

Preface

We live in an age of perplexity. Undoubtedly also, we live in an age in flight from perplexity. How can one say this, when the advances of scientific knowing accumulate by the day? Is this not satisfying enough testament to our indomitable curiosity and will to know? Are we not moving inexorably to more and more complete knowledge, driven ever onward by perplexity, not by flight from it?

It is true. Our knowledge of things grows, there is hardly a thing that escapes our curiosity, we have devised efficient means for probing this thing, that thing. We can look forward to knowing more and more. And yet we are still disquieted. In all this expanse of knowing, we are missing something, and we know it, even when we deny it.

What is this perplexity? A prevalent notion is that perplexity is the same as curiosity, and that a disciplined harnessing of our intellectual powers will solve all problems, resolve all curiosity. But this, I believe, is not perplexity at all. Suppose you insist that perplexity is just such curiosity. There is still another perplexity, beyond all determinate cognition. This perplexity is more elusive, more worrying, more indeterminate and resistant to technical mastery. This perplexity stirs a disturbing mindfulness at the heart of our being, bringing us to arrest before the enigma of being.

We might know everything about things, but we might know nothing about this enigma. Perplexity is in another dimension to determinate cognition. One might say it flanks our determinate cognition on the extremes. At one extreme, perplexity is prior to definite curiosity about this and that thing, as an indeterminate opening to being as other to us, and as arousing as yet undetermined thought. At the other extreme, perplexity succeeds definite cognition as the disquieted mindfulness that being in its otherness has not been conceptually mastered by this cognition. Perplexity precedes determinate curiosity and exceeds determinate cognition.

This excess itself perplexes us, and perhaps will always perplex us. Moreover, this precedent opening of mindfulness is itself exceeding perplexing, since relative to the rest of things, it is unprecedented. Human mindfulness, in the fullness of its range before the enigma of being, and in the quality of its troubled thought, is unprecedented. There is nothing quite like it in the rest of nature. Some will argue, I know, that our mindfulness is simply a refinement of the adjustment to things we share with other animals. No doubt much of our knowing serves such adaptation. But the *disproportion* of our mindfulness, the excess of our perplexity gives the lie to this reduction. The reduction is itself in fugue from that perplexity and its disquiet. Ironically, the fugue from perplexity could not be at all, had not perplexity in a more ultimate sense made possible the definite curiosity and determinate cognition, of which the theory of adaptation is one instance.

One major desire in this work is to explore what this disproportionate mindfulness is. The perplexity in question might better be called "metaphysical perplexity." This is distinguished from scientific and common sense curiosity in that it asks questions about what precedes and exceeds the determinate intelligibilities of science and common sense. We are fugitive from perplexity because perplexity is intolerably perplexing, in so far as it *does not fit* into the determinate intelligibilities of science and common sense. Normally we think that to be is to be determinate and that to be determinate is to be intelligible. But there are indeterminacies of being that resist the categories of science and common sense, and which are not for that reason merely unintelligible. Nor are they merely indefinite, again as if they lack intelligibility. These indeterminacies of being are more than determinate, are overdetermined. We might call them "overdeterminacies of being." They exceed every determinate category, but yet incite our further perplexed thinking, just in this exceeding.

In a way, our flight from perplexity makes strange sense, given our insistence that all intelligibility is *not* perplexing. For what happens in train of this insistence? We are forced to shore up the clarity of our intelligibility by incessant denial of the groping perplexity out of which the intelligibility emerges. And then we forget how astonishing it is that the intelligible is intelligible *at all*. Why not unintelligibility, senselessness? That intelligibility is intelligible at all is not itself an item of determinate intelligibility. The question is in another dimension, as is the astonishment. Like the unprecedented disproportion of human mindfulness, and the astonishing enigma of the being there of beings, it, too, is not properly minded.

I believe we must reflect on the significance of these overdeterminacies of being. For our very perplexity concerning perplexity can lead to the exact opposite to flight, namely, the precipitation of the metaphysical mindfulness that will ask those questions at the boundary of determinate intelligibility.

Perplexity about perplexity precipitates the question of ultimacy. Of this question we are also evasive. We live in an age of perplexity, not because we have heroically followed our perplexity about ultimacy, but precisely because we have not followed. We live in an age of perplexity, precisely because we are *not* perplexed by ultimacy.

Is our perplexed mindfulness shadowed by the question of ultimacy? How is it? What is this question? This I want to explore. Since we live in an anti-metaphysical age in which many professional philosophers find even the question of ultimacy embarrassing, it is no easy task to turn on that shadow and welcome it into converse. But converse with it we must. Those who prefer to face forward resolutely towards the neon sun of scientific enlightenment will wonder if we are talking with nothing, or perhaps with ourselves, or our own shadow. They would have to turn from *that* sun to understand that the shadow cast by the question of ultimacy is thrown by an *other* sun. Scientific enlightenment will see only a blank emptiness in the sky, and will not see that this blank emptiness is also a shadow of the sun they do not see. Relative to the blank emptiness, we seem to lack even *our own* shadow. This lack should give us pause, make us wonder whether, after all, something ultimate is being missed. Let there be emptiness in the heavens, let even our shadow be dissolved on earth, still our perplexity is not dissolved. It is a seedling of foreboding that something is amiss, that perhaps we are remiss.

If this seems cryptic, it is because it is cryptic, and the signs are difficult to interpret. This happens to be true of our encounter with everything important. Initially it is perplexing and makes no sense to us. I hope to make some sense. But my mode of making sense will not be just the statement of some univocal thesis, and the production of univocal argument and evidence. In a work complementary to this, I have tried to develop my understanding in as systematic a fashion as is possible, and appropriate to the matters at issue.[1] But I believe there is also a necessary nonsystematic side to philosophy. Granting this other side, the present work consists of an interlocking set of metaphysical meditations in which I return again and again to perplexity about ultimacy.

Or rather it is the perplexity about ultimacy that returns again and again, often when we most think we have at last put it in place. Thought takes form in the between: Now I circle around a tangled issue, now I take this angle, now that, now a theme ruminated on earlier returns in a new light and context, now a sudden breakthrough of new insight is given to one,

---

1. *Being and the Between* (Albany: SUNY Press, 1995). I should say that in *Being and the Between* I distinguish astonishment and perplexity. For strategic reasons that distinction is not to the fore in the present work; nevertheless it is very important, with significant systematic repercussions, which *Being and the Between* explores.

or a new saying is vouchsafed, or indeed a new darkness descends on one. In real philosophizing one can be exalted by thinking, one can be humbled by it. One can be exalted and humbled at one and the same time.

The different chapters can be briefly described. Chapter 1 is by way of introduction. The introduction is both existential and systematic: existential relative to the context in life out of which my reflections on the between emerged; systematic relative to a succinct statement of the metaxological view of being. Like any philosopher I have hesitations about speaking in the first person singular. Yet given what I want to say, it is necessary to speak in the singular voice, even when one voices themes whose import extends beyond the singular. This chapter manifests some of the traces of its own origin.

Chapter 2 takes up the issue of perplexity relative to the experience of being at a loss, as manifested in the tragic. Again, while we speak from the between, our perplexity extends us to the extremes, and mindfulness of the tragic is of great power to face us with our flight from perplexity, and with the inescapability of a mindfulness beyond the determinate intelligibilities of science and common sense. The experience of being at a loss in face of the tragic forces us to rethink the very nature of philosophical mindfulness.

Chapter 3 takes up what I call the "idiocy of being," where "idiocy" is used with some reference to its Greek sense of the "intimate," the "private." I want to say that idiotic being is not at all merely idiotic, just as the idiosyncratic is not merely idiosyncratic. I explore the enigma of selfhood, at the edge of determinate intelligibility, as well as the field of communication, within which the intimacy of being is shaped. Familiar themes from a variety of traditional ways of understanding selfhood and singularity are thought anew in light of the idiocy of being.

Chapter 4 is devoted to what I call "agapeic mind." Here I examine different formations of mindfulness, objective, subjective, what I call "erotic mindfulness" as a foil to agapeic mind. I address the question: Does mindfulness transcend itself out of lack or indigence, or from a perplexing fullness that is overdetermined? I try to explore the power of mindfulness to be radically self-transcending, and to be mindful for the other as other. The exploration makes reference to many of the major understandings of mind in the tradition of philosophy. And yet again the chapter is meditative, and takes on a character other than expository or interpretative or argumentative, when the theme dictates it. The meaning of mindfulness cannot be confined to a technical problem in professional epistemology but extends to our entire sense of being in its otherness.

Chapter 5 is on ultimacy and perplexity. One might have gotten the impression that earlier chapters deal with more intractable issues, while agapeic mind, so to say, sunnily affirms the power of self-transcendence to be for the other as other. This would be too simple by far, and the recurrence of perplexity in its more resistant moods can never be obviated. The significance of honest skepticism is addressed relative to the ground of reason. I make an approach to questions about groundlessness, contingency, absurdity, God. It is in this chapter that a greater effort begins to state something about the ultimate as other to us, most familiarly perhaps in terms of the thought of God. The thought makes a call on us that we be truthful in as ultimate a fashion as possible. And this requirement is barely touched, if touched at all, by our power in constructing formally correct arguments.

This concern is continued in the final chapter on agapeic being. I seek to address the question of ultimacy in relation to the issue of being and the good. What is the being of the good? What does it mean to say "to be is good." "It is good"—what is the meaning of this startling saying? Is something of ultimacy given here for thought? Agapeic being might be seen as the ontological counterpart or partner to agapeic mind, though it would be very wrong to counterpart them simplistically as complementary poles. They always are involved in community, though the community between them has to be traversed with radical perplexity, not immune from visitations by darkness and desolation. And yet we cannot consent ultimately to darkness and desolation as the final word.

I am conscious that, at times, I am trying to give some definition to what up to now has lacked a name, or perhaps lost its name—such as the idiocy of being, or agapeic mind. Of course, I do try to address other more familiar views. But I have had the feeling of moving into unexplored territory. I do not say this in order to stake some claim to originality. Sometimes I sensed that the territory I moved in was wild. Sometimes I had the intimation that perhaps paths might have been there once, and that our modern flight from metaphysical perplexity led to overgrowth and the obscuration of ancient ways. If much of what I say seems to me presently nameless, let there be more ancient names, and I will rejoice if they are reentered in the book of the living.

I want to thank William Eastman, director of SUNY Press, for his great encouragement and support over the years. I did some work on this book (as well as *Being and the Between*) in the academic year 1992–1993, while a Fulbright Research Fellow, as well as Visiting Professor, at the Higher Institute of Philosophy, Katholieke Universiteit Leuven. Again I want to thank the Fulbright Commission in Belgium, especially Mrs Margaret Nicholson and Mrs Alice Allington for their hospitality and help. I also want to thank Professor Carlos Steel, President of the Institute, both for his generous support and valued friendship. I would like to mark my gratitude to Finula Collins and Michael Commane for the hospitality of their houses in Ireland, the first in Inchydoney, West Cork, the second in Castlegregory, Kerry. Some of the present reflections took shape in those places, and owe something to the places, as well as to the generosity of these friends. I owe a debt of gratitude that cannot be measured to my wife Maria, and to my children, William Óg, Hugh, and Oisín. I dedicate the book to them.

Chapter 1 was originally an essay of intellectual autobiography, introducing the volume of CLIO, vol. 20, no. 4, summer 1991, devoted to discussion of my work. I thank the editor, Clark Butler for permission to reproduce. Chapter 2 appeared in *Tragedy and Philosophy*, ed. N. Georgopoulos (London: Macmillan, 1993).

Chapter 1

Being Between:
By Way of Introduction

1. *Ecce Homo!* What a depth of affrontery in Nietzsche's self-apotheo-sis! How we squirm before it! I see Aristotle swinging away in distaste. I fancy Spinoza loudly whispering—*Caute!* I hear Kant hissing—*Schwärmer!* I imagine Hegel's face stony with conceptual embarrassment. Can one, dare one talk about oneself, diffident about the disdain of the fathers?

What is Nietzsche's provocation? Philosophers are averse to advancing their singular selves right to the fore of the picture. We would fade into the neutral, public universal. We are anxiously equivocal about saying "I think." Let Descartes claim "I think therefore I am" as his first indubitable truth, nevertheless we show ingrained reluctance to identify our being with our thinking. Instead the "I think" seeks its home in "consciousness in general." The "I am" becomes "being in general"—the indigent of Hegel's categorial logic.

Can "I am," "I think" be given a modulation different to the Cartesian or idealistic one? Outside self-apotheosis, beyond self-sublation, I will try to be honest—something impossible. This is already a lie. But I will try.

I want to say: I think. I want to say: I am. But I cannot quite. Philo-sophical uneasiness gnaws. Why? One can stress the I; one can stress the thought. Stress the latter and the I masks itself behind the universal. Stress the former and the universal dissolves into the confession of personal idio-syncrasy. In one way or other, philosophers have always been between these poles. The unavoidable unease springs from the tension of their togetherness. One wants to be true to both, but they tug against each other.

The mask of the universal is public, hence in strain with the mask of thinker as singular. Hegel might stand for the first; Nietzsche for the second.

Nevertheless, both thinkers, and others too, can be read as *between* the two masks and indeed being both at once. Thus Socrates: a very singular self presenting himself as the representative of the rational ideal, the universal. He apologizes for himself as a philosopher, and one can only properly apologize for oneself; nevertheless his self-apology is for a way of being in quest of the ideal that would be a universal standard for all, for none. He philosophizes in between.

I have managed to begin without talking too directly about myself. But already *in medias res* the idea of "being between" comes to manifestation. In what follows I, too, must find a middle between merely idiosyncratic particularity and anonymous universality. Since the idea of being between is central to my thought and being, I revert to myself. I see my thought as concerned with this idea of being between, in the existential and systematic senses I will outline. I begin with the first.

2. I was born in Ireland and lived there for the first twenty-three years of my life.—I am now 40[1]—whether a Dante-esque middle I cannot say. My being Irish shapes my thought. My family background contains no philosophical prefigurements; and I can offer no convincing sociological explanation for why I philosophize. But there was a strong religious influence in my life, both in my family and in the wider society. I grew up in the Middle Ages, an Irish Catholic, fostered on a sense of the mystery of God and God's ways, on a sympathy for the rejected and the outsider whom we cannot judge not to be God's favored, fostered, too, on an esteem that God's creation, nature, was good. I cannot identify the piety I inherited with Hegel's unhappy consciousness, though there were traces of the latter. The sense of divine transcendence from the Catholic tradition was balanced by a pagan appreciation of the mystery of nature itself, the sensuous being-there of the world in its sometimes unbearable beauty, its reassuring persistence and its elegiac evanescence.

When as a boy I studied the poetry of the English Romantics, especially Wordsworth, there was no abstraction in the latter's sense of one's trembling delight in and before nature. No feeling enforced a dualistic opposition between the beauty of the world and the transcendent mystery of God. The two flowed into each other. When later I read and prayed the Psalms, I was opened to the same in the sublime songs of David. I still cannot see an affirmation of God's transcendence as a downgrading of the astonishing beauty and goodness of the world. I cannot accept the Hegelian or Marxist or Nietzschean critique of transcendence; most certainly not the latter two who

---

1. This first appeared in 1991

enforce a choice between this world and God's transcendence. Staying true to the between implies a rejection of that enforcement. I still ponder the possibility that only the latter transcendence, suitably understood, allows us to grant the value of particular things, just in their intimate particularity. One rises on a bright morning with the darkness blown away, and it is hard not to think that the world is an ever fresh marvel, a miracle of absolute particularity. That esteem is still with me, though time can wear the ability to see what is there and to sing and to praise it.

But growing up was not rhapsody. I recall being between two extremes: mathematics and poetry. The study of mathematics, physics, and mechanics was mind-opening. I was deeply impressed by the power of ordered thinking which these disciplines embodied. Even then I remember once asking my physics teacher—he had just set out on the blackboard an astonishing system of intricate equations—why the laws governing light were thus so and not otherwise. The curt answer I received: "Why is the grass green?" My teacher answered a question with another question which dismissed the first question.

But I was asking about the ground of nature's lawfulness, though I did not then know it, nor did my teacher. I know now that I was asking a metaphysical question about physics. The question came *spontaneously*—I was not corrupted by the tradition of philosophy or ontotheology or "metaphysics of presence." What at fifteen did I know about these things? Nothing. I was just struck into astonishment and perplexity that natural phenomena would be governed by what seemed like such mathematically precise formulae. While impressed by mathematical physics, my mind was never confined within mathematical order.

Being between mathematics and poetry, between mathematical science and metaphysics came home to me in the troubled reading of *Hamlet*. The study of *Hamlet* deeply influenced me around the age of fifteen with the brooding power of thought as metaphysical. Hamlet lived a condition of uneasy inwardness that the ordered precisions of mathematics cannot encompass. Out of the selfless consolations of the mathematical universal, Hamlet brought me back to the singularity of the troubled mind. The time was out of joint for Hamlet; the middle was fractured. In that fractured middle, Hamlet was a thinker of despair; ultimately despair is radically singular. Hamlet says: "What should such fellows as I do crawling between earth and heaven? We are arrant knaves all; believe none of us" (*Hamlet* III, i, 128–130). There is no geometry of this "crawling between." In the fractured middle, he was a thinker of the extremes, a thinker also of a different elusive thread of providence beyond despair, for there's significance in the fall of a sparrow. I still think that tragic art precipitates a deeper metaphysical perplexity than even the marvel of mathematical or quasi-mathematical order in the world. But the tension of these two will return.

When I was seventeen, I spent a little less than a year as a novice in the Dominican order, religious brotherhood of Aquinas. I took and still take religion with ultimate seriousness. I considered becoming a priest because of this. I do not know what I was then like. I recently met a fellow novice who had persevered in the priesthood—an accidental meeting in Rome, twenty years later. It was like meeting a ghost, a ghost that reminded me of a ghost of myself. He said I always argued that one had to keep "the whole picture" before one and not get lost in trivial details; he also said I had a kind of passionate impatience.

I had a certain kind of faith then. To have faith, however, can be dangerous; it can degenerate into a kind of spiritual arrogance. Would I have developed in that direction? I think spiritual arrogance is the thing to be rooted out of the soul. At some level I am sure that I thought I was loved by God. Where did this come from? From the fact that my mother and father loved me? From the fact that I was intellectually talented? But I never knew I was intellectually gifted until to my own surprise I won a scholarship at the age of ten. I had initially refused to be in the scholarship class (affectionately known as the "schol class") and had taken myself back to the ordinary class. Without official permission I simply decamped back to the ranks of academic averageness. I was returned unwillingly to the "schol class." And to my surprise I was successful.

I was never unintelligent. But I never really felt that there was any special status to this. I do not think it was intellectual talent that drove me to philosophy, even though I knew I was not untalented. Again I performed well in exams across the divide between the sciences and the humanities. I could just as easily have been a scientist as a philosopher—if intellectual talent was all that was at stake. In fact, when I initially signed up for my college degree, I enrolled in the engineering faculty because my scores in mathematics and physics and chemistry was so high, and the conventional advice was that an engineering degree was superior to an arts degree. Superior here meant: you will make money. This was after I left the Dominicans. I was accepted for engineering in a restricted class. I did not stay beyond a few weeks but transferred to the liberal arts faculty. Why? I simply decided to follow my heart's desire at that time—to study poetry, possibly write some.

I wanted to do a degree in English to allow me to read the poets. I also took philosophy. Within the first year I discovered that the way poetry was taught did not answer the impatience of my thinking. I wanted to think, and poetry was presented as some ineffable gift that seized a few favored ones, recognizable only to the initiated. I now admit that great creators, in poetry, in philosophy, elsewhere, may be marked by enigmatic gifts. But this view is easily used in the self-serving connivance of mediocre talents. I found that my teachers of poetry did not seem capable of protracted thinking; perhaps I was unjust to them. Great poetry exhibits a spiritual seriousness which can shame the thought of some philosophers. But then poetry was presented as if it had nothing to do with thought.

This approach is stupid, but it was the fashionable anti-intellectual imagism of the day. I did not lose interest in poetry. I took a joint honors degree, a double major in English and philosophy, and later continued my interest in philosophical aesthetics. But at the age of eighteen, I suspect, I dedicated myself to philosophy with a fervor not entirely unlike the religious seriousness I exhibited the previous year in the Dominican novitiate. This is why I say it was not just intellectual talent that brought me to philosophy. It was the search for an answer to some of the fundamental questions of being. The drive to such answers is not a purely intellectual matter. And when one is appropriately involved as a singular I, the mind itself becomes activated in modes that are not merely intellectual. Thinking undergoes an existential transfiguration.

Hence, a plurality of different modes of being between that marked my development: Religiously I was between Catholicism and a certain pagan celebration of the earth. Then I was between religion and philosophy in that the upsurgence of the need to think drove me out of simple faith, and yet the merely analytical intellect had to be overcome to open up the richness of being that faith previously offered. I was between science and art, the engineer and the poet: the engineer with compass and log tables could not match the poet in speaking to the soul, but then the poet's singing seemed to soothe and finally stifle hard thought.

3. I dwell briefly on the philosophical import of some of these modes of being between. First consider the tension between religion and science. I mentioned my exposure to Wordsworth's poetry of nature. As set forth through that poetry, and Wordsworth's is only one example, albeit very powerful, nature comes to appearance as charged with value. It may even be the sign of an other origin, the concretion of an energy of being that moves us to wonder and to rejoice. By contrast, scientific reason seems to make cold the world, depersonalize the thereness of things, discharge all energy in impersonal forces in motion. It devalues the world in the literal sense of extruding from consideration all questions of value inherent in the being of things themselves. The ultimate result can be a nihilistic scientism. This nihilism is more pervasive than is realized. Reason seems to rob thought and life of an ultimate ground of value.

The world is charged with the grandeur of God, Hopkins wrote. If the development of mind disenchants the world, one may find oneself between God's world and the impersonal universe of scientific reason. One might acquiesce in this disenchantment, or take flight from it by arresting thought.

If one wants to remain true to the between, something other than acquies-
cence or flight is needed. One will have to reconsider the matter Nietzsche
raises in connection with nihilism. In response to nihilism Nietzsche saw the
need to recharge the world through what he calls a "transvaluation of values." I do not endorse Nietzsche's way of doing this; I do agree about the
urgency of what he sought. There are many places in my work where this is
an absolutely central matter for thought.

Some of the fundamental problems of modernity were understood very
profoundly by the great Romantics. It may be fashionable now to dismiss
Romanticism, and there are difficulties with some of its characteristic strategies, in the main, I believe, because of the ambiguous heritage of idealism
which is still with us. The Romanticism that is dismissed is a sentimentalized, bowdlerized Romanticism. Moreover, the issue at stake here is not merely
aesthetic. It concerns the very ground of value, the issue of being and the
good. These matters will return.

Why not turn one's back on scientific thought? Why not throw in one's
lot with poetry? I could not do this, perhaps partly because I always found
something unacceptable about the anti-intellectualism of the poets in Ireland. Their fear of thought or their inability to think was sometimes expressed as a pseudo-superior irritation with the merely analytical intellect.
We murder to dissect. Yes, this is true. There are forms of thought that are
homicidal. The question then is whether there are forms of thought that are
beyond murder. Philosophy, I believed, was capable of that thinking. If I ever
was to write poetry, it would have to be poetry that did not call for a
sacrificium intellectus. The poet and the priest were in a strange collusion in
Ireland: For the many, faith; for the cultured elite, poetry; for none, real
philosophy. I mean real hard thinking about the great issues of the spirit,
which are also the great issues of poetry and religion.

It is not enough just to say: I believe philosophy is capable of this
thinking. One has to do the thinking: not sing invocations to possibility,
but work to bring forth the realization of the promise. In *Philosophy and its
Others*[2] (more so than in *Desire, Dialectic and Otherness*[3]), I have tried to
enact what I call a "plurivocal philosophy": a philosophical thinking that is
not reductive of all the voices of meaning to one overriding logical voice; a
thinking that listens to what is other to more standard forms of philosophical
thinking; a philosophy that lets its own voice be reformulated under the

---

2. William Desmond, *Philosophy and its Others: Ways of Being and Mind* (Albany:
SUNY Press, 1990).
3. William Desmond, *Desire, Dialectic and Otherness: An Essay on Origins* (New
Haven: Yale University Press, 1987).

impact of philosophy's own significant others, like religion, science, art. Plurivocal philosophy tries to get beyond all this sterile caricaturing. A thinker has to have something of the poet, priest, scientist in him all together.

Hence, in *Philosophy and its Others* I sometimes speak as a philosophical poet or poetic philosopher. This is what I call: "thought singing its other." Here we need to be as much on guard about *philosophers* as about poets. For there are philosophers who *collude* with the poets to enforce the stereotypical opposition of poetry and philosophy. Readers of *Philosophy and its Others* will know that I take writing very seriously. The philosopher is as much a guardian of language as is the poet, and as respectful of the word as the priest claims to be. What else has the philosopher but words. "Words, words, words," says Hamlet (*Hamlet* II, ii, 195); this is the condition of the self. I refuse to concede that there is one warranted way of writing philosophy. There is no Platonic paradigm of writing written in heaven, and to which the professional philosopher has to conform.

Every act of genuine thought is an adventure, an attempt to say. The form of the saying is the very articulation of what is being said. A genuine act of philosophical thinking is such that it is almost impossible to separate form and content. When we summarize a thinker's doctrine we have performed just that separation. We have packaged the original articulation of thought, and made it currency to be passed around the economy of mind. The singularity of great thinkers becomes the more evident the closer we get to their living thought, and the more we also find it impossible conceptually to package this thought.

It is a cliché one hears: He writes well (take Santayana, as an example), but he is a literary philosopher, not a hard thinker. As if to be a hard philosopher you had to be a barbaric writer. This is nonsense, of course. This is to be taken in by the smoke and mirrors of *another* philosophical rhetoric posing as an anti-rhetoric. Really good writing is the last emergence of painful and struggling thought. *Ars est celare artem.* Some philosophers speak as if poetry were soft; yes there is a soft poetry—this is bad poetry. Similarly there can be a soft literary philosophy and this can be mediocre philosophy. There can also be a putatively hard philosophizing which one discovers, once having pierced the crust of concepts, to be an almost empty formalism. The thinness of thought of some hard technical philosophy, evident once translated into nontechnical terms, sometimes disconcerts one with the final softness of hardness.

A philosopher, like Nietzsche, is attacked as a "mere poet." What is a "mere" poet? Such jibes are complete *philosophical misunderstandings* of the spiritual greatness possible for poetry. We philosophers need the courage to write properly. But there is no a priori transcendental form of writing. There is no absolute authority dictating that we think or write in this or that form. This freedom, too, is related to what I call "plurivocal philosophy."

4. Even in my undergraduate studies in philosophy (1969–1972) at University College Cork there was a certain element of being between. At that time, talk about the rapprochement of Continental and analytical philosophy was not as fashionable as it was to become. Academic philosophy in Ireland epitomized this divide: some academics, and especially those in Trinity College Dublin looked to England, to Oxford and Cambridge; other academics looked to the Continent. The National University, of which University College Cork was a constituent college, was a secular institution, though traditionally it was thought to be Catholic, while Trinity was Protestant. Many academics in the National University looked to places like Paris and Louvain, instead of Cambridge and Oxford. As an undergraduate I was extensively exposed to both traditions, as well as to the history of philosophy and Aristotelian-Thomism. The bent of my soul was towards Europe. But since I wrote and thought in English, inevitably this meant some confrontation with Anglo-Saxon philosophy. I would say that as an undergraduate I had as much of David Hume as Thomas Aquinas, as of Heidegger and Sartre.

Eventually—and this was all done like a peregrinator or sleepwalker, since I did not altogether know what I was doing—I sailed into this between by not going to Great Britain or Europe for graduate studies. I came to the United States to study in a department with a reputation for European philosophy! America provided the home outside Ireland where the divide between England and the Continent could be—I do not say reconciled—but passed by. The bent of my soul is still towards the Continental tradition, since I think it is more deeply continuous with the great tradition of philosophy and is more radically self-conscious of the project of philosophy, more radically questioning about the whole nature of the philosophical enterprise.

For my M.A. in Cork, with Garret Barden as my supervisor, I wrote a dissertation on the concept of imagination in Collingwood. When I came to Penn State, I discovered that Hegel's idealism was much meatier than Collingwood's, presenting an enormous challenge to thought. This was coupled with intensive reading in the tradition of metaphysics. I found a shift of interests from aesthetics to metaphysical questions. I could have written a dissertation on Hegel but did not. I felt a certain urgent sense to locate where I stood, or might stand. With Carl Vaught as director, I wrote a dissertation called "The World as Image and Original." In retrospect this was the first draft of *Desire, Dialectic and Otherness*. The major ideas of the latter were already extensively articulated in the dissertation.

My main concern could be put thus: I was especially concerned with the attenuation of otherness and transcendence in modern philosophy, and most radically in the Hegelian system. I have never been able to accept the caricatures of heteronomy, transcendence, imputed to Plato or to the Medievals, whether by Hegel or Nietzsche or other post-Kantians. The great speculative thinkers of the classical and medieval world are still of interest to me. I think the Kantian and post-Kantian critique of metaphysics may be helpful for the workhorses of metaphysics, like Wolff and Baumgarten, where metaphysics has already been packaged into scholastic manageability. But the thorough-breds of pre-Kantian metaphysics cannot be dismissed so quickly as "dog-matic metaphysicians." Any thinker worth his salt tries to plumb skepticism to its deepest and most acid-filled abyss—deeper even than Kant, who drew back in alarm from the extremities of skepticism. There is something laugh-able about thinking of Plato as a dogmatic metaphysician, as if he were an academic scholastic.

Yet I recognized that there was a fundamental truth to the modern turn to the self, and in a qualified sense to transcendental philosophy generally. I wanted to take something like a transcendental starting point, in a generous sense, but not end up in an immanent idealism, where the other as other is redefined merely as a functional term of the "for-self." I wanted to pass through the self and rethink what I took as the legitimate metaphysical impulses of premodern philosophers. I did not, and still do not want to offer historical studies of thinkers. I am interested in the matter in question, and in those thinkers who have profoundly thought the matter in question. In-evitably then my work has a strong systematic side: the philosophical per-plexities themselves are the focus, not the interpretation of figures, though this last is not excluded.

In *Desire, Dialectic and Otherness* a certain hermeneutics of desire pro-vides the dynamic vehicle for this project. The book offers an unfolding of thought, structured around the fourfold sense of being that I will outline in the next section. I was especially self-conscious of the fact that some of the great metaphysicians like Plato could not be interpreted in accord with an ideal of the merely abstractive intellect. Hence my emphasis on desire has very little to do with an empiricist understanding. It recalls, though it does not finally duplicate, the Platonic emphasis on philosophical eros. My intent was not to end up with a hermeneutics of desire which was the metaphysical apotheosis of the *for-the-self*. I wanted to stress desire as a metaphysical open-ing to being, being in its otherness, as well as the self-development of the human being in its own ineluctable search for its own wholeness. I thought that this opening to the other needed a fundamental reversal of some of the modern presuppositions about otherness and transcendence. This reversal could not be persuasively performed by a scholarly study of the texts of other philosophers. The *Sache selbst* had to be addressed. Only if thus addressed, could we be in a strong position to read the stated views of the other philosophers.

This has been my general philosophical practice since: On the one hand, a dedication to the systematic and nonsystematic exploration of the thing itself, regardless of what philosophers have said about the matter. This is very difficult, for it sometimes means thinking without any guides, thinking about the otherness of the matter at issue, with nothing to guide one but a desire for honesty before being and a willingness to let that otherness confound one, unsettle one. Then, on the other hand, a need for a deeper hermeneutical self-consciousness about the essential metaphysical possibilities of the philosophical tradition. This means trying to get to know as best as possible the thought of the great philosophers; to think and rethink their ideas—not as dead schemas in a museum of thought but as the provocative and living thought of the best minds from whom we continue to learn. The thought of a genuine philosopher has a certain inexhaustibility. Hence my more systematic and independent work is complemented by a variety of studies of other thinkers. Sometimes the systematic and the hermeneutical come together. In developing a position in itself, one ought to have in one's bones a hidden knowledge of the philosophical possibilities of millennia.

5. In *Desire, Dialectic and Otherness*, I developed a fourfold sense of being, a brief outline of which may be helpful. This provides a recurrent systematic framework for my ideas. It will also indicate why I chose the theme of being between to name the existential matrix which nourishes the more systematic project. There is no claim to a closed system. System is for me an after-the-fact articulation of the matter that must be allowed to take its own shape. System does not dictate to the unfolding matter what form it should take. This means that system is always open to its own possible dismantling, especially in so far as the system is open within itself to the acknowledgment of modes of being and mind that are other to complete conceptualization.

This is important because despite the strong systematic side to my work, there is an equally strong side which takes system to the limit, stands at the edge of all system. We sometimes need modes of saying that are other to systematic saying. These sayings seem idiotic to system, where idiotic carries connotation of the Greek "*idios*"—the private, the intimate, what is not completely available in terms of the public universal. The between has an idiotic as well as systematic articulation. The first corresponds to the mask of singularity, the second to the mask of universality, the two masks of the philosopher, mentioned at the beginning. Their tension is evident in *Philosophy and its Others*, but a careful reading of *Desire, Dialectic and Otherness* will uncover the same thing.

I develop what I call the "metaxological sense of being," in contrast to the univocal, the equivocal, and the dialectical senses. This idea derives from the Greek *metaxu*, meaning middle, intermediate, between, and *logos*, meaning discourse, speech, articulate account. The metaxological sense of being is concerned with a *logos* of the *metaxu*, a discourse of the "between," the middle. This *metaxu* is suggested, for instance, by the discussion of eros in the *Symposium*, though I do not subscribe to everything said there. Let me make the following points.

Eros articulates the self, and if we grant Socrates' account, eros initially lacks what it seeks. But the restlessness of eros in the middle cannot stop short at any finite entity or concern; ultimately it is a restlessness for the ultimate. The pursuit of the ultimate itself testifies to a positive power of being in the self; it cannot be mere lack that drives desire beyond lack; it is the original power of being that constitutes the self as openness to what is other to itself; the dunamis of eros reveals a self-transcending openness to transcendence as other to desire itself.

There is possible an understanding of the *metaxu* which imposes no static definition on the middle. The latter becomes that in which and through which we have our being, but the articulating of our desiring being in the middle shows itself as an ineluctable quest of ultimacy. The middle as a dynamic field and the desiring energizing of our being there point beyond themselves. Here I would exploit Augustine's description of the double nature of his own quest for ultimacy: *ab exterioribus ad interiora, ab inferioribus ad superiora*; from the exterior to the interior, from the inferior to the superior. I interpret this to mean the following. In the middle of things—the exteriors—we come to know the dunamis of our own being as an interior middle, a mediating self-transcending power of openness. This is the first movement. The second movement is: in the interior middle, within the self-transcending urgence of desire, there is an opening to an other, more ultimate than ourselves. We are the interior urgency of ultimacy, this is ultimacy as the superior. This superior ultimate is not identical with our own erotic self-mediation; it is irreducible to us and mediates with us—the inferior—through the agapeic excess of its own unequalizable pleni-tude. So, in fact, this second movement also allows the possibility of a double mediation: our own erotic quest of the ultimate; the ingression of the ultimate as a superior other that interplays with the middle out of its own excessive transcendence.

I cannot do justice to such a difficult matter here. But I am particularly concerned not to collapse the ultimate in its transcendence into human self-transcendence. Yet I do not want to underplay the importance of the latter. Hence to articulate the relation of self and what is other to it, we need a certain complex balance of unity and plurality, identity and difference, sameness and distinction. Hegel's answer—the middle is dialectical—offers a powerful articulation of the interplay of self and other, but I think that in the end it collapses the difference between the ultimate in its transcendence and our own self-transcendence. The middle as metaxological, as I develop this, is such as to make impossible this collapse, for it articulates an irreducibly double intermediation.

If our intermediate condition of being is inadequately interpreted either by totalizing holisms of the sort attributed to Hegel, this does not mean we have to opt for the discontinuous plurality we find in deconstructive thought, indeed in Wittgensteinian pluralism. There is more openness and recalcitrant otherness in the middle than totalizing holism grants, more continuity and community of being than deconstructive pluralism allows. I concede the contemporary concern with difference and plurality, nevertheless I am uneasy with the sometimes sterile obsession with discontinuity. Our very encounter with otherness and discontinuity forces us to raise the question of the meaning of the community of being. Deconstructive thought very obviously, and Wittgensteinian pluralism less overtly, perpetuate the post-Cartesian and post-Nietzschean taboo on the question of ultimacy. This is, in part, attributable to an intellectual anxiety that is reactive to idealistic totalisms, as if the latter held an unchallengeable monopoly on the thought of the ultimate. It does not, as my invocation and questioning of Hegel is intended to indicate. If the middle is a certain community of being that sustains otherness, we must go beyond a philosophy of merely asserted difference, as well as any metaphysics of totalizing unity, for this ultimately suppresses differences and hence also real community.

I define the metaxological view in its dynamic interrelation to three other senses of being, namely, the univocal, equivocal, and dialectical senses, each of which has bearing on the question of ultimacy.

The first sense, the *univocal* puts the stress on simple sameness, hence on unmediated unity. The ontological sense of univocity is to be found in all metaphysics indebted to Parmenides, from Plato to Spinoza and Hegel. The logical sense of univocity pervades all the heirs of Aristotle with his insistence that to be intelligible is to be determinate: to be intelligible is to be a determinate *tode ti*. Examples could be multiplied, but modern positivism could be mentioned as making a reductive use of the ideal of univocity against metaphysics. I do not deny a role to univocity in any hermeneutics of being, but alone it is not enough, and it can wreak havoc if erected into the ideal before which metaphysics must bend the knee. It does not do proper justice to the complex differences we need to take into account, and forgets the great truth of a deeper side to Aristotle when he said: *to on legetai pollachōs*, being is said in many ways. I have already noted some inadequate consequences of univocity with respect to the question of the ultimate.

The *equivocal* sense of being, by contrast, calls attention to aspects of unmediated difference, or perhaps zones of tension and ambiguity that resist any simple reduction to univocal unity. Thus, a feeling for the equivocal often helps us recognize the rich ambiguity in the intermediate being of things. Of course, we can so cling to equivocity that we turn our backs on any effort to think though the ambiguities. We fail at absolutely univocal mediation, so we give up on mindful mediation. Content with an endlessly reiterated equivocity, we claim to celebrate sheer plurality, but this is devoid of the promise of any deeper relatedness. Plurality then does not condition community, but becomes a dispersal of beings that is merely fragmenting. While the deconstructionist is extremely critical of the philosophical ideal of univocal unity, in a reactive move he risks this kind of equivocal thinking. Even the effort to *raise* the question of the ultimate is sharply dismissed as mere nostalgia for the univocal absolute of the "metaphysics of presence," or "ontotheology."

Say what you may, the question of ultimacy will not vanish into either its univocal reduction or its equivocal deconstruction. The third sense of being, the *dialectical* sense, can be stated relative to univocity and equivocity, though it is more complex than either. The dialectical sense recognizes the self-transcending dynamism of thought in its restless surpassing of limits, whether they be the fixations of being by univocal thought, or the dissolute, unmediated differences of equivocal thought. The dialectical sense knows the impossibility of avoiding the question of the ultimate, if we remain true to this self-surpassing dynamism of thought. This is one of Hegel's great insights. We are here also allowed to see the vacillation between univocity and equivocity that marks Kant's antinomies. Kant's thought of the antinomies anxiously oscillates between the Scylla of univocal reduction and Carybdis of equivocal deconstruction. Kant remains dissatisfied with both extremes, sought an indirect way beyond them, but he never quite could get beyond them with a clear intellectual conscience. In his own way, Kant was aware of the indeterminate ontological perplexity, but clung to the ideal of univocal intelligibility out of fear that this indeterminacy might be merely equivocal.

Philosophy must not run away from the potentially antinomic character of thinking. The antinomic character of completely determinate thinking, in fact, provides a major impetus to perplexity about ultimacy. Finite, univocalizing thought in the long run generates its own self-contradiction. Dialectical thinking does not run away from this antinomic condition but tries to think it through more radically. Hence it shares something with deconstructive thought, in that both raise serious questions about the finality of the ideal of univocal unity and any privileged stress on simple unmediated sameness. But there are different forms of dialectic, not all merely negative. Negative dialectic of the sort espoused by Adorno shares quite a lot with Derrida's deconstructive thinking in their courting of equivocity against univocity, and in their refusal of anything like the Hegelian speculative unity. I am not advocating the latter, but it is not clear if the former transcend an endlessly repeated oscillation back and forth between univocity and equivocity. A dialectic which is not merely negative must be diffident with respect to any merely equivocal thought.

I put it this way: ambiguity is not only to be acknowledged, it is to be mediated, *thought through* in as mindful a way as is possible. Unlike deconstructionist thought, the dialectical sense of being suggests the genuine possibility of mediating equivocal difference. One reason why we cannot rest with unmediated difference is that it engenders a sense of alienating antithesis or dualistic opposition. One can see here the power of dialectical thinking to subvert the dualistic oppositions, for instance between time and eternity, said to beset the tradition of metaphysics. Dualistic opposition and equivocal difference subvert themselves, as does mere univocity, if we think the matter through. The possible togetherness of the opposites, indeed the passing of one side into the other, is opened up by the dialectical sense.

The fundamental difficulty here concerns the precise character of this "togetherness." This togetherness defines the community of being, of the self and the other in their likeness and in their difference. To be in the middle is to be articulated in and by this togetherness. We cannot say what the middle is unless we can say something about this togetherness of beings. Again both the middle and the togetherness are dynamic—dynamic relatings of beings that themselves are energized by the original dunamis of being. A fundamental limitation I find with the dialectical sense, and this I find in Hegel and other idealist dialecticians, is that it encourages a tendency to interpret *all* mediation primarily in terms of *self-mediation*. The togetherness of self and other and their intermediation is, in the end, seen in the light of a certain privileging of self-mediation. This privileging of dialectical self-mediation continues the traditional metaphysical apotheosis of thought thinking *itself*, and so is shadowed by the ideal of univocity that it seems to transcend so trenchantly.

The dialectical sense grants the need to mediate equivocal difference; but this is done by reducing *all otherness* to a form subordinated to the putative primacy of such absolute self-mediation. The doubleness of self and other is not then properly sustained as articulating a togetherness that is irreducibly plural; it becomes dialectically converted in a dualism that is to be mediated and included in a higher and more embracing process of self-mediation. Such a dialectic converts the mediation of self and other into two sides of a more embracing and singular process of total self-mediation. The thought of everything other to thought risks getting finally reduced to a moment of thought thinking itself. Thus, Hegel's speculative unity is marked by, as we might call it, a kind of "dialectical univocity."

The metaxological sense of being is not the antithesis of dialectic. It is antithetical to any such reduction of otherness, and to the reduction of a pluralized intermediation to any monistic self-mediation. The togetherness is to be articulated with a different stress on otherness. The space of the middle is open to a double mediation, a double that is no dualistic opposition. This was part of my intention in invoking Augustine's extremely suggestive formulation above. The middle is plurally mediated: it can be mediated from the side of the dialectical self; but also it can be mediated from the side of an otherness that is not to be reduced to a moment of self-mediation. Even Hegel held that the other mediates the middle; but for him this mediation invariably turns out to be a penultimate, hence, subordinate moment of a more ultimate process of dialectical self-mediation; indeed mediation by the other turns out, in the end, to be a mediation of the self in the form of *its own* otherness, and hence not the mediation of an irreducible other at all.

The complex "between" as articulating a metaxological sense of the togetherness of self and other cannot to be understood in terms of such an encompassing dialectical self-mediation, even granting the latter all its internal complexity. The "between" grants otherness its irreducible otherness. If otherness is to be mediated, and it is to the best extent possible, it must be mediated in terms other than dialectical self-mediation. The latter reduces the plurality of forms of mediation to one essential form that encompasses all the others. The shade of univocity rises again.

Metaxological intermediation is itself plural. There is an affirmative sense of the *double* that cannot be spoken of simply as a dualistic opposition. Nor is the other simply the self in the form of its own otherness. Our intermediation with certain others cannot be included in dialectical self-mediation. The mediation of the metaxological between cannot be exhausted either by the mediation of the self or the mediation of the other. Neither side can claim to mediate entirely the complex between. The "whole" is not a whole in the sense of a conceptual monologue with itself; it is a plurivocal community of voices in interplay just in their genuine otherness. This community is not a totality but an "open whole."

The double mediation of the metaxological means that genuine speculative mind must be both self-mediating and also open to the intermediation between thought and what is other to thought, precisely as other. This is not to reject the appropriate contribution from the univocal, equivocal and dialectical senses. It does mean that the deepest openness of speculative mind demands the impossibility of the final closure of thought by itself and in itself. Speculative perplexity is concerned with the mindful thought of being, and if the thought of being is metaxological, we are charged with a double imperative: thought must think itself; thought must think what is other to thought.

When thought thinking itself privileges only its own internal self-coherence, it is tempted to renege on potentially dissident forms of otherness that resist complete conceptualization. In modern philosophy this temptation follows from Descartes' classic formulation *"cogito me cogitare"*—a subjectivistic version of Aristotle's *noēsis noēseōs*, answering in its own way to the requisite self-mediation of thinking. When we elevate this into *the* essential form of thought, we produce a contraction of metaphysical openness to otherness. Thus, in the subsequent history of modern philosophy, we find that speculative perplexity is transformed into an endemic sense of mind's alienation from being's otherness. If we absolutize self-mediating thinking, the otherness of being is now reduced to a mindless dualistic opposite; or alternatively, it is dialectically dominated by an idealistic self-mediation; or it is simply mindlessly let be in its unmediated thereness; or it is irrationally celebrated in its brute facticity by post-idealistic philosophy. All of these are interwoven with the devaluation of being, discussed previously.

To think the middle and ultimacy means to struggle against every attempted closure of thought on itself. The *second* exigency of thought—that it be genuinely open to the otherness of being, even in forms dissident to complete conceptualization—must be allowed its freedom. For this second exigency reflects the indeterminate openness of ontological perplexity. And perhaps some contemporary accusations against speculation find their basis in a tendency of metaphysics to absolutize the first exigency of thought thinking itself. From this absolutization follows a certain logicism where metaphysicians create grand structures of conceptual abstractions without any community with being in its otherness. I see the significance of this second exigency and its indeterminate perplexity in its call for speculative *honesty*: philosophy may find its self-mediations ruptured by forms of otherness that its categories cannot completely master.

Speculative mindfulness need not be the conceptual monologue of thought thinking itself. The impact of otherness may strain the voice of thought into a perplexed saying that takes it to the edge of univocal and dialectical logos, if not beyond. The limit of the middle need not be a merely negative line of demarcation that says: so far, but no further, nothing more. It may become a place of meeting where the mind in perplexity genuinely opens itself to what the ultimate as other brings, on its own terms, to the metaxological between.

6. The Irish generally find it hard to leave Ireland, though they also have been adventurers, wanderers. Most have left because of economic necessity. I left because of a mixture of economic and intellectual necessity. I could have studied in England or perhaps Europe. When I came to America to a program with a nonanalytical focus, this coming for me constituted a movement between two worlds. My Irish world was then at the edge of modernity vis-à-vis technology and traditional religious values. America was a different country of the spirit. It did not have that smallness and intimacy of community one finds in Ireland. I was between my rootedness in a particu-

lar place, Cork, that I loved and still do, and the sense that there is an unmastered world of otherness beyond this; this sense of being between was heightened by coming to America.

I went through the move as an exile and was often homesick. In contemporary Continental philosophy one of the current buzzwords is "nostalgia." It is hurled as an abuse against thinkers who supposedly long to return to the comforting self-sameness of the womb of being, unable to stand their difference before the uncontrolled heterogeneity of the decentered world. The critique of metaphysics as an ideology of identity, presence and so on, is tied up with this word "nostalgia." I have no difficulty admitting the sentimentalized lack of honesty that can accompany some forms of "nostalgia." But there is a kind of avant-garde braggadocio which play acts with "nostalgia." This play acting has no real knowledge of the tension, war and pain, and stressed longing between sameness and otherness. My patience is thin with those who posture about exile and home, dismissing the desire to be at home with being as mere cowardly nostalgia. I can understand Socrates' refusal to leave Athens: exile would have been a kind of death; I can understand this existentially as well as intellectually. It would require a mindless gall to dismiss Socrates' refusal to leave as "nostalgia."

I was between two worlds. In time I came to be relatively at home in my new country—relatively since a sense of dislocation never entirely deserted me nor has done so to this day. I live between two worlds and there is no *Aufhebung* that would unite the two into a seamless unity. I have been in exile from the first home; and in the outside there is not a second home, but a search to be at home with being even in this stressed between.

After completing my studies at Penn State, and after teaching for a year (1978–1979) at St. Bonaventure's in upstate New York, we returned to Ireland, intending to settle there and make a home. We stayed for three years, but primarily for a mixture of economic and intellectual reasons I returned to America and Loyola College in Baltimore where I have been ever since. My life has been a series of crossings and crisscrossings in the between, and sometimes with respect to extremities of belonging and exclusion that stress the middle. There need be nothing middling, temperate about this middle.[4]

---

4. Since I wrote this in 1991, I and my family find ourselves undertaking another crossing. I am now Professor of Philosophy, and Director of the International Program in Philosophy at the Higher Institute of Philosophy at Katholieke Universiteit Leuven (Louvain) in Belgium. Given what I said above about Continental and Anglo-American philosophy, perhaps there is something fortuitous in this. Moreover, there is a deep historical connection between Ireland and Leuven, dating back many centuries.

The between become a kind of outside in the middle itself. There is an alienation from one's initial ground, yet also a liberation from a thoughtless immersion in the initial ground. There is a call to a being-at-home in not being-at-home. Thought itself is alienating, and unavoidably alienating. Is there any thinking that is not alienating? I do not mean a thought that overcomes alienation *simpliciter*. I doubt there is any such as long as we live. I mean a thought that dwells with and lives in the alien, non-reductively, and yet without turning into the wretched unhappy consciousness of Hegel. I side with Pascal when he reminds us of our double condition of wretchedness and greatness. There is no escape from wretchedness; but greatness in part consists in an honesty about wretchedness. Hegel is less than fully honest about the truth of wretchedness in his discussion of the figure of the unhappy consciousness.

Moreover, this between is not only an outside in the middle. There is a certain beyondness to it that is idiotic—idiotic in the sense of intimate, as other to the cold stony gaze of the neutral objectifying universal. This idiot intimacy cannot ever entirely appear in the public universal. If the philosopher thinks of himself as the high priest of the public universal he will twist before this idiocy and intimacy. This I have tried to suggest in my most recent writing: honesty demands that we not pretend that there is no such thing, even as we find it extraordinarily difficult to communicate it; one has to be something of a poet to do so effectively; but the main thing is a kind of honesty. Honesty itself is idiotic; there is no system of honesty; one is honest; I am honest or not. Honesty is an elemental intimacy of hard simplicity and openness that some manifest. No science or system or technique will guarantee it; it is a quality of character in its deepest intimacy of mindfulness and being; this is why honesty is a source of greatness.

Honesty is also a source of wretchedness. Honesty generates skepticism in philosophy; but too often the skeptics then blow it by wasting the honesty in futile parlor games of dismantling the positions of others, in an intellectual eristic. The most horrifying honesty, skepticism, is the one that searches the abyss of inwardness, the idiotic this of the thinker, for the lies and ruses and self-deceiving rancors and festering bile that lie hidden in the soul. Precondition of being an honest philosopher: skepticism about the crud corrupting mind, desire to be rid of that crud. And one may find that one cannot purify oneself on one's own.

Philosophers talk about truth and reason, perhaps even absolute truth or absolute knowing. The skeptical rejoinder is not easy to stifle: we know nothing. Honesty points to the condition of being between. It need not be imprisoned in either these extremes: the extreme that hubristically claims more than it can deliver; the extreme that dismisses philosophy as an old swindle of the human mind that masks its emptiness in swelling ideals.

Honesty's intermediate nature reflects the metaxological character of being. If we are honest, or trying to be honest, we let ourselves open to the truth, be it what it may; honesty presupposes a possible willing submission to what may be other to our heart's desire; hence honesty demands a certain unconditional respect for the truth, should we be able to encounter it. But honesty reverts on the human being, implicating the existential dimension to the philosophical quest for truth. I am between the possibility of knowing the truth and my repeated temptation to be closed against the truth. Honesty is a middle condition which need not possess the truth, but it is not thereby closed to the truth. Rather it is marked by its own truth of being, which is not the truth, but a willingness to be truthful. So the singular self can be truthful even when it does not possess the truth. This also suggests the need to move beyond the dualistic opposition of the honest singular self and the impersonal truth, existence and science. The between moves us to a further mediation which is other than the reduction of the universal to the particular, other than the absorption of the particular in the universal.

I was talking about being between America and Ireland. To anyone who has not gone through it, it is almost impossible to communicate the pain of being uprooted. I had lived in America for five years in the 1970s. One would think that I would smoothly fit into life again. Returning was like a kind of death, rather than a new beginning. Or: there was a new beginning but it was shadowed by a death. It took years to come to terms with this, and the trace of death is written on my thought ever since. For one who knows what I am talking about, this is no hyperbole or melodrama—being uprooted in an almost literal sense, like a tree that cannot draw sap up from the soil; and yet the tree lives on without that energy that should flow into it, unasked. I was between a plurality of worlds, each defined by their own intrinsic resources and limits, none reducible to the other, and neither reducible to a third principle or world. My experience of thus dwelling in the between deepened my quest for a non-Hegelian philosophy of community and otherness, and a double without *Aufhebung*. When we leave the immediate home we do not return to it dialectically; there is no dialectical return. There is called for a different commemorative living of the home, but always out of the distance of one's difference and the otherness of the home.

When one returns to the first home, one's eyes have been doubled, and one sees the same thing differently. One sees the home in a doubled way, in a redoubled way. There is no simple univocal home ever more. Again the great task is to find a way of being-at-home in this not being-at-home. I think this is coincident with the metaphysical destiny of being human. We are native to the world/ we are strangers in the world. We are at home with being/ we can never be completely at home with being. We are double. The doubleness has to be lived in its stress. Perhaps we may turn the stress into a tension that drives a creative act. So by this paradoxical being-at-home in not being-at-home, I do not intend a mere equivocation. Nor do I mean it as a dialectical *Aufhebung* of our not being-at-home into a more encompassing home of thought thinking itself. I mean being wounded by exile, difference, distance, suffering. I mean singing in the wound. I mean letting the suffering of the otherness of being become the occasion of a great affirmation of being, a singing of being in its otherness, as for ever beyond us, and yet as always our home.

7. My first published book was *Art and the Absolute.*[5] It was generally well received by Hegelians. They especially liked my critique of deconstruction, which the deconstructionists did not like. I would now say that for strategic reasons I pulled some punches about Hegel. I was tired of caricatures of Hegel. It is silly the way Hegel has been so many times overcome by mediocre minds. All one has to do is grind out a few clichés from Marx or Heidegger or Derrida; and presto!—Hegel is put in his place. I found this ridiculous, and still find it ridiculous, even though I criticize Hegel. Hence, I wanted to write a book which gave Hegel a run for his money. I wanted to read him with an eye as much on the thing itself as on texts. I wanted to read him clean of that hermeneutics of suspicion whose evil eye on the thought of an other brings forth a still born interpretation of that other. I wanted to explore the possibility of an open dialectic, an open interplay of art, religion, and philosophy. Granted, the desire for this open dialectic reflects my own desire to reinterpret dialectic. Nevertheless, I found and still find significant ambiguity in Hegel's enterprise, sufficient to offer room for some such openness.

I never did deny that we might need something else to do justice to a more robust sense of otherness and a different sense of openness, as note 6, p. 190, should make very plain. That note was the advance advertisement for *Desire, Dialectic and Otherness. Art and the Absolute* was written *after* the major articulation of the systematic concepts of *Desire, Dialectic and Otherness* were developed (in "The World as Image and Original"). I was a post-Hegelian before being an Hegelian and again publicly becoming a post-Hegelian. The matter is simple: one has a purpose in writing a book; one cannot say everything; ever act of saying is necessarily a silence about some other things; the fact that one says little about these other things does not mean that one has nothing to say about them, or no thought about them. Giving Hegel a run for

---

5. William Desmond, *Art and the Absolute: A Study of Hegel's Aesthetics* (Albany: SUNY Press, 1986).

his money frees one from that sterile rancor, too rampant today, towards Hegel and the tradition of philosophy. Being generous to the other, does not mean one adores the other thinker, or that one is incapable of differing in thought. The themes of *Art and the Absolute* reflect my own concerns: the community of art, religion, and philosophy; the nature of concreteness; atheism and humanism; the problem of nihilism; the metaphysical significance of art and beauty relative to the devaluation of the world in modernity; evil, the negative, the issue of the transfiguration of the ugly . . .

I have already said something about *Desire, Dialectic and Otherness* where the above fourfold sense of being is developed. Some readers have found it a difficult book. I do not know what one says to this, except to hope for careful, patient readers. It is a systematic work, but in no merely static sense, since the systematic structure emerges from the unfolding of a metaphysical hermeneutics of human desire that becomes progressively more complex and rich. The first part of the book moves through the univocal, the equivocal senses of being to an open sense of dialectical self-mediation. The second part moves beyond dialectical self-mediation into a more fully articulated development of the metaxological community of being. It culminates in its final part in a speculative meditation on the ultimate ground of the metaxological community of being in terms of what I call the "absolute original." The book is one that has to be read once as a whole, in order to be seen for what it does, namely, instantiate the very double mediation of the metaxological that it articulates and defends. Perhaps because of its difficulty, perhaps, too, because it does not fit into any contemporary camp, whether analytical or Continental, perhaps because of its refusal to bow to the current fashions, it has yet to receive the attention it deserves.

Philosophy and its Others is, in one sense, a sequel to *Desire, Dialectic and Otherness*. In certain respects, it presupposes the availability of a more austere statement of the metaxological standpoint, though it can be read in independence of the previous book. My problem there was not simply to unfold this standpoint, but to ask about its truth relative to the fundamental ways of being and mind. Since the reader will find some summary of its contents in the essays to follow,[6] I will confine myself to some general statements.

If the voice of *Desire, Dialectic and Otherness* is perhaps closer to Hegel, at least the Hegel of the *Phenomenology*, the voice of *Philosophy and its Others* is more Nietzschean, perhaps even Platonic. It might seems strange to couple

---

6. See Merold Westphal's "William Desmond's Humpty Dumpty Hegelianism" *CLIO*, vol. 20, no. 4, summer 1991, 353–370; and Stephen Houlgate's "William Desmond on Philosophy and its Others," *ibid.*, 371–391.

Nietzsche and Plato, so seemingly antithetical as philosophers. Contrary to this antithesis, however, I think that Plato and Nietzsche are the philosopher-poets. Moreover, more than any other thinkers both exemplify what I call "plurivocal philosophizing." If the palm were to go to any it would go to Plato for exemplifying the inner urgency of philosophy, between "poetry" and "system." Plato is nothing or nobody—he never appears directly in his dialogues. Yet he is everyone and each of his personae. He says everything and says nothing. He appears in none of his characters and yet he appears in all of them. As a philosophical poet he has no univocal identity, yet as a dialogical thinker he is not merely equivocal. As a plurivocal thinker he is metaxological.

In *Philosophy and its Others*, I wanted to develop the metaxological view such as to bring philosophical thought into closer proximity to human life, a proximity being progressively lost by philosophy's academic professionalization. The work is systematic and yet goes to the limit of system. I underline the importance of its subtitle: "Ways of Being and Mind." The fundamental metaphysical issues of being and mind are here at stake. There is a desire to stay true to the phenomenological richness of concreteness. While systematic it tries to articulate a plurivocal philosophy. Against the cliché of the conversation of mankind, against the professionalization of philosophy, I wrote in a manner that tries to break down the bureaucratic functionalization of the aesthetic, the religious, the ethical, and the philosophical. The opening chapter, entitled "Philosophy and its Others: On Ways of Being Philosophical," tries to recover the many voices of philosophy in terms of a plurality of self-images that have influenced the philosopher in the past and present: these self-images include the scholar, the technician, the scientist, the poet, the priest, the revolutionary, the hero, and the sage.

There are then substantial chapters on "Being Aesthetic," "Being Religious," and "Being Ethical," respectively. The last two chapters, entitled "Being Mindful: Thought Thinking its Other," and "Being Mindful: Thought Singing its Other," try to think philosophically beyond the functional divisions, in a plurivocal philosophizing which seeks to gather some of the voices of philosophy into some kind of a community of articulation. In another sense, I am concerned with the question of nihilism and the breakdown of the aesthetic, the religious, and the ethical. What I call "thought singing its other" is a response to the issue previously noted of recharging being with some sense of inherent ontological value. Here the voice of the poet is essential, but not a merely aestheticist poet: a poet marked by the urgency of ultimacy that we find in being religious, and of respect for intrinsic value such as we find in being ethical.

Again I found unavoidable some effort to say the this as this. I could not suppress the idiotic, the intimacy of being and an ineluctable yet non-indigent sense of particularity. These latter ask for some wariness of the stock forms of linguistic communication. When honesty is at stake, who gives the orders? We must shed the prejudice that we are professional technicians with only one skill to which we must stick, on pain of excommunication from the guild. The freedom of spirit of philosophy is surely other than any professional expertise or technē. This is not to disparage expertise but to refuse its idolization. Sometimes one writes in many ways, indirectly, even in a systematic way that hides system. I fear one can write too well. The reader might mistake the ease with which he reads for an ease of understanding what is actually at work in the text. Everything is so smooth that one thinks one understands what is going on. The moment of felt illumination may be the moment of unfelt ignorance. Philosophical writing can have a certain silence and reserve built into it, a hard and elemental simplicity.

Again one chafes at the chains that we create for ourselves. One would think that, say, the journal article were a Platonic form, determining a priori the exposition of philosophical ideas or scholarship. What if it is a prisonhouse wherein we creatures of custom take up habitation? What about the need for daring, for audacity in thought, for simple elemental honesty about the fundamental perplexities of being? No graduate school education, no method or technique, no hermeneutical panacea, no deconstructive skill, will guarantee the simple elemental honesty of a perplexed human being. We learn a game while loading ourselves up with chains; when someone tries to remove the chains, we protest that this is not playing the game, that this is not philosophy. Were Socrates to look for a job today, he would fail dismally—no books, no articles, no fellowships, no honors, no system, no scholarly expertise, not even ABD; just an irritating malcontent who would end up annoying all the professionals. And yet we wax eloquent about our respect for the Delphic gnōthi sautón!

Is there something post-modern about this? I do not think of myself as a post-modern. If what I say has any relevance to what is now going on—and I would be disingenuous to deny that I think it does—this is not primarily because I keep my ear to the ground to hear the muffled tramplings of the Zeitgeist. It is because I think there is a matter to be thought which all the philosophers have tried to think. By almost a process of cultural osmosis we pick up what is in the air in our own time, and are shaped by it. Only by a great discipline and opening of spirit and mind do we begin to hear what some of the great thinkers have tried to say. The latter is by far the harder openness to what is other. Hence, my dismay when the hermeneutics of suspicion towards the tradition makes it all but impossible to hear what those others were trying to say, all the while declaiming its uncompromisable openness to the other. Thus, the instrument of the Zeitgeist congratulates itself. One does not try to be original in philosophy; one tries to be honest. The most effective way to be original in an age that has made a social conformity out of the rhetoric of originality is, I suspect, through the wearing, bruising struggle for spiritual honesty.

So I am at odds with some of the pervasive attitudes of post-Hegelian thought about the tradition of metaphysics, without necessarily subscribing to Hegel's view of speculative philosophy. I sum up these attitudes in a Nietzschean formulation: to Hell with Plato! Let us take Plato now as a figure for the despised ontotheology, metaphysics of presence. I find that certain stock characterizations pass currency as established truths, characterizations derivative primarily from Nietzsche and not from Plato himself. A direct reading of Plato and other metaphysicians yields far more nuance and complexity. I find that those who totalize the tradition accuse the tradition of totalizing thought.

In *Beyond Hegel and Dialectic*,[7] I develop some of these ideas. This book consists of six meditative essays on themes relevant to the limits of philosophy and Hegel. These themes include: speculation and historicism, and the middle between time and eternity; the relation of philosophy and religion, in the light of cult and representation; dialectic, evil and the idiocy of the monstrous; deconstruction and dialectic relative to logos and the mockery of philosophy; philosophy's ability to laugh at itself. This is not just a book on Hegel. I am concerned with a rethinking of speculative philosophy along the lines of the metaxological sense of being, hence Hegel is my major interlocutor in so far as he privileges dialectical self-mediation. The work is a dialogue and confrontation between the dialectical and the metaxological senses of being. Overall I am between Hegel and his critics in this sense. I have more respect for Hegel and systematic philosophy than his critics. Nevertheless, I acknowledge the legitimate questions to be put to Hegel. I am very critical of Hegel from a metaxological standpoint. But I am unsure if the questions have been put in the best way. Philosophy has not been completed by Hegel. And the old metaphysical questions are the ever-new perplexities of present living thinking.

8. Where do I go from here? It is always rash to make promises. But there are some promises one makes rashly to provoke oneself later into redeeming them. Here are three hopes. First, I would like to develop the fourfold sense of being in a systematic work on metaphysics where I take up the major themes of the philosophical tradition. There are already many suggestions in this direction in *Desire, Dialectic and Otherness*. Second, I would like the develop the fourfold sense of being relative to the good in a

7. William Desmond, *Beyond Hegel and Dialectic: Speculation, Cult and Comedy* (Albany: SUNY Press, 1992).

work on ethics. The chapter "Being Ethical" in *Philosophy and its Others* contains the outline of that development *in nuce*. Third, I would like to write a work on God and gods in which I develop the fourfold sense relative to the pluralistic nature of religious life and the non-univocity of the idea of the ultimate; I would like to undertake a metaxological reconstruction of some of the traditional "proofs," better called "ways" to God.[8]

Where do I go from here? One is tempted sometimes like Socrates to turn to poetry. Perhaps I will, perhaps I will not. In the aftermath of post-modernism, one becomes wary of mere aestheticism, without spiritual seriousness. Now I do not have a choice. I philosophize from a kind of inner necessity; when that inner compulsion dries up, I will stop. There is no a priori limit to this inner spring of thought. My experience has been this: The more one thinks, the more one is overcome by an ontological perplexity, a sense of the burden of the mystery, such that all saying, ever the most able, is a stammering. The more I know in the sense of determinate knowing, the more a different indeterminate perplexity springs up. I know a lot; my curiosity about many things is relatively well satisfied; but I now think that there is a different, second astonishment or perplexity beyond determinate intellectual curiosity. This is an indeterminate perplexity before the "whole," in some ways a formless astonishment, as if one were groping one's way in a darkness that was too deep, or a light that was excessive and hence blinding and disorienting; groping one's way like a blind man, though one can clearly locate all the determinate objects in one's environment.

This condition is all but the reverse of Kant's in this sense: Repeatedly Kant laments the "mere random groping" of metaphysics prior to his own putting of metaphysics on "the secure path of science." I think that beyond all determinate science there is a groping that indicates a more radical metaphysical struggle. This groping suffers from an essential perplexity about the meaning of being that give the thinker a kind of metaphysical migraine, or insomnia. To this perplexity one cannot give any definitive univocal answer; to this perplexity one must return again and again. No, it is rather that such a perplexity returns to one again and again, and does not wait the permission of a scientific warrant.

There is no definite answer because the question does not concern a univocal puzzle with a one determinate answer. Instead of the secure path of science, this second metaphysical thinking is buoyed up on a sea of indeterminate perplexity. We may construct categories which allow manipulation of this part or region of the matrix. But such categories also delimit, hence

---

8. I have now tried to fulfill the first rash promise in *Being and the Between*. The two other rash promises must still be redeemed!

distort—distort both the excess of mind itself, and the excess of being in its otherness. Such categories invariably falsify the metaphysical perplexity if they do not carry in themselves some memory or reminder of the matrix of being's excess out of which they are crystallized. Philosophical categories, when they are the articulation of metaphysical perplexity, must themselves be between univocal determination and openness to this excess.

I am in the between of life, the middle. I know where I am and I do not know where I am. The appalling feeling comes over me that despite the astounding achievements of science in determinate knowing, we are as babes relative to the metaphysical enigmas of being. It is a horrifying feeling that there is a sense in which we really know nothing, that all our knowledge is a kind of veil of Maya. This is utterly repugnant to the confidence of rationalism, completely blasphemous to anyone with even a trace of positivism, inexcusably anathema to political progressives who extol in modernity the rational amelioration of social life. I cannot escape an absolutely oppressive sense that something is missing, that we know nothing, that we are not seeing what is there, that we do not really see anything. I do not say this like Dostoevski's Underground Man who sticks out his tongue at the pieties of reason. I say it as one who thinks that reason defines one of the highest nobilities of human existence. But it is reason that drives one to this further honesty about the second perplexity. And that second perplexity seems to consume all the hard won consolations of the first, determinate knowing.

Chapter 2

Being at a Loss:
On Philosophy and the Tragic

1. Howl, howl, howl, howl! . . .

A violently reiterated Howl is not the usual way to initiate a philosophical meditation. Neither Aristotle's list of categories nor Kant's table make mention of any Howl. Hegel's *Science of Logic* contains no concept corresponding to Howl. There is no Platonic *eidos* of Howl. Indeed the Howl seems to shout down, shout against all categories, drowning out the civilities of reason in its brute explosiveness. Perhaps we might think of the cynics, the dog-philosophers as not silencing the Howl. But Hegel saw nothing much in Diogenes, bastard offspring of Socrates. Nor did he take much notice of Diogenes' self-description: the watchdog of Zeus. And many philosophers are much more Hegelian than they realize, or care to know. We will shrug it off. With sweet reason on our side, we will say: Why have a bad conscience in turning from the Howl? Where can Howling find its place in the ideal speech situation? This Howl is no voice in the grand "conversation of mankind." The rest is philosophical silence.

Yet this Howl is different. A silence that merely shrugs it off betrays philosophy. For this Howl breaks forth as one of the great conceptless voices in the "conversation of mankind." Perhaps it would be better to say the Howl is a "transconceptual voice." Thus, we keep alive this ambiguity: Is the Howl other than conceptual, being empty of concepts, or is it more than every concept, hence full of a challenge philosophy must strain to think? For this reiterated Howl is the agonized voice of Lear, coming on stage with the dead body of Cordelia in his arms.

Howl, howl, howl, howl! O, you are men of stones:
Had I your tongues and eyes, I'd use them so
That heaven's vault should crack. She's gone for ever.
I know when one is dead and when one lives;
She's dead as earth. (*King Lear* V, iii, 259–63)

The philosopher has no category of Howl. Who then are the men of
stones? Is Spinoza a man of stones in describing his philosophical desire thus:
Not to laugh, not to weep, not to detest, but only to understand? Is this what
philosophy will do? Give us eyes and tongues, but eyes and tongues that are
stones? We cannot, we will not speak about this Howl. We will be silent
about heaven. Will we, like Anaxagoras, turn the sun into a god of stone?
How then will we look on life and death? As if philosophical reason had
nothing to do with life or death? And where then are our categories for that
simple phrase that assaults the disarrayed mind: "For Ever"?

Lear's Howl is a transconceptual voice in the "conversation of mankind" that not only ruptures all logical systems but also threatens the very
basis of that civilized conversation. It threatens, not because it will not hear
the other, but rather from excess of hearing, from excess of exposure to an
otherness that destroys every human self-sufficiency. Can philosophy listen
to this Howl and not risk the ruin of thinking? For when one hears that
Howl a crushing night descends wherein the mind is threatened with black-
ing out or going blank. The mind shudders, as if a dark abyss had opened and
swallowed all sense. Rational mind undergoes a liquefaction in which all
intelligibility seem to be reclaimed by a malign formlessness. There is anguish before this Howl.

The Howl is an outcry. It reminds us of the great outcry of Dostoevski,
in the howl of Ivan Karamazov, against the suffering of innocent children.
What is the source of this outcry? Why listen to it? Thinking too much on
it—will it not make us mad? Like Lear's Howl, it issues forth from a depth of
our exposed being that seem to elude conceptual encapsulation. The Psalm
says it: *De profundis ad te Domine clamavi*. But what are those depths, what
cries out from those depths? The Howl as an outcry is a cry from the heart.
But what is a cry from the heart? What otherness has stirred the heart to this
outcry? Must philosophy default here? Can there be a systematic science of
such cries? Would not a systematic pretense be nonsense, a folly of logic?
Such a cry, such an outcry, is elemental. If logic would that it were not heard,
if it tried to stifle the outcry, would not logic prove itself to be metaphysical
madness? Does the outcry need tragic saying? Can tragic art alone make us
hear this Howl?

Our listening to the agony of Lear's outcry is not yet over. Have the
men of stones the tongues and eyes for this savage saying:

And my poor fool is hanged: no, no, no, life?
Why should a dog, a horse, a rat, have life,
And thou no breath at all? Thou'lt come no more,
Never, never, never, never, never (*King Lear* V, iii, 307–310).

This Never is an absolutely crushing word.[1] Perhaps never has the word Never been uttered as crushingly as by Lear. Can philosophical dialectics take us into this Never, beyond this Never? Can the universal of logic or Hegel's world-history ever unharden the irrevocability of Lear's savage, reiterated Never? What can philosophy ever tell Lear, what alleviation give him in his elemental grief? What consolation could the Platonic *eidos*, or Husserl's *strenge Wissenschaft* ever offer? What, to reverse hearer and listener, does the conceptless voice of tragedy tell philosophy? What can we philosophers hear in this Howl, in this For Ever, in this Never? In their metaphysical horror is there incitement to think about essential and unavoidable enigmas—tragic enigmas forcing philosophy to its own extremes where its concepts begin to break down? Can philosophical mind break through to a deeper metaphysical thinking even in this breakdown?

2. I step back from the edge to approach these questions thus. First I will speak of philosophy and the tragic, most especially in relation to Plato, considered by many, Nietzsche not least, to be the archenemy of tragedy. I will say that this is too simplistic: philosophy has a complex, plurivocal identity, not reducible to scientific cognition, though not exclusive of rational cognition. Philosophy can be especially attentive to certain fundamental tensions between determinate knowing and significant indeterminacies of being beyond encapsulation in specific concepts. Subsequently, I will reflect on such tensions in relation to Lear's Never and the related notions it calls forth.

I am not primarily interested in tragedy as a problem in aesthetics. Modern aesthetics tends to be too much in the grip of an aestheticism that compartmentalizes art: in its excessive insistence that art is art, that art is for art's sake, that art is resistant to any intrusion from what is other to art, post-Kantian aesthetics ends up divorcing art from its origin in the fundamental

---

1. Shakespeare scholars argue about the difference between the Folio (1623) and the Quarto (1608) editions. In the Folio there are 5 nevers, in the Quarto 3 nevers. As the reader will come to realize, for purposes of the metaphysical reflection undertaken here, the difference between 3 and 5 is not of ultimate significance. One never can be enough, Once is enough. I thank Robert Miola for bringing to my attention the point about the different editions.

creative and tragic powers of human existence. In elevating art into a false self-sufficiency, it ends up diminishing art's metaphysical power. This power interests me. I ask: What is it about *being* that is revealed by the tragic? More specifically, what does it mean to be in the guise of *being at a loss*? Tragedy reveals one of the ultimate forms of being at a loss. In a tragic situation we were faced with boundaries from which there is no escape. We are backed against a wall, as it were. We are pushed without easy recourse into a dead end of being. How we are, and what we do in this *cul de sac*, is revealing of what it is to be.

If my interest is metaphysical, I immediately add that metaphysics here escapes the stock Heideggerian charge of "metaphysics of presence." As is well known, Heideggerians accuse all of metaphysics, from Plato to Nietzsche, of being some form of the "metaphysics of presence." I say: If metaphysics can meditate on the tragic in the guise of being at a loss, then it is ridiculous to see all this as "metaphysics of presence." Being at a loss shows tragic experience as already deconstructing the "metaphysics of presence." True, there is a philosophical tendency that would immediately want to convert being at a loss into some totally rational picture, see the loss as a mere prelude to a positive founding, a being refound, a new foundation, and so on.

I believe metaphysical reflection is capable of a more complex response. Being at a loss is not a mere absence, relative to which a dialectical interplay can be quickly initiated. Here an absence does not dialectically provoke its contrary presence, such that tragedy would be the play of absence and presence, with the presence more clearly grasped by the philosopher than by the tragic artist or the person undergoing the tragic. This again is too simple. Certain exposures to being at a loss seems to be unsurpassable in the direction of a positive finding that we can articulate on this side of going under into death. Or: a certain suffering knowing of being at a loss may itself be what is affirmative in tragic undergoing. Metaphysical meditation on that suffering knowing is solicited.

We begin to see the emergence of the crucial tension between philosophy and the tragic. Traditionally philosophy has presented itself as the quest for a rational account, indeed a rational account of being in the most comprehensive sense: a logos of the whole. The implicit presupposition of this entire quest is that being as a whole is ultimately intelligible. Should we think radically enough, should we take our logos, logic to the ultimate boundary, then being as a whole will reveal itself as available for intelligence, for reason. *To gar auto noein esti te kai einai*: to be and to think are one and the same. This utterance of Parmenides (frag. 3) seems to be the complete antipodes of Lear's Howl. Parmenides' saying is susceptible of a number of interpretations, but these are not the point here. The point is that philosophy seems driven by the conviction, should we say faith, that being is not ultimately tragic. True reason will never be at a loss; true reason will be the intelligent *finding* of the deep logical intelligibility that is inherent in the nature of things.

Philosophy does not deny that enigmatic and recalcitrant events do strike us, or that, to all appearances, we do experience being at a loss. But these are often seen as the ambiguous, perhaps duplicitous appearances that a more penetrating mindfulness will surpass. Parmenides says (frag. 6): the many wander like hordes that are double-headed, *dikranoi*: two headed, in two minds, at a loss what to think one way or the other. The many do not find being but are beings at a loss for logos—they cannot say what being means. Appearances appear tragic but being in itself is not tragic. In being in itself there is no loss. Hence Parmenides' description of being (frag. 8)—a well-rounded sphere, neither more here nor less there, but homogeneous throughout, without gaps or ruptures. The description of beauty in itself in Plato's *Symposium* reiterates the apotheosis of such being without loss, beyond all lack. Time is the sphere of loss, for time is a perpetual perishing, time is decay, decrease, decease. Death is the ultimate loss of being, and the ultimate before which we experience being at a loss. Parmenidean pure being is deathless.

When philosophy sees itself as a complete rational finding, beyond being at a loss, it predominantly thinks of itself as a science. To be scientific is to be capable of giving a determinate account of things, a logos of a *tode ti*. Systematic science would be the apotheosis of never being at a loss. To every perplexity, every enigma, there would be a determinate response to be made. If philosophy were exclusively systematic science, it would ultimately be a systematic exclusion of the tragic. For in principle one should never be at a loss in systematic science. If one were radically at a loss, the suspicion would surface that the scientific claims for complete determinate intelligibility were questionable.

Suppose, by contrast, we think now of some great tragic heroes in relation to their *knowing*. Consider Oedipus' will to know: he refuses not to know the truth, but the truth was too much; in an excess of dark knowing, he must blind himself to continue. He may be personally guiltless but his knowledge, self-knowledge, brings measureless suffering, not *eudaimonia*, as Socrates suggests knowing will bring. Consider Hamlet: he, too, is marked by a thirst for knowing that goes to the boundary of man's metaphysical predicaments; he knows and does not know that his father was murdered; he alone bears the burden of knowing/not knowing; he has to put an antic disposition on, use the mask of madness to deal with his wrenching situation; his knowing is not that the real is the rational *sub specie aeternitatis*; his is the cursed knowledge that "the time is out of joint." Where is the consolation in this knowing? His knowing essentially puts him at a loss what to believe as genuine, who to trust, what to do. All his knowledge brings is suffering. Yet both knowing and suffering are unavoidable.

Consider Lear again: the cushioned King has to become unsheltered to the extremities, stripped to his elemental humanity before the powerful elements, endure his passage through a madness more knowing than his regal sanity; and at the end there is the Howl and the Never that assault the calm of our philosophic faith in the basic intelligibility, indeed value of being. Lear's tragic knowing brings him to the condition of being utterly at a loss. The Howl says it all, namely, that Lear does not know what to say: the public communicability of discourse retracts before the horror and all intelligible saying seems to founder. Tragedy brings a knowing that shatters every naive faith in the intelligibility and worth of being or saying. Is philosophical mind then at a loss? What can it think about such extremities of being at a loss?

No doubt about it, philosophy has a strong eros to overcome loss, not to be at a loss, to place reason where tragedy faces rupture. What then do we do with the devastation of losing, with being bewildered by loss? What does the philosopher do, for instance, with the erosion of being that time inexorably works? I say the philosopher because I want to underscore the singularity of the philosopher as a living thinker. A propensity of philosophers has been to displace reason's attention from the singularity of the philosopher to the putative universality of philosophy as such. The consolation of the logical universal usurps the idiocy of the singular as singular. Again I use the term idiocy in the Greek sense of *idios*: an intimacy of being at the edge of, if not outside, the system of public reality, an intimacy not indifferently available to anyone and everyone. (This idiocy will be important below in discussing the Never.) What of this idiocy of the particular philosopher as particular? The philosopher as a particular human being is washed away by the erosions of time. To be is to be bound to a process of genesis that not only brings into being but always brings about the demise of being. The erosion of the being of the particular, the loss of being for the particular is ontologically constitutive for every particular being. This cannot be denied.

Indeed I claim that we are marked as metaphysical beings, as well as tragic beings, only because this ontology of loss is intimately known by us. If we did not intimately know being at a loss, it is not clear we could fully raise the question of being in any other sense. Nor could we be characterized as beings who undergo or behold the tragic, or who bespeak the tragic in works of art and religion. Obviously the sense of the tragic is only possible in a human world; but it is not possible in a merely humanistic world, where what is radically other to the human is not given its proper due. Tragedy arises because we become mindful that there are rupturing others that inescapably disrupt, destroy any sense of ontological self-sufficiency that human beings might feel or claim on behalf of their own being. We are metaphysical beings in the measure that the tragic breaks through, in the measure that we know our being to be one that loses itself, that loses its way. We know that our way of being is unavoidably a way of loss. Being at a loss is a more deeply constitutive dimension to being human than might initially be suspected.

Wherever possible we try to stand our ground before being at a loss. Philosophy can be a mindfulness that tries to find its way in loss. It can be a finding of being in the losing of being, a mindfulness that thoughtfully tries to be at home with being in being at a loss. Here the identity of philosophy that emerges is other to its identity as systematic science. Losing, failure, breakdown, the eruption of the indeterminate are acknowledged as absolutely essential here. Logic offers no final answer with being at a loss. Nevertheless, one tries philosophically to speak of loss as essential, without reducing loss to the logical consolation of a conceptual essence.

So it would be very wrong to think that philosophy must always simplistically displace metaphysical concern from the rupture of loss towards the neutral logical universal. The situation has never been one of simple opposition or "either/or." In my remarks now to follow, with respect to the view that philosophy has no simple univocal identity, I will speak of Socrates and Plato, to a lesser extent Nietzsche and Hegel. Philosophy has a more complex plural identity which includes but is not exhausted by the will to systematic science. What is *more* than systematic science in philosophical mindfulness is related to the metaphysical meaning of being at a loss, and hence also to the tragic.

Thus, one way to read Plato is as a strongly Parmenidean thinker: the doubleheaded nature of the doxic many is not to be taken seriously, especially if one has seen the circular self-suffcent plenitude of being in itself, absolute being without loss. Yet the doubleheadedness reappears in Platonic philosophy. Philosophy reduplicates a plurality that the Parmenidean ideal ostensibly leaves behind.

This is the tension. On the one hand, related to the Parmenidean ideal, we find a logicist concern with contradiction: contradiction is the doubleheadedness in thought that philosophy shuns. Hence, the allergy to equivocal language, double language that is potentially duplicitious. Logos will try to disarm or expose the duplicity of equivocity by formulating all questions of being in sheerly univocal terms: there is one meaning and one meaning only. But then, on the other hand, we must grant in Plato the articulation of *positive plurality* as constitutive of genuine philosophical dialogue. Nor is such dialogue just a smooth seamless exchange between a philosopher and others. It is born out of perplexity: someone is at a loss what to think and asks another for his views or response. The experience of being at a loss drives a philosophical dialogue, and needs the plurality of its constituent voices. Many voices, many heads are necessary to respond to the condition of being at a loss. Hence, the plurality of voices in difference or contradiction is not necessarily a merely negative thing. In response to being at a loss, plurivocity constitutively energizes the very dynamism of philosophical interplay and exchange.

But you will say: this is the negative dialectic that inevitably will subvert itself; the being at a loss drives beyond itself through the inherent momentum of logos as dialectically unfolding; the negativity of loss will negate itself and produce a positive finding. Thus, the faith in logos is preserved and we always end up with a rational account beyond all loss. But if so, why do so many dialogues end in an impasse, an *aporia*: they end up at a loss. This is glaringly at odds with all those clichés of Plato as the "metaphysician of presence" *par excellence*. The dialogue drives logos to a new height of articulation, but also to a deeper acknowledgment of being at a loss. Logos in *aporia*, logos at an impasse: these are constitutive for the Platonic sense of philosophical thinking. It is as if the wonder that is said to be the originating pathos of the philosopher *reappears* after he has done his best job in giving a determinate logos. The indeterminate perplexity reappears, wonder resurrects itself, in a different sense of being at a loss, now at the limit of logos iself.

I find it peculiar that Aristotle is often honored as the philosopher of tragedy in the ancient world. His *philosophical practise* is antithetical to Plato's here. In a far more insistent way, Aristotle wants a determinate logos of a determinate somewhat, a *tode ti*. This is why he rejects the philosophical appeal to myth. This is why, when he reiterates Plato on wonder, one suspects that wonder has been dimmed into intellectual curiosity, the telos of which is not a deepening of metaphysical astonishment, but the dispelling of curiosity in a determinate answer to a determinate question. Aristotle significantly invokes *geometry* when claiming that the acquisition of knowledge issues in a *reversal* of wonder (see *Meta.*, I, 983a15–25). (I will remark below on "geometry" and tragedy. It is significant that Husserl links philosophy and geometry, not only in *Ideas*, but even in the *Crisis*. He is only one of many sons of Aristotle respecting "geometry.") If Platonic wonder can be deepened but not dispelled, this is because being at a loss can be bespoken but never eradicated. Why? Because man as metaphysical is an *indeterminate question* to which no determinate answer will ever reply or correspond. If there is to be an answer, it must somehow include the truth of indeterminacy itself.

The greatness of being at a loss, of running into an *aporia*, is precisely its reminder that just this indeterminate openness is ontologically constitutive of the human being. A totally determinate science, in claiming to give a complete explanation, would actually be a falsification of this ontological truth of the being of the human. Its very success would be its most radical failure. All we have to do is becomes self-conscious of this and the force of being at a loss reinserts itself into philosophical discourse again. This is always happening in philosophy. No sooner does it make some claim to knowing, but there begins the process of deconstructing the completeness or adequacy of this claim. In finding its way, philosophy immediately initiates a way of losing that thenceforth subverts its own provisional peace. Philosophical mind's true and enduring condition is one of metaphysical insomnia.

The anti-philosophical philosophy of deconstruction does some of its main business in bringing philosophy to *aporia*: making philosophy acknowledge that it, too, in the end, is brought to loss; that thought is being at a loss which sometimes hides its own loss in dialectical rationalizations. Of course, there is some truth in this. But I say: philosophy has *already* always been at this point: always at a loss. This is the very perplexity that generates thought, that, in turn, is always deconstructing itself. This, too, reflects the skeptical principle in all genuine thinking. Those least infected by the skeptical principle are the minnows of the philosophical tradition. Hence, deconstruction fishes best with the small fry of thinking, not the sharks. To reduce Plato's sense of logos and *aporia* to the metaphysics of presence is to draw in a net empty of Plato the philosophical shark. As a developed philosophical strategy, skepticism is nothing but mind's alertness to its own being at a loss before perplexities it finds intractible. Philosophical mind comes to know itself in its own breakdown. It can also break through into thought beyond breakdown. Skepticism, like deconstruction, tends to give us breakdown without breakthrough.

When logos runs up against an *aporia*, different responses are possible. One might deny that the *aporia* is really an *aporia*, and redefine it as a merely temporary block on reason; reason will eventually find a way beyond and in the end there will be no beyond, there will be no other to reason. This is one typical philosophical strategy: there will be no others to philosophy, since all reason has to do is continue, and the other will no longer be other, because it will be conceptualized, will be thought. The other of thought, in being thought, will be thought once again, and so it will not be the other of thought. We end up back with Parmenides. And so philosophy will meet itself again at the end of the road. The god of this philosophy cannot include the tragic, because the ultimate picture will be thought simply thinking itself; there will be no loss, no self-loss; all will be embraced in the circle of self-thinking thought.

Another response is silence. The rest is silence, it says at the end of Hamlet. Philosophers have known the power of silence. I name but two: the younger Wittgenstein in the *Tractatus*: logic falls silent in the face of the mystical; Aquinas at the end of his life when he refused to continue to write and said of his work "It seems to me as so much straw." Being philosophically at a loss and silence are intertwined. But silence, like being, like being at a loss, can be "said" in many ways. There is the empty silence of meaninglessness. There is the silence of an acknowledging, full of reverent respect before the other. There is a silence of despair. There is a silence of peace beyond measure. There is a tragic silence: this is a transconceptual silence that rends the silence, all silences, the conceptless silence of Lear's Howl.

It seems to me that the great systems of philosophy are encircled by a silence that they do not, perhaps cannot name. The silence that circles the system, the philosopher, turns his speech of clear concepts into the chiaroscuro of the tragic. But the philosopher as idiot can be haunted by this silence; this can make him *more* than systematic scientist. The unsaid haunts all saying; but some saying carries the silence of the unsaid in itself. This is most evident when the philosopher is also a poet. Plato and Nietzsche are the two great examples. Their thought is plurivocal; thinking is not the monologue of *noēsis noēseōs*, or Hegel's self-thinking Idea.

Thus tragedy raises the question of philosophical silence in philosophy's very lucid speech itself. We probe the philosopher when we ask about his silence: What does his speech avoid, what does his speech respect, what does his speech ignore, what does his speech dread to say? All such questions call for an awareness of the different modalities of philosophical silence. Consider Spinoza's motto *Caute!*, his one word of command, or perhaps warning. Who is he commanding or warning? Of what is he afraid? What then does the motto mean? Many possible things, all beyond univocal logos. The tragic itself is always beyond univocal logic.

One thing we do not want at the limit of tragedy is the chatter of conceptual analysis that thinks it has the measure of an enigma when it makes a verbal distinction. At the opposite extreme to this analytical evasion, there is the possibility I develop in *Philosophy and its Others*: not only thought trying to think its other; but thought trying to sing its other. To say how the Howl turns into song is too large a theme here, though I will offer a few hints at the end.[2]

I return to Plato as a philosopher who thought in the shadow of the tragic. I do not simply mean the shadow of Greek tragedy, though this is true. He was concerned especially with tragedy as a religious drama in which appears the inscrutable will of the gods, even in the mask of their resistance

---

2. See *Philosophy and its Others*, chapter 6 on thought singing its other. Nietzsche speaks of the birth of tragedy from the spirit of music. It is not entirely clear how, in Nietzsche himself, something like Lear's Howl might turn into Nietzschean music. How do we get from the Howl to the music? On what I call "aesthetic theodicy and the transfiguration of the ugly" in Nietzsche and also Hegel, see *Art and the Absolute*, 150–159.

to reason. The wrath of the god that mocks the pretensions of human reason
was something deeply disturbing to the implicit faith of philosophy, namely
that being, at its deepest and most ultimate, is intelligible. God is not envi-
ous is the refrain in the *Timaeus*, a refrain reiterated by Aristotle, by Aquinas
and significantly by Hegel himself. Hegel says it because he holds God to be
self-disclosive: there will be no enigma in the ultimate which resists the
approach of reason; God is simply reason and the nature of reason is to
manifest itself, reveal itself, make itself available to the philosophical mind.
Likewise Plato was concerned to purify the gods of the masks of irrationality
they seemed to wear in tragedy.

For the suffering in ancient tragedy has a sacred modulation; what is at
stake is sacred suffering, and the tragic hero is not out of the ambit of the
sacrificial victim of the gods. If one's basic faith is that being is transparently
intelligible to mind, this sacred violence of the holy provokes shudders.
Where is the *epistēmē* of this sacred violence? If the gods are infected with
such an otherness to reason, an otherness violating to reason, we seem to
peer into an ultimate arbitrariness in the nature of things. At bottom being
does not appear completely intelligible to the tragic vision.

Moreover, there was the proximate tragedy of Socrates. The man who
seems most rational meets a death that seems least reasonable, with respect
to both justice and truth. Platonic philosophizing sought to penetrate Socrates'
tragedy to the intelligibility, the life of reason at work in this philosophical
life, in the loss of this life in a senseless death. If the life of reason cannot be
found to be at work in this life here and now, then for Plato the loss is also
the loss of the here and now. The work of reason will be said to transcend
this life. And as the work of reason transcends this life, so in fact must it
transcend this death. Again we see the desire to save philosophy's faith in
intelligibility. The problem is that, if we anticipate ultimate reason and justice beyond this life and death, we then return, in some form, to the question
of the ultimate light or darkness of the gods. Plato knew this too; else he
would not have Socrates tell the myth of Er.

Plato wants to see the light. Nietzsche did not see *this* light. At the
bottom of things he saw darkness. At its deepest the nature of things is such
as to give rise to horror; in itself being is not intelligible. Still reflecting
Schopenhauer, the bottom of things is a dark origin, in Nietzsche's case, a
Dionysian origin that erupts and is given shape in the tragic drama, but
which in itself exceeds all form, for it is the forming power which in itself is
formless.[3] That is, the ground of being for Nietzsche, what he calls *das Ureine*

---

3. William Desmond, "Schopenhauer, Art and the Dark Origin," in *Schopenhauer*,
Eric von der Luft, ed. (Mellen Press: Lewistown, 1988), 101–122.

in the *Birth of Tragedy*, is not intelligible in itself. Intelligibility is a consoling construction of concepts that we and philosophers like Socrates create as a shield from too violent an encounter with the Dioysian will to power behind it all.

A major point here is: Schopenhauer says the Will is on *the other side* of the principle of sufficient reason; so in a sense there is no sufficient reason for the ultimate Will. Nietzsche runs swiftly with this insight in relation to philosophy and the tragic: the ultimate origin is beyond the principle of sufficient reason; and hence to the extent that philosophy is contained by this principle, it cannot properly think the tragic. There is a suffering that comes through in the tragic that exceeds the ministration of the principle of sufficient reason. In face of this suffering we need art more fundamentally than philosophy.

Who, for Nietzsche, embodies the principle of sufficient reason? Socrates, of course. Socrates wants to disarm the a-rationality of the tragic, neutralize in universals the sacred suffering that springs from the dark Dionysian origin and that the tragic drama makes present, that tragic drama celebrates. Philosophy fakes its own being at a loss, disguising its conceptual consolations as "truth." Tragedy looks into this fearful darkness, yet it bespeaks this darkness with a certain celebrating joy. This joy is our brief salvation from despair and meaningless suffering. It is our encounter with death and our unreserved yes to being, despite the destruction and the terrible. Deep down life is inexpressibly joyful: this is what the tragic says to Nietzsche. Philosophy is treasonous to this suffering and this joy; it turns away from both towards the abstraction and the concept; Socrates offers in dialectics his therapy for the darkness of life. For Nietzsche this is the epitome of philosophy's impotence, its ineptitude before the tragic.

This is not Nietzsche's last word about philosophy and the tragic. If this is Nietzsche's judgment on traditional philosophy, it is not his judgment on the promise of philosophy. He himself clearly wanted to be the first Dionysian philosopher, the first philosopher of the tragic, the first tragic philosopher. Philosophy in the tragic age of the Greeks was already marked by this promise, only to be aborted, nipped in the bud by Socrates and Plato. But even Socrates was a masked Dionysian: he, too, suffered from life; he, too, wanted a saying of being that would enable the transfiguration of being, in a manner analogous to the transfiguration of life and death that the sacred suffering of the tragedy enacts. The antithesis of tragedy and philosophy is not an ultimate antithesis, though clearly the way to transcend this antithesis cannot lead us back to Socrates and Plato and their heirs—so Nietzsche thinks.

Once again the relation of philosophy and the tragic raises the question about the very identity of philosophy, and indeed, after Nietzsche, its future identity. Can philosophy honestly name the otherness of the tragic without disarming its horror or neutralizing its challenge by means of its conceptualizing appropriation? If philosophy can try to think the tragic, must it redefine its modes of thinking, such that it opens itself to what may resist its categories, perhaps ever cause their breakdown? Would not this also demand a rethinking of the relation of the poet and philosopher, and in a form that finds the Platonic view unsatisfactory? Or must we also be cautious with Plato here too? Is not Plato's philosophizing also a mask of the tragic poet?

Nietzsche's views force us to make a more general remark in line with earlier points about systematic science, namely: if the scientific view were completely applicable to the whole of being, there would be no room for the tragic. Scientific mind treats being as valueless in itself. The question of the worth of what is, the very worthiness of being, does not directly arise for it. This question points to a convergence of metaphysics (as asking about the meaning and truth of being) and ethics (as asking about the goodness of being). [In Nietzsche's case, metaphysics and ethics are subsumed into aesthetics.] The tragic exposes mind to a radical experience of being at a loss. Ingredient in this loss is the possible loss of the worth of being: the horrifying possibility is brought before us, not only that being lacks an ultimate intelligibility, but that at bottom it is worthless, it is valueless.

Tragic experience seems to suffer being as drained of any value. Being is, but is as nothing. Better not to be at all, perhaps: a saying Nietzsche repeated after Schopenhauer, who himself repeated the Greek Silenus, companion of Dionysus, and the figure to whom the drunken Alcibiades compares the enigmatic Socrates. Metaphysics tries to be mindful of such issues, science does not. Science is itself a mode of mind that devalues being, drains being of value: the being there of the world is taken for granted as a given fact; the being there of what is arouses no ontological astonishment, or metaphysical nausea, or aesthetic jubilation, or religious celebration. Scientism—in claiming that science will answer for the whole—is thus identical with nihilism: the assertion of the valuelessness of being. Nietzsche himself understood this, and blamed philosophy for being the remote source of this nihilistic scientism, which paradoxically is driven by hatred of the tragic, that is, epistemological dread of its suffering knowing. The paradox is that the scientistic impulse presents itself as beyond love and hate. In fact its "love of truth" hides a hatred of the tragic for its recalcitrance to conceptual encapsulation.

The silence of science returns philosophy to the saying of art. The metaphysical question does arise in art, and painfully in tragic art: a great hero comes to nothing, his being is shown to come to nothing. In this loss of being what then is the worth of being? What is worthy being when all being, even the greatest, seems inexorably to come to nothing? Science has nothing to say about such questions. There can never be a science of the tragic, and were the scientific mentality to try to impose its norms on the totality, the result would have to be a blindness to, a denial of, perhaps a repression of tragic experience. The irony here is that this repression embodies a metaphysical violence that has its own implicitly tragic dimension. We normally do not couple Spinoza and metaphysical violence, the noble Spinoza who in austere purity of mind philosophizes *sub specie aeternitatis*. Yet there is such violence in Spinoza's claim to treat human beings and their emotions like he would treat solids, planes, and circles. This sounds high-minded, since the philosopher seems willing to sacrifice the pettiness of his restricted ego purely for disinterested truth. But such a putative will to truth is potentially a violent repression of the truth of the tragic. There is no geometry of the tragic. When philosophy thinks it is the geometry of the tragic, this is tragic for philosophy.

I think Plato knew this. Over the entrance to his Academy is said to have hung the saying: Let no one enter who has not studied geometry! Yes, but this does not say, *only* geometry; nor that once having entered, all modes of mindfulness will be reduced to geometry. Again I reiterate that the philosopher's self-identity can be forged in a deep awareness of being at a loss. This is relevant here. A crucial place where the limits of logos comes up in Plato's dialogues is the *Phaedo*. Socrates is in prison on the eve of death. He accepts that there is no escape, no way out for him. Is this death tragic? Is the philosopher at a loss in the face of it? Will geometry help one through the portal of dying? Where is the geometry of death?

I am within traditional respectability in raising the issue of philosophy and the tragic here. Certainly Hegel, even panlogist Hegel, thought of Socrates' death in tragic terms. Dialectical reason is at work even in tragic death. For Hegel there is a clash of two justified principles or powers. Socrates embodies the new principle of subjectivity: inward thought makes claim to absoluteness over against the social substance. Against this thinking stands the social substance itself, whose unreflective ethical *Sittlichkeit* was the fundamental ethical embodiment of the people's *Geist* at its most ultimate— religiously and aesthetically, as well as ethically. Both those powers have their justification, but the emergence of the first from the second produces an inevitable clash between the two and the downfall of both. The unreflective ethical *Sittlichkeit* was at a loss what to do with Socrates as embodying the radical freedom of thought; Socrates himself was at a loss in asking ethical questions in a form to which traditional *Sittlichkeit* could not answer. This double being at a loss necessitates for Hegel the loss of both as distinct opposites and their falling to the ground. Socrates was guilty for Hegel; but Athens itself was infected with the spirit it condemned in Socrates and so in this sense was condemning itself. It was already unknowingly in the spiral of dissolution that the Socratic spirit represented—the dissolving powers of thought before which nothing seems to stand. Thinking brings us a loss of unreflective tradition, shows what is hitherto accepted and lived as coming to nothing.

Hegel's view is very illuminating in its dialectical sense of the together-ness of opposites. But I am not interested in displacing the tragic issue onto a neutral universal, not interested in displacing the issue from the particular philosopher to the stage of world-history or to philosophy as systematic sci-ence. Ultimately, for Hegel, the particularity of Socrates and his death is *world-historically redeemed* as preparing a more thoroughgoing victory for rea-son in history. Hegel displays the philosopher's faith in the final ascendency of rational intelligibility. Universal spirit as world-historical is the victor. But what of the tragedy of Socrates as *this* philosopher? What redeems the death of this particular self as idiot?

Plato is deeper here and more revealing for our purposes. He presents Socrates as a particular human thinker. Socrates explicitly says in the *Apol-ogy* (32a) that to survive as a philosopher it was necessary for him to live as an idiot (*idioteuein*). He would have been dead earlier if he had not lived as an idiot. Thus he outlived "the sects and packs of great ones that ebb and flow by the moon," as Lear—about to be imprisoned and become "God's spy"—calls the factions of feverish politics, the world-historical mighty. Plato's Socrates does not give us systematic science or a world-historical account in exoneration of his philosophy, his life. We are given an apology for an *indi-vidual life*. Though that life involved the search for the universal, the life itself was the mindful existing of a *this*. Only a *this* can apologize; a universal does not apologize, nor does it live the inviolable inwardness of an ethical life. This latter is part of Socrates' tragedy. There is no way to make sense of the enigma of Socrates if we think that his life was exhausted by a logicist obsession with the ideality of universal definition. One does not live or die for such a definition. The ideal sought must be different to a definition encapsulated in any logical category.

Socrates' death makes us reconsider the enigma of his life as philosophi-cal. We begin to sense that there was something ineradicably *Once* about this life. Death revealed to us, to Plato, the Once of this life, in confronting us with its Never: once Socrates was but now never more. Why was Plato too sick to attend the dying Socrates? What was this sickness before death? Is there any "geometry" to heal it? Can we imagine Plato howling: Why should a rat, a horse, a dog have life, and Socrates no life at all? Will Socrates ever come again? The answer is: Never, never, never! Hegel will say to this: No, no, no! Socrates will always come again. But he will not come as *this* Socrates, but as universal thought. But Plato knew: *that* is not Socrates. It is Socrates as a this that concerns us; it is Socrates as a this that apologizes for philoso-phy; it is not the universal using Socrates as an instrument that apologizes; it is not the Socratic spirit. Socrates says: I, I, I and the I is ineradicably singular, irreplaceable. There was only one Socrates, one and one only, even though this unique singular claims to speak on behalf of the universal.

It is for this I, not for philosophy as such, that we cry at the end of the *Phaedo*. At the end, we weep for an *other*; it is the death of the *other*, Socrates, the beloved other that had his friends and Plato at a loss. (Below we will see that it is the death of the beloved other, Cordelia, that pushes Lear to the most extreme loss.) The tragic issue is not just concern with *my* death à la Heidegger, but with the death of the other—Marcel and Levinas would agree. But perhaps the deepest moment in the *Phaedo* is when Socrates covers his face after taking the poison, and his body began to mortify, petrify with the advancing poison, as if becoming stone. The universal has no face; the universal Socratic spirit has no eyes wherein terror or fear or exhaltation or consent might appear. But Socrates as idiot, as an irreplaceable this, has a face, has eyes.

Why must those eyes be veiled? What was in those eyes of the dying Socrates? Composure? Terror? Did Socrates crack in the face of the Never, all his previous arguments about immortality notwithstanding? Did the impersonal universal lose its power in this final moment? Or do the eyes have to be covered up because the eyes reveal the absolute singularity of the person, the absolute particularity of the philosopher? The death of the singular philosopher, the veiling of the eyes in the final moment, is completely enigmatic to philosophy as systematic science. There are no concepts within any system that can tell us about those eyes looking on death, looking out of death, on life.

The I as idiotic is in the eye in a manner that is evident nowhere else. The idiocy of the I is its ontological intimacy, and this intimacy of being appears in the eye. In the face of death, the eye is the place where the face may manifest the person's yes or no to being, to death, to the Never, to the Once—if indeed this yes or no come to manifestation at all. Socrates' eyes are covered because there is no public universal that can encapsulate what might have appeared in them. You might say: terror appeared, and then imply that terror is public; we all share terror; terror before death is universal. True. But this is beside the point in relation to the intimacy of the eyes, their idiocy from the point of view of the universal, its stony eyes.

Consider how, regardless entirely of death, we find it extremely difficult to hold a person's eyes; there is a dangerous ambiguity about eye to eye contact. How much more powerful is the dangerous ambiguity when the living survivor is making contact with the eye of the dying one. What passes from eye to eye, what metaphysical terror is there in this communication, what metaphysical consent? What passes between the eyes is an intimacy of being which no impersonal universal can ever bespeak. This is why Plato, the poet-philosopher, gives us an *image* here, not an impersonal universal.

The manner in which Plato covers the eyes is a stroke of philosophical genius. There is nothing to compare to it in all philosophical literature. Plato says nothing; but the writing of this silent gesture before death, witnesses what cannot be said.

I note here how visitors to Nietzsche after his breakdown frequently commented on his *eyes*. The visitors seemed to see in Nietzsche's eyes a *knowing beyond sanity*, that invariably shook them in a brief disruptive revelation. The terrible eyes struck them in every sense, as if the dead eyes, the mad eyes were the eyes of tragic wisdom; and then just as quickly the veil would be redrawn and the vacant face of idiocy would look out at them.[4] I note, too, the prominence of the theme of eyes in *King Lear*: sight and blindness, "reason in madness." We recoil at the horror of Gloucester's plucked eyes, empty sockets like Oedipus' gouged eyes—gouged with the malignant cry "Out vile jelly where is thy lustre now?" Is this all that the eyes and the ontological intimacy of the I are: vile jelly? Were Socrates' eyes, Nietzsche's eyes just vile jelly—where is their lustre now?

Lear advises Gloucester: "Get thee glass eyes." Gloucester already knows: "I have no way and therefore want no eyes; I stumbled when I saw" (*King Lear* IV, i, 18–19). Death opens the eyes of weeping. Weeping eyes cannot be understood in terms of Sartre's Look; the actuality of weeping is totally inexplicable in Sartre's reduction of the promise of the eye to the Look. The Look is the apotheosis of the eyes of stones, the Gorgon's eyes that turn to stone. But stones do not weep. Nor does "geometry." Only flesh weeps. Only flesh knows the tragic.

By contrast with Hegel's *Aufhebung* of Socrates' particularity into the world-historical universal, Plato offers us the singularity of an apology, even though the life apologized for may include the search for a universal more than personal. The philosopher is often between these extremes, tempted to sacrifice the first to the second. The artist is also between these extremes, but his temptation is perhaps the reverse, the sacrifice of the promise of the universal for the singular. Both need each other to allow the epiphany of universality in singularity, as well as a non-reductive acknowledgment of the singular as singular: to name the singular without reduction, and to grant the universal without dessication. In trying to find the middle, the lure of the extremes will be differently modulated by the artist and the philosopher.

If Plato does not offer an Hegelian *Aufhebung*, this does not mean we lose all faith in logos. Death is the place/noplace where the philosopher's

---

4. On the eyes of the mad Nietzsche as seen by some visitors, see *Conversations with Nietzsche: A Life in the Words of His Contemporaries*, ed. and introd. Sander L. Gilman, trans. David J. Parent (New York: Oxford University Press, 1987), 242, 246, 247.

extreme being at a loss is manifest. In the thought of death we try to think what cannot be thought, for to think the thought of one's death is to think oneself as being. Logically, we are caught in an *aporia*. Existentially, we are faced with the temptation to give up on logos. Hence, it is here that we find Socrates' warning in the *Phaedo* against misology. This is extremely significant. I see it as Plato's/Socrates' gesture that philosophical logos must not simply give up before the ultimate experience of loss. Being at a loss before the loss of being—this is impending death. The philosopher's response cannot be a question of conceptual chatter continuing. What does one do at this point, if anything? What can one say?

Socrates gesture of philosophical *faith* is to continue talking. I stress that the talking is not logically univocal but irreducibly plurivocal. Philosophical speaking has more than one mode, more than the argumentative statement of thesis and evidence. Apart from the significant fact that the Platonic dialogue itself is more than a logicist monologue, within this dialogue Socrates suggests the possible need of philosophical song or music. He himself blends with the swan of death, the songbird of Apollo. This again evidences a view of philosophy very different to systematic science. Song and system cannot collapse into one totality. It is true that Socrates offers different "logical" arguments with regard to immortality. But these are logically easy to trouble, as Socrates himself grants. On being logically troubled, and in the face of the consternation of his interlocutors, Socrates goes so far as to compare his philosophical speech to incantations and charms. Finally, Socrates offers a myth.

Songs, charms, arguments, myths—different voices of a plurivocal philosopher. There is no one voice in the face of death, in the face of being. Why this plurality of different voices? Because Plato is a plurivocal philosopher, responding to the living/dying philosopher as a plurivocal this. Socrates was like a *father* to his friends who, bereft of him, would be as orphans the rest of their life (*Phaedo*, 116a). Nor can we forget the weeping of Xantippe. And then the silence—"best to die in silence," Socrates suggests (*Phaedo*, 117e)—and the masterful gesture of covering the eyes, as death creeps over the body. The *covered* eyes: Are they the eyes of death? Are they the extra eyes of posthumous mind (see below), mind looking on being from beyond the ultimate loss? Are they the eyes of a Never that crushes all hope of a beyond? Socrates is dead, dead as earth. Then the eyes *uncovered*: staring, fixed, immobilized, stones; their once vibrant presence extinguished, never to come, never; dead as earth.

This is not logic; this is not system; this is not the abstract universal. All of this is an image, a philosophical icon. At one level the image says: Philosophy must go on. But at another level it cautions: It can only go on if it is honest about loss, if it keeps before its thinking the image of death, the memory of the dead.

3. I said before that there is no geometry of the tragic. Nor is there a geometry of death or of the memory of the dead. I have also denied that philosophy can be reduced to the determinate cognition of the determinate. "Geometry" would be a figure for totally determinate or determinable knowing that seeks utterly determinate intelligibility. That there is more to philosophy as plurivocal, I now want to illustrate in terms of a non-geometrical meditation on Lear's Never. In trying to think through this Never, there opens up both a sense of metaphysical horror and of ontological astonishment. We again face the issue of the value of being, questioned in an extremity of being at a loss.

Metaphysics, I think, is always shadowed by the Never. In turn, the Never is unthinkable without a sense of what I will call the "*Once*" and the "*That it is*" of a being. Need philosophy flee this shadow into universal cognition? Does tragedy stay closer to the truth of the Once, the Never, the "That it is?" Beyond all determination, all self-determination, tragic loss is not recuperable at a finite level. There is a loss of being that transcends finiteness, an *aporia* that allows no surpassing at the level of finite determinacy. How are we to think of this loss beyond finitude, since it take shape in finitude? It is beyond because is entails *being at a loss before finitude itself*. Is this being at a loss before finitude a loss beyond finitude, pointing to the other of finitude? Is the Never ever softened in an everafter that allows some recuperation of meaning?

We must relate the Once and the Never to the "That it is." A being is, and is but once, and then is no more—never. Only we know this, only we. This is why the human being is the metaphysical being. Tragic and metaphysical knowing of being at a loss are only possible for a human being, not for a rat, a dog, a horse. It is not simply that we are capable of rising intellectually to the impersonal universal. This is true. But there is a more intimate kind of knowing where metaphysics and the tragic overlap. This takes shape in response to the Once and the Never: the gratuity of mortal being, the necessity that it pass out of being, lose its being in time, the chance we are offered to say thanks in the interval of the Once, before the night of the never more, thanks for the gift of time itself.

When Lear says Never, we hear him beseeching why a certain being should have being at all. Why should a rat, a dog, a horse have life and thou no life at all? He is addressing a particular thou. We recall Hamlet's fateful question: to be or not to be. But the metaphysical question assumes a more violent form after Lear's Howl. When we try to think about his savage Never, thinking becomes faint, become lightheaded, as if it were about to swoon, to undergo a blackout. For the Never names the irrevocable and the irrecoverable. It names them irrevocably.

We are here at an extreme extreme. It is like the cliff that Gloucester is induced to see in his mind's eye: "How fearful/And dizzy 'tis to cast one's eyes so low!. . . . I'll look no more,/Lest my brain turn, and the deficient sight/ Topple down headlong" (*King Lear* IV, vi, 11–12, 22–24). Gloucester's cliff, like the metaphysical enigma of being, is a cliff of the mind. At the edge of the Never, one is overcome by a kind of metaphysical vertigo, as though one were about to throw oneself off the mind's own cliff or ridge. It is as if one were to undergo a death by the thinking of this sheer abyss. One has to be blinded, like Gloucester, to surrender oneself to it.

That Lear addresses a thou, indicates that the Never presupposes a certain attunement to the singularity of the singular. The Never invokes the sheer "That it is" of a singular being, the being of Cordelia—not the being of an indifferent thing, not being as an anonymous universal. It is this being as particular, the idiotic being, the intimate being of Cordelia as the singularly loved child of Lear. Again I use "idiotic" in a sense related to the Greek *idios*: an intimacy of being not indifferently available to anyone and everyone, a neutral public.

The thought is this: Cordelia came into being, offspring of the father, marvel of a child, loved beyond measure by the father, though the father was also foolish and cruel. The singularity of her "That she is" is not replaceable by the being of anyone else or anything else. The being of the "That she is" is not substitutable for any other "That it is." The "That it is" of any this or that is a singular metaphysical marvel. This is the sheer being there of a thing, or a self, or a human being. This sheer being there is enigmatic. It floats on the void, in that the shadow of its possible not-being haunts its sheer being there. The "That it is" is shadowed by its own possibility of never being again. Together the Never and the "That it is" point to a certain absolute singularity of a Once. That Cordelia is in being, that this "That she is" is unrepeatable, irreplaceable, that this sheer being there will in time not be there evermore, all of these point to the time of the particular being as an absolutely singular Once.

The difficulty for the logicist mind is that it thinks in terms of concepts or genera or classes or universals or sets which are precisely tailored to the repeatable, the non-unique, what is not singular but what the singular shares with all other instances of the same genus or universal or class or set. The logicist mind shuns the idiocy of being there. So the sense of being that is carried by the "That it is," by the Once of the "That it is," by the irrevocability of the Never that is the destiny of the mortal singular being—all of this is deeply recalcitrant to logical conceptualization. The very act of conceptualization, by its very nature, displaces us from the singular as singular: something remains about this that is idiotic to the logical universal.

I stand on the shore and see the flow of wave after wave; they form, crest and crash on the sand. I struggle to identify a particular wave as particular. The sun glints for a moment on a singular form, but in the same moment, the form is deforming, reforming, endlessly ushered elsewhere, endlessly othered by the undying energy of the sea. I cannot fix the This that is Once, and then is

Never again. It briefly rises to the surface of the sea, and flowing into another, it subsides into the maternal waters again. I say: the wave. And I see many waves; they all are waves; all are instances of a common genus; big and small, angry and smooth. But the glint of particularity is no sooner received than it vanishes. There is joy in the glint, but terror in the vanishing. The glint of particularity is the singularity of that wave, the self of a this. Try to fix it, mind cannot. Mind is at a loss, it passes by the mind, and yet it is known as passing by. It is noted in the passing of its thisness. The human being, child of time, is the glint that mindfully arises and vanishes on the maternal sea of being. Nor need the passing be smooth transition; it may be abrupt violence.

Can we be mindful of the Once as the sheer now of being now? The Once reveals a particular that, in being, is in a process of perishing, but that as determinate spills over our every effort at fixed determination. I do not think of this "spilling over" in a merely negative light: it is not an indefinite vagueness that should be philosophically replaced by a determinate concept. The particular resists conceptual determination because of its ontological richness. It "spills over" because it is the concretion of "more" than determinate being.

This means rejecting Hegel's view of the matter. Hegel's discussion of sense-certainty in the *Phenomenology* seems to reduplicate and answer the difficulty I have here. Hegel repeatedly claims to show that the immediate is mediated, that to name the particular is always to invoke a discourse of universals: the this becomes a universal this; the now becomes a universal now, time; the here becomes a universal here, space, and so on. Hegel essentially subjugates the sheer being there of a being to a set of universals which are then said both to articulate and give us the truth of the original immediate this. Sheer ontological astonishment, perhaps secretly terror-tinged, before the sheer being there of a being is immediately covered up with a net of concepts. The rest of the *Phenomenology* will continue the cover-up and claim that this cover-up is simply the process of completing philosophy as a science of systematic determinate knowing. A similar point will apply to Hegel's *Logic* where being is the emptiest of universals and hardly distinguishable from nothing into which it dialectically must dissolve.

The sense I am struggling to say of Once and Never and the sheer "There it is" of a this, is at a tangent to Hegel's. It grows from a conception of philosophy different to the Hegelian one of scientific system, with its stress upon the determinate knowing of the determinate. Unlike Hegel's consciousness and sense-certainty, Lear, the father loves the child as a sheer this. The love of the parent reveals an ontology of singularity that is unremittingly attentive to the this as this. The this is not simply an instance of a universal; in parental love the metaphysical fragility of the this is known. The metaphysical frailty is the sense that this being has a singular being that was never before and never will be again as this, sheer onceness, sheer unrepeatability. No being or universal can substitute for this being, ever, never.

This metaphysical frailty concretizes the sense that the Once is shadowed by the never more. Never more is ontological necessary to the definition of the "more" of the "Once" as non-repeatable. My sense of the particular as *idios* demands we see it as its own world unto itself, but it is not a bare or indigent particular. Quite to the contrary: it is more, not less than any abstract universal. Nor is this sense of the nothing that comes with the Never the same as Hegelian negation. For Hegel's "nothing" is caught up in the dynamism of determinate negation, hence every negation will yield a positive result. If there is an outcome with the Never, it is not that Hegelian one.

My point is not to deny mind's need of universal structures; this is part of all philosophy. The point rather is not to falsify certain particulars by something like Hegel's dialectic of sense-certainty. It will not do to say that all immediacy is mediated and, *mirabile dictu*, the dialectical dynamism presses relentlessly forward again. Some particulars take root in one's being and cannot be uprooted without violence. There are particulars that, as it were, hook into one's throat, and struggle as one may, one cannot pull them out. The Never hooks into the throat of thought and rasps the smoothness of its conceptual voice. It cuts into philosophy, making a wound that may never be entirely healed. Particulars which are idiotic, intimates of being, have a certain inward otherness, invisible to any form of objective thinking. This intimacy of being resists objectifiable identification, is other, idiotic to objective thinking. It resists total saying in determinate concepts, resists being brought out completely into the public domain of conceptual discursivity.

The Once, the Never and the "That it is" mean that there is and will be no repetition. Being as the "That it is," floating once on the nothingness whence it came and whither to our eyes it is once again returned—all of this is idiotic. The Never thus says a No to Nietzsche's eternal recurrence and its once more. The Once is a no to this eternal recurrence too, I think. Every unique particular, that is, everything, will never be repeated. There is only once, and once only. If there is an eternity it must be radically other. It cannot be a repetition, for even repetition would be other than what it repeated, and the once would renew itself as other than what it once was. This is what is implied by a metaphysics of agapeic creation.[5]

---

5. Is there any sense in which the idea of *sub specie aeternitatis* has some applicability here? Even Spinoza says: We feel and experience ourselves to be eternal. Do we need a sense of time's other, traditionally called eternity, to make sense of the Once and Never of our time? Here eternity could not mean the impersonal universal, the eternity of dead ideas. It would have to be something like the living conversation of mind that outlives time, as in Socrates' dream of the other world: this other world is not simply the world of ideas, but of *thises*—*particular* heroic humans to whom Socrates wants to talk. On the critique of "static eternity" see *Desire, Dialectic and Otherness*, chapter 4.

We might here think of the irreplaceability of the This in terms of Job's second children. Surely we miss something absolutely fundamental if we think that a second set of children can replace or substitute for the first children that are dead? We miss the unrepeatability of the Once. Perhaps there is here something that is ever escaping from us. We are in the process of loss always and we do not even know it. Even as we think we master this or that, this other or that other is slipping from us and mostly we do know it not. Tragedy brings home the permeability of all being by loss: to be is to be at a loss.

This view may not apply thus in the world of means and ends, of pragmatic utility. But that world is one of the replaceable: one thing can substitute for another, one thing might be as useful as another and for an end outside itself. Such a world lacks in intrinsic values, lacks the irreplaceable, the unrepeatable. The tragic shows that the instrumentalized world feeds off a flattened ontology. The world of utility is a narrowing and a falsification of being. Tragedy involves the destruction of the instrumental illusion. Every quotidian value comes under stress, if not destruction. Even the highest instrumental values of regal politics are seen as less than ultimate. Lear will be stripped to his majesty and then stripped of his humanity, and will have nothing left. And there will be more insight through this "nothing" than through all the regal power of the instrumental world.

In that sense, world-history can be a lie from the standpoint of tragic knowing. This is why there is a kind of "Hegelianism" for which the intimacy of the tragic is a closed world, for it sees things too much in terms of the public arena of world-history. It cannot comprehend the idiot wisdom of a Lear.[6] It does not touch the extremity of what is seen and said there. Perhaps there is no "place" for this in human existence. Perhaps we can only die after beginning to see what is revealed here; die or be utterly transformed. But this transformation would be death also to the instrumentalized self. It would be a blank, horrifying emptiness; the instrumentalized self would see nothing, nothing there.

The judgment coming from that "place" would say: Never, never, never— and you have lived this lie, and now must break, break absolutely, or you die a different death. Thus, we might liken tragic insight to a process of being drowned: the air of everyday instrumentalities is withdrawn, we cannot breathe, we are being asphyxiated by a knowing that we cannot process, cannot digest. We are being brought under, going under, undergoing, in shock from a lightning bolt out of the Once and the Never. Yeats once said: "black out; Heaven blazing into the head." This black knowledge is a blindness, a madness, a death, a howl, as when a knife pierces one.

---

6. On idiot wisdom, see *Philosophy and its Others*, chapter 6.

The Never then is at the antipodes of Hegel's *Aufhebung*. The Hegelian negation as determinate negativity is always prelude to the *Aufhebung*. As I before said: Never is a crushing word; Never is *the* crushing word. But what does it mean to be crushed? Is there a dialectical account of being crushed? Being crushed is like a retraction of the energy of being into an inarticulate void, not a determinate negation. It is like a stunning blow to the head: one may never recover from the metaphysical concussion received. Once hit, one will always be concussed by this Never; one will always, evermore find it difficult to keep one's balance. One's being has lost its equilibrium, is always in danger of tilting over and itself falling into the abyss. The mind staggers like a drunken man. This is madness from the point of view of philosophy's official image. But was there not sometimes a secret metaphysical staggering in the great philosophers, Hegel included?

Lear was once a kind of Hegelian himself in thinking of being in terms of the public stage of the kingdom, the Hegelian universal of world-history. Exiled from this stage, pressed through madness, Lear discovered the intimacy of being, the wisdom of its idiocy. In effect Lear rejects Hegelian dialectic in saying to Cordelia, still alive, that they would take upon themselves "the mystery of things,/As if we were God's spies; and we'll wear out,/ In a walled prison, packs and sects of great ones/ That ebb and flow by th' moon" (*King Lear* V, iii, 17–20). There are no final mysteries for Hegel's dialectical concept. Can we call Hegel "God's spy" when he compared his *Science of Logic* to God's thoughts before the creation of nature and finite spirit? No. The *Logic* is silent about what Lear sees. Hegel's God, as the world spirit of world-history, dialectically ebbs and flows by the moon, borne in devouring time by the packs and sects of great ones, Hegel's world-historical nations and individuals. Hegel's dialectical theodicy fails for all Lears, mute before the elemental grief of father and mothers, mute before murdered children, the Golgotha of the intimacy of singularity. The rational comfort of dialectics does not comfort.

The idiocy of the Never as lived from within brings home the intimacy of horror. This intimacy is at the limit of sense, and our response to it is itself at the limit of sense. We experience here a metaphysical helplessness which we ought not to euphemize or fake with the bustle of psuedo-explanatory discourse. No rationalization will ever do away with this being at a loss. Here is a destructuring indeterminacy, a negative otherness that resists total recuperation in the logic of dialectical concepts, a collapse of the energy of being, a metaphysical oppression that resists being reduced to any mediated account.

When one comes to the edge of the Never, one looks over into nothing. It is an edge of being that is no edge, for the other of being here is not a simple negation of being. It is the irrevocable revocation of being: the nothingness of being as beyond being and yet as the destiny of mortal being. But paradoxically the "nothing" of the Never is "too much," a dark excess of irrevocable revocation of being. This dark excess is beyond the dialectical economy of Hegel's system of determinate negation. It is an indeterminate negation which is yet quite determinate—for it is this self that will die or is dead—but indeterminate because the very determinacy of the Once is itself the intractable enigma or mystery. The *tode ti* is here an idiotic particular because it cannot be subsumed into a universal without betrayal of its thisness. Precisely as a determinate *tode ti* it is recalcitrant to conceptual determination, either in its thisness or in its possible universality. A different thought of the This is required than either an Aristotelian or Hegelian one.

Here we might compare Lear and Abraham. This is entirely relevant, for the invocation of Abraham served Kierkegaard well to charge the Hegelian system with its betrayal of the This. Unlike Lear, Abraham was *asked* to kill his child, sacrifice his son. Bear in mind: Abraham has a child in old age. Presuming that his eyes were not already stones, one imagines the aged father, the father preparing for death, looking upon Isaac with a sense of the sheer Once of his being there. Isaac was a gift out of nothing. Abraham must have intimately known the metaphysical density of the Once, the irreplaceable This, indeed the idiocy of its gift given the extemity of his own age—the madness of an old father, but a madness gifted by God for whom all things are possible. Again we cannot make sense of the Never without a sense of this absolute Once. Here a metaphysics of creation is deeper than a dialectical logic of the self-generating Idea. The latter does not allow for sufficiently radical otherness, and hence for sufficient newness, oneness, as does the former.

When God asks Abraham to kill his son, the violence in this request is unparalled: the irreplaceable is to be destroyed, to be treated as if it were nothing. But ontologically this is impossible. There is a sense in which even God cannot undo His work, once given the otherness of its being created. Though the This was a gift out of nothing, once in being, the This is absolutely irreplaceable—all the more evident too, given the extremity of Abraham's age. God cannot undo this, even though He order the death of the This. Yet Abraham consents to God's attempted revocation of the irrevocable. Abraham now stood at the edge of the Never. In some sense, he faced into the Never as the result of his own willingness, his own choice, and so must have consented to its crushing burden. His is willing to give up the Once of Isaac. I cannot conceive of his willingness except as invaded by metaphysical nausea and horror. Sickness of heart inundates him but it must be kept down, smothered in silence before God. This silence horrified and obsessed Kierkegaard. He wanted to admire the silence but secretly had to stifle his own nausea before the horror.

Lear cannot smother his rage in silence, though he prays for patience. He prays for patience because he is being crushed. He cries out in his intolerable loss. Perhaps he cries out because the regal I of Lear was not yet dead in

him. Yet this regal I is part of the glory of human particularity, humble or
hubristic, its glint of free selfhood. Lear does not willingly go up to be
crushed by the Never. It visits him, even though his own foolish acts offered
the welcome to it in the form in which it did come upon him. Abraham is
willing to be crushed and yet has faith that beyond the Once and the Never
is God and His promise. This sense of the beyond is not thus evident in Lear.
Nor is Lear given back his Cordelia as Abraham is given back his Isaac.[7]

   Can we discover any alleviation at all in this contemplation of the
Never. As one possible approach, I suggest we consider Dostoevski's experience of, as it were, outliving his own death. The younger Dostoevski was
condemned to death for subversive politics. As a condemned criminal I
think of him as living with the thought of the Never. On the morning of
his death, he faced the Never: never again the sun rising, never again the
fragrance of the air, never to hear birdsong at dawn, never again the face of
a familiar loved one: never, never, never. On the morning of his execution,
Dostoevski was already half over the edge of death, already thinking, trying
to think what cannot be thought. We know the rest of the story: absolute
reversal from death to life—the absolute surprise of reprieve, the shock of
the impossible. Dostoevski experienced being pulled back again into life,
but not without the taste of the unthinkable. I think of this as like the
violent shock of being brought back to life, like a resurrection from the
dead. Instead of never being again, he was given back the Once again:
once again to be, to live.

   The metaphysical consolation, such as it is, is this: The sheer "once
there is" of being at all strikes home. Dostoevski sensed the sweetness of the
morning air, as if for the first time, as if never before, as if the sheer moment
of resurrection to life resurrected all life to its virginal freshness. It is like the
fairy tale that begins: Once upon a time. This Once recalls the mythic time
of such an aboriginal freshness of being, the time of the origin beyond all
time, the time out of time of creation from nothing as pure gift. The resurrected Dostoevski must have rubbed his eyes: I am here. I am. It is. It is
inexpressibly good to be, simply to be.

   This "I am" is not the "I am" of Descartes' *cogito ergo sum*, I think
therefore I am. This resurrected "I am" is one that the power of thought,
purely on its own, cannot bring into life, back into life. This "I am" comes as
a gift from an unnamed other. This "I am" testifies to a gift of being from the
other than no thought thinking itself could ever conceive as *being*. Not *cogito*

---

7. The theme of patience is very important, both for *King Lear* and our reflection
here. It would require another meditation. I do make some remarks below in chapters
4 and 6.

ergo sum; but I was as dead, as nothing; but now I am, in a reversal from death to life, from never to once again; a reversal that pure self-thinking thought cannot effect or indeed conceive. This "I am" is a release from the prison-house of immanent subjectivity, a release towards the otherness of being because of the gift of being from the other. Encounter with, or being brushed by the Never resurrects the Once in its splendor. The value of tragic insight offers itself in the precipitation of this ontological joy. One must sing "I am." I must sing the "to be" of being as gift.

There begins Dostoevski's initiation into what in *Philosophy and its Others* I call "posthumous mind:"[8] a thinking of being as if from beyond death, being in the worthiness of its present joy. Tragic insight crosses over from life to death, and looks back on life, crosses back and lives life otherwise: life in death, the Once resurrected. Dying, and yet to look on being there with the extra eye of death: this is what I call posthumous mind. The eye of death has been added to the mortal living one; henceforth one is split between the here and the beyond, the Once and the never more, and the more that may be beyond the Never, beyond life and death. The theme of being at a loss returns. It seems one must lose everything to be able to see anything properly. One must be brought to a complete loss to be able to see things once, and once again. To see the simple "there it is" of what is: to see the marvel; to sing the marvel of being. "Thy life's a miracle," the son Edgar tells the father Gloucester, after the blinded father has fallen into the abyss of mind. The beloved father, too, is for the exiled son an irreplaceable This.

And yet Lear's Howl comes back again and again and the word "marvel" sticks in the throat. Where is the song then? Lear's Never seems to give us, not horror and pity à la Aristotle, but horror without the pity, pitiless horror.[9] At the end of *King Lear*, there is no resurrection of the Once. Nevertheless, looking on Lear, we are made to ponder the possible resurrection of the Once. The horror of *King Lear* is that this resurrection seems to have *already* occurred when Lear and Cordelia are taken to prison and Lear speaks of being "God's spies." Lear is actually as if dead by this time. He speaks as if from a condition of posthumous mind. On waking to Cordelia's presence, Lear actually says: "You do me wrong to take me out o'th' grave: / Thou art a

---

8. On "posthumous mind," see *Philosophy and its Others*, especially 278ff., 300, 304, 368n20; also on posthumous mind in relation to metaphysical thinking, see *Being and the Between*, chapter 1.

9. Hence the difficulty sometimes felt in staging the final death scene. Shakespeare's sources have a restoration and happy ending. In the eighteenth century, the ending sometimes was changed. Dr. Johnson said that the death of Cordelia was so shocking that we would want to avoid it if we could.

soul in bliss. . . . Where have I been? Where am I? Fair daylight?" (*King Lear* IV, vii, 45–46, 52). Fair daylight—the words recall the restoration of elemental being for Dostoevski. But then all of this is snatched from us in the Howl, Howl, Howl. We thought we had crossed over to death and returned. Kent says: "He but usurped his life" (*King Lear* V, iii, 319). But Lear has actually to cross over into death itself. We cannot really outlive time in time itself. The ontological enigma of death has to be endured. "Men must endure / Their going hence, even as their coming hither; / Ripeness is all" (*King Lear* V, iii, 9–11). The irreplaceable cannot be replaced.

Through the tragic suffering of being at a loss, the question rises again to torment the philosopher: If one has ever been brushed by metaphysical astonishment before the Once or metaphysical horror before the Never, why should we confine the irreplaceable only to the loved particular? Why should not a rat, a dog, a horse evoke the same sense of ontological enigma? Why not explode Hegel's dialectics of sense-certainty with the mystery of a rat's being—or for that matter Krug's pen. This is perhaps a variation on Parmenides' question to young Socrates about dirt and the *eide*. Hegel runs away from the dirt of Krug's pen. Plato is better again in making Parmenides tell Socrates that philosophy, too, must think the hair, mud and dirt, the repugnancies of being from which at first reason recoils (*Parmenides*, 130c–e).

Thus, in a deep sense, and with the blessings of untragic Parmenides, there is no reason at all why philosophy should despise the being of a rat. True: the beloved This is for us the place where most often the enigma of being breaks through. The metaphysician can ask: Why should a rat, a dog, a horse have being at all? They, too, exhibit their sheer "That it is." Though we might eat them as meat, in themselves they live the intimacy of being in their own way, every entity a gift out of nothing by agapeic being. But when I turn thus from the beloved This to the despised This, from the child to the rat, the point is not at all for philosophy's eyes to become as rational stones. It is for philosophy to be the metaphysical thinking of agapeic mind.

Chapter 3

The Idiocy of Being

1. Idiotic Singularity

Philosophers sometimes exhibit a species of metaphysical anxiety when singularity is taken as ultimate. Yet the question arises: Is there a kind of absolute singularity, particularly in relation to selfhood, a singularity at the edge of inclusion in any conceptual system? Is there a certain thisness to self which from the standpoint of universal science is idiotic? Is there not something idiotic about this singularity that strains logos? I do not say that it must send metaphysics sulking away in misology. Rather it strains logos to the limit of any neutral universalism, hence demands modes of saying other to more traditional discursive ways. I want to explore this idiocy of being, both in terms of its availability to discursive articulation, and its recalcitrance to complete univocal determination.

Two extremes often define the issue. On the one hand, selfhood is interpreted in predominantly atomistic terms, terms continuous with the individualism pervasive in Western modernity. The individual is seen as a center of desire who calculates self-interest in a larger neutral context to maximize the options for its own gratification. There is here a privatization of self continuous with the turn to inwardness of the Cartesian *cogito*, and with the devaluation of external being into a valueless *res extensa*. Society provides the social surrogate of the neutral context wherein the individual as the atom of self-interested desire pursues the maximization of its satisfactions. The atom of self is transposed from Descartes' thinking thing into a desiring thing; but desire itself is interpreted in narrow terms of calculated self-satisfaction. It has nothing to do with, say, the divine abandon of Platonic eros.

While today this atomistic view is under criticism, it still constitutes the presupposition of much ethical debate, particularly in liberal and utilitarian thought. Relative to this criticism the second extreme emerges. In repudiation of this privatized atom, selfhood is said to be socially constituted. Society is not a neutral framework, but the very originating ethos within which the particular person comes to be himself or herself. There are strengths to this view, especially as a corrective to the atomistic privatization, but there are problems too. Most glaring is the danger of reducing the person merely to a construct of the network of social relations. The person becomes nothing in itself, and its intimate singularity vanishes in a tissue of larger public forces. I think we must reject this publication of the person. It risks a social leveling which is the outward correlative of the privatized leveling we find in the first atomistic theory. We must find a way beyond a privacy that trivialized inwardness and a publicity that also trivializes inwardness in a social holism that dissolves irreducible singularity.

What does such a way suggest? It suggests that every self is doubly mediated. What is this double mediation? First, every person constitutes its own integrity of being; as a dynamic center of being, every person is self-mediating; it is the promise, more or less realized, of a constitutive relatedness to self. Then there is the second mediation. This denies the closure of the first self-mediation, for the being of personhood is defined in a web of intermediating relativity with others. Intermediation with the other stresses the openness of the *inter*, the between, as straining against every closure on itself of self-mediation.

The truth of the first mediation was glimpsed even in the Cartesian *cogito*, albeit in somewhat abstract form. Marking self there is a certain irreducible self-relativity. Consciousness and self-consciousness do not constitute self, as the view coming from Locke and his heirs implies. Such a view says that a relatively stable, relatively provisional personal identity is constituted by an association of memories, impressions, and so on. I think we must say that consciousness and self-consciousness presuppose the power of a more basic self-relativity. We could not be conscious of ourselves did we not presuppose this more fundamental sense of the integrity of selfhood.

The constructed unity of self of empiricism is itself only possible given a prior sense of unity that is the ability to be self-conscious of the fact that all these experiences are *my* experiences. The mineness does not come from the experiences, but is presupposed by them. A more original sense of self is presupposed by experience as its, you might say, transcendental condition of possibility. When Hume looked into himself and found no self, it was Hume himself who found no self. Hume already had to have had this prior sense of himself in order to look at all, and in order to be able to know that he found nothing. His discovery of no static substantial self presupposed a prior sense of self, perhaps to be described in other than static substantialist terms.

I return to this matter below, but for now it is enough to say that this prior sense of self is not static substance but a dynamical original power of self-articulation and self-relation. The dynamical power at stake in the particular self makes it such that it must develop its own self-mediation to realize the promise of what it means to be its own singular self. We become ourselves, but we are already ourselves; and we become the selves we already are, because we are not the self we might be, given the promise of being that is given to us as being this person. The person is the power of self-mediation, rich in itself: a beginning and end, a beginning as a source of activity out of itself; an end, in that the self is in quest of its own mediated integrity or wholeness; a middle in that the self is just this dynamical mediating power that mediates with itself.

But—and the point is crucial—this is just the first mediation, self-mediation. There is a second mediation that answers to the second alternative above mentioned which emphasizes the network of relativity that socially shapes the self. For self-mediation is not closed on itself. It may become so, but its very nature as free is, in fact, to open itself to what is other to itself. We are marked by a certain desirous form of being: we desire to be, and we desire to be ourselves by entering into a variety of mediating relations with what is other to ourselves. Self-mediation is not self-sufficiency; we need the other to be ourselves; hence our power of self-mediation is born into, and given over to a community of being, where every effort to close self-mediation is ultimately undermined. This second mediation coexists with self-mediation, and always strains the latter's temptation to closure on itself. We are what we are, not only through ourselves and our own activity, but also through our relatedness to others and the welcome into the community of being that other persons offer to us. We become what we are in virtue of the welcome of the other.

Nevertheless, the danger of a closed self-mediation is matched by the danger of underplaying the singularity of self-mediation. The self then becomes merely a function of a network of social relations already at work in community; apart from this network it is all but nothing; it dissolves into this web of relations. This view makes the self nothing in itself by defining everything relative to mediation with the other. This amnesia of the idiotic singularity of self is a great danger with contemporary efforts to break with the merely atomistic view.

2. The Anxiety of the Philosopher, the Consolation of the Universal

Why when one speaks of irreducible singularity do philosophers get uneasy? Why this anxiety? We see our task as making sense of being in its widest and most general aspects. We make sense thus by the uses of categorial schemes. These unavoidably involve determinate concepts with a certain universal range of reference. We claim to want to make sense of selfhood, not of this self, not of that self. And yet there is something about being a self that invokes just the "this" of singularity.

Many examples could be adduced. I will mention Socrates' conversation with Euthyphro as very revealing. When asked about the nature of piety, Euthyphro first answered in these terms: "Piety is what I am doing." For Socrates this is not just the wrong answer, but shows an inability even to conceive of the right form of the philosophical question. It is not what I am doing that is the issue, but the general concept or idea that is more than any particular, and that perhaps a particular may instantiate but with which it cannot be identical. Later Euthyphro succeeds, at least partially, in satisfying Socrates. He raises his sights beyond particularity towards more and more encompassing universal perspectives. But at the end, he collapses back into a less than universalistic perspective, indicating his inability to sustain the philosophical drive beyond particularity. Euthyphro fails because he cannot forget his "I." He cannot forget what he is doing. He cannot forget himself.

My question is: Perhaps Euthyphro has a truth on his side that must be approached with a little more respect? Perhaps there is something about singularity that can never be completely rendered in the universality of the concept? Perhaps this singularity also asks us to reformulate what a community of being is. I say a community of being, not a community of concepts, which is perhaps the limit for some philosophers. Our anxiety with the singular as singular stems from our inability to formulate it in a system of universal categories. We seem to be reduced to an inarticulate gesture towards its thisness. Our anxiety is that outside of a system of universal categories and their possible completeness we are always threatened by such an idiotic inarticulacy. Let us call this threat "the autism of being": a blank face that seems empty of intelligibility, mocking our busy explanatory schemes with a recalcitrant muteness. I do not think this has to be the outcome, though it is one possible outcome that ought not to be dismissed immediately.

Let me offer a second example. In the opening chapter of his *Phenomenology*, Hegel offers his famous discussion of sense certainty. Essentially what Hegel claims is that the putative inarticulate richness of sense-certainty, its gesture towards a radical "this-here-now," is impossible to sustain. The minute we start to gesture towards a "this-here-now" we are implicated in a process of mediation. Once in this process we find ourselves caught up in the momentum of the universal. Then the "this" expands before us from its putative muteness, or autism: the "now" becomes a universal "now" and invokes the more englobing idea of time; the "here" becomes a universal "here" of space. Overall, mediation places the initial "this-here-now" in the more encompassing framework of a public space of categorial intelligibility.

I agree on the unavoidability of mediation, and that with its advent the call of the universal makes itself heard. The question is whether there still is something about the singular that remains unmediated in terms of the mediation of the universal category. It is not that there is no mediation, but perhaps the immediacy of the "this" calls for a different mediation than the Socratic *eidos* or Hegelian universal. Perhaps it calls for a mindful respect towards the "this" as "this," and in a manner in tension with the dialectical transposition, whether Socratic or Hegelian.

Again a philosophical anxiety emerges here. In this regard, Hegel is only a late heir of Socrates: the same drive from particularity to universality is evidenced in their way of putting the philosophical question. I do not think this exhausts the philosophical question. I believe Plato/Socrates would agree, though perhaps not Hegel. Hegel runs with the "logocentric" strain of Socratism and forgets that in Plato there are other articulated strategies for acknowledging the "this" as "this." There are also strategies, other than logicist ones, for suggesting a sense of the universal. These include the resort to myth and the very casting of the unfolding of philosophical thinking in the drama of dialogue.

Moreover, it is important to remind ourselves again that Socrates offers an *apology* for his philosophical life. As I have suggested before, an apology is ineluctably singular, even when the singular self who apologizes also claims to pursue the life of universal thought. To defend his own singular self, Socrates must talk about himself in self-justification, just like Euthyphro. He must remember himself in the singularity of his philosophical life, what he has done, what he is doing now even under threat of death, what he will continue to do, as this singular Socrates, even into the other world. He tells the story of himself as this singular I. No abstract universal will save him or justify him against an accusation that is also ineluctably singular and personal. Again, it is especially significant for the present point that he forthrightly says that he would not have survived to his present old age if he had not lived as an idiot (*idioteuein*). An apology for a life of philosophy is idiotic. Even to justify philosophy as a life of universal thought, there is no way finally to avoid the idiocy of being.

By contrast, Hegel wants there to be nothing idiotic about philosophy, about thought. He sees the self-mediation of the particular as yielding its self-identity, via the mediation of the universal, to a network of interrelations with others; inevitably it is absorbed into the larger whole which constitutes its truth; its truth for itself is attenuated in this larger whole. This is why atomistic theories are antithetical to Hegelian thought, and why contemporary defenders of social holism often gain much sustenance from Hegel or Hegelian modes of thinking, even though the dread name of Hegel is never mentioned.

As a distinctive center of the original energy of being, the self mediates with itself and intermediates with what is other than itself. In this sense it is always *between* an inarticulate inwardness and the public world of social relations. Nevertheless, there is something about its own self-mediation that it cannot completely mediate. There is a certain inward otherness that can never be entirely reduced to a determinate articulation. The power of self-being has a certain positive indeterminacy: as an origin of self-articulation, the source itself is overdetermined; it is not a mere indefiniteness, but a particularization of the original power of being as excess and plenitude. It is impossible to isolate absolutely the self from the others, but the deeper we delve into the power of being that constitutes self, the more we come across an indeterminate power that is prior to any determination and that exceeds every determination, whether effected by the self itself, or by the social networks of relations which consolidates its communal identity. This is the ontological power of original selfness.

This inexhaustibility of selfhood, exceeding determination, conceptual or social, is the idiocy of its being. This is at the edge of determinate intelligibility, but it is not senseless. Quite to the contrary, it calls for the utmost in discerning mindfulness. I believe it is *made* senseless, if our only way of making intelligible sense is dominated exclusively by determinate universal categories. Hegel is blind to this truth of the idiotic "this." He has no patience with it. It is immediately dissolved into the dialectical universal.

We might perhaps be less resistant to Hegel's move if it concerned a particular of nature to which we might be indifferent, or an indifferent thing like Krug's pen. But what if the "this" is a person, if the "this" is a *beloved* "this"? A beloved "this" is one in whom this intimacy of being is manifested as *beyond* atomistic separation, and social dissolution into an exclusively communal identity. A beloved "this" forces on us the thought of irreducible singularity. Recall again Lear's love for Cordelia. Lear loves Cordelia in the thisness of this "this"; he does not love Cordelia as representative of a universal humanity. Cordelia's love also is not for the father as father or as king but for the father as just this singular father. There is a love that is concentrated on the singular as singular. This is not to close it off from what is other to this singular, but that is not the point. Likewise, we might again recall Abraham's love for Isaac. Does Abraham love Isaac as Isaac, and this despite the horrifying thing God asks of Abraham? Does he love him only as the bearer of the future race promised to him? The horrifying thought in the very intimacy of horror, I suggest, is not the possible end to the future race, but the sacrifice of this singular I. This is Isaac my son; his blood will be spattered on the rock; his flesh will be cold and his eyes will be stones. Death calls to mind this singularity. His singularity is irreplaceable. It has no substitute. This is the horror of the father.

Where can we accommodate this irreplaceable "this" in a logic of universals? Any standard atomistic conception offers no help. It trivializes the "this" as "this"; it neutralizes it. Nor is there any way one can love the "this" as "this," in the sense at stake, if everything is to be calculated according to "rational" self-interest. The atomistic conception flattens the intimacy of being. Likewise, a universal holism produces a flattened conception. The tragic depth of Cordelia's death as a beloved "this" and the extremity of Lear's response is outside any logic of nameless public universals, or any socially constructed identity. This tragic depth exceeds the flattenings of atomism and social holism, and yet the very intimacy of being of the beloved singular calls for some acknowledgement of this depth. Neither the empiricist or the idealist alternatives do justice to the reality of thisness or the community of being which supports the "this" in its intermediations with others.

I take with great seriousness Kierkegaard's point about inwardness, namely, its final hiddenness. Beyond a certain type of mediation, beyond thought even, Abraham's silence is a kind of "mediation" beyond Hegelian mediation. I say this knowing that Kierkegaard rejects the language of mediation at this point, I think because he mistakenly believed that Hegelian mediation exhausted all the possibilities of mediation. This is not true.

For there is nothing emptily mute here. Neither Lear's Howl nor Abraham's silence are the autism of being; they are full of significance in excess of conceptual mediation. And do not say I contradict myself because I *speak* about what exceeds conceptual mediation. I am talking about the idiocy of being; hence the saying is public in its own way. The difficulty is finding the best way to say this idiocy without flattening its excess. The idiocy has its own *communicative* power. Likewise, both the Biblical story and Shakespeare's work are ways of saying that are not flattening, ways that must earn the respect of the mindful philosopher.

It should be clear, then, that by the idiocy of singularity I intend no privatistic atomism, though I do mean a privacy of the intimate. I intend it also in this sense: there is a certain excess of being characteristic of what it means to be a self, which can never be completely objectified in an entirely determinate way. This is an affirmative overdetermination. Thus, the "presence" of a self can be understood to point to this all but incommunicable intimacy of being; and yet this all but incommunicable intimacy, in fact, is at the very origin of genuine communicability. In many current debates "presence" is defined in the critique of the so-called metaphysics of presence, but this meaning is almost the exact opposite to what I intend: "presence" as the reduction of being to a completely available univocity and determinacy; "presence" as completely transparent and available for intellectual consumption by Cartesian conceptions. This is a wrong contraction of the idiocy of being as intimacy.

"Presence" is something shimmering and elusive. We know what it is before we say anything, though when we try to say exactly what it is, we know not what it is. Nor is this unexpected, because presence is an excess of being. It is the promise of self-transcendence that is especially characteristic of personal being, though it is prefigured in all being. This shimmer of presence, as the elusiveness of intimacy, is an indeterminacy in a positive sense, and might perhaps be called absence too: absence in the sense that there is no one definitive thing, univocal determinate entity that completely answers the call of what is here at play. Presence is absence, if our sense of being is completely ruled by the logic of a rigid univocity. The indeterminacy of selfhood is ultimately grounded in a freedom of being which can never be reduced to one determination or even an ensemble of determinations, since in itself it is a very source of determination. The origin of determination is itself indeterminate in this dynamic, open sense. This is absence, but only because the atomistic logic of a flattened privacy, in insisting that self be a completely determinate entity, sees nothing there, cannot see anything there.

This happens to Hume, for instance, when he looks inside himself for personal identity. He expects to find some univocal self. But there is no such thing. He concludes that the self is nothing. But since he still has a feeling of self—and of course he has to have such feeling, because always and willy nilly he is an idiotic self—he must seek to construct a self from the pandemonium of fleeting impressions. Of course, to define self-identity relative to this construction is question-begging, because a more original sense of self must be presupposed as the *constructing source*, which associates and brings together into congeries, the plurality of putatively discrete impressions. No self could be constructed from impressions, if this more original sense of self was not presupposed. For no impression could be felt as "mine" without this more original sense. Thus, the whole process of constructing a derivative self-identity floats on this intimacy of elusive selfhood which the constructed self ostensibly denies.

The Humean dissolution of the self is not unlike the post-structuralist denial of self and its deconstruction of the transcendental ego. Resort to the transcendental ego is marked by its own effort to reconstruct "presence" in terms of a universal ego, or a formal logical universal, or logical condition, free of all empirical particularity. But none of this is true presence at all. Consciousness in general, presence in general—this is a contradiction in terms. Presence always turns on some sense of the intimacy of particularity. And so this resort to the transcendental ego can be a repetition of the philosopher's penchant for flight from the particular into the universal. The consolations of consciousness in general are false alleviations of the burden of singularity as my singularity. To shed oneself of oneself in the neutral universal of mind in general—this is one of the great illusions of idealism.

Again I do not want to deny the universal, but we must rethink it in terms that do not sacrifice idiotic singularity. The deconstruction of the transcendental ego does not get us to the intimacy of presence, since presence is reduced to univocal determinacy, and the deconstructionist, like the empiricist, sees no such presence, sees nothing there. But the intimacy of being, while not completely articulable in determinate univocal fashion, is communicable; it is communication itself. We are thus pointed to the deeper meaning of presence. Presence is self-communication; presence is already a vector of intimacy which is self-transcending, a vector that goes towards the other, even for the other. Presence is outside of itself, other than itself, because it is the self-communication of an original center of being to an other that too, in its own right, is presence, is self-communication. Presence lives the doubleness of being, between self-mediation and intermediation with the other.

We need, then, an other idea of the universal that cannot be just the Platonic *eidos*, nor the immanent Aristotelian form, nor the consciousness in general of idealism, certainly not the *flatus vocis* of nominalism.[1] This other universal is not one term of a logical or ontological antithesis. It is the happening of the between. This universal is the community of the between where presence meets presence. This universal is the community of the middle, that space where being ceases to be an anonymous thereness, where self and other, each in their self-communication and their communication with the other, cross and crisscross. If the idiocy of personhood in its singularity is self-communicating presence, we are always beyond univocal presence, and the two, self and other, always go together. This universal is a community of being wherein idiotic particulars meet, in a meeting that is not a logical conjunction or an empirical contiguity, but a mindful being-together that is ineluctably ethical. There is no "being-with" without the intimacy of being.

3. Elemental Idiocy, Self Before Self

I will come to this community, but now I want to look more carefully at this prior sense of self, as well as a number of related conceptions. The elemental I, presupposed by all subsequently "constructed" selves, reappears in different experiences like pain, pleasure, insomnia. But the "root" is not the Cartesian "I think" or any version of it. It is not a preflective *cogito*. It is a prereflective idiocy, prior to all *cogitos*, and all determinate thinking.

---

1. The trouble with nominalism is not its emphasis on particularity, but its univocal diminishment of the this.

Since Descartes we have been wont to think in terms of the antithesis of subject and object, out of which antithesis emerges an understanding of mind as essentially objectifying. The world of being-other is there, as having been made an object for the subject. The difficulty then is that this objectifying mind has to account for *itself*, and as *other* than an objectified thing. The subject objectifies being, but this objectification of being-other, when then applied to the self, objectifies the subject, and in essence the subject as subject vanishes. Thus, the intimacy of being is dissolved in the modern antithesis of subject and object.

Reacting to this a variety of existential views were developed, and rightly. Objectifying mind leads to the self-forgetfulness of the mind that is effecting the objectification. There is an oblivion of self in the very success of self as objective mind. Such objectification may have some relative justification when applied to beings other than human beings, but with the latter something other is required. This is, in part, why Kierkegaard will claim that truth is subjectivity. He and other existentialists have been criticized for overstating the case against objective mind, and for ambiguity with respect to subjectivity itself. Such criticisms are not the issue now, though the issue is, at least in some respects, the proper interpretation of the truth of subjectivity itself.

The danger with the existential and related reactions to objectifying mind is that their response is still determined, to some extent, by the antithesis of subject and object that, as we saw, led to the forgetfulness of self. If we fail to think beyond this antithesis, and simply recoil from objective mind back to subjectivity as its antithesis, we will still be in thrall to the antithesis, and in some form or other, we will repeat the problem. For instance, we may counterpose a subjective irrationalism to an objective rationalism, or a merely solitary privacy to the alienating public space of the other, now called the crowd, or the herd, or *das Man*. The prior sense of self, the intimacy of being, the community of being, and the mindfulness more fundamental than subjective, objective or instrumental mind, will still not have been thought.

The distinction between subject and object is made possible by a sense of selfhood and community prior to the objectifying consciousness that lives in the distinction between itself and what is other.[2] Consider the common analogy of mind and eye. The mind/eye that sees, knows that it sees and what it sees; but the eye does not see itself as an eye in the same way it sees its objects. It later knows itself as an eye, later than its knowing what it sees, and that it sees. Eye here is not meant as an organ simply, but as power of

---

2. I now focus on self, later on community; also see later chapters on agapeic mind and being.

seeing, the power of an energy, an acting. It does not have to be known for it to be; its being what it is presupposes all instances of knowing. To see itself as an eye it looks in the mirror, but what it sees in the mirror is a reflection of itself, never absolutely itself. Its self-knowing in the mirror is derivative from a prior being with itself. There is presupposed a sense of self-relativity prior to all self-recognition in the otherness of the mirror. Otherwise it could not see and say: that reflection is *me*. The crucial word is recognition: there is a knowing of itself *again*, hence a second knowing, a recognition, but this knowing again is as if for the *first time*.

How do we understand this paradox of the second being known as if it were the first? Or the first coming to be known explicitly as if it were the second? The answer seems to be: prior to this explicit seeing of self in its reflection, this recognition of self, the self already pre-explicitly knew itself. This prior self is what I am calling the idiot self. A singularization of the energy of being is *with itself* in a primordial and original way. The idiotic self is an elemental being with itself. It is irreducible. Call it atomic, if you will, in the sense of indivisible, in the sense of *individuum*. It cannot be split in the sense of *atomos*. Nevertheless, a univocal logic of identity cannot be applied to it. For this unsplittable, elemental I can be *doubled*. It is a "one" that can be a "two" or a "three," indeed can diversify and multiply itself, and we cannot assign a univocal determinate limit to the number of self-multiplications. The univocal mind will say that this is crazy. But indeed it can double itself, for how else would it be capable of self-recognition, which is just the happening of the I that we are interpreting? In self-recognition, the self both cognizes and is cognized, recognizes and is recognized. It is not in external antithesis to an objective thing; it is as "subject" its own "object." The double, even the antithesis, is within it, rather than simply external.

This enigmatic power to be such a double, to be self-doubling, cannot be accommodated to the model of an external dualism of subject and object. At work in the heart of elemental selfness, there is an original power of self-transcendence and relativity to what is other. Idealism has shown greater insight here than is currently admitted to its credit. I add that I do not interpret this self-doubling as just the power to appropriate what is other to the self and hence to interiorize it within the immanent closure of an encompassing subjectivity that overreaches both sides of the antithesis of subject and object. Immanent self-transcendence does not exhaust the meaning of transcendence, just as objectified externality does not exhaust the meaning of otherness, or of being there as other.

Yet we must agree with idealism. There is, we might say, a complex coil of self around itself, that is elusive, transcending and articulating, and that cannot be made intelligible on the univocal logic that is applicable to objectified thinghood. The "being doubled" that we see in self-recognition points to the elemental self-articulation of the idiotic I. Every articulation of the elemental is in its own way elemental. But against the closure on itself of the coil of self around itself, the self-articulation of this original energy is a self-transcendence that is already a mode of "being with." From the outset the meaning of community as "being with" is not to be conceived in terms of a transcending subjectivity that encompasses within itself the two sides of subject and object.

Elemental self-transcendence and community are inseparable, so much so that an elemental "being-with" is constitutive of the idiotic I itself. The nature of the intimate self is "being with": being with self, and being with what is other to self. But "being with" is not to be first interpreted on the model of objective or even reflective knowing. There is a more primordial "being with," that is not reduced to the "being with," or togetherness of objectified entities, whether of an ego or an external object (these latter came later), or to the "being with" of the self with itself in the self-recognition—the latter is also later crystalized by reflection out of the first elemental being with itself of the idiotic I.

This idiotic self comes to more manifest expression with the *aesthetic I*— aesthetic in its ancient and widest connotation concerning sensible and sensitive being.[3] Being-there as other is given as aesthetic presencing; so also the sense of self is emergent as aesthetically intimated. By the aesthetic self I mean the self in the prereflective and preobjective feeling of itself as fleshed. There is a being with self in the element of the body. There is intimacy to the flesh.

Thus, my body is not a possession; its myness is not that of a piece of property. There is first no distance on this flesh that might allow one to speak of its ownness in terms of property. My body is properly mine in an appropriateness beyond all property and appropriation. My flesh is proper to me but not as a possession. The body is elementally my own. The very notion of property is derivative from this more elemental "owning."

Thus, the slave is not just a piece of property, or one deprived of owning property. These points may be true, but more fundamentally the slave is deprived of the freedom of his body which is the freedom of himself. He is deprived of himself since another disposes of his body. He is not allowed to own his body. In truth, he still *is* his own idiotic and aesthetic self, beyond every appropriation of his body by another. This entails an ownness of owning beyond all property relations. This body is proper to no one but the I, in the radical singularity of its own idiotic intimacy. Even the slave has this ownness that he keeps to himself, that is absolutely other to his owner. Here is the germ of the freedom that, in the end, is the promise of fuller freedom

---

3. On idiotic and aesthetic selving, see *Being and the Between*, chapter 10.

in the community of being. This radical ownness must remain undefeated, integral even though wounded, if finally the owning of the slaveowner is to be overcome.

In primary aesthetic feeling, there is presence to self which initially is a felt self-presence. This does not at all mean that it is determinately known as such. It is lived self-presence. We feel ourselves; or rather we sense ourselves as in a sea of aesthetic presence; we make no initial distinction between the external as an aesthetic presence and ourselves, our bodies, as aesthetic presence. This is why the opposition of subject and object comes later, and why it is a mistake to take it as original. There is in the flesh an immediacy of self which is not separately subjectified over against the world as an objectified otherness. We do not know in an objectified way if what is intimated in sense is the immediacy of the self or of the other. Sometimes it is felt as the immediacy of self, sometimes of other-being. An infant feels the other as himself, sometimes feels himself as the other. There is no objectified distinction. This is the most rudimentary of all self-intimacies, and it is barely articulable, given what looks like a kind of promiscuous univocity that marks the absence of distinction between the self and the other. It is, if you will, an equivocal univocity, though it is not known as such, and hence is not a self-conscious equivocity.

There is a lived presence of the self to itself, and of the self to things. There is an intimacy of immediate mind between the self and itself, the self and external things or others. There is the stream of minding as in process, and yet as present to itself. This minding is lived from within, prior to all more sophisticated acts of mind; it is also always the being with itself of self in every subsequent act of minding. This is the self as aware prior to self-awareness. It is hard to separate awareness from self-awareness, since here we are trying to refer to awareness as *self-aware prior to self-awareness*. Obviously, the distinction cannot be rigid. Self-consciousness as thematically directed and as self-reflective comes later, when the self has already developed its own powers of articulation and mediation, when it also has entered into a myriad of explicit relations with what is other to itself, or discovered itself to be thus involved, even though initially it does not know this involvement.

It is very difficult to talk about this self-awareness prior to determinate awareness of self. Consider how the "*con,*" "*cum*" of consciousness carries the meaning of "with." The "being with" can be with what is other to self. It can also be the self as immediately with itself. This is what is here in question. The intimate self is already a relation, a "being with." But this relation that constitutes singularity is not univocally single. There is a "being with" that is a prereflective self-relativity. The idiotic singularity is this.

To speak thus already seems to imply the splitting of the self into the self-knowing and the self known . But, in fact, the "self-knowing," such as it is, does not occur in such a split as thus objectified. The idiotic "self-knowing" of the singularity has an *intimation* of a double. That is, there is no univocal prereflective self, though the prereflective self is the hearer of the call of a double: its intimacy with itself is also an intimation of the otherness that will call on it more insistently as it grows in its own self-mediation. What then of the unity of self? Is the singularity a split unity from the outset? I prefer to say that it is, from the origin, the promise of a double mediation. To be the singular promise of a double mediation need not necessitate a dualism of the self in itself and the self for itself, or again between the self for itself and the self for others.

So we might venture that there is enigma at the center, the root; the enigma is not first in the circumference. The source of the light is dark. The source of self-consciousness is not a self-transparent light around which the shadows fall. The center and the source is the mystery. The light is dark to itself. There is an original power to be that is singularized in this self. The original intimacy with self is sensed as a certain unique energy of existence, a unique flavor of the energy of selving: the energy of being is sensed as the being at work of selving. There is the inward thisness as the prereflective mineness. We see this in the way a child says "mine." Existence reveals itself as an irreducible insistence of self, and this insistence as a "mine," as a "this," as a flavor of "this," a savor, a taste individuated. We taste only ourselves in this radically intimate way; we can have an intimation of the intimacy of another self.[4]

I savor self, I can savor self even in the domestications of habitual sameness. I may be an insipidity this morning, but I feel it as inescapably mine. I may be an exhilaration this moment, and I feel it and no one

---

4. Consider these instances: the stubborn will of a child, a selfness that emerges almost from the start; the child throwing a tantrum; the child saying "mine" also says "no"—self-insistence as elemental. This sense of I is not a construct of power; it is an emergence of power, out of which subsequent shapes of self are constructed. Think of the openness of this first emergence: the child may think you can see right into it; it will shout "stop looking at me." It will come to know that its intimacy is not thus on immediate show for the other.

Or consider this other example from a later stage: blushing. When we blush the intimacy surges in the body itself, and the blood goes to the face or drains from it. We blush when something has touched the intimacy of being; and of course, the blush can be one of modesty or one of shame. The blush is a return of the elemental I , and it cannot be explained in terms of any construct of self, since it emerges just in the chinks of armor in a particular construction of self. Something intimate is touched through the chinks of self-protection. No theory of the self as just a construct can fully explain the elemental surge of self that courses through the flesh in the blush.

knows, sometimes not even I myself. Or I am worn down; I am the wear of time. Or I savor self as a hidden hope, a dream hovering on the edge of time's desert, a mirage, a sign. Or I cannot stand myself, I flee myself; but I am myself fleeing. My escape is my escape and there is no escape. There are ruses and distraction. There are pretenses which try not to savor self. I am disgusted with myself; I am disgust; I taste its nausea as a drink I cannot stomach; I cannot stomach myself; my self-being revolts at itself, finds itself revolting. And yet in all this wretched innerness there is something astonishingly great. Being sick at self, being sick at heart— what other I in nature is sick thus, with a sickness of spirit? What other I shows this stress of innerness—an I that might go mad with the nuance of its own spirit?

A revelation of this savor of self can come, for instance, in the experience of insomnia. I wake in the middle of the night. I am floating in a disturbing darkness, vaguely sinister, or muffled in ambiguity, one knows not where one is determinately. There is the indistinct threat of the indistinct world to the elemental self-being that is nowhere and nothing. Waking to the night and its terrors, the child knows it is nothing definite; in itself it knows not who it is; there is nothing definite on the walls of its room, on the sides of its crib, in the room's empty air; there is nothing definite and yet it is alive with presence and pulsates. The child cries out for another, and the comfort is simply to be touched, the hand of another, touched by elemental presence. The community of the reassuring touch dispells the sinister. We die, we will die like children. Death is the final idiocy of being. We may howl, or go into it with yes.

When the older self wakes to its sleeplessness, it may be calmer and more enduring, but it is the same as the child, only it feels sure that day will come. Day does not always come. Nor does the comforting touch that re-kindles its trust in the good of being, or the being of the good. Perhaps the insomnia is endless, beyond night and beyond day, a dry burning patience of seeking that works on and on, even out of eyesight or earshot; or burrowing below self-consciousness it infects one's being, like a virus soundlessly spreading. What if, qua philosopher, one knows the day is also the night continued, and the insomnia is a metaphysical perplexity just at that equivocal pulsating of being? There is nothing; there is being; in the ambiguity between the two, the self is stripped of its own determinate formations, when it wakes. It has retracted from its roles of the day. It has no role, only a tired and weary selfness that would be rid of itself, and be welcomed into the comfort of sleep. At the zero point it cannot rid itself of itself, cannot retract that final step back into its own body. It has to endure itself and the ponderous presence, the burden of being awake. The stripped self is made sleepless by its own perplexity.

4. Idiot Being and Indeterminacy

I hear an exasperated query: Do you not then, just like Hume or the deconstructionist, lead us darkly along the path of dissolution? Is the point then the vaporization of all determinacy? I do not think so. The original power to be a self is articulated. Desire erupts in the idiotic self, it surges up in the flesh, elementally and unbidden. It comes to be shaped in a process of selving. Instead of the dissolution of determinacy, there is the fuller unfolding of this power to be into a distinctive self with a plurality of determinate self-manifestations. The singular self mediates with itself and intermediates with what is other to itself. It freely determines itself by being other to what it presently is, and by working towards the ideal it would become through its own self-determination.

The energy of self is carried by desire, as well as articulated by it; and this selving is not first known in self-reflection; it is known in its desiring. It is already desiring before it knows that it is desiring, and what it is desiring. It only knows itself by having been first propelled into a curve of self-transcendence, discovering itself determinately in this curve. There is incessant determining but no complete self-determination. What we crystalize in objectification is always only something of the fullness of what is ongoing in the energizing of selving; it is not the fullness. The indeterminacy of determining, and the impossibility of complete self-determination, already intimates in the roots of self an openness to being as beyond self-determining being.

While desire is energized in a singular self, it is never simply univocal, but pluralizes itself in its own forms. I mention two formations as especially important, namely, erotic and agapeic self-transcendence. These correspond to the two mediations—self-mediation and intermediation with the other. The self of erotic transcendence surpasses itself towards the other, but mediates with the other to mediate its own self-completion; the other is finally for the self; hence erotic self-transcendence is never entirely released from the self-insistence of existence. Agapeic self-transcendence, by contrast, is a surpassing of self towards the other that is for the other; it more fully redeems the promise of community carried by the second mediation, the intermediation with other-being as other; it is a love of the other that is not self-insistent in the first sense. There is both erotic and agapeic promise in the intimacy of being, in the idiocy of selfhood.[5]

---

5. I will have more to say of these in later chapters. In *Being and the Between*, the movement from the idiotic to the aesthetic to the erotic to the agapeic self is more systematically set out.

My main emphasis now is not on these determinations, but on an indeterminate sense of self that precedes every determination. If we demand a
univocally determinate self, we will deny such an indeterminate sense. Do
we not vanish into vagueness without this univocal determinacy? I think it is
the exact opposite: If we insist that selfhood from the origin is univocally
determinate, then when we try to determine what that self is, we dissolve in
an indeterminacy that has nothing positive about it. Likewise, if we conceive
of selfhood on a reflective model, then subject and object are taken as already articulated, and a presupposition of a determinate self is already effective in every subsequent thought. If we think through the implication of
these determinate and reflective models, we cannot sustain them, without
either begging the question or an infinite regress.

I first take the reflective model. It begs the question. Why? If we talk
about the self as self-reflective, then this self must have a sense of itself as
both the subject and the object of the reflection. But in order to recognize
itself as the one portrayed in the object as reflection, it must already have a
sense of itself that allows it just to *recognize* itself. When I look in the mirror,
and see a face there, I could never recognize that face as *my own*, did I not
already have some sense of what was my own, my own identity, prior to the
image that appears in the mirror. Without this prior sense of my own self, the
image in the mirror would always appear as the face of a stranger, never my
face. I would never see myself in the image. Self-recognition in the mirror
presupposes a sense of self-knowing that is prior to the self-reflective phase.

Consider the infinite regress: Suppose you say that self-identity still can
only be gained from a reflection, then the problem of identifying my self in
this reflection will presuppose a sense of self as already having been identified, and this will ask for another reflection, and then another sense of self,
and another reflection, and so on and on and on. We get a hall of mirrors of
infinitely regressing reflections and originals, and no original self. But this is
nonsense since the ability to talk about such a hall of mirrors itself presupposes an original self. Thus, for instance, the deconstructionist conveniently
forgets himself in deconstructing the self, forgets the living self necessary to
make sense of the deconstruction of the self. I think this infinite regress can
be reinterpreted in a more positive light. It points to an inexhaustible reserve
to the recesses of idiocy that ever elude complete objectification, that is
suggested by objectifications of self but never univocally captured by such
objectification. The prereflective self is not a univocal atom but an idiotic
overdetermined power of being.

Suppose we turn to views that insist on determinacy. What we find is a
parallel argument relative to the empirical ego. The empiricist will insist that
to be intelligible is to be determinate, and that to be determinate is to be
given in determinate sense experience. In what determinate experience is

the determinate self given? In none completely. We might then say that there is nothing there but a stream of impressions, an infinite succession of experience following experience. The empiricist will then say there is no self. But this stream is a degenerating form of the infinitude of self. It is a generation without a genesis, an issue without a source, a kaleidescope of images of an original that is denied to be, hence, images of nothing, hence not even images, for an image that images nothing is not an image, it is itself nothing. The infinite succession of experiences degrades into the self/nonself that is nothing.

The empiricist disdains to become entangled in some of the deeper perplexities his deconstruction of the self precipitates. Perhaps because of a scientistic faith, or a common sense moderation, he flees such perplexities. Others will be less lacking in philosophical intrepidity. For instance, we can here get various forms of the self as erotic. Consider the Sartrean self as nothingness, as empty and lacking in itself. The infinite restlessness of desire degrades into an equivocal intentionality; it becomes, for instance, the eroticism of Don Juan, the conquest of one sexed thing after another, and so on to infinity, *ad nauseam*. Instead of univocal determinacy the self's infinity appears, but it is nauseating. Indeterminacy appears here in entirely negative form. With self reduced to empty erotic subjectivity, the outcome is an infinitude that nauseates rather than fulfills.[6]

Deconstruction and empiricism, in fact, are closer to each other than appears on the surface. Neither may be too comfortable with the closeness, but both operate within the context of the univocity of being, albeit in very different ways. They exhibit different attitudes towards the self as univocal. Deconstruction takes apart this univocity in a project of dismantling and overcoming metaphysics. Empiricism dissolves the univocal self in its search for that univocal self: it finds none. It, too, ends in a burning of the books of metaphysics—to use Hume's metaphor—just as does deconstruction. From a scientistic beginning, from an anti-scientistic beginning, each recommends to us the *auto da fé* of metaphysics and theology. Both are infected by

---

6. If we must reject the inflated selfhood of "romantic" subjectivity, yet even relative to this overblown self, we must defend the infinite inwardness of the self. The latter demands a respect for the intimacy of being, free from any imperialistic puffing up of subjectivity. This respect cannot be grounded in the deflationary self or atomistic views. The latter lacks rich inherent integrity; it has aggregational identity in a mass. Even were we to speak here of parts and wholes, the parts are flat, and the whole little more than a facade. Behind the facade, predatory individualism still swells, and will to power inevitably fills the vacuum of the idiotic. And so in time, the deflationary atom becomes again the self-inflationary individual. The atomic monad becomes Thrasymachus *revivus*.

equivocity, for neither is possible without the unnamed idiocy of being which their conceptual superstructures pass over.

Traditionally the resort to the transcendental ego in Kant and other idealists was to avoid this equivocation: the incoherence of the denial of self, by the self. And yet the intimacy of being is not a form or a logical possibility, nor is it only a constituting, synthesizing activity—it is the source of this activity as exceeding this constituting activity. The formalism of transcendentalism reconstitutes the univocal sense at a level of higher universality; hence, the transcendental self is nothing empirical but other; it certainly is not personal; it is consciousness in general. Thus, Kant will say (*Critique of Pure Reason*, B 157): "I am conscious of myself in general in the synthesis of the multiplicity of representations, therefore in the synthetic original unity of apperception, not as I appear to myself, neither as I am in myself, but only to the extent that I am. This representation is thinking, not intuition."[7] It is not intuition, for Kant holds, with empiricism, that the only intuition is sensuous; there is no intellectual intuition.

Kant's universal form of consciousness in general lacks the intimacy of being. Indeed it is in flight from the idiocy of being. Far from this idiocy being the idealistic "for itself" of the transcendental ego, the transcendental ego presupposes the intimacy of self. Nor is the idiocy simply for-itself; nor is it an epistemological ego. Nor is it quite Kant's noumenal self: this is simply an unknown X, given a purely indigent characterization, set in dualistic opposition with the phenomenal ego. I think we must reject the indigent characterization as well as the dualism: the intimacy is communicated; the intimacy is overdetermined, a plenitude, the promise of the agapeic self. Yet it remains mysterious and enigmatic; so it must be interpreted. And perhaps this is part of the positive truth of Kant's "unknowable." Still he reduces the double to a dualism, such that the enigma cannot appear in any shape or form. This is not true to the idiocy of being.

Put otherwise, flight from the idiot self to the transcendental self will undo itself when the latter takes a formalistic shape. In the past, there then followed a flight *from* transcendental formalism, and also in a more hidden way from the idiotic self, to the *historicized* self. Instead of the logical or transcendental universal, the truth of being is then sought in the historicist or world-historical universal. The historicized self is not the idiot or intimate self. There is a historical shaping of selfhood—this I do not deny at all. The overdetermined energy of selfhood has a certain formlessness in itself; it can become many things, take on many shapes, can become a plurality of forms,

---

7. Note the tension here between consciousness in general, and the stress on the "that I am." How to reconcile this generality and singularity?

multiplied even against each other. Time is necessary for the self to become itself. The past is the having become of the idiotic self, necessary to give it concrete ballast in the present of its open venture; the future is necessary for the self to come to itself in terms of the ideals it sets for itself. All the complexities of temporal becoming are to be upheld, but the idiotic self is not the product of historical genesis simply. Nor is it a *telos* which in the end we will finally reach. It is an elemental source that is never left behind, not a goal projected at or beyond the end of time. There is an ahistorical idiocy to the self that shadows the self as historically constituted. The ground of the historical self is the idiotic self; and this idiotic self is never left behind.

It seems to me there is danger of tremendous dishonesty with respect to the historicized self. Consider: a person becomes a king, an emperor, a mighty ruler in world history; he constitutes his self as a great and powerful master; he rules over all; his subjects tremble; his enemies cringe; he swells with his self-articulating power, an erotic sovereign. He is Alexander, or Caesar, or Lear, or Stalin. Yet when the sun goes down and this mighty self lies down to rest in the night, he must strip. What is there? Fleshed vulnerability of the intimate self. I am lord of the universe; I lie down to sleep, and I am a breathing vegetable.

Fitful with power, I sleep restlessly, but in the dark I awake. The darkness is the formlessness of being. There is nothing distinct or distinguishable or distinguished in it. In the silence my distinguishing marks melt. I am alone in the formless dark, a formless self, a cry of self, an idiot center of pain and hope, or hate, or anguish, or regret. The vulnerable idiocy emerges when there are none of the props that support the historicized identity. The determinations of the day are retracted. I am as nothing, though I am not nothing. I am a well of longing. I am a sink of sin and sporadic repentance. I am a cauldron of envy and plot. I may remember sunshine in an open meadow of childhood; and, for no reason I can say, I am shaken to the roots by the memory. I may be many of these things. Without the props of day I may sink beneath the surface of muteness into an autism of being. Or my silence in sleeplessness may just be a cry from the abyss. I am an abyss in the abyss of night. The helplessness that lies prone, this is the idiot self. And the king, too, is that idiot. Of course, morning comes, distinctions return, I am distinguished again. The tremors of the night grow quiet; the lord of the earth lords once more.

The patience of night is closer to the truth of self-being than is the self-assurance of day. The lording is a lie. The flight to will to power of the historicized self is fearful of the idiocy of the night, though the flight has produced its own darker night. History will assure itself with the daylight confidence of enlightenment, but it lies about the idiot self and the abyss of the night that it forgets or represses. The silencing of intimacy in world-history produces, in the extreme, the howl of the death camps.

World-history has perhaps been modernity's biggest metaphysical lie. The idiot self reminds us of a simple truth: We come into the light out of a darkness of origin; that I am at all—this, too, is idiotic. We go back through a darkness of death, into a light, or a different night, or nothing, we do not know. The first and the last are metaphysical enigmas; the middle is an enigma of intimacy; and the lie of its mastery by world history is a flight from a mystery that chastens our hubris. History absolutized is perdition. The kingdom of heaven is idiotic, for idiots only.

5. Idiotic Self-Relativity

I mean no intemperance, so I will speak soberly of what might be called "idiotic self-relativity." It seems we cannot deny an elemental self-relativity, for it is the basis of our every effort to make sense. If the I were not self-related, it would not know that it had made sense. It must be aware of *what* it had done, to know *that* it had made sense, and this would be impossible did it not relate to itself with the relevant mindfulness. Do animals have this self-relativity? One cannot exclude some self-relativity, but it does not reach the range of human self-mediation which is immeasurably wider, indeed of a different order of being. Human desire is freely self-mediating. It is not simply biologically determined in a more or less univocal way. One might say that animal desire is pointillistic: it seeks this, this, this, and so on. This succession of this, this, this . . . would be an image of futility for the human being. This is why we substitute the phrase "*ad nauseam*" for the "and so on." In our procession along an infinite succession of desires, we become mindful of the succession and of ourselves in the succession. There is the promise of mediating self-relativity implicit in the succession all along. The free range of self-relativity, and the possibilities of self-mediation transform animal appetition into human desire as free being for self.

This self-relativity is not a mechanism; it is in act, as an action, an acting. Again there is something elemental about this being in act and acting; it is not reducible to something else. This is where the idiotic I germinates a determinate self-reflexive self. It is the ground of the empirical ego—the empirical ego is already a determination of the more original idiot self. Difficult though it is, we can talk about this origin; it is not an autism of being. Nor is this origin an object; and yet it can objectify itself; it is self-objectifying; and as self-objectifying it must be more than an object, for in the object it can come to recognize itself, self again. The process of self-objectification is necessary for the full articulation of the origin, but the origin must have some intimate sense of itself prior to self-objectification; otherwise the self-objectification could not recognize itself as such, as self. But the original self cannot be simply a product of the return of the I from its self-objectification. It cannot be simply the product of self-objectification; for then it would be self-presupposing, which is just the point which seems to be denied, if the self is simply the product of self-objectification.

The I acts upon itself: it is the acting and the act and the action; and it knows itself as the same I in all of this. Yet it knows that there is a difference between itself and all its actions, for its power of being is exhausted by none of its actions. Is the idiotic I just thought thinking itself? No, for its intimacy with the other is always already there from the outset. The I is aesthetically concrete in its embodiment; its intimate presence there can be a radiation that welcomes, or withdraws, or even threatens. There is no problem of epistemological solipsism. The sayability and unsayability of the idiotic I is not this problem. This intimacy of being and its unsayability is not a problem but a metaphysical enigma. A problem is a determinate question with the possibilitiy of a determinate answer. A metaphysical enigma is an indeterminate perplexity to which no one determinate univocal answer can be ever adequate. Every determinate answer points beyond this univocal answer to the deepening of the enigma, to dwelling further with what eludes complete conceptual mastery.

Am I talking of something like Fichte's intellectual intuition of the immediate self? Fichte is Kant's heir, though he refuses Kant's prohibition on intellectual intuition. Fichte's I is the principle of thinking in general; already the transcendental displacement beyond the idiotic I takes place. Yet Fichte does help us, especially if we see the meaning of "intuition" in a particular light. Consider the root of "intuition" in the word *intus*, the inner, the intimate. The intimacy of being, the "*intus*," is implied in intuition, indeed to such an extent that philosophers have been extremely alarmed by claims of intuition. These, it is said, are merely idiosyncratic; they are not publicly warrantable. But, of course they are idiotic, precisely because, if there are intuitions, they go right to the heart of the intimate self which resists objectification and hence manipulable availability. If we understand the "*intus*" and the "*idios*" with the requisite metaphysical complexity, any unqualified rejection of intuition founders. Rather the elusiveness of the truth of metaphysical mindfulness calls all the more for recognition. Nor need there be any intent to use "intuition" as a mask to disguise lack of philosophical honesty.

Of course, intuition too often has been misleadingly objectified in terms of the paradigm of visual perception. From this paradigm intuition gets narrowed to the perception of a determinate object. Thus, intuition loses its essential reference to the intimate, and becomes contracted into a narrow determinate epistemological act. While this is not the place to offer the account, it could be shown that this contracted intuition is the objectification of a much more rich and complex mindfulness that is not marked by the univocal boundaries the objectifying account implies. Visual perception is a determination of mindfulness, articulated out of a more indeterminate aesthetic, fleshed mindfulness. This latter precedes and exceeds visual perception, and plays over the milieu of the determinate perception as a definite act of seeing. The intimacy of being is still at work even in objectified perceptual intuition.

Were we to speak of an intuition of self, this would be an indeterminate intuition in an even more radical sense. For it could not be the intuition of a determinate object. This again is what Hume found. But he failed to understand adequately the meaning of what he found, or rather did not find. If we retain the notion of intuition, its meaning would have to be rethought in terms of the intimacy of being. The intimacy means there is a coincidence with self, before non-coincidence, yet with an intimation of the non-self. It is this primordial, internally intricate coincidence that is awakened to philosophical mindfulness in intuition. I cannot completely abstract from the I; but the I is never a solipsism; self-relativity floats on a sea of sensed otherness; the idiotic I lives in a fleshed aesthetic mindfulness. Thus, the primal self-relativity of the I cannot be the infinite self-relation of the idealistic ego which merely thinks the other out of its own thought of itself. The idealistic ego is finally an erotic I that only excites itself: this is an onanistic intimacy. The self-generation of this ego is an auto-eroticism; its self-becoming is always out of itself, and always through itself and always for itself; it never escapes the circle of auto-eroticism, no matter how wide that circle may be swelled. There is not hetero-eroticism and certainly not agapeic transcendence that goes beyond the circle of erotic sameness towards the other as other.

The spontaneity of the I is not infinite in act. The I is a finite particular creature, not a God. This is the whole point of its absolute singularity. Of this the idiocy of its being serves as a reminder, calls its creaturehood back to mind. The idealistic ego, especially that of Fichte—is a false interpretation of self-relativity to the extent that it elevates this into the absolute—literally *ab-solo*, from itself alone. The solitaire game of this absolute self-relating would absolve it from the other. Thus, Fichte found it intolerable for the self to be explained by another, even God; hence his attack on the notion of a created self.[8] This absolution of self-relativity from the other is plain wrong. We can avoid it by recovering the idiocy of the intimate, even while acknowledging something strange and other and enigmatic about selfhood.

---

8. This attack helped launch the famous *Atheismusstreit*.

6. Idiotic Freedom

The issue can also be approached in terms of freedom. If there is an indeterminacy to the idiot I that is original, "original" does not imply atomic substance but source of origination. The original indeterminate I is free as an originative source of being. I want to suggest that this is not just freedom as self-producing. We find this latter concept in idealistic and existentialist thought, but it is very equivocal. If there is any self-production, it is not a creation from nothing. The self must *already be* for it to produce. The self is a creation, but not first a self-creation. If it were the latter, you would have the absurdity of its lack of itself being the original of itself. The lack would be the original, and hence nothing would be the original source.

We might say that lack is itself originative only because it points us back to a plenitude of being that, in articulating itself, comes to know its own lack in the form of need and desire for the other. The lack is energized by a more originary power of being. Freedom is not ultimately erotic, nor simply for the self. Put otherwise, the indeterminate freedom of the idiot I is not autonomy. For the intimacy of being is double, hence its being for itself is also heteronomous. Freedom as originative indetermination is agapeic, in that it can be for the other, and for the self in so far as it is free for the good. The self is created for itself to be the promise of self-creation that is the promise of being for the other. It is an agapeic creation that may create beyond itself, both erotically and agapeically.

Freedom cannot be reduced to a determinate power. A determinate power produces a determinate product, and a certain univocal causality binds source and effect together. Such univocal causality is found throughout nature, as it is in human existence. Relative to this univocal causality we have the power to predict determinately the consequent from the prior: with the one goes the other, according to a well-defined, determinate relationship.[9] This is not so with freedom: there is an idiocy to freedom as beyond the intelligible structures of univocal, causal determination. In freedom there is no univocal causality binding the prior and the posterior. The idiocy of being is a loosening of the bonds of determinacy. To be free in itself, the source of freedom must be beyond univocal determination; for it cannot be fixed. And it cannot be fixed because it is a fixing or source of fixing, a shaping and not at first a shaped product. There is something elusive about this unfixed fixing, this shaping beyond shape, this open determining beyond determining. It is very difficult to make it intelligible, precisely because we tend to think of "making intelligible" as a process of

---

9. See Desmond, *Being and the Between*, chapter 9 on causality.

fixing a determinate structure. To render a reality intelligible is then to determine the indeterminate. But with freedom we cannot do this completely. So there is something unintelligible about the original freedom, if intelligibility is exhausted by determinate structure.[10]

Of course, we need to keep in mind that the process of making determinate intelligibility, qua process, is not itself a determinate intelligibility. It involves reference to a determining intelligence, an action of doing the intelligible, of being the intelligible, of being the energy of intelligence that understands the intelligibility of the structure. Thus, even the effort to fix determinate intelligibility is itself participant in a process that cannot be completely fixed. We are always at the edge of determinate intelligibility with freedom. Each of us in the innerness of our intimacy is the very ontological taste of freedom. This taste of freedom is elemental in not being derived from other finite determinations. But this does not mean that it is self-derived simply, a completely autonomous self-production. Put as concisely as possible: Freedom is given to itself elementally, and only gives itself

---

10. If there is no univocal causality with freedom, is it all equivocal? In a qualified sense, yes. We inhabit a domain of ambiguity where nothing is immutably fixed. The unfixity of the realm of freedom is unsettling, challenging to self-determination. But the equivocity is an ambiguity to be mediated. Freedom flowers in the mediation of the equivocal, especially the equivocation of desire. This is like a labyrinth. Is there an Ariadne's thread? In one sense, nothing but the frail idiotic self. The intimate self can lose itself in the labyrinth. But it is also always a promise. Otherwise we are empty selves, nothings to be filled with the junk of advertisers, or the slogans of the political propagandists. Then we are nothing in ourselves, and only something in virtue of what a dominating heteronomy imposes on us. There are too many examples of this emptying out of the self in modernity. In the extreme, it leads to the torturer for whom there is no indefeasible intimacy. I know it may seem extreme to say it, but some advertising can be a distant cousin of torture, when it sets out to break down the self, make it suggestible, amenable to . . . whatever . . . to anything at all. It does not matter how you fill in the emptiness. It is all the one, since it is all indifferently different. In principle, and at a certain extreme, there is a ghastly convergence between electric shock and this use of the electronic image. There is a decomposition of the self, production of a dark equivocality of desire where the self does not know what it desires, does not know what it does know. This is the barbarism of idiocy. And then the void is filled up, desire reformed from formlessness. This is a perverse parody of creation—making the subject anew, giving it to itself out of nothing, giving it to itself as the kitsch of consumption. This cult of novelty is metaphysical violence on the self. "Creativity" becomes the destruction of the self, the intimate singularity. A self, as with the torturer, is made no longer to trust the truth of self. This is a variation of the hellish circle of the evil genius of Descartes. Man now plays the role of the evil genius, the swindler of desire, for power, or profit, toying with the idiot self.

to itself, because it is first idiotically given to itself. Its intimacy with itself is itself the gift of original being as other to itself. It is idiotic not only in its acting, but in its being, that is, in its being given to itself, simply to be itself, and then to produce itself and to produce beyond itself.

We need metaphysical mindfulness of what is thus ongoing, in order to be recalled from objective intelligibility to the intelligencing self. But here, too, we come across something paradoxical relative to the ideal of univocal intelligibility. Intelligence is a reading between (*inter-legere*): the *inter* is there in both intelligibility and intelligence. To be between, there is something more to intelligence than any determinate, univocal intelligibility. This means there is something about intelligence that is not completely intelligible. There is something about determinate know-ing that is not known determinately. There is something about this or that determinate act of freedom that is not reducible to this or that determination. There is something about mindfulness that escapes its own minding. Minding escapes its own complete self-mediation; it is other to itself in the very act of grasping itself or what is other. It exceeds itself in its very appropriation of itself. Its own self-appropriation is given to it out of this excess, a gift that it quickly forgets when its concentrates exclusively on its own power of appropriation. Its identity is other to its every identification, and yet it is simply this process of identification which is never-to-be-absolutized.

The reference to the excess of indeterminacy as other, in the innerness of intimacy, suggests a source of creation beyond the self itself as source of origination. In a word, there is an other origin transcending the self as origin. The self as origin is itself an origin beyond the lack revealed in desire. This origin as plenitude of indeterminacy particularizes the self as this self. This particularization does not univocalize self; it determines it to self-determina-tion as always open. The particular self is given to itself by an original indeterminacy that, as idiotic, is never exhausted because there is always more to it that exceeds all finite determination.

Of course, there is a proper sense of our *infinite lack* we cannot deny: the human self is not God. Out of this lack arises the erotic articulation of the self, namely, the search of itself and the other in its own self-transcendence, with the view to achieving the promise of its own wholeness. But there is a different transcendence of the self from the side of the agape of being. Then the excess as "more" (not a lack) reveals the potential for agapeic mind and willingness. The idiotic self expresses itself as a double willingness: self-willing, as its own insistence of being; good will as the willingness to sacrifice the self-insistence for the other. This second willing is a making sacred of the idiotic self as for the other. The sacrificial self becomes a sacred self, though it is still an idiotic self.

7. Community and Idiotic Being

How is the idiocy of being compatible with the idea of community? Is any move from the first to the second possible? I want suggest that there is no move from the first to the second, since the two are always together, though the togetherness of the two can take different forms.

Consider the following. There is no community without communication, but there are many modes of communication, all relative to different modes of "being with."[11] Suppose we reflect on what we deem an intimate conversation with another person. In such a conversation we already transcend solipsistic privatization. The point could be made that the intimacy of being makes possible, as it is also articulated by and communicated in, this being *intimate with*. As I have said, intimacy is itself a mode of "being with," one that is not completely objectifiable, since it is the self in its lived innerness that is present in this communication. Both the inwardness and the "with" are complexly modulated by this "being with." Our togetherness with the others, when it is a mode of being intimate with, transforms the meaning of socially defined identity. Intimacy is not something that has to be "in here" or "out there" in any determinable spatial sense. Being intimate with is a mode of being there with the others that can be inward, or outward, or both at the same time. True, it can never be merely outward; intimacy always requires an energization of inwardness. A purely outward intimacy makes no sense, though there could be a more purely inward intimacy. Outward intimacy is the transformation of outwardness by this energizing of the promise of inwardness as self-communication, communication for and with the other.

This transformation of outwardness into presence beyond objectification is evident, for instance, when something about the other "touches" us. What is this? What touches? What is touched? This "being touched" need not be physical, though it may be that too. A handshake transforms the space of the between; it may be warm, or limp, or reluctant; one might feel that the hand was offered as an object without presence, and one made contact with a fish. A self retracts into itself and out of its hand, even as it offers its hand—it does not offer itself. The retraction of presence is felt in the intimacy of being, but in the mode of the draining away of self into a wan absence. Contrariwise, a single word of intimacy may touch us to the depths of our being. The intimacy of the other beyond objectification passes in a communication that energizes the promise of our own intimacy of being. A certain physical touch, too, can astonishingly transform the interchange of presence between two selves, erstwhile there just as stones.

---

11. There are many modes of being together, hence many formations of community; on this more fully, see *Being and the Between*, chapter 11.

The happening of idiotic "being with" is easily deformed. Not only is aesthetic discernment and intelligent discrimination necessary, but also finesse of spirit. We show a lack of this if we conceive of the intimate and the public as dualistic opposites. Of course, these may be opposed, and often are in modern culture. A contracted privatism coexists with a devitalized togetherness. What is called "public" becomes a neutered space, indifferently available for all atoms of privatized desire. This neutralization of public space attenuates the original energy of being in an objective manner that matches the same attenuation in the subjectivity of the private atoms that function within the space.

Community, properly speaking, is marked by a certain intimacy of being that, like freedom, is impossible to reduce to univocal determination. Think of the following: How we sometimes wonder as to what makes distinctive *this particular people*, say the Russians or the Japanese. What makes it to be *this* people, so particularly its own? An often suggested answer is that the particularity of a people is defined by a certain shared spirit, their own *esprit*. We know, of course, that this can harbor danger,[12] but the crucial point is that this *esprit* cannot be completely objectified. We cannot say univocally that just this or that aspect is the spirit that makes the people this peculiar people. Often this spirit never appears into notice beyond its day to day being at work. For the most part it is revealed in some extraordinary crisis, say, the death or assassination of the head of state, or in the celebration of a victory, in war or sport. As to what exactly is revealed, in such an outpouring of celebration or mourning, we cannot completely conceptualize it. There is an excess to objective conceptualization, because a community is marked by a nonobjective intimacy of being.

In everyday life this is taken for granted. Frequently only its rupture gives one some sense of it. Consider another example, that of the exile or emmigrant. One leaves one's own country and people for a new country and people. Before leaving, one lived in the intimacy of being of the first home. Now having left this nonobjectifiable intimacy, one painfully begins to get a sense of an elusive sense of everyday togetherness that previously was com-

---

12. Derrida offers some reflections on this in relation to Heidegger. I make some remarks on Heidegger's politics in relation to the world-historical universal, and tortured religion in *Beyond Hegel and Dialectic*, 43–55. Because the spirit of a people is bound up with the intimacy or idiocy of being, delivering lectures against "chauvinism," "nationalism," or some such, in the name of enlightenment rationality shows a peculiar lack of enlightenment. There is much more at play here, for good and for evil, dangerous yet of promise, than any rationalistic preaching can comprehend.

pletely taken for granted. This now haunts one, as no longer there. One undergoes its previously powerful presence in its present absence. The rupture allows the space for pained mindfulness of what was at work, but not noted. The same thing happens with the loss or death of a beloved one. Bereavement brings a contraction of the energy of being, once supported by the nonobjectifiable intimacy with the now dead other. While one was thus supported, one did not advert to its being at work.

If the intimate and the communal need not contradict each other, why then are they so frequently opposed? An important part of the answer is, I believe, that we objectify the intimacy of being by instrumentalizing it. Not surprisingly, the coarsening of the intimacy of being is pervasive in Western instrumental societies. This is ironical since these societies are heirs to spiritual traditions that stress the unique singularity of the person. But when that stress is coupled with a will to instrumentalize being, the space of the public is voided of inherent value, and the outer loses the aura of communal intimacy. We may believe for a while that the self in its inner privacy will be the sanctuary of inherent value. This retreat into the so-called sanctuary of privacy is widespread in instrumentalized societies, but it is in flight from the effects of the instrumentalization, which it cannot escape entirely. For it brings into the intimacy of being the same orientation to being that defines the instrumentalized society. This instrumentalization will eventually corrode this privacy also, and the private will be denied its intimacy. The communal and personal intimacy are so bound together that the instrumental devaluation of being produces the same despoiling of inherent value in one as in the other.

We then say: Nothing is sacred anymore. The intrinsic worth of the other, of the self in its idiotic singularity, of the other in its idiotic intimacy—these have to be respected in a noninstrumental way before the nonobjective radiance of communication is granted its right of place. The phrase "Nothing is sacred" invokes the idea of the holy, and a desecration. The language is not mere metaphor or hyperbole. Loss of the intimacy of being entails a desecration of the sacred spaces of being where the communal and the personal meet. A complete desacralization of being would produce the destruction of the intimacy of being and also the disintegration of "being with," in any sense deeper than a mere being alongside the other. In the beginning and in the end, the intimacy of "being with" is inseparable from being religious. The word *religio* itself communicates this in its naming of a bond of relatedness and a tie of trust. The intimacy of sacred communion is in the depth of the idiocy of being. Were this depth entirely desecrated, the distinctive personal "being with" of human community would wither at the roots.

Let me take a somewhat different approach. Think of architectural places. These are public spaces, almost always with a functional purpose. A building is the instrument of a community in that sense. But even in this instrumentalization of lived space, there can be a transformation of the instrumentalization in the direction of the intimacy of being. There are architectural spaces where a rich sense of human intimacy is present or allowed to be. I do not simply mean intimacy of quantitative scale. It is true that the larger quantitative scale becomes, the more difficult it is to preserve the sense of intimacy. Even here one might claim that where the traces of the sacred are, there more fully is conserved the intimacy of being.

Think of the space of intimacy created by a medieval cathedral. Considered on a purely quantitative scale this would seem to squash personal presence in its singularity, and yet it does not. Compare this with the monstrosities dreamt of by the Nazis, as by Albert Speer, or the use of monstrous space at the Nüremberg rallies. The immensity of space here was to dissolve the singularity of self in a visceral surge of togetherness. It aesthetically shaped the intimacy of a people, at a level below discriminating mindfulness. This public space produced an idiocy of being that brought to the surface the dark togetherness of a people, feeling its power in an orchestrated surge of self-excitation. This surge was earthed in the figure of the Führer. Here we see the darkness of the intimacy of being, exploited by a public space, instrumentally wrought to whip a gathering into a *volkisch* frenzy. The power of spirit, touching the intimacy, is equivocal. It can be twisted into an idolatrous worship of the people or its leader. The Führer becomes the One in whom all differences are dissolved, the locus of what I call an absorbing god, of the people itself as an absorbing god.

By contrast, the immensity of the architectural space in the cathedral served to focus the soul on itself initially, to help it recollect its spirit in the intimacy of prayer. The self is to remember who it is, as a creature before God, God who is not an absorbing Moloch, but an agapeic absolute who does not dissolve the differences of creatures, but loves them in the singularity of their singularity. Having welcomed this return to the nonobjectifiable self, the space shapes a second mediation: there is a transcendence towards the other, as the self is drawn out of itself by the movement of the space upwards, vertically. The surge of spirit is caught up in the space that points vertically beyond towards transcendence as other. There is a movement of self-recollection from exterior distraction to interior respose, then a movement in the intimacy of the soul to the superiority of transcendence. Nor does transcendence dissolve the community as public or excite it into hubristic self-assertion. The sacred place is the communal space of a people. There is no dissolving of singularity into the one leader. There is journeying together, on the pilgrimage of finitude. The tourist, voyeur of sacred spaces, knows nothing of this pilgrimage. Camera snapshot: still of the scene, click of the metallic eye; the intimacy of being is not revealed. The space of intimacy, as communicating a being with, calls for participation.

The point, then, is that a public space can be marked as welcoming both the singularity of the person and its relativity to what is other. In different degrees, it can concretize the intimacy of being. This concretization need not be an objectification; it can be the sensuous manifestation of the promise of that community of presence. Were a building a merely neutral instrumental space, it would foster the degrading of this promise. The promise is itself degraded into predatory opportunism in a network of transactions, wherein the self can maximize its self-interested options. A space devoid of value is the lack of an ethos. It is the profanation of space, and incites profanation. It is little wonder that such profane spaces foster selves devoid of reverence and respect. How profane the modern city often is, how lacking in intimacy its spaces and denizens! Is it any wonder that these denizens flee into a privacy shuttered against the other, now also profaned into a threat?

The genuinely public space, as soliciting the promise of a community of presence, is a space of *betweenness* where the self, even in the idiocy of its singularity, feels it can be at home, at home with the other. Home—this is the most elusive word; this is the word of intimacy. Home is a word of mystery. It is a word that cannot have one univocal meaning, and yet it is not merely equivocal. When we are at home, we know we are there, though we cannot say completely in clear discursive conceptions where we are, and what it means to be there. A community is the public home of the idiot self. Home may not finally exist in this world. It may be what the religious call the kingdom of heaven. Yet only by preserving the intimacy of being will we keep alive the promise of this kingdom. In its light, there might be something hellish about a perfectly functioning modern state, one that lived by nothing but the instrumentalization of being. The sinister nature of its perfection would just be that everything seems to be functioning absolutely efficiently. But the elemental human presence as self-manifestation and self-communication would be absent. In that functional perfection, we would be lost, the kingdom would be lost. There would be no people. There would be no home.

We cannot protest too loudly against the functionalization of being that still proceeds apace in Western capitalist societies, notwithstanding all our protests of the inalienable rights of the individual. The mystery of selfhood, beyond every function, has to be reaffirmed. This is its idiocy as a value in itself and as a being for itself. With Marxist communism now in ignominious retreat, the collectivist totalization seems to have been repudiated. Yet the danger that the latter magnified into world-historical visibility is the same danger facing the increasingly functionalized societies of the West—the failure to understand fully the public space of community in the requisite terms of the intimacy of being. The totalitarian states rushed over the irreducible singularity much more violently than does the capitalist West. There privacy is let be to a greater extent, though often in the form of self-distraction or ethical neglect. But the singularity of self is still dominantly understood as an exploitative, or to-be-exploited, unit of productive, instrumental power.

The logical and ontological basis for the violence is a mistaken, rather incomplete, understanding of the relation of singularity to universality. What I mean is that the Marxist communization is an heir of the Hegelian move from particularity to universality. The communist state may purport to be the concrete universal, but this concrete universal failed to let be the singular in its intimacy. This universal, supposedly concrete, is still not concrete enough to open itself to the inward otherness of idiotic selfhood. Marxism and capitalism share in the same functionalization of being. Both reveal related pragmatic appropriations of the philosopher's flight to the universal: the universal will no longer be merely contemplated; it will be practically enacted in the reconstruction of community, in accord with a certain ideal of rationality. But if this universal is an abstraction, the reconstruction will inevitability share in the poverty of the abstraction. The metaphysical danger is forgetfulness that this is an abstraction, hence a possible distorting source of community in its concrete promise.

Against functional and world-historical amnesia, surely the philosopher must remember who and what we are? What we are is a promise, always frail, ever threatened. The promise must be kept in mind, even if it cannot be contained within a conceptual system, or a society constructed according to an idolatry of function. If it is at the edge of rationalization, it is not any the less real, or lacking in supreme interest to thought. A certain kind of metaphysical thinking may really only begin just at this edge. There may be something idiotic about metaphysics as a thinking beyond systematic categorial science. This idiocy of thinking need not be a philosopher's anxiety, or indeed terror. Thought may find a home there, there where it is not at home in the world-historical abstraction.

Such thinking inevitably has an ethical and political dimension. Idiocy is politically powerful, just in its political powerlessness. This is a truth to human being relevant to ethics and politics that is tangential to, in a different dimension to, that of world-historical or systematic universality. From the standpoint of the pragmatic and logical truth of the latter, the former may be the real metaphysical truth. Relative to this, pragmatic truth may be a lie, ultimately. Systematic truth may be systematically incomplete. What may be suitable for certain pragmatic and conceptual domestications of middle being, may dissemble the depths of middle being, its heights or extremities, all intimated through the idiocy of being.

In premodern thought the functionalization of being was less systematic; nor was the instrumentalization of all areas of being conceived as a global project of rational and technical mastery. Thus, ancient and medieval *theōria* promises more of an open contemplative vigilance for the manifestation of the intimacy of being; the elusive presence of being there in the enigma of its being there. Metaphysical thinking cannot be divorced from the ethical: the double mediation of the self preserves its inherent value as a this, and yet points to it as a deep down appeal for dignity, an appeal showing its coimplication with other selves. A metaphysical rethinking of this intimacy forces us to think the ground of ethical dignity. And in this ethical appeal one notes again the inseparability of the communal and the idiotic. An appeal goes out towards the other, but it always has an intimacy to it, something of the elemental thereness of the singular self in its vulnerable being for-itself. An appeal is an exposure to the other wherein we ask the other to be *with* us. It invokes the second intermediation of the other. Appeal cannot be reduced to singular self-mediation. Nor do atomistic selves appeal. Likewise, on atomistic terms no real explanation of irreducible dignity is possible.

8. The Intimacy of Torture, Love

I want to illustrate the matter relative to two opposed shapings of the intimacy of being: torture and love. Love and torture are coeval with human being, yet the instrumentalization of being in modernity has affected both. We find widespread use of torture, even while it is rejected widely; we find widespread cheapening of love, while eros is publicly exploited more and more profanely.

In the violence of torture, one has to say that there is a peculiar intimacy between the torturer and his victim. This is an asymmetrical "being with": the torturer wants to break into the intimacy of the victim, as a robber breaks into another's house. Meanwhile, the victim is to have no recourse. He is despoiled by another who hides his own idiocy, or puts it at the services of destroying the intimacy of the victim.

The torturer, let us say, wants to extract information from another by force. We say "extracts," and there is an aggression in the word. Think of the extraction of minerals from the earth. Not incidentally, in premodern cultures miners were looked on with a certain ambiguous awe: mining skirted the edge of desecration—the earth itself as mother was plundered, violated. The earth itself had an intimacy, an innerness on which the act of mining as extraction encroached. The miners would perform certain rituals to propitiate the earth for possible violation.

Bacon now is frequently cited for his image of the new science as putting nature on the rack, putting it to the torture to force it to yield its secrets. To put to the torture was an ancient means of testing a person in a juridical ordeal of truth. But if truth comes to light by way of torture, can we be so sure that the "hidden" has in truth been conquered, or finally dispelled in any entirely determinate knowing? Suppose there are intimacies of being, not just relative to the self, but to the whole of being? Suppose that these, by their very essence, resist the truth of torture? The truth of torture would then be a metaphysical violence, one oblivious to the violence of its knowing, so far from self-disclosure has it driven the mystery of being. Such violent knowing would actually produce its own autism of being.

With torture of the human being, violence or the threat of it becomes a way of forcing the intimacy of being to yield up what it withholds. This very forcing often has the effect of driving the intimacy into a deeper recess of self, into an idiocy that ever retreats beyond the encapsulation of the encroacher. This retreat of the intimate into its own reserve may infuriate the torturer. Alternatively, the torturer may be fooled or satisfied with "truths" that are divulged to him from a less intimate layer of being.

Apply the analogy more generally—as indeed Bacon does. Suppose determinate scientific knowing did find nature yielding determinate truths to it; but suppose that its entire objectifying approach also produces the retreat of the intimacy of being back into reserves that no objectifying knowing can ever reach. Suppose we are satisfied with such truths. Would we not be fooled into thinking that now we have gotten to the truth of being? In fact, this truth of being, true as it is, would be untrue to being, relative to the mystery of its more intimate reserves of possibility. The power of objective knowing would be impotence before the mystery of being, and this power would not even suspect its impotence. Of course, the very suggestion that there is an intimacy of being beyond its objective power will be derided as "mystification." There can be nothing more there because, of course, objective knowing can see nothing further there. Or it might be greeted with epistemological aggression: the self-defense of objective knowing becomes a hatred of any suggestion that finally it is metaphysically powerless or inept.

With torture of the human, the torturer clearly hates the suggestion of his own powerlessness. The relation of torturer and victim is at the edge of the elemental: it is the very will of the victim to retain himself, to keep himself to himself; it is the root will of one against the root will of the other. It is a war of elemental selves, in which one side has all the weapons of objectification, while the other side has nothing at all, except the idiocy of selfhood in its irreducible intimacy. The torturer wants to destroy that inward otherness of the victim in its irreducible intimacy.

For the torturer, sophisticated in the infernal art, the point is not to kill the other; it is to violate the intimacy of the inward otherness. With some persons this inward otherness may be sufficiently strong, or stubborn, or unyielding, so much so that its drives the torturer into a fury of negation. Death is a defeat of the torturer's intent to desecrate the intimacy of being of the other. So he develops a finesse in degradation. He creates techniques of demeaning objectification, submitting the victim to trials *in extremis*, which devalue his body into a locus of indignity. Degrading the other is for purposes of perverting freedom at its most intimate. The perverse pleasure of torture is in the *forced cry of helplessness*. For the cry of helplessness is an appeal *in extremis*. The extreme appeal communicates "enough, no more"; it asks the torturer to let be. The appeal to be let be is a groan of submission just short of physical death, and yet it comes close to destroying selfhood in its idiocy, that is, its resistance to determinate objectification. Or the appeal may be in the silent eyes that say "enough, no more." The eyes or the groan say "Please"—they helplessly plead against the despoiling of the inward intimacy. Torture seeks the degradation of the vulnerability of appeal.

If torture is a hatred of hiddenness, it is the other's hiddenness that is hated, while the torturer keeps himself to himself in his own hiddenness. ("Keeping oneself to oneself" is another expression of the elemental self-relativity I spoke of previously.) The torturer wants to objectify the other, but seeks himself to escape beyond all objectification. Torture is profanation of the mystery of selfhood, mystery which the torturer reserves for himself alone. Hence the attack will be on the most intimate parts of the body, and not just against the parts most vulnerable to pain and suffering, though in fact the most intimate and the most vulnerable tend to coincide. The mouth will be pillaged, as in extracting teeth without anaesthetic, or exposing and probing the roots of nerves in the gums. The violation of mouth makes the victim helpless to cry out; even the appeal of the body will be stifled. Or the assault will be against those parts of the flesh most vulnerable to uncovering and nakedness. The "private parts" become the focus of this hatred of hiddenness.

The private, intimate parts used to be called the *pudenda*, the shameful parts. My point does not concern whether there is an inappropriate shame about the body; there is. But shame is the shadow of the sense of modesty which is the incarnate expression of the intimate reserve of the self: the freedom not to be forced into the open against one's will. The torturer wants to shame that freedom in degrading the private parts. The private parts are ambiguous, in being both most sensitive to touch and most subject to pain. This ambiguity provides the opening in the flesh for the torturer to launch his assault on the intimacy, not only of the body, but of self-being. It is the intimacy of self-being that is shamed in the shaming of the shameful parts.

Think of the elemental neccesity of the body having to relieve itself. Think of our vulnerability in this, and the demands of modesty and dignity that we do this in private and alone. Its idiocy asks intimacy. But one is deprived of this by the torturer. It is mocked. Of course, foul horrors, worse by far, and nameless, are visited on the intimacy of the flesh. Schopenhauer spoke of the genitals as the metaphysical organs. And while his metaphysics needs modification, we can say that the torturer's violation of the private parts is essentially a metaphysical assault.

Desecration is again the proper word for what is here effected: not just violence on the body, not just the assault on dignity, nor just the destruction of inherent worth, but the trampling on the trace of infinity in the idiocy of the self. There is to be nothing sacred at all. Torture serves the kingdom of death that hates every trace of the divine. Torture incarnates a metaphysical necrophilia. But necrophilia, we must remember, is a mode of "being with": it is being with the dead, it is community with death. The complete desecration of the intimacy of being would be the necrophiliac community with death.

If we now turn to love, compare the groan of tortured pain to the groan of erotic pleasure. Qua sounds there might be little quantitative difference between the two. Even qua groans of pain and pleasure there might seem little between them: both involve retractions of selfhood to the elemental; both are idiotic and at the edge of conceptual mediation. But one bespeaks a going beyond oneself in self-transcending, the other communicates a silencing of self-transcendence that coerces the intimate self back into the unbearable void of its own suffering. Nor are the groans mere immediacies that are indefinite, or empty of meaning. They are elementals that are already overdetermined, and bespeak in a complex togetherness between self and other.

In love, as opposed to torture, we find respect for the reserve of the beloved who is allowed to be in its own intimacy of being. The other will be let recede, since freedom is the allowance of withdrawal. The modesty of love is the mindfulness that self-disclosure moves on an equivocal boundary, where the intimacy of being opens itself to possible acceptance or despoliation. Modesty guards the intimacy of selfhood in its infinite reserve. Love lets that modesty be; there is no profanation in love. If the intimacy is to come to self-disclosure, this must be let be as genuinely free for itself. Love then is a welcoming of the intimacy that never forces. Such a forcing would force modesty back over the other side of self-disclosure, even though, on the surface, the appearance of self-disclosure might seem unbroken.

We all have experienced those surprising moments in conversation when suddenly we realize that the other is no longer there, even though the talking continues. The other communicates but has withdrawn from the communication; the intimacy of being has reserved itself. Or we communicate with another, and there are moments when we know we have just leaped over a gap or abyss whose silence has been disguised by the slight quickening of breath, or of the pace of speaking. The surface is all self-disclosure, but we are startled by subtle indeterminacies requiring extraordinary finesse to hear, indeterminacies into whose space the intimacy of the self has been withdrawn. Indeed there may be intimacies into which the idiotic self is so withdrawn that they are secret to its own self-consciousness. This self creates a conversation within itself which hides other silences wherein a deeper intimacy of selfhood has been retracted. Love of the other may be necessary to reopen these retractions. On its own the self may be unable to open up its own closures on itself.

In love we find the self-opening of the other towards one's own self-opening. There is no way to force the other to reveal and give itself with the longed-for presence. Every effort to force the lover, betrays the love and the lover. Hence there can be no technique of love, though technique may produce the simulacrum of love. It will work on the surface of intimacy, but already this signals the death of intimacy. The intimacy of being by its very nature is absolutely reserved to technique. Where technique is, the idiocy of selfhood is not, and there is no love. I might, of course, be deceived by the simulacrum technique produces. I do not know it but I am objectified and manipulated. I am "taken in," as we say. I am seduced or let myself be seduced. The heart is such a great need of love that it will give itself up thus. Its being taken in, its giving itself up may be deluded. Even this delusion will mimic the essential giving of oneself over to the other. One *lets oneself be deceived*, though in another recess of the intimacy of being, one is not entirely deceived. Such self-deception is a hiding from oneself what one recess of intimacy knows, knows beyond the intimacy of being that is closer to honest mindfulness.

Opposed to the forced submission of the torture victim, the giving up and giving over of love will be a willing giving to the other. If subsequently this willing is shown to be betrayed, the experience can be crushing. The idiocy of being comes out here too. The self retracts its trust. Being crushed, or disappointed, or betrayed, all these reveal the intimacy of being in a reversal of the directionality of self-opening transcendence. As there is no technique, there is no systematic science relative to being crushed, or being disappointed, or being betrayed. They are idiotic, outside system. One need only think about how the wound of a significant disappointment, just in its closeness to the heart, may significantly influence the entire life, the destiny of someone. Others may have no inkling of how that wound so decisively shaped the self-becoming of that person. It may become hidden even from the self it so shapes, so close to the self it eludes self-knowledge.

There can be a certain betrayal of trust that is metaphysically indistinguishable from torture. In each such case, the inward otherness of the intimate self is crushed. This is why the betrayed person may feel himself "tortured by the betrayal," so deep may run the sense of violation. If a friend or parent or spouse betrays one, the energy of self-trancendence that comes alive in trust may be reversed and the intimate self be sent into a tailspin of withdrawal. It recoils back on itself, away from any giving over of itself to the other. The more intimate the given trust, the more violent the betrayal on innerness, the more convulsive the retreat. In another sense, the torture of betrayal can be more crushing than the torture of torture. The torturer is explicitly an enemy, does not present himself as friend. But in the betrayal of trust, it is the intimacy of the friend, the intimacy of an intimate, that has wounded us, or being wounded by us.

9. The Field of Intimacy

The idiocy of being cannot be confined to closed innerness because there is a *field* of intimacy. Singular figures, significant particulars haunt one's world. These are not items in one's environment, nor simply "significant others." They emanate a texture of real presence. A person inhabits one's world to the point of also inhabiting the intimacy of one's own being. The other radiates a certain aura, shimmers in a space of thereness in an entirely personal and unique way. The language of the senses seems unavoidable. There is a musk of self, a shining of self. There is a radiance of intimacy that is idiotic.

I am sitting in an empty room, my back to the door. Of a sudden I know I am not alone. There is a tingle along the bones, a presence sensed before sensed by eye or ear or touch or smell. A presence is intimated before announced, known before identified, identified before named. This is a knowing of the other's presence that is not a determinate knowing. How do I know that the emptiness is no longer empty? It is as if my solitude is a field of intimacy, and as a field of intimacy it is not a field of solitude. It is a space of intimacy into which another steps as a radiance of intimacy. The field of intimacy is modified by this radiance of the other, even before the other is determinately known, communicated simply by being there, even before being announced. Or there is an "announcement" of the other self that is prior to all determinate announcements. The very being there is a self. The self is this immediate announcement of presence, a presence that is absence, if all announcements are reduced to objectifiable determination.

The field of intimacy is filled with the entrance of an unknown other who, in stepping into it, radiates a difference and communicates indeterminately beyond all sensory and cognitive determination. Of course, the unknown other may be known, for I may know who is behind me, unseen, as yet unrecognized. I exclaim: "It is you—I knew it all along!" This happens; we all know this happens; and there is an excess to determination in this intimation of the other. How does a room change when another enters thus? Travelers in a remote wilderness experience something similar when they come upon unmistakeable traces—the tingle along the spine, not devoid of foreboding, says: the presence of the human.

In the pragmatic world the strangeness of presence settles into habitual presence. Sameness receives primary notice; singularity shades off into the background. This is the daily averaging of singularities. The self of the other is standardized in relatively predictable roles, domesticated by long familiarity. We say we have a handle on that person. The word "handle" names well the instrumentalization of selfhood, its manipulability, literally its availability to handling (manus: the hand). In this pragmatic order, the self of idiotic singularity is a nothing. It is a no place, a self that cannot be placed. Nor can the field of intimacy be placed in that order. It is another place. I can domesticate the singularity of others, the others can do it to me, I can do it to myself. The "nothingness" of self-being strikes one as strange, outside the economy of habitual manipulation.

And yet, even in the domestication of presence, the intimacy of self radiates into relatedness to the other, for the other radiates an intimacy of its own into the between. Whether we domesticate it or not, the between is the field of intimacy. Suppose we lose a long accepted friend. Now the unique aura of this other is not there any more. The field of intimacy is shaken. The sense of absence is the sense of presence mourned. I grieve the loss of this intimate self; I grieve what was all but nothing in the pragmatic world of habitual sameness. But it was there then, at play all along. Now I see it. The absence of passing away puts me in mind of the presence that was then absent to mind, just because it was so present. We were too close to real presence: not close, we were in it as a field. Death and loss and distance allow us to sense what was there all along, but missed all along, in its being taken for granted. When we miss it in loss, we then begin to find it, perhaps even for the first time. Of course, the finding is quickly lost, since the singularity of the intimate is hard to fix, beyond its recall in the form of memorable similarities. The pragmatic order quickly regains its sway—as if there were no mystery to all this presencing and withdrawing, this unmasterable coming and going.

The field of intimacy is not confined to human being. Other beings have their singularity, their radiance, their aura of ontological presence. Think of the difference between a scientific account of, say, a natural environment and a poetic celebration of place or landscape. We can give a more or less scientific account of a place in terms of its geology, its geography, the botany of its flora and fauna, the biology of its inhabitants. But in the poetic rendition, the intimacy of place transcends the particularities of environment, made intelligible by a set of universals common to other similar environments. It is this place, not that, which is celebrated. It is loved in the singularity of its singularity.

A person can come to love a place in such a way that a rapport is set up between him and it, and the things of daily commerce within that place. A human being can have a peculiar tenderness towards a place, as if the place claimed him as home, as if he belonged to the place, rather than the place belonging to him. This being at home in the place of home is the community of the intimacy of being. An artist speaks the word of home in that sense, science does not. Science tries to think of place placelessly, in the name of an anonymous space. The speaking of the artist is agapeic naming. It speaks the singular name.

This rapport is brought to mind in the loss of a place. The loss of place can be a loss of self. One has lost one's place; one is retracted to the idiocy of one's own being, again at a loss, because one has lost the rapport with the otherness of the place. What is this rapport? We are at ease in a place, or disturbed by it; we breath its air; the place presses on one, impresses itself, or fails to communicate. We speak of the spirit of a place as its genius. This has been lost in the modern instrumentalization of place. There is no time to find our home in the elusive, evanescent, shimmering of happening.

In the place of home, there is a passing back and forth between oneself and the place. One is abroad in the place; one is not in oneself; there is no Cartesian innerness; one finds an intimacy at play in the between. I look at the mountain and I am spread out on it; I gaze at the sea and I am turmoiled by its roil; I am out of myself in place. And place implaces itself in me; the mountain is within. The mountain consumes me, towers over me, is an admonishment. There is no dualism—the restless sea sings in me.

Is this a complete equivocation? I prefer to think of it as a creative doubleness, in the sense of a doubling or redoubling of one in the other. In the between, I and other pass into each other, and are able to be both. There is a "being both." There is a community beyond univocity; there is a being both without a dialectical subordination of one to the other; I would call it a metaxological double. We can live this and not know it. The metaxological names the manyness of what is there in the intimacy of the inexhaustible this.

10. Idiotic Likening

One cannot deny the gap of communication between someone mindful of the field of the intimate and someone dwelling predominantly in the world of habitual sameness. It is hard to get through to the second what is at play there. I can try to communicate, but the communication cannot be successful if it is confined to generalities. Success only comes if my interlocutor calls upon the memory of the idiotic in his or her own life, and recognizes that I, too, am somewhere *like that*.

"Like that"—what does this mean? "Likeness" suggests a number of possibilities, but two main ones are relevant here. First, likeness can be the instrument of a generality, a means towards an anonymous universal. A is like B because both share in a similar characteristic, C, which is singular to neither. Hence, their likeness points to a commonness other to the singularity of either; this likeness subordinates the singularity of both.

A second possibility is this: "likeness" can be a reminder of singularity, and so point in a very different direction to commonality as defined in terms of anonymous universality. A is like B, and the likeness means that the singularity of A and B is like, precisely in a community of irreducible singularities. To say "we are the same" means "we are both irreplaceable." We are alike in that each of us in community is an absolute singularity, even in our relativity. This likeness is a relativity that frees the sameness from reduction, and returns each singulairity back to its singularity again. This likeness of community is a sameness that dissolves reductive homogeneity, a sameness that releases its own homogeneity back to irreducible heterogeneity.

In the first case, when I say to you "It was like this," likeness does name an intermediate condition—it is, so to say, a halfway house towards a common characteristic that will function as the sign of a generality. My friend's child has died. I say:—oh yes, I once lost a child. Or consider Claudius telling Hamlet that the death of fathers is such a likeness, such a generality. The tale of generations is the common story of lost fathers and grieving sons, repeated again and again—all said by Claudius with the intent to rob the singularity of Hamlet's grief of its singular intimacy. They are all alike means here: they are all the same really, indifferently the same. The commonness of the universal admonishes Hamlet to put off his unmanly grief and become a stone.

It is worth looking a little more closely. Hamlet's mother give him this advice:

> Gertrude: Do not forever with thy lids
> Seek for thy noble father in the dust.
> Thou knows't 'tis common; all that lives must die,
> Passing through nature to eternity.

Hamlet: Aye, Madam, 'tis common.
Gertrude: If it be,
            Why seems it so particular with thee? (*Hamlet* I, ii, 69–75)

Note the contrast of the common with the particular, and the buttress-
ing of the power of the former by appeal to nature and eternity—true certainly, but not true to the particularity of a grief, and hence untrue. Hamlet
rejects the "seeming" particularity of his grief. "Seems, Madam. Nay it is. I
know not 'seems'." He is, in fact, speaking of the idiocy of being when he
goes on to say: "But I have that within which passes show/These but the
trappings and the suits of woe." This is intimacy beyond objectification.
    Claudius repeats the lesson of the common:

            But, you must know, your father lost a father,
            That father lost, lost his, . . . (*Hamlet* I, ii, 89–90)

But he, fratricide, usurper, incestuous seducer, goes further: he arraigns
the singularity of Hamlet's grief before eternal necessity, before Heaven itself:

            But to persever
            In obstinate condolement is a course
            Of impious stubbornness; 'tis unmanly grief;
            It shows a will most incorrect to heaven,
            A heart unfortified, a mind impatient,
            An understanding simple and unschool'd.
            For what we know must be and is as common
            As any the most vulgar thing to sense,
            Why should we in our peevish opposition
            Take it to heart? Fie! 'Tis a fault to heaven,
            A fault againt the dead, a fault to nature,
            To reason most absurd, whose common theme
            Is death of fathers, and who still hath cried,
            From the first corse till he that died today,
            "This must be so." (*Hamlet* I, ii, 92-106)

    It is interesting how the *how* of a saying can corrupt the truth of a said.
Note how Claudius instrumentalizes the intimacy of being in the interests of
his own will to power. He uses almost exactly the opposite argument with
Laertius, when he loses his father (see, *Hamlet* IV, vii, 108ff.). He manipu-
lates Laertius by whipping up the singularity of his grief to make him want to
kill Hamlet ("To cut his throat i' th' church." *Hamlet* IV, vii, 127), and so
accomplish Claudius' own aim.
    As a philosophy, stoicism suggests a similar petrification of the intimate,
when it reduces the death of a child to a general theme in the human

condition. It happens to us all. Death has become an It—the singularity of every death is neutralized, because universalized. The Stoic enjoins a retreat to the innerness of selfhood where he claims to find a fastness and security beyond the vicissitudes of externality. And yet he risks reification of the "like this" into oblivion of the intimacy of being. Stoic self-security is undermined by what a less neutering return to innerness reveals: the idiocy of being upsets all inner self-security of the sort the Stoic craves. For in the idiocy of being, there is an otherness of innerness which heightens mindfulness of the frailty of singular being, not only the vulnerability of its own self, but the fragility of the other.

This is even more so, when we mind self and other as singulars of infinite worth. The sheer "onceness" of the I, which a drop of infected water will maim or drive mad or kill, makes us less ontologically secure rather than more. The sheer "onceness" of singularity floats as if it were an absolute center of being over the abyss of nothing. This absolute center is all but nothing; and yet in its absolute vulnerability it is not nothing: it is. There is no security in this: "It is." For the idiocy of being means: It was not once, it is now for the while of the between, it will not be once again.

So in case of the second possibility above noted, the words "like this," can be said otherwise than as a pointer to the neutral universal. The likeness points to the this as this, not to the sameness as a sameness. Like you I lost a father; but the thisness of my grief puts me in mind, not of grief as a generality, but of the thisness of this grief that now racks you. There is a community here, and it is through the likeness of an intimacy. The between is itself qualified by an intimacy which is not the exclusive possession of you or I. This qualification, in fact, constitutes community as personal. Silence and reserve are also necessary. The habitual words of consolation are dangerous. For it is not just their standardized content that is the important thing, but the who and the how of their saying.

I say: "My sympathies to you"—standardized consolation. But the very "this" of the person saying, and the "this" of the how of saying, all these make an enormous difference to the commonality that comes to be in the word of solidarity. For I can say all the right words, but in an absolutely wrong way—then the word of solidarity fails, even in its visible success. Example: A priest at a funeral speaks all the right words of ritual consolation. But he speaks the right words as an ecclesiastical functionary, not as an I. But it is a singular I that is dead, and singular mourning Is that survive. It is the community of intimacy created by common grief that calls for address with the word of solidarity. But the word of community is uttered functionally by a functionary. All the right words now become all the wrong words, from the standpoint of the thisness of this grief.

Determinate scientific universals articulate, to the best extent possible, the habitual samenesses, both of things and of our thinking. Things have their habits; our thinking has its habits. These are the publicly standardized modes of commonness. All this is proper to the intelligibility of beings. But this is not all. There are ways of being and mind proper to self-being and other-being, on the other side of the standardized sameness. Such is the likeness that is a gesture of welcome towards memory of the intimate. Thus, through the remembered grief which cannot be shared, there is a sharing of a grief. The comforter tries to be the bearer of shared grief towards this person in the particularity of their grief. This likening, this sharing is agapeic.

The first sense of likeness may be made the basis of a "scientific" psychology whose "findings" may be more or less true, relative to some standardized version of humanity. But this is radically incomplete relative to the idiocy of selfhood, and radically false, if it holds it has the truth of selfhood. The second sense of likeness is the essential basis of a community of being that does not disrespect the intimate; it grieves and rejoices with it; it points to home, even in the agony of not being at home. This "likening" hears the call of a beyond that is beyond all likeness, and with which we are in community. This demands agapeic mind, be it in philosophy, or in life itself.

11. Idiotic Metaphysics

I will shortly turn to agapeic mind, but let me conclude with a remark on the significance of the above for philosophical saying. Nietzsche claimed that the opposition of Plato and Homer was life's basic antagonism. I doubt that Plato would grant the antagonism as Nietzsche stated it. For there is a *philosophical art* that, even in its logical pursuit of the universal, seeks not to betray the singular in its proper singularity, nor the community of saying even between antagonistic human seekers. This art is suggested by the Platonic dialogue itself. It is as if Plato himself is the *internal* tension between art and science. Plato reveals the tense communication of "Plato" and "Homer," in Nietzsche's sense.

The standard opposition of art and science is presented in terms of the contrast of the particular and the universal. It seems to me that the idiocy of being demands a kind of metaphysical thinking transcending this standard contrast. Science does have a drift towards the general, even when its evidences are garnered from the particularities of the given. It tends towards general explanatory schemes or cognitions that intend a universal range of reference, none of which are to be confined to the particular as particular.

Art genuinely evidences a tolerance of otherness and embodies a rich way of naming the "this" as "this."[13] Nietzsche is so far right. It is not that philosophers must give up general analysis and become writers of poems. They may do this, but this is still to accept the standard contrast. Rather the sense of being manifest with the idiocy of the "this" must be let pose its challenge to philosophy, must be let seep into the sources of thinking its otherness.

No prescription can be offered of the thinking that might result, were we to allow the idiotic to seep into metaphysical mindfulness. There can be no method or analytical technique here. The intimacy of being points to an idiotic source beyond determinate thinking. To ask for a method would be already to determine this source, in advance of the challenge it might pose to metaphysics, and hence to domesticate this challenge before it is even allowed to pose itself. We do not give up determinate thought, but this source in idiocy must be let sprout, and in the determination of metaphysical thinking itself. Certainly the categorial pigeonholing of art and philosophy must be suspended. This is not to advocate their confused promiscuity, but a certain philosophical fidelity. The fidelity may sometimes demand resort to metaphysical metaphors, or concepts that are mindful of their own imagistic nature.

If the idiocy of being makes an intimate claim on the philosopher, one cannot escape into the thought of mind in general. The singularity of the philosopher has to be acknowledged. One must deny oneself the consolation of denying oneself. Even such a consolation is equivocal, since one is still oneself as consciousness in general, even while claiming to have put oneself aside as *this* thinker. Paradox is hard to avoid, for there is a kind of loss of self in the return to singularity; but this is not a return to the ego, but to the I as abroad in the field of the intimacy of being. In other words, there is an energizing of the sources of agapeic mind which loves the particular as particular, and as for itself, and not simply for the subjective ego. The "loss" of self in the idiocy of self is just this willingness of the singular I to be mindfulness for the other, to be this singular source of radical self-transcendence towards the other in its otherness. This is what I call agapeic mind, not nameless mind in general. Properly speaking, metaphysical thinking and aesthetic openness both are concretions of agapeic mind, which is mindfulness for the other in its otherness, and yet also in its community with the intimacy of the I.

It is relevant to recall again Plato's repeated reliance on the story and image. This is not a mere concession to the many, who are incapable of the pure selfless thought of unindividualized *eidē*. It is a necessity because we

---

13. On this tolerance of otherness, see *Philosophy and its Others*, 102–109.

philosophize in the middle. The middle requires of metaphysics some articulation of the *concrete texture of being there*, through the particularities of the image and the likenings of myth. The self as singular is philosophically put to the test in the middle. Nor is it by accident that so many Platonic dialogues are given the titles of proper names. One might expect dialogues to be named in terms of the general themes said to be their subject matter. And yet the proper name of the singular interlocutor is offered as the identifying mark of the philosophical conversation. The proper name points to the self as a "this," just as a "this": he is on stage in the drama of the dialogue, itself a community of intimacy, since it is the very deepest selves of the interlocutors that is put to the test of conversation, of philosophical communication. The abstract universal is only one "character" in this much more complex and rich drama of philosophical dialogue.

This community of aesthetic and metaphysical mindfulness, and both as different expressions of agapeic mind, point us also beyond science to the affiliation of philosophy and religion. Religion offers us the ultimate images of ultimacy. Of these we must be metaphysically mindful. We are called to restore to mindfulness a certain religious respect for the "this" as "this." Ultimately I believe it is impossible to do justice to the "this" as "this" outside of a metaphysics of creation as agapeic. The ultimate origin is an agapeic source that gives the finite other its being, not for the origin itself, but for the finite being as other in its own right. The finite entity is let be in its thisness as other and its own. The intimacy of being, we might say, is the memory of God's creative breath that sustains every being as a singular "this."

While I do not want to suggest an "aestheticization" of being, in the more normal sense of "aesthetic," in some ways *music* is the art that most restores us to the idiocy of being.[14] Music touches us at a depth below and beyond self-consciousness. Through it sound the voices of the silent intimacy of being. No doubt, musicologists will point out the intricacies of formal structure involved in music. They will resurrect their Pythagorean ancestry and see the link between *ta musika* and *ta mathematika*. No question, there is intelligible structure in music proximate to mathematical determinacy. But the living performance is not the structure. It is the aesthetic sounding of the intimacy of being, given form in the score. This is something always other, in

---

14. Relative to a previously discussed theme, we see an expression of this at two extremes: music, it is said, is the language of love, though it can be used to seduce; then there is a technique used by torturers, whereby the prisoner or hostage is subjected to a background of "white noise" for days on end, to pulverize the intimacy of being, drive its idiocy to the point of despair and madness.

that every performance more or less redeems the music, or betrays it, but no performance exhausts it, though the score is the same. The playing of the music is the thing, and there is something beyond mathematical system about this play. It is a happening of the idiocy of being itself. We play it, or find ourselves in its being played. It comes upon us when we listen attentively to it; it carries us, though we have to let ourselves be open to it. We have to have ears to hear, and this is no biological function but is a condition of the intimacy of being. Having ears is to have a heart that listens. We are taken out of ourselves by listening, transported into openness.

The music that comes closest to the condition of prayer is closest to the intimacy of being, for such music is the word of intimacy with the sacred other. In such music, it is as if the sound dissolves into an infinitely upward movement towards transcendence. It catches us in the vector of transcendence; and we are moved from depths we cannot comprehend, moved towards an other we cannot determinate. Neither the inner depths that stir, nor the other that draws can be univocally determined, yet while in the milieu of the music, they are together.

Prayer may be the deepest enactment of the intimacy of being; for the praying self is the most idiotic. It is senseless and yet divines sense beyond sense. It is given over, yet it is the audacity of trust. It is elemental vulnerability and appeal, elemental perplexity and consent, elemental confession and renewal, elemental adoration and fragile glory. It demands nothing, yet waits in expectation of all good. This is the infinity of the simple. Augustine said that God was *intimior intimo meo*. This is the intimacy of being beyond the ego, and beyond the intimacy of self. It is the idiocy of God. Of God we are made mindful in an idiot wisdom. If death is the final idiocy in the between, then the only way to die is with a proper prayer. We may spend a life looking for the proper prayer. Can idiotic metaphysics close its mind to this audacity and this appeal?

Chapter 4

Agapeic Mind

1. The Community of Being and Mind?

Is there a community between mind and being? If so, how does it agree with being between, being at a loss, and the idiocy of being? What is its character? How do we speak of it? Does the field of the intimacy of being suggest something of it? Is it bound up with that mysterious word "home?"

This is an old and elemental metaphysical question. It is also a perennially renewed perplexity. Parmenides' affiliation (frag. 3) of *noein* and *estin*, thinking and being, suggests the question—though he says they are *auto*, same, where we ask about community. Nor has the question been definitively solved, and put in place. At the height of contemporary science, Einstein remained perplexed by a version of it.[1] If never definitively answered, yet it ever recurs, and to it we also must recur, with perhaps a deepening of the proper perplexity.

Such perplexity is qualified by our sense of *difference* to the rest of being. Testaments to this include the unquestioning dualism of commonsense, as well as the scientistic hubris going with a conceptual dualism of mind and nature. These issue in two opposite results: on one hand, the objectivism of denatured mind, relative to nature; on the other hand, the subjectivism of

---

1. A. Einstein, *Sidelights on Relativity* (New York: Dover, 1983), 28: "How is it that mathematics, being a product of human thought which is independent of experience, is so admirably appropriate to the objects of reality." Also A. Einstein, *Ideas and Opinions* (New York: Bonanza Books, 1954), 292: "The world of our sense experience is comprehensible. The fact that it is comprehensible is a miracle."

denatured mind, relative to mind itself. These extremes have formed the legacy of post-Cartesian philosophy. They reflectively accentuate the dualistic difference of commonsense into a systematic alienation of mind from being in its otherness, and of mind from itself in its own deeper intimacy of being.

It is now increasingly recognized that this legacy is used up, bankrupt. It is the inheritance of an ontological deracination. The question then is: What resources do we have after this judgment of bankruptcy? Is there any source of renewal, exceeding this inheritance, or perhaps preceding it? We are brought again to question the community between mind and being.

The renewal begins minimally in the recognition that no conceptual reflection of being is absolutely autonomous or self-determining; rather it originates in a prereflective mediation, an already given togetherness of mind and being. This togetherness is not exhausted by the conceptualizations of being that science or philosophy produce, though these can be mediated transformations of it. Thus, the acknowledgment that science originates in the *Lebenswelt*, for example, by Husserl and others, is one expression of what is at issue. Does this expression go far enough? Does not the *Lebenswelt* itself raise the question of a more originary community of mind and being which shapes the possibility of the *Lebenswelt* itself? Does not the modern reflective mediation all throughout carry with it the residues of its own dualistic starting point? Must we rethink the prereflective community of being, prior to both scientist and commonsense dualism, rethink not only the commonsense community of being, but a more originary sense of ontological community?

Objective, subjective, and transcendental mind will not suffice, for they are subsequent to this prior community. We must rethink the dynamism of minding as an orientation to being; we must rethink the otherness of being, as both for itself and for this minding. To this end, I propose an exploration of what I call "agapeic mind." The matter, of course, has ramifications other than the deracinated mediations of post-Cartesian thought. Agapeic mind can find expression in aesthetic, in religious, in ethical form, in metaphysical form. No neutral condition or monological state of affairs is intended by the activity of being mindful. I explore a mode of mindfulness in which thinking is for the sake of the other, thinking for the sake of what is other to thought itself.

Traditionally *agapē* is a form of love, often contrasted with *eros*, and also with *philia*. These contrasts are not irrelevant, with a relevance I will specify as the occasion demands. Agapeic mind names a mode of thought thinking what is other to thought, in which there is a release of thinking from itself towards the other as other. At stake is the power of mind to transcend itself. The point to be explored is whether and how, in this transcending, mindfulness is already in community with being-other towards which it transcends.

There are different modes of this self-transcendence, including that of what I will call "erotic mind." By contrast to agapeic mind, by erotic mind I will mean a relativity of mind to what is other to self, but a relativity that subsumes what is other into the self-relativity of the mind seeking its own self-satisfaction and self-certainty. Erotic mind goes to the other beyond itself, but its self-transcendence is impelled by its own lack which it would fill by appropriating the other. Its relativity to the other serves this fulfillment of its own initial lack. The truth of the other affords the truth of self-fulfillment.

The truth of agapeic mind is not this self-satisfaction. It includes a disquiet about every such self-satisfaction, a perplexity before the other it cannot include in its own conceptual schema, a loss of self-certainty, and at best a trust that its motion towards the other calls for a faithfulness beyond guarantees. Traditionally philosophers have often favored erotic mind, since this coheres with the very strong desire to make thinking absolutely self-consistent, and so to glorify thought thinking itself as the ultimate, and the philosophical god.

In terms of the fourfold sense of being, objective mind is dominantly tied to the ideal of univocity; subjective mind easily lends itself to the equivocity of being; erotic mind corresponds to the dialectical sense; the metaxological view finds its expression in agapeic mind. I will start by following the movement of this fourfold. It is not simply that we are moving towards agapeic mind and metaxological being; these are already in play, and in some way taking shape. We are trying to move back deeper, and more intensively, and closer to the original community of mind and being.

2. Objective and Subjective Mind

Frequently we think of the truth of mind in terms of the ideal of objectivity. Mind is truthful when it is true to the state of affairs that holds objectively, regardless of what subjective mind may think. This contrast of objective and subjective mind operates as a winnowing sieve whereby the chaff and wheat are separated. Subjective mind is usually taken to imply a failure of self-transcendence. Though this language might not be used, nevertheless, self-transcendence is held to be the accomplishment of objective mind. We think of objective mind as having successfully mastered, or put aside certain subjective impulses, or idiosyncratic factors that interfere with understanding the matter before us, purely as it is in itself and for itself, regardless of our personal desire. Objective mind is considered true to the matter as other, precisely because it has surmounted or extirpated desire.

Objective mind thus might be coupled with a certain *ascetic* ideal of knowing. Nietzsche immediately comes to mind as subjecting science as "ascetic" to severe criticism. Perhaps also we might think, in more subdued terms, of the contemporary critique of the so-called myth of the given. Ascetic mind, objective mind is mind claiming the power to be mindless, that is, not to be there, when it clearly is, to be as *nothing* in registering without alteration the pure objectivity of the real.

By contrast, agapeic mind seems to suggest a coupling of a mode of love and knowing. At this point we should not make too much of this, until a number of essential cautions and qualifications have been put in place. In an important regard I do not reject what is intended by the above description of objective mind. However, this description ironically is prey to equivocations. Let me elaborate.

One might claim that there is a sense in which the mind is nothing. The mind makes itself count for nothing in the process of letting the real in its otherness play on it, play for itself, and then play for it. But this peculiar power to be as nothing is paradoxically joined with the power to open up to all otherness. Somehow the soul is the all (*to pan*)—Aristotle said, in words as cryptic as any oracle of Heraclitus. He never quite explained the "somehow" (*pos*). We might say that agapeic mind is an interpretation of this "somehow." Mindfulness, the minding of being, reveals a power of being in the self which is an energy of being: it is the being at-work (*en-ergon*) of being, minding being. As the energy of being we are, it is articulated as our desire to know. But the desire to know is a beginning. There emerges the wonder and originary perplexity that will later become determinately articulated into different forms of knowing. Mind is plurally articulated, but prior to each determinate articulation is this astonishment and originary desire of perplexed openness. This indeterminate opening also outlives every determinate specification which constitutes this mode of knowing or that mode of knowing. Desire to know precedes determinate knowing, is specified and relatively satisfied by this and that form of determinate knowing, but it exceeds or transcends every such articulate specification of itself.

Objective knowing is *one* particular specification of this originary energy of desiring mindfulness. It is one particular specification that imposes on desire a strict regime, an austere ideal of exclusive univocity. It excludes impulses wayward or distracting to the thought of the matter at stake. Objective mind, as ascetical knowing, insists on a certain suppression of desire. The suppression seems blanket, and the ascetical knower may speak in strong dictatorial terms. In fact, the suppression can always only be partial and provisional. For desire itself is pluriform. It may well be the case that certain modes of desire are inappropriate to the matter being minded. For example, there is a very appropriate exclusion of idiosyncratic desire in the case of mathematical knowing. Two and two is four, and it is so regardless of how one feels about the matter, and regardless of what opinions one might want to share: the univocity and abstractness of the matter rightly dictate an exclusion of certain modes of self-being that simply are irrelevant.

There is this other crucial point, however. Mathematical knowing is still the doing of a self, and the desire of the mathematically specified self is not entirely out of play. The mathematician—and the greater the mathematical genius, the more this is true—is driven by a passion for mathematical precision and truth. But the passion for mathematical truth is not itself a mathematical truth. Were we to try to articulate the passion of the mathematician in purely mathematical terms we would fail dismally. In that regard, the mathematician who thinks that *everything* can be explained mathematically is blind to the glaring fact, namely, that his own driven passion for absolute mathematical truth is not itself an instance of mathematical knowing or truth. In this discrepancy between the passion of the mathematician and mathematical truth, the mathematical mind exceeds itself. It shows itself as a concretion of self-transcendence.

More generally, the objective mind that would ascetically extirpate all desire cannot explain its own desire for truth, nor indeed the sometimes dictatorial way it insists on its own monolinear tracking of the dunamis of mind. Objective mind articulates the desire to know, but objective mind cannot comprehend this desire itself, for it is one specification of this desire, albeit a paradoxical one that seems to want to deny entirely the relevance of desire as self-transcendence to the venture of knowing.

The dunamis of mind is an eros for truth and being; it is also more than an eros, it is the promise of an agape of truth and being. In any case, the dunamis is not to be extirpated but realized in its proper shape. Objective knowing may claim to suppress eros, in the putative interests of knowing the other neutrally, without subjective interference. In fact, the ascetical suppression of eros is equivocal. Perhaps one may have a sublimation of this eros in objective selflessness, but this is the caution: This selfless sublimation in the interests of a univocal objectivity courts its own equivocal subjectivism.

What I mean is that ascetical objectivity, instead of being desire's suppression, may be the secret, hence equivocal elevation of a dominating desire, perhaps even a desire to dominate, masking itself as the pure neutral openness to the thinking of the other. Far from letting the other be as other, objective knowing may serve to subject the other to its own constraining abstractions. It may hide its own secret will to power, as Nietzsche saw. The objective scientist, like the ascetical priest, masters himself in order to be able more effectively to master the others. Knowing is power, it will be said.

But here this is not the power of agapeic mind. There is a different release towards the other in the latter, a release concerning which Nietzsche, good diagnostician, proved a flawed healer.

Objective knowing is a doing of the self that unfolds into a community of self and other. One might suggest that true objectivity is found in the universal as the metaxological community of being. Since objective knowing is finally not faceless or anonymous, it is also subjective, in that it makes a call on the knower to become a certain kind of mindful self. Mind operates in the between: between subjectivity and objectivity, between selfhood and community, between perplexity and truth, between separateness and participation. Even in objective knowing it is impossible to overlook the work of agapeic mind. We are reminded of the participatory nature even of the seemingly observational, spectatorial attitude of objectivity.

Consider again the passion for truth. This is all the more importunate, the more energized becomes the will to know the truth for itself. A great scientist is a highly energized passion for truth. This passion imposes strictures that are essentially ethical, the ethical strictures of being truthful to truth. Such a scientist would be as truthful as possible, even when she or he does not possess the truth. One must tell the truth as best one can, often if it goes against oneself and some of one's heart's desires. One must be honest: a metaxological condition where the unconditional requirement of openness to the truth imposes itself on a self who does not possess the truth, and who may be tempted to erect his own view into the truth, in order to possess the conceptual means to feel at home with being in its otherness, prematurely. Such honesty is between subject and object; the otherness of truth lays its charge on the self, who charges himself to be true to self as seeker, and as called by the truth to openness to what is other.

We also find the seeds of agapeic mind in the scientist's emplacement in the community of fellow scientists. Dishonesty will corrupt this community: one must not sin against the others, for instance, by falsifying data. The ethical element in objective knowing is evident also in the dedication of the scientist to a worthy and noble enterprise. One gives oneself over to an intellectual calling. I am not talking about the technician or scientist who hires himself out, for example, to do research to produce more efficient weapons of destruction. Devotion, commitment, the giving of oneself, surrender to a project that is larger than one's small self: all of these are virtues that require self-transcendence.

One does not say "my science," yet in one's ability to put one's self aside, one reveals a larger self that strives to take into account the reality and the thoughts of the others. This humility before the community of others is not a squashing of the self but its enlargement. This is not its swelling self-aggrandizement, but its release from its previous narrowness, and with this release its widened ability to understand the other on its own terms, out of its otherness as other. We are pointed beyond the stock characterizations of objective knowing to agapeic mind as participant in the metaxological community of being. Truth is public relative to the latter, but this publicity is not antithetical to the private in the sense of the intimacy or idiocy of being. Truth is found in community, but the truth of community is itself as complex as the nature of agapeic mind.

I can also state the issue from the side of the otherness of being. This is not exhausted by objectified outerness. Thus, to grant the energy of agapeic mind in objective knowing is to break with what Husserl calls the "natural attitude" in its reduction of being to an objectified externality. It is also to anticipate surpassing the bifurcation of the "is" and the "ought." We need not devalue being in an imperialistic neutering. Even the putative neutering of being by objective mind is a low grade expression of agapeic mind, in that this neutering is motivated by the desire to be true to being, without the false superimposition of human valuations on things.

This is to the good, but incomplete. For this "neutrality" reveals an eros for truth, while covering over the extent of its cognitive participation in a network of ethical values, which the theory itself is incapable of explaining. There is an existential/ethical side to objective knowing as participatory in a community of mind and being. Objective knowing counsels detachment, disinterest. But these are ambiguous counsels, since they seem to deny the *value* of objective inquiry itself. In fact, they *specify equivocally* some of the virtues of that inquiry. Inquiry is an interest in the truth, and an attachment to its demand, even when it contradicts our interests and attachments. But this cognitive interest and attachment are still ours, ours as mindful being, open to the call of the truth of things. All being mindful is ethical, including objective mindfulness. There is no way completely to disinfect the "is" of value. There are always glimmers of the agapeic sense of being.

Consider here the empiricist influence on the ideal of objective mind. The power of empiricism is its reluctance to grant as real anything that is not somehow given in experience. Experience is itself tied to our bodily being in the world. The senses are the epistemological organs by which what is other to self makes its impression on us, and through which we know it as it is, if we know it at all. Of course, classical empiricism was influenced by reflective awareness of the potential duplicity of the senses, as when something seems to be so but is not, such as the "rising" of the sun. Its ideal of objectivity was formulated in terms of primary and secondary qualities. Cold objectivity was denuded of the charged thereness of being that we find in the aesthetic presencing of things. As it turns out, primary qualities are *mediated intellectual interpretations* of being as matter. Yet even in this intellectual reconstruction of experience, the ideal of grounding objectivity in experience, and hence in the body, was not abandoned.

This provides, I suggest, a source for the glimmer of agapeic being. For reawakened mindfulness of the body reveals it to be significantly other to the intellectual construct that passes for the "body" and "sense-experience" in the regime of objective mind. The body is aesthetic opening to being other to the self; it is aesthetic self-transcendence. As such it cannot be completely objectified. The aesthetic body is already the flesh of mindfulness, the incarnation of self-transcendence. On this incarnation of self-transcendence, all objective knowing at some point depends, but this dependency is occluded, the very originating source of objective mind is forgotten, and objective mind wrongly takes itself for the epitome of autonomous knowing.

A similar point applies to sensible being as other to the self. I imply no mere "subjectification" of knowing in this reminder of embodied knowing as aesthetic self-transcendence. We are aesthetic beings within the world of being as aesthetic presencing. The body is also our place of insertion in otherness, of difference and community. It may set us off from the other, but it also offers the world its entrance into our self. The body is the given place of intermediation, which is neither subjective or objective but both.

Why are the languages of subjectivity and objectivity not adequate to express this intermediation? I suggest that the senses are the flesh of agapeic mind; they exist for the other; they are about the other, even when, as sensitive, they wake up to themselves as receptive; the doubleness of the metaxological community is at work in the flesh. Here we find paradoxes of nearness and distance, relatedness and separateness, even with respect to objectified outerness. The sensuous world is the appearance of the surplus of an agape of being. Givenness is the aesthetic body of this surplus. The body is *in the middle of* the aesthetic agape. Thus, not accidentally we say that the eye *feasts* on light, colors, shapes; the ear feasts on sounds; the nose feasts on aromas; the hand, the skin feasts on the touch of the other. Mostly we are not awakened to this touch; we sleep on in the feast—earth, sky, water, air, fire—touch of the elemental, that touches elementally.

All of this, it will be said, is "too much" for objective mind. True, but there are different responses possible to this excess. The aesthetic body celebrates it, celebrates in it. Objective mind, for the most part, is a univocalizing rationalizing that sees in this excess an unsatisfying ambiguity of being that it wants to reduce to clear and definite determinations, expressed if possible with the precision of mathematical univocity. To objectify being is to univocalize it. But this is to entrench dualism by rigid separation of the subjective and objective. This entrenched dualism is incompatible with the community between mind and being which is presupposed by the truth of objective mind. Inevitably, then, objective mind often leads to misinterpretations, both of the transcending dynamism of self-being (which it tends to subjectify), and the transcendence of other-being (which it tends to objectify).

Objective mind may even understand itself as a kind of "God's eye view," as it has been called, or the "view from nowhere." These imply an idealized detachment from the idiosyncrasy of subjectivity, as well as the conditioned vagaries of historical context. They have been criticized as idealizations untrue to the concrete complexities of actual knowing, abstractions from the truth of such knowing and its context-bound historicity. The issue is large and, as one might expect, full on revealing complications on which I offer a few remarks.

No doubt, our finiteness has to be remembered. God also must be remembered. But there's the rub. Who is the "God" of the so-called "God's eye view?" "God" is here the idealized projection of an absolutized objective mind. "God" is the absolute voyeur, though a strange voyeur, since he does not seem to take any pleasure in watching. What he sees is not good or bad, hateful or lovable, vile or noble, pitiful or tragic or intoxicating or joyful; it is neutrally just there. He does not behold creation and say: "It is good, it is very good." This is the "God" of a kind of dead mind, a mind that really minds nothing. For to mind something really is to be alive to its being, with the utmost possible in attentive discernment.

Analytical philosophers who use this notion of the "God's eye view" seem not to notice that they have reproduced a very flat version of an impassible, deistic divinity. The implied "theology" is unsophisticated and crude. It will come as a surprise to them to be told they are dubious theologians. They have prided themselves on being free of "all that nonsense." It is not true. They are more deeply immeshed in dubious theology the more they think themselves free of it. A truer sense of the "God's eye view" would be that of a divine agapeic mind, hence not neutral, or detached, or voyeuristically spectatorial, and not necessarily cybernetic or mathematizing either.

Likewise, the "view from nowhere" has been derided, but there may be more to it than its scoffers, even its defenders realize. I am thinking of a free mind that has struggled to loose itself from its own enclosure, that is, willing to see the matter from the view of the other, indeed willing to put its mind in the place of a plurality of others. Such a mind is, in a sense, from nowhere, in its availability to a plurality of other views that do not coincide with, or serve its own self-interest. The "view from nowhere" might also be understood as the view of mind that has faced into *death*, and that has been purged by the void into a different, released lucidity: an honesty beyond death, or at least struggling to transcend the fear of death that is also fear of truth, truth as shattering one's own self-enclosure.

There are overtones of posthumous mind here, as indeed of agapeic mind. I will say more about mind and death below. I now say that the "view from nowhere," such as it is, is only possible because of the self-transcending power of mind, the fact that it is no fixed determinate thing, that its life is to be other, to be beyond all finite determinations, and hence to be free from enclosure. The "place" of that mind is indeed here and now as an ineradicable singularity, but it is also "nowhere," as an ecstasy of mind that is itself in just its being beyond itself.

The point is not irrelevant to the arguments between realists and antirealists in recent analytical philosophy of science. Realists are committed to a belief in an objective state of affairs out there to which our knowing can correspond. Antirealists attenuate the sense of an externally fixed reality towards which mind moves in a move beyond itself—there is a stress on the internal practices involved in knowing itself, the immanent activities that define a practice or community of scientists.[2] In such antirealism we see a reaction to the ideal of pure objectivity, and a variation of the theme of erotic mind (see below). This is revealed in the antirealist stress on the *pragmatics* of knowing, allied with a predominant sense of the *self-relativity* of the practise or discourse. There is no real understanding of the question of agapeic mind.

The analytical realists are not in a much better situation. Most such realists tend to a physicalist view, itself defined by the univocal sense of being: there is a fixed reality out there, to which corresponds one unique set of univocal descriptions, the complete unambiguous knowing of which is the goal of science. On this physicalist univocalizing of being, I think there is no basis for understanding the being of mind as self-transcending, hence of agapeic mind.

But the real is not exhausted by the univocal sense of being, as is clearly evident in the aesthetic presencing of beings, and in the reality of the self-transcending dynamism of minding itself. This transcending is perplexing, and resists physicalist reduction. Aesthetic presencing also resists physicalist reduction, for every such reduction is already an infidelity to the fullness of physical givenness. Physicalist reduction lives from an excision of what is not subsumable into its conceptual predetermination of being. It is a truncation both of the self-transcending of mind and of the transcendence of being-other. It lives off the power of agapeic mind even as it denies it, just as what we might call its "abstract of being" lives off the agape of being-other, even as this, too, is being denied.

Of course, most practicing scientists rightly accept some version of "realism." There is here a better *pragmatic* grasp (though not necessarily a philosophically reflective grasp) of the desire to know *beyond* self, of the implicitly agapeic self-transcending power of knowing. Anti-realism is not any simple

---

2. This second sort is qualified by Putnam's "internal realism," which he also likens to Kant's "transcendental idealism."

subjectivism, but it does risk a devious subjectivism writ large, a kind of communal subjectivism. The subject of knowing becomes the scientific community, its practices and "research-programs," or perhaps now the larger historical cultural community, but we never entirely get beyond the self-mediation of this community. If all we know in the end is ourselves, albeit rebaptised as the community of inquirers, the entire project is a long-term swindle. The "long run" is only the indefinite postponment of honesty about the epistemic swindle.

I am not disagreeing with the emphasis on community, but I do disagree with the sense of community as exclusively defined by an internal or immanent set of practices. This seems hard to distinguish from the apotheosis of a communal self-relation or self-mediation. Then the ruptures of otherness out of transcendence are denied or excluded, when not domesticated. The "realistic" conviction of an other beyond knowing is the promise of a breath of fresh air from surprising transcendence. The anti-realist seems not to know it, and would hate it if he did know it, but *Hegel* thought through the essence of his view, with far greater insight and thoroughness and intellectual audacity. The truth of the whole is dialectical self-mediation, or the truth of being is the dialectically self-mediating whole; the community of mind and being is a dialectically self-mediating whole.

What we discover here is a dialectical absolutization of the erotic mind. In Hegel's system, absolute mind is an erotic absolute. By contrast, I offer the metaxological interpretation to point to a different self-transcendence that does not domesticate the transcendence of the other. Community has to be interpreted agapeically to allow for the realism of otherness and our knowing of it. The real also has to be interpreted metaxologically, and not just in terms of an unstable dialectic of the univocal and equivocal. The "absolute" also has to be rethought agapeically.

3. Erotic Mind

But what would erotic mind be? At the outset, let it be said that we here have a crucial shaping of self-transcendence. The dynamic of erotic minding follows this structure: from the experience of lack, through the quest for an appropriate object to requite the lack, to possession or appropriation of that object, and thence to fulfillment and the overcoming of lack; in this appropriating of the object, there is a return of mind to itself, both as completing itself and as being completed, through possession of the object. Hence, erotic possession is mediated self-possession, self-possession mediated through the other.

Let me put this epistemically. The experience of epistemic lack emerges with the consciousness of ignorance. I seem to know nothing, I lack the knowledge of something. This lack is not a material void, but sensed as the deficiency or insufficiency of the perplexed I. I am ignorant; but I come to know this ignorance in the very energizing of the mind itself and its eros; I come to know my mind as seeking what it lacks. Ignorance is thus permeated by epistemic desire when ignorance is sensed as such. I say "sensed," because initially what is at play lacks fully determinate articulation. This desire, in turn, energizes the quest for the knowing of what would overcome the initial, inchoate lack. The quest of knowledge is then a process of self-transcending: transcending the lack in the ignorant knower; transcending the enclosure of that self within itself; transcending the relatively inchoate to the relatively articulate, transcending the indefinite to the determinate.

I am lacking and I seek what I lack. But I must look beyond myself as lack, for as lacking I cannot through myself supply what I need. Thus, eros articulates the dynamism that drives out beyond self in its quest of the reality that, on being known, overcomes the initial lack. But in thrusting beyond, the seeking knower enters into a middle space between itself and what is beyond itself; its own erotic quest places it in this between. The middle is inhabited dynamically. In this between, mind is not only a principle of self-transcendence, but also one of mediation with what is other to itself.

Here one might look at the implied erotics in the notion of thinking as a "conceiving." Something is conceived and coming to birth. The metaphor of conceiving entails an image of the seed that carries the further growth implicitly in itself, but that needs the fertilizing contact or ingression from something other, to be set in motion for its own self-development or self-articulation. When the process of gestation is advanced, an articulation of the conception may be uttered, come to light, brought to birth.

The proposition may articulate this articulation, or more generally, a public saying or communication. I mention the latter, since the former can be too restrictive in enclosing what the issue of mindfulness may be: the issue may be a communication, and hence a coming out of self into the between, as a relativity of the self and the other. Propositional communication is but one mode of articulation, albeit one especially favored by objective mind, and more generally, by any outlook that seeks to render the meaning of being in dominantly univocal terms. The proposition lends itself objectively to the inspection of the univocal mind. Its usefulness is that it can be detached from its own source of origination. But this is also the danger; it is abstracted from the more complex conceptual process of the erotics of mind.

A proposition treated in abstraction from this process is like a child treated as if it were born without parents. We may have its functional name and identity but may be lacking the name of its more intimate identity.

Objective mind, as it were, wants to rebaptise orphan communications as fully autonomous issue. Nevertheless, all communication, propositional included, is within community, whether the community of mindful communicators, or the community of mind and being. Even in the putative autonomous proposition, the traces of its orphanage are carried in the copula, the "is," that joins subject and object. Propositions are proposals and copulations. The erotics of the joining of mind and being seems inescapable.

Consider this illustration of mind as erotic, that is, as thrust into the between, as an energy both of self-transcendence and of mediation with what is other. I hear a bang. I am shocked into curiosity. What in Heaven's name was that? The question articulates my lack: I do not know what that bang is, what caused it, what it might portend. I respond: attentively, apprehensively I look around; I concentrate on its possible reasons, or causes, or sources. This responding is my *being outside* myself: I am other to what I was just two seconds ago, now foraging in the world of otherness for a reason or cause or source. . . . I am engrossed in the other, absorbed in the effort to absorb what is there, and what is relevant to my lack. Being outside myself in this middle, being other to myself in this middle—these testify to the dynamic of self-transcending, which is the very power of minding itself. Mind is the power of self-othering, in response to a perplexity that comes to it from the otherness of being beyond itself.

If in this self-othering I seek to overcome my lack, this is not all. My alert gaze swings through the field of vision; my ears strain to listen to the surrounds. Eyes and ears are beyond themselves, embodiments of self-transcendence, reconnoitering the between. I turn to my left and see the black cloud. I say: A clap of thunder, by Jove! I know now. In identifying the source of perplexity in the otherness of the between, I may possess it mentally, now as information that I may conceptually put in its place (though perhaps not *its* place, perhaps in *my* place). My mediation with its otherness, in the self-transcending movement in the middle, ends with an epistemic identification of the disturbing difference. I mark the source, and on being satisfied with the knowledge, I return to a relative equilibrium of self-possession. My mediation with the unknown, my successful transformation of the unknown into the known, allows me to mediate with my own perplexing lack, mediate with myself. My eros for the unknown, in being satisfied, allows me to be satisfied with myself again, allows me to be at home with being, in being at home with myself.

There are ambiguities in all of this, of course. Notice especially the stress on the appropriation of the object. Erotic mind is driven by *its own lack* and it is driven beyond itself to overcome *its own* lack. Its motivation is for the self; the other is for the self and the return to self-relatedness of the knower; the knower seeks itself to be satisfied, in its relativity to the other;

116*Perplexity and Ultimacy*

the other is not there simply for itself; it serves as the medium by which the knower returns to itself, not to the first naïveté or ignorance, but enriched by its passage in and through the other. In a word, for erotic mind, knowing is essentially the mediated appropriation of the other.

Other limitations follow. Thus mind can easily become seen as instrumental: erotic mind can make mind and the other into means to an end. Is the end mindfulness itself? Sometimes yes, sometimes no. It is possible to argue that the answer is yes with, for instance, Aristotle's *noēsis tes noēseōs*, or Hegel's self-thinking Idea. Mind is driven to self-completion, and there rests in the ever renewed circle of its own dynamic self-mediation. Self-minding is both means and end. This view is not immune from criticism, especially in so far as self-minding makes the other a means to its own self-mediation, but it is superior to a more thoroughly instrumentalized view. In the latter, mind is essentially a means, and not both means and end. The circle of self-thinking thought is broken, but not with the result of a more radical release towards the other, as in agapeic mind. Rather the circle is broken because something other than mind serves as the end, for which mind is a means.

The example I will cite is Nietzsche's view of knowing as will to power. This is just one example, but in modern philosophy many instances of the romance of power and knowing could be cited. Once again note that here mind is erotic; but now mind and eros are *disjoined*, in that mind serves as the instrument of an eros that is not itself mindful. This eros is christened will to power, and mind serves this eros; mind is only a disguised form of this will to power. Not only is mind here instrumentalized, but the otherness of being is also a means to an end. The end is the beginning, the source: the alogical powers that precede the emergence of mind, say the will, or the id, or the forces of social production. The other is for the mind, the mind is for this eros, this eros is for the self, this self is itself the expression of powers, not themselves within the self-mediating power of the self. In all cases, mind as for the other as other is ultimately denied. Even the self cannot be properly for itself; for push this line of thinking in a certain direction, and minding is but foam on the surface of the ocean of an otherness, and this is no agapeic otherness, but perhaps an indifferent, perhaps a hostile power.

Erotic mind, in this above regard, clearly breaks with the neutralism of objective mind. Thus, Nietzsche attacked the "immaculate perception" doctrine. He has many followers, most recently in French thought, who criticize the myth of scientific objectivity and its complicity in structures of power and domination. But does Nietzsche's critique or theirs escapes the economy of power? One suspects that while this version of erotic mind dissolves the self-possession of mind, and offers some equivocal release vis-à-vis objective knowing, yet there is no breakthrough to the agape of being. This critique is the disillusion of objective knowing, but its eros remains within a circle of concepts which do not really release mind towards the other. What it reveals is one equivocal side of objective knowing as neutral univocity. A lot of contemporary discussion of foundationalism and deconstruction is determined by this, so to say, equivocity of objective, univocal knowing.

I think we must acknowledge that there are partial truths here to be acknowledged. For when we deal with finite entities as determinate objects, it is in order that we take up the appropriate relation to them. A certain appropriating of the other is not *always* out of place. We get a sense of things, we put them in their place, and their place is often defined relative to our needs and interests, and not in any narrow sense either. We appropriate determinate objects; we make use of them; they often are means to ends that are not intrinsic to their being. With the proper qualifications, we do enter into a system of exchange with things; they give themselves to us for our use. Life would be obviously impossible without this.

In a way, things are very practically *generous* to us, and we are not always grateful for their usefulness. I can envisage a proper use of things in which we render our thanks for their humble everyday gift. Already an openness to the agapeic infiltrates this thanks, or at least begins to glimmer on the borders of the instrumental. When we give thanks for food, for example, we acknowledge the generosity of the giver, just in the act of using it for our own self-survival, self-satisfaction. We are released towards its otherness, even though we must consume it. We dignify the instrumental with this reminder of, this gratitude for, what in its being is beyond instrumentalization.

The danger of an excessive objectification is perennial: food, the body, the sensuous as such, even the mind and spirit, all these we may seek to make the object of a manipulative technique. This can yield a debasement of erotic mind, against which the equivocality of erotic mind cannot always sufficiently guard itself. Eros is inherently ambiguous. It can be instrumentalized as a will to power which degrades the other into an object of its own self-aggrandizement. Eros can also be partner to a more radical self-transcendence. The passion of knowing may carry the self out of itself, in an ecstasy which finds itself surprised by the other. It may bow before this other, instead of forcing the other to bow before it.

Erotic mind is in interplay with the other, and in the best sense, it is aroused to the promise of the other. Born in desire, it may open up the other, in a way that a less insistent familiarity fails to do. Its arousal is a measure of its passion for the truth of being. It may be pervaded by the anticipation of the other in terms of itself, yet in dynamically carrying though its anticipation, it may find itself surprised, even overcome, by the other. By contrast, the instrumentalization of erotic knowing makes sure that it will never really be surprised by the other. There will be no marvel. For marvel, surprise, the unexpected dispossess the seeker of any pretense to be completely on a par with what is sought. Erotic mind must give itself over to the other in order to secure its own self-relation. It may find that this giving over upends every efforts to secure such self-relation. Erotic mind may turn into something else again.

Consider the classical account of eros in Plato's *Symposium*. Notable here is the pluriform nature of eros. Notable also is the flowering of a more pervasive eros in mindfulness of the beloved other, and more specifically in philosophical mindfulness. As the highest mindfulness philosophy is a con-cretization of eros. The movement of this eros is from the self as lacking, though a realization that absolute lack makes no sense relative to mind, since ignorance known as such is a condition of being between: between knowing nothing at all, and between the possession of absolute knowing. Erotic mind is in the between, stressed by the extremities that pull it downward to the silence of the beast and upwards to the serenity of the god.

As erotic mindfulness philosophy moves from the intermediate soul towards the Good as the absolute other. In this movement we discover a *co-implication* of self and other. The notion of a monadic self is nonsense, if mind is erotic. Moreover, in dynamic desire—understood here in terms of the infinite sweep of human self-transcendence—the other participates in the unfolding of the self, even if the latter self mistakenly thinks of the overall movement as simply its own self-unfolding. The *ruse of eros*, I think, is precisely to equivocate on the primacy of self-articulation. For the self-articulation would be impossible without a community between the self and the other, which self-articulation seems to subordinate, but which it cannot.

The other infiltrates desire, and always invites the possibility of a *rever-sal* of priority between self and other. I say "invite," but I could say "wel-come" in some cases, where the co-implicated other has out of itself already activated its own agapeic power. But the invitation is there, sleeping when not roused. In sum, it is crucially important, relative to the equivocality of eros, to be discerning enough to distinguish between the erotic mind that becomes an objectifying will to power, and the erotic mind that, in growing in itself, grows in its awareness of the co-implication of self and other. The first can distort, indeed block the promise of self-transcendence; the latter points beyond itself to agapeic mind.

4. Agapeic Mind

Let me now attempt to speak of agapeic mind. Are we confined to the "egocentric predicament?" Is there a transcending of mindfulness beyond this, beyond subjective, objective, and erotic mind? What I want to explore is a generosity of mind beyond lack, an openness beyond need, a vigilance with respect to the beyond, beyond self-interest. My claim is not that humans ever *completely* embody such agapeic mindfulness, yet in our failure, we are aware of the ideal at stake, even if its demand is only episodically approximated. It says something essential about what we are, and the promise of what we are to be. Again we cannot avoid our intermediate condition, between our finitude and an absolute demand. Agapeic mind expresses something that is both a regulative ideal and an ontological reality, somehow constitutive of our most intimate being. There is no direct univocal way to say this. Given the nature of the case, my path will have to twist and turn in a sometimes serpentine way.

How think the possibility of mindfulness that, in some elusive sense, is from the beginning already defined by a certain fullness, and not simply by lack? Full of what? It cannot be full of different kinds of determinate knowledge, knowing everything about this and that. This is impossible. Yet mind can be implicitly informed by an enigmatic sense of the "whole," and this prior to all determinate knowing, and more than every item of determinate knowledge. Thus, agapeic mind is related to the *second indeterminate perplexity*. The latter is not a specific curiosity about a determinate problem, but is activated beyond even the answers to such specific problems.[3] If it is activated beyond such answers, it suggests that there is more at play in minding, even *before* the specific questions such answers meet.

Suppose we take our sights from Aristotle's previously cited saying that somehow the soul is everything. The soul is not a determinate form since it is the power to receive determinate form in itself. Aristotle might equally have said that the soul is everything, because somehow it is nothing. How then something, indeed everything, and nothing? This: the mind is nothing because it is no thing; it is in excess of every thing; it manifests self-transcending dynamism. If it were simply a univocal determinate thing, there is no way we could explain this self-transcending power. And we need to acknowledge this power, even if perhaps we cannot completely explain it. We must acknowledge it because if knowing is a relativity of self and other, we have to explain how the self is outside of itself in this relativity. The self as mindfulness enters the middle between itself and the other, mediates this difference and constitutes a self-aware relativity. This, of course, is only one

---

3. As I will argue in subsequent chapters, it must be activated to raise the question of the ultimate, to raise mind beyond its immersion in finite knowing and projects, all of which are finally defined within a system of instrumentalities, of means relative to ends, not of origins out of which things arise, not of finalities that cannot be converted into mere means.

side of the matter, since the other *gives itself* into the middle also, and mind-fulness relative to the other is doubled over to meet this giving of the other. In any case, a thing that is beyond itself is not a completely determinate univocal thing. It is a thing that is a no thing. It is a determination of indeterminacy. This indeterminacy can be given a number of modulations. Consistent with the paradoxical language that is called on to conjoin seeming opposites, this indeterminacy is the nothing that is also the more, as the original of the self-transcending power of minding.

Consider how, when I mind something, I am no longer simply myself; in minding a thing, my mind is about that thing. Example: I am driving a car and someone shouts: "Mind the child!" Mindlessly—so it seems—I swerve and avoid the child. But the seeming mindlessness is really minding that forgets itself by being catapulted out of itself, by its being rivetted on the other. I forget myself in minding the child. But this forgetfulness is just the activation of myself as sheer mindfulness of the other. I give myself, am given over, to its life as other. I become that life, at least partially. Mind is free of itself, released from itself but as itself, engrossed in the other which it becomes, even as it makes itself nothing for the other's sake. This enigmatic power of becoming the other is possible on the basis of the mind being a kind of free nothing, a creative indeterminacy that can assume, without subsuming, the being of the other.

This nothing of creative indeterminacy will receive different interpretations, depending on whether we see mind as erotic or agapeic. This nothing is granted in both. In erotic mind, the nothing is the lack of indefiniteness which has to be overcome in a process that makes the indefinite progressively definite. The nothing is defined through a process of self-definition which appropriates the determinate other, and uses the definiteness of the known other to confer increasing definition on the self-developing mind.

And this, of course, is ingredient in the maturation of mind. Mind can overcome indefiniteness through a dual process: One, reaching out to determinate objects which, on being known by mind, give the mind itself the definition of the thing known—mind becomes determinate in knowing determinate things. Two, through a process of self-development that goes along with increase of determinate knowing; for in knowing definite things the mind comes to self-awareness of itself, as precisely a power of definition, and hence knows itself as self-defining. Hegel's account of mind is erotic in this sense. He combines these two senses of definition, coupling them with an understanding of the negativity of mind. The nothing determines itself through

---

4. Keats suggested something of the point when he spoke of the poet's "negative capability." But *all* minding is marked by the promise of "negative capability," and more.

a process of self-development, which itself goes along with increasing knowledge of determinate things. We culminate with an understanding of the nothing as self-determining negativity, and of mind as in possession of itself in its appropriation of the other.

When we turn to agapeic mind, we find a different sense of the nothing and indeterminacy. The indeterminacy is not just the lacking indefinite; it rather refers to a sense of plenitude that undergirds even the lack of the indefinite. Indeed, the lack of self-determining negativity is itself only possible because it is grounded in an affirmative power of being. We desire, seek, quest, not just because we lack, but because we *are*, and we are as the power to be self-articulating. We are the positive power to overcome our own lack because we are already a particular concretion of the plenitude of being. A sense of plentitude is written into even the indigence of our lacking and needy form of being. The indeterminacy is not merely an indefiniteness to be given complete determination; the nothing is not a negativity that is completely self-determining. The otherness of the power of being intrudes at the beginning, in the middle, and it outlives our end.

This otherness calls for a different affirmative relation right from the outset. The call is coeval with our being, indeed it is prior to the self-articulation of being for which we claim autonomy. The power to be self-articulating is given and called forth, called forth by the otherness of being, *before the self can call itself forth*. In a word, there is a prior giving of self-determination which is not self-determining. This giving is from a surplus of plenitude, not from an indefinite lack. The movement of mind is not impelled by a doubting that insists on being allayed by self-certainty. The nothing of agapeic mind is awakened in an expectancy that is not self-insistent. This expectancy is not an epistemological defect. It is the desert of an elemental love of being.

Previously, I hinted at this love in relation to the way the senses feast on the agape of being as aesthetic presencing. But the point can be applied to philosophy itself—commonly viewed as the opposite extreme to aesthetic feasting. Philosophy might be an agapeic knowing. This relates to the metaxological view and its double mediation. The first movement of mind (but this does not mean absolutely first) is from the self to the other but for the other, perhaps even to the point of sacrifice of self. "Sacrifice" here is meant metaphorically. This is the death of the self in the knowing of the other. Eros has been described in terms of "the little death," and one sees the point. But one might say that if agape is more truly death, it is also more truly life, in that one is nothing, the other is all. The second movement concerns openness to the return from the other to the self. This is not a return to the self of itself; it is the self-revelation of the other to the self. In agapeic alert the other may come out of itself. This is *its* unfolding, not mine, *its self-unfolding* as given for the self, given in return from the other as other. The coming of the other is welcomed.

And so the directionality of agapeic minding is not linear in any straightforward sense. It demands a patient thinking, a staying with the being that is before it. This is not, as it were, an apathetic patience; it is an active patience. It is a watching, where watching implies a ready attentiveness for what may break cover before one, and come out of itself and towards one. It is a vigilance. To be vigilant means to be willing to wait, to be patient in the sense of letting things take their own time, unfold in their own time, and not be forced into premature, hence false, revelation. To be vigilant also means to be in a state of high alert. The patient thinking of agapeic mind is this state of high alert that paradoxically has nothing insistent about it. It demands a strange mix of active mind and patient readiness, energy of being and of being nothing.

The movement of agapeic mind can sometimes be a kind of hovering, or expectation, or solicitation. Expectation: one is not sure what will emerge. As stillness overcomes the mind—the movement is a movement of stillness, of quietness—one is waiting. Hovering over the middle: waiting for the spirit of the place or event. One may miss it; there are no guarantees. It may be too subtle; it may be so obvious, and we look in the wrong place or way. The time of the self may be out with the time of the other. They cross, but do not cross.

I am in a place called Inchydoney, near Clonakilty, West Cork. I look out at the sea and watch. The waves come in, retreat, come in, retreat; there is the background murmur of a low whoosh. On the other side of the bay, the hill is a motley of greens; there is fog on the horizon. I have just offered a set of simple empirical observations. These might be confirmed by anyone at all who would occupy the position I now occupy, who would step into my perspective or something relatively close to it. The empirical observations are relatively anonymous in that respect. Anyone might make them.

But now consider: I might offer these observations as I pass through this place. I drive to Inchydoney in my car, get out, make a number of observations, like a few quick snapshots, and drive on, drive away. The mind has served as a good registering instrument but is barely touched by the scene. Instead I have come here, and have stayed. I have been here a time now. This is the staying that is important, and the giving of time to mind to loose itself, the giving of time to the things before one. With such a giving of mind and things a chance to be themselves, with this mindful giving of time to things, the self-same observations can cease to be simply neutral descriptions. The self comes to sink into a place with time; the place tends to pass over into the mind. The mind is in the place; the place is in mind. This is a deeper mediation of the self and world than the minimally implicated observation of one who passes through the middle. The one who passes through, if he does not have enough time, merely surfaces, skims over, instrumentalized the middle. The interplay between self and world is superficial, albeit correct, accurate, even exact.

Not so simple with the one who mindfully stays with the place. Agapeic mind must stay with that kind of patience, for only then can there come to realization a deeper relatedness between the minding and the showing in the world. The greens of the hills are gestures, signatures of difference; the sound of the waves voice the endurance and impermanence of things; the fog on the horizon is the line of indeterminacy beyond which hides mystery. The mystery is not in here, or out there; it is here and there and nowhere. The mind must be steeped in the things, sink into the things; alternatively, the things must become tinged with minding, become presences, lively or brooding, but presences, not neutral objects. Presences seep beyond their own determinate boundaries and communicate their implication with their surrounds. Agapeic mind goes out to such presences; things present themselves, out of themselves to agapeic mind.

And so as a noninstrumental vigilance, agapeic mind is not an interfering mode of thought. Or, since the human mind almost unavoidably is interfering, it is an effort to still that self-insistent will to interfere with the other. The presencing of the other is often reduced to its determinate thereness. We identify it as an object by pinning down this its determinate particularity. In the process we diminish the suggestion of something more in the thing. We want to see the things as simply that determinate presence and nothing more. In fact, no thing is simply that thing and nothing more. In itself it concretizes an energy of being that is individualized in things but that exceeds every such concretion. Every such concretion reminds us of this "more" that it concretizes and that it is not fully, that it does not exhaust.

Relative to other things, we find the seepage of this more in the presencing of the thing to things beyond itself. No thing, we find, exists univocally in itself; its very identity is shaped in its relativity to other things; it is outside of itself in this relativity; its presencing to the world is its passage beyond rigid univocal identity into the community of others; the presencing of things is their mute communication of an identity that is revealed in relativity, and that in a way celebrates self and relativity together. The flower sings to the hill on which its grows; the wind dances with the grasses that it enlivens, quickens; the birds glory in the sky that gives them freedom; the heavens rejoice in these open spaces of unconstrained liberty. The community of being sings, sings silently. Presencing is the silent word; or there is no silence really. Agapeic mind tries to be attuned to the voices of otherness. Attuned to the "more" in the determinate things, it welcomes its freedom, calls it forth. The yes to things of the agapeic mind somehow confirms their identity, redeems their presencing.

Let me try to put the point by recalling the mythic story of the Adamic naming. What would this be? It would be a naming unlike anything since the Fall. For since the Fall our naming of things always is implicated in domination, in robbing things of their divine freedom, in the interests of making them subject to our fallen freedom, itself a parody of divine freedom. What would it mean to say that the first Adamic naming was an agapeic naming? It would mean such naming freed things to be themselves more fully. It would give them their being in a completer way. It would say: "It is granted." The name would be a granting that said: "Here is the promise of being; it is given." It was as if God left the creation open in its promise, allowing us to call forth something of that promise in agapeic naming. *Now* our naming does not call forth the promise of freedom, except rarely. *Now* our names use that promise of others for ourselves, and deflect it from its own being fully for itself.

The first Adamic naming suggests the co-creation of the human being, our agapeic yes in the middle to the middle, that confirms the things in the identity the Creator gives them. Adamic naming would help God create perfection. God's agape lets be this open space of freedom, lets it be for us as other to Himself, letting us be ourselves, inviting us to be agapeic beings that let other beings be for themselves. One might say that this is the creative love of creation that descends to the love of consecrated particularity. And this is ingredient in what I imply by agapeic mind—love of the particular as particular. And the latter is not at all the univocal identity that shrinks back into itself, but shows the energy of the "more" by which the thing becomes itself, in the sweep of its own self-transcendence into the middle of the universal community of being. But then, too, we cannot neglect to remember the always possible peril of the Golem.

What all this implies, I think, is a rethinking of "givenness" in terms other than fixed univocal presence. The giving of the "more" in the given is there to be recovered. Our thinking on "the given" has to stand outside the standard terms of contemporary discussion. The other is not objectified by agapeic mind but let be, though not indifferently. It is granted in its otherness, granted to be itself in its otherness. It is granted, it is given, *datur*. It is a *datum*, a being given. But it is not the mind that gives it; it is given because it is allowed to give itself; and we say, "It is granted." We assent to the self-giving of what is there, and we give ourselves over to the middle space of meeting the other, as it comes into that middle place. We say yes in the middle; the affirmation "it is," *esti* is consent to the community of the middle. This "is" is the agape of the copula.

I want to mention briefly a significant implication for philosophical mindfulness, namely, the need for a hermeneutical *generosity*. What would this require? It would ask of us: Seek the strength in the other, the point of ripeness, or if not that, seek the promise of ripeness in the other. And if one seeks the good in the other, do not define this good simply in terms of its congruence with oneself; let this promise of the good of the other emerge; welcome and make way for its emergence for itself. Is mindless naïveté being counseled? Certainly it is not intended. The negative is not blinked. Were it, we would have a mindfulness mushed in sentimental good will. Rather we must discern something beyond the equivocity of erotic mind.

Recall how erotic mind is ambiguous, how in one mode it can lend itself to an objectifying instrumentalism. It is out of this ambiguity that erotic mind can generate a hermeneutics of suspicion. This means: the other is not beloved; the other relative to will to power is a potential threat, or curb on my self-possession; hence erotic mind must be wary of the other; its own self-possession may be subverted by this otherness beyond mastery. It may not only be wary and suspicious, it may hate, its hatred expressed in an ever more vehement will to dominate the other. Erotic mind, passing through this hermeneutics of suspicion, can end up in a kind of sadistic mindfulness, for which being-other must passively lay itself down like a masochist. Sartre's philosophy, I suppose, epitomizes this sadistic mind most clearly.

Even though the hermeneutics of suspicion parades in a posture of superiority, it is infected with a sense of its own lack, and it turns to the other as a means of assuaging this lack. But the way it assuages this lack, and justifies itself and its own superiority, is not by seeing the good in the other, but by suspecting the wrong in the other, the disvalue for the self of the other that subverts absolute self-possession. Agapeic mind, as expressed out of a hermeneutics of generosity, is out of joint with this. It seeks a home in the good in the other. Its very anticipation of this tends to draw forth this good. And this, of course, can be mimicked by the hermeneutics of suspicion: suspicion will find its own prejudice self-confirming; the other deemed suspect unfolds suspiciously, the other treated as a threat come to one as a threat. By contrast, generosity of mind is at home in a granting of the worthiness of being. It does not insist that other-being justify itself, before the judgmental gaze of an imperious or possessive knowing. A freedom is afforded the other, at least the promise of this freedom is held out from the outset.

This also implies that the polemic between traditionalists or post-Nietzschean deconstructionists finally has about it something sterile. We are not involved in an erotic struggle for tradition or against it. This is why we need an agapeic hermeneutics, both in relation to traditional and contemporary thought. The only way to meet this need is to cultivate agapeic mind vis-`a-vis the matter itself, beyond the struggle of contemporaneity with tradition. Contemporary thought is not to be scorned, but since its dominant hermeneutics tends to suspicion about the past, we need the corrective of

agapeic mind relative to the dead philosophers. This would be the act of generous thinking that would give life to the dead, bring the dead back from their
death, bring their thought alive in the present again. Rethinking them would be
an act of memorial love. Agapeic remembering would not simply reshape them
in our own image. It would allow the contemporary thinker to be reshaped in the
image of their otherness. Hermeneutical generosity brings the dead back to life.

I imagine myself as dead. I imagine I go to the house of the dead where
Plato, Heraclitus, Aquinas, Hegel, and many more now are. In the house of
the dead, I as dead must talk with the dead. How do I talk with these dead
philosophers? Do I bring them "up to date" about the "metaphysics of presence" or "ontotheology" or "the linguistic turn" or "the textual revolution"
or "deconstruction" or whatever? Do I hector them on their faults, on their
being surpassed, or being hopelessly "out of touch?" Were I to do so, I can
imagine a piercing look of generous surprise on the face, say, of Plato. The
face silently questions me: *Who is this?*

And would the dead be harsh with us? Are we being honest with the
dead when we flog them with polemical fury? I can imagine a silence falling
on the gathered dead when a recently arrived dead one, still fresh from an
academic conference, goes into full flight in the mode of the hermeneutics of
suspicion. A pause of hush, a lull in talk, again a silence of surprise: How is
the truth thus served? Is this the service of the truth? And then I imagine a
different measure of conversation being quietly resumed.

Agapeic mind does not ask: How will I judge the dead? It asks of itself:
How will I be judged by the dead who were great? This is why one strives for
a generous hermeneutics, putting oneself in their place, in their otherness.
One tries to comprehend their greatness in its otherness, not simply refash-
ioning this in the image of one's sometimes narrower concerns. The dead are
really beyond being made instruments of my self, they are beyond being
simply for me. I must be released towards them differently, to be worthy of
them and the service of truth.

5. No, Mind and Mine

I hear a grating protestation: Are you not fantasizing on an ideal? Is it
not the case that we humans are the most pressing self-insistence in the
whole of creation? I agree, and moreover, I connect your protest to the idiocy
of being.[5] I think of the child beginning its process of becoming itself, and

---

5. Relative to this idiocy, remember the "mineness" is also a "being with," hence
inseparable from community: this other sense of "mine," which is "not mine," is
relevant here.

how the self-insistence of will presents itself with an undeniable stubborness.
Two of the major words, first, elemental words, are "no" and "mine." The self
as will, as insistence of being, as "mine" against the "not-mine"—these surface almost immediately in human existence, and never leave it. It is only
too true that much subsequent self-development is just the serpentine unfolding of these two words: "no," "mine." Some reflection on this is needed.

"No" is obviously related to the nothing. It is a specification of the
original indeterminacy of being. There is a freedom of being beyond univocity
which shows the power of negation, shows the self as the power of negation.
Thus, the "no" allows the self to set itself off from what is other to itself,
allows it to differentiate the world into this, and then not this, not that, and
so on. The word "and" which conjoins the plurality of things and events
would be meaningless without the "not" that sets the things apart into their
distinct identities. The "no" identifies things, even as it allows the no-sayer
to come into a sense of its own identity. There would be no articulated world
without the "no." Does not all of this tell against the idea of agapeic mind,
and from the outset? Does it not mean that, at best, we have a complex
erotic mind, where the "for-self" develops intricate ruses of overcoming and
negating, but all leading back to that other elemental word "mine?"

For indeed the "no" and "mine" are inseparable. When I know that I
can say "no," and not just once, but again and again; and when I know that
it is I that says "no," know that I am this power of negation, *I know that
nothing can stop me* from saying "no." For I will mutter it silently even if fear
shuts me up. I can say "no" in the sullenness of silent eyes, in the stiffness of
a withdrawn body. I can say "no" in a smirk that dismisses. I can say "no" by
saying "yes." When I come to know all this, I know myself as free, and as
free, the delicious taste of "mineness" comes to offer itself. I am I; I am not
the other. There is something elemental here—something idiotic, singularly
intimate beyond complete determination.

The difficulty, of course, is that the movement of separation in the "no"
also opens up the terror of the will, even in the intoxication of free difference. I am I, but I, too, am also other. There is a space of void between me
and the other, and this space of void brings home to me my lack, my need,
my nothingness, my emptiness. Freedom is then tasted as an intoxicated
emptiness. This is why I think I must say "mine" again and again. I think I
must reach across the void between me and others and claim them. In
claiming them as mine, I think I claim my freedom again. But I do not claim
my freedom agapeically, but always for myself, and the other serves this claim
of the self about itself. In a word, the other confirms my "mine." The rudi-
ments of the drama are revealed clearly with children. They have not yet
learned to disguise the raw nakedness of the "mine" and the "no." They will
learn to do this; for the "yes" and the "yours" will not be gainsaid. But the

"no" and "mine" will not sleep. They will continue their disguised work, even under the disarming incognito, or alias, of altruism.

In Freud's inability to understand genuine altruism, we find his incapacity to think beyond this clandestine work. Agapeic mindfulness was an impossibility for him, since the self-insistence of the human, in its "no" and its "mine," finally determines the whole story, in the beginning and in the end. In the middle, we cast around for alleviation of the distress engendered by encounter between such self-insistence and a universe indifferent, very often hostile. There is nothing but eros in Freud, sly eros complicating the "no" and "mine," never eros that comes to the border of celebrating being's agape. At the border of eros is death, *thanatos*, indeed all along eros is inseparable from *thanatos*. But this is not the death that gives itself into the agape of being. There is no agapeic good will at all. If Freud were right, every affirmation "It is good" would mean "It is good for me." It is not the goodness that counts, but ultimately the "for me." Retracted from its further unfolding into agapeic self-transcendence, eros becomes intertwined with *thanatos*, but this now as the "no" to being that retracts back into itself, into its own finally empty "mine."

Freud is only a modern example of a view which has had multiple adherents in all eras. While the picture of human being is bleak, it has its pathetic truth, in that much of our lives are thus. The noise of the self-insistent I squawks its "no" and "mine" above the music of everything else. We can finally have nothing but contempt for this squawking I, that is to say, for ourselves, if this is all we are. *Le moi est haïssable*, Pascal said. This, too, is true. It is true because this self is untrue. We recognize it as hateful, because there is more. It is the promise of "more," even as it squawks. And we are pathetic, though the pathos is not the patience of the agapeic mind. It is the sad sight of the empty self that stamps its foot to convince the earth that does not move, that scowls and shakes its fist at the heavens that still smile. This is the indigent self: a shiver of helplessness before a hostile world, a shiver of subjectivity that turns itself into a shout of aggressive self-insistence.

Freud did not notice that, if this was the "bottom line," science as knowledge of the other, regardless of self-insistence, was an impossibility. Freud's own claim about psychoanalysis as true science presupposes the possibility of something like agapeic mind. Or is psychoanalysis as science itself another shiver of helplessness, another shout of "no" and "mine."[6] If so, it

---

6. Some recent "revisionist" interpretations of Freud himself, as quite other to a kind of secular saint, an unimpeachable crusader for truth, lend strong support to this possibility.

can make no claim for itself as true. If no, then we have to revise the picture of human possibility presented by pychoanalysis itself: if the psychoanalyst is a true scientist, he must be other to the picture of the human being as radically self-insistent. The truth of psychoanalysis depends on the *genuine self-transcendence* of true thought, of agapeic mind, something that is denied as possible by psychoanalysis. It will not do to say that scientific truth "sublimates" the core self-insistence. This is not self-transcending mind, only another clandestine self-insistence. The "truths" of psychoanalysis make the truth of psychoanalysis impossible.

The case is analogous to the previously mentioned instance of mathematical knowing. Mathematical knowing is not itself a mathematical truth. The mathematician's passion for truth cannot be accommodated to a mathematical truth; the mathematician studying equations or numbers is not himself an equation or number. Likewise, the psychoanalyst claiming to know the truth of the human cannot be, if his claim is true, an instance of the truth he claims to discover in human existence. He or she must be something more, there must be something more; but this something more cannot be accommodated to the theory. If the theory is right, there can be no true theories, for a true theory goes beyond radical self-insistence. If the theory is wrong, we get the same opening up of a possible orientation to being that goes beyond self-insistence. We get the possibility of agapeic mind, a more radical transcendence of "no" and "mine" and their complex ruses of domination.

And do not slip away with the excuse that self-referential argument is a cheap logician's trick that pulls conclusions from concepts, like rabbits from hats. The use of this mode of self-referential argument is absolutely to the point, for the claim at issue is that there is nothing beyond self-reference, self-relation. The use of self-referential argument precisely shows the breakdown of the absolutization of self-reference. Something more is already at work in self-reference, in self-insistence. All the self-referential argument does is absolutize self-insistence, and in doing so shows the impossibility of absolute self-insistence. It shows the being at work of something other all along, and absolutely necessary for the ruses of self-insistence to continue to work their sneaky perpetuation.

Here the self-referential argument is no logical gimmick, but an elemental confrontation of the self with itself, wherein it discovers something at work other than what it says, or claims is at work. This is honesty about the self, working to deconstruct the absolutization of self-insistence. There is a freedom and necessity at work beyond the "no" and the "mine." What is other appears if we dwell with the matter of self, that is, if we stay patiently with the thought. And to do this is, of course, to be mindful in a potentially agapeic way, once again.

6. Mindfulness Beyond Lack

I want to turn again to the question: How can mind be beyond lack, be somehow already full? If mind were already full, it must be somehow fulfilled at the beginning. But does not fulfillment come at the end of a search, rather than at the beginning? And is not this what most impresses us about mind: we are in search, and in search because we lack what we need to fulfill mind's eros? How think at all of mind as already somehow full?

Here are some relevant considerations, some made with reference to thinkers at two extremes of metaphysical commitment, namely, Plato and Heidegger. Long ago Plato (as we see from the *Meno*, and elsewhere) was attentive to the issue, and puts the essential question: If we are in search, how do we recognize what we seek, did we not already have some sense of what we seek? If we did not have this prior sense of what we seek, we could not seek it at all in the first place. Contrariwise, if we do have this prior sense, why do we seek at all, since we already seem to have what we seek, and we cannot really seek what we already have? There are complex, not to say paradoxical, circlings of mind here. They have been rebaptised as the hermeneutical circle in our time, not least by Heidegger.

If we were completely outside the relativity to being of mindfulness, we could never have mindfulness of being at all. We start, not with a void nothing, but with an implicit relativity to the goal of our quest. The quest cannot be denied, but the unwinding of its pathway requires careful interpretation. The quest is not a linear passage from nothing to something, from a lack to a fulfillment. It is the passage from a paradoxical lack that points deeper than lack to a more positive condition of being. This other condition is one of being between: we are between the unknowing lack of the beast, and the knowing beyond all lack of the god. The intermediate nature of mindfulness means we could not recognize the truth we seek in the middle were we not already implicated with the truth, were we not already in the truth. The seeker is already rich with a richness beyond lack, though this richness impels him to a more articulated expression of what is at play in this prior plenitude.

The seeking of truth, it would seem, is made possible by an already effective relativity of mind and being. If absolute alienation involved hatred of the truth, even hatred has to acknowledge, hence relate to, that which it would utterly destroy. Alienation from truth is still within the intermediate condition of relativity to the truth of being. We are within this relativity even when we betray it, or err from it, or lie against it, or are cheated of it. The goal of fulfillment is already at work from the origin, for if it were not at work, the process of explicit passage from origin to more fully articulated end could not take place at all. If mindfulness is shaped in a self-transcendence, the goal it seeks enters the very institution of self-transcending, right from the start.

How can an end shape a beginning? The end must be already at work in the beginning in a more positive way than can be captured in the language of lack. Something of this is imaged in the Platonic account of the parentage of eros (*Symposium*, 203a ff.): the mother of eros is Penia or poverty, and the father is Poros, contrivance, resourse (son of cunning, Metis). But Poros is presented to us as a god drunk with nectar at the celebration by the gods of the birthday of Aphrodite. Poros stumbles from the feast of the gods, and while sleeping in the garden of Zeus, Penia, the mother of eros, sleeps with him. Eros is conceived of their union. Thus, eros has an origin in the intoxicated fullness of a sleeping divinity, as well as in the resourcefulness of indigent wakefulness. Divine drunkenness and festivity, the agape of the gods, a feast of plenty, is also embodied in the generation of eros. Nor is eros simply death-bound; mingled with death, there is something deathless (*athanatos*) in the process of generation (see 203e). Eros will not seek death but the good as its end, and the good as agape of being will have been at work in its search from the origin. It loves the good because it is already originated from a love that is with the good.

So we must say that the picture of erotic mind as moving from lack to fulfillment is itself lacking. To think of mind in erotic terms presupposes a more original power of being at work from the beginning. An origin that from the beginning is articulated in terms of plenitude rather than lack simply, I call an agapeic origin. Such an origination does not proceed simply from lack to plenitude, but from plenitude to plenitude, or from plenitude/ lack to plenitude.

I admit to the difficulty of finding the adequate words here. A perfection is a perfection, one says. A perfection will express itself as perfection, not absolutely, but after its kind. How then can a perfection express itself incompletely or imperfectly? Nevertheless, it seems necessary to say that the human being as mindful is, in some sense, an ontological perfection, whose being, even while incomplete and lacking and in search, yet expresses a certain ontological wholeness of being. The being of the human is not perfection absolutely; neverthless, there is a proper finite wholeness—an ontological perfection, not a perfection of completed activity. This ontological perfection is in the first place the gift of being. Our mindful being is given to be, by the gift of original being as agapeic.

Much more needs to be said on this, but consider here how Heidegger rightly speaks of a prereflective awareness of being. Yet his understanding of this is not shaped by deep meditation on any primal "It is good." His is a sunless northern world compared to Plato's sunlit mediterranean world. Plato's world was closer to the place traditionally ascribed to Eden. Plato implies that we are already, in some mysterious way, at home with the truth. At a remove from the "It is good," Heidegger thinks that *Angst* before nothingness, faced in our always impending death, reawakens us to the enigma of being. This privileging of the encounter with the absolute lack of being through the nothing marks Heidegger's thought as more erotic than agapeic. Hence also the privileging of futurity and the resolute will. The residues of idealism in his version of erotic mind as *Sorge* does not sufficiently guard against the "for-self" of *Dasein* seeking to assert itself over the relativity that is always already at work. So he will say things like: "Dasein exists for the sake of itself."[7] This makes it hard to grant agapeic mind, where being for-the-other is allowed to come into its own. It makes it hard to see the very dynamism of lacking being as an incomplete expression of a fullness already at work. Yet Heidegger did struggle with equivocations in the erotics of thinking. In the later Heidegger there is a sense of the origin as giving, and a sense of awaiting this giving, a waiting beyond willful interfering. This is more reminiscent of agapeic mind.

What Heidegger calls this prereflective awareness I would call the "immediacy of metaxological mindfulness of the community of being." Being is articulated in community; a community is a mode of relativity; all things live and move and have their being in community. Every entity is double: it is for itself as an individual particularization of the energy of being; and it is related to all other entities within the complexly articulated milieu of its own being— here it is for the other, or the other is for it, though there be no explicit knowing of this. There is no absolutely pure "for-self," since self-mediation is itself inseparable from the network of relations that define intermediation with the others, and of the others with it. In that self-mediation is situated in this network of relativity to the others, self-mediation comes to be within the community of being as metaxological. This is not to deny an irreducibility to the self, but to say that it is given its "for-itself" out of the more primal metaxological community. The givenness of the "for-itself" points back to the implicitly agapeic dimension of the metaxological community. The "for-itself" may erotically pursue its own self-fulfilling identity, but this erotic self-fulfillment is again first given to the self out of the community of the others.

This suggests a reversal of views that stress the primacy of self-interest, such as we find in Hobbes, Sartre, Freud, utilitarianism. Ultimately self-interest and its pursuit are derivatives of a movement of being within community that allows or gives the "for-self" in its otherness to other selves. The possibility of

---

7. M. Heidegger, *The Essence of Reason*, trans. Terence Malick (Evanston: Northwestern University Press, 1969), 31.

being for-self is given to the self from a more original community of otherness which gives the self its being, as other to all the others. To claim self-interest as ultimate is to fail to understand the nature of things. The claim to ultimacy is, at best, an abstraction from the fullness, at worst the elevation of a false identity into an absolute that ultimately cannot sustain claims made on its behalf. There is a failure to understand the community of being.

Moreover, when this is propagated as the truth of being for humans, we perpetuate a lie that is destructive of the nature of things. We may seem to think outside the community, and by the lack of mindfulness we put ourselves outside the community, but there is really no outside of that sort. Instead we make a wound in the fullness of relativity. Everything, in direct or remote ways, in immediate or very mediated ways, is involved with everything else. There is no ultimate "for-self," or there is an ultimate "for-self" but this is most radical in the intimacy of being that reveals the singular as free. Relativity is not a static network of structural relations. It is a dynamic interplay between centers of being that are in the energetic interplay of the community of creation.

Heidegger's claim of a prereflective awareness of being is a minimal one, though he does try to reflect on, hence speak out, what it implies. He would not like the word "mind" perhaps, but it need not have any Cartesian connotations. What he calls *Denken*, I call "being mindful." In asking about the meaning of being, what is at stake is the nature of the community of mind and being, *Denken* and *Sein*. How then can mind be in search and yet be full in some sense prior to lack? Mind is in community with being from the origin, the community is metaxological and as such it gives the "for-self" its otherness. This being as given is a gift of the agapeic origin; agapeic originality is constitutive of the being of the given; mind is the promise of an articulated saying of this gift of agapeic originality. Redeeming the promise is the quest.

Plato conceives of our coming to time, of our being given to time, out of a community with true being, defined in terms of the eternal Ideas. This coming is from the fullness of eternity to the forgetfulness of time. Hence mind is in this respect full, though it does not first know it in time; hence knowing in time is *anamnēsis*, being reminded. This profound answer is full of ambiguous twists and turns. Mindfulness is memorial. Obviously, this is not empirical or historical memory of time's contingencies, but the ultimate mindfulness that knows the community of the soul with true being. This is metaphysical knowing. Mindfulness is metaphysical memory.

Memorial knowing celebrates a bond already there, even though the being memorialized may not be there. For example, I memorialize the dead; the dead are not here; yet I am reminded of my bond with the dead, and my own implication with a community beyond the immediacy of presence. Thus, the philosopher's interest in death is an interest in life, and the ultimate bonds of being that are perpetually escaping notice. Philosophy as memorial mindfulness is a way of remembering to notice. The forgetful condition of time is a fugitive condition. It is being in a fugue state.

Socrates does not call philosophy the preparation for death but its practise. How does one practise death? Certainly it has something to do with release of the soul from the enclosure of the "for-self," and its transcendence towards the being-other of the ultimate. Just as the eye is itself in being bathed in light, the eye of the soul is to be released into the element of the Good. Plato quite clearly hints at a philosophical will to *transfigure* death. No doubt, this might sound hyperbolic, and cautious commentators will consign it to the "mythic," or preserve a studied silence. The silence hardly helps. We speak about the so-called theory of Ideas, and the Ideas have been interpreted as dead immutable eternity, death installed in eternity. But there is more to the Ideas than this. We can fail to appreciate an entirely different desire to see death overcome through eternity. Eternity would not be the installation of death on the throne of the ultimate. The ultimate, that is to say, the Good would be what gives us *eternally to will life as good*, to consent to the good of being even in death, perhaps beyond death. Plato and Nietzsche are here quite kindred, despite Nietzsche's caricature of Plato. Philosophy as the practise of death is not metaphysical necrophilia but the memorializing mindfulness of our ultimate bond with the Good.

Interestingly, the story of time for Heidegger is also one of forgetting. Heidegger is very anti-Platonic on the surface, but some of his philosophical moves duplicate Plato. A major difference is the excision of the reference of human transcendence to eternity. This excision, however, does not preclude the working of a surrogate eternity: His Being does the work of time and eternity. Heidegger's Being, as I understand it, turns out to be an unstable mixture of the origin as agapeic and the origin as erotic. Erotic origin: Time is a self-manifesting/self-occluding "eternity," needing the human being for the articulation of its epochal mittences; Being comes mindfully to itself in us. Thus, we find the influence of Nietzsche's nay-saying to eternity, and the shadow of Hegel's absolute, realizing itself in human self-consciousness. Yet Heidegger wanted to keep open the difference of Being and beings in a manner not incompatible with the origin as agapeic. His effort to think Being from Being, as an effort to overcome the "for-self," to think the other out of the other—these are potentially agapeic, as is also his sense thinking as thanking.[8]

---

8. See *Beyond Hegel and Dialectic*, 43–55 for remarks on Heidegger's sense of origin; also Desmond, "Rethinking the Origin: Hegel and Nietzsche," in *Hegel and Hermeneutics*, ed. Shaun Gallagher (Albany: SUNY, to appear).

The current influence of Nietzsche and Heidegger has contributed to a standard picture of Plato as nihilist. Platonic reminiscence is turned into an erotic mind that is *metaphysically aggressive*: time is a fall from the One, and the lack of time comes to dominate our efforts to be at home with being here. Nietzsche's attack itself seeks a self-affirmative eros as will to power in time itself. I do not think he adequately conceives of agapeic affirmation. There is too much of the "for-self," legacy of the self-assertion of modernity and the idealistic tradition that Nietzsche never entirely transcended in his song of self. The early Heidegger ambivalently sang that song, though the later Heidegger tried to escape the untruth of its forced strain.

Another, more generous interpretation of Plato remembers the Good, and offers a different way to think metaphysical memory. The truth of eros is told in a myth which is the memorial story of the origin. As I already pointed out, eros has a mingled ancestry in Poros and Penia. The trace of divine festivity is in the very conception of eros, when Penia sleeps with the drunken Poros who has stumbled intoxicated from the feast of the gods. This trace of the agape of the gods is an origin *before* the awakening of eros to its own beginning in lack. We could say that if the gods had not had a good time in the festive agape, there would be no human eros at all. Eros is marked by hidden memory of the divine feast. What is a good time? What makes time good? This is a major metaphysical question. Eros and agape are two ways of thinking the goodness of time, of thinking what makes a good time.

Metaphysical memory is being reminded of the Good. Being reminded, our thinking again comes to be endless: there is no finite end to it. And yet there is a fullness to it from the outset; the lack of a finite end to it is the intimation of an inexhaustible promise. I call the Good the "agapeic origin." The Platonic image of the Sun suggests the inexhaustible radiance, self-exceeding of the origin. *Omnia bonum diffusivum sui*, was the wise common-place of premodern philosophy. It expressed the recognition of the generosity of the Good, its agape for the other. The Sun is the giver of life and light and growth. This is what is granted. Time is not a mere fall into ontological indigence. It is the most perfect possible creation. It is said quite clearly in the *Timaeus* that the Demiurge made the world as perfect as possible. The *goodness* of the derived cosmos is the god's primary care.

Not is Plato forgetful of our fugue state. As prisoners of the Cave, our condition is one of metaphysical forgetfullness. Oblivion to our community with true being is the pervasive condition of the unenlightened. Our mindful being images the eternal original, images its agape in our self-transcending eros and agape towards the primal and ultimate Good. In the fugue of the Cave, there is the inversion of the image as a being "for-itself," the retraction of its relativity to the absolute original beyond itself. Thus, we need not interpret Platonic *anamnēsis*, as Levinas seems to suggest, as closed within itself. Quite the opposite, there is a porosity to transcendence beyond thought, even when we do not think its otherness. Granted there are passages where the dialogue of the soul with itself alone is said to constitute thought. But again this is a dialogue, not a monologue, a dialogue because always open to the rupture by transcendence of the self-enclosed soul. Reminiscence implies that a bond with the other is already constitutive of the self. Memory is not self-remembering simply. This constitutive bond with true being is prior to self-remembering, prior to our encounters with particular others in time, prior to the formation of a particular soul in time. This prior other is eternity.

Even if Plato equivocates between the static univocity of the Ideas, and the dynamic originality of the Good, there is a never abandoned commitment to think and rethink the Good as constitutive of a prior community of being, in which the worth of granted being is not forgotten. Remembrance of the Good is the highest *anamnēsis*. When the prisoner is turned around in the Cave, ultimately it is the redirection of mindfulness towards the Good that is absolutely decisive, not his new discrimination between shadow and substance, even lower and higher. These offer new lights on finite being, but do not necessitate the transformation of outlook that must come if finite being is finally seen in the light of the Good. And it is in this light, that the good of the cosmos is affirmed by the Demiurge in the *Timaeus*, affirmed indeed in an all but hyperbolic way.[9]

The doctrine of *anamnēsis* might seem merely geometrical if we think of the *Meno*, where geometrical truth is called forth, solicited by Socrates. But the matter is metaphysical and ethical, concerning not just the structure, but the worth of being. *Anamnēsis* takes us beyond the dichotomy of ontology and ethics which Levinas defends, but I will say more on this below. The memory of mindfulness is not a merely epistemological theory. As an ethical orientation to being, it says that a certain metaphysics of the Good already constitutes our being, before we wake up to ourselves as lacking, that is, as

---

9. How could one possibly, in a Nietzschean vein, think of Plato as devaluing the cosmos when in the *Timaeus* he pictures the Demiurge as fashioning the cosmos as a visible work of art, the best, the most beautiful possible, even granting the recalcitrance and vagaries of the Errant cause. Recall Plato's philosophical art and the eikonic nature of the cosmos: "It is everyway necessary that the cosmos be an eikon of something *(pasa anankē ton cosmon eikona tinos einai)" Timaeus*, 29b1–2. Plato suggests something not at all unlike what Neitzsche calls an "aesthetic theodicy." The cosmos itself is called a sensible god, "an aesthetic god that images the intelligible *(eikon tou noētou theos aisthētos) Timaeus* 92c. Notice also the superlative language of praise for the worthiness of this cosmos: *megistos kai aristos kallistos te kai teleōtatos gegonen eis ouranos hode monogenes ōn*; most great and best and most beautiful and most perfect in its generation, even this one heaven singular of its kind *(ibid.)*.

erotic. There is nothing merely intellectualistic about this. The conversion or *periagōgē* of the entire soul is at stake, since the primal being of the soul is in play. The struggle of the elemental self is at stake in the overcoming of the forgetfulness that comes with absorption in finitude. The remembering self must remember at the level of its own elemental being, the level at which it is primally given to itself, freshly granted to be from its origin in eternity.

Is this why children display the elemental agape of wonder, indeterminately before Being and beings? Is this why they exhibit a more or less indeterminate trust that will later darken and narrow itself only to those others that have proved themselves for the self? The first trust for the other is defined spontaneously in the prior bond with the community of being. The enlightened self is the remembering self, but remembering is an act of transformation that breaks through, mindfully now, the enclosure of the "for-self." It reverses the "for-self" into a being beyond self of eros and agape. This remembering self is the self who becomes the new willingness beyond will to power, the new readiness that reaches down into the very roots of self-being to the bond with the other at work from the origin.

I recall Leibniz' notion of the preestablished harmony of being. This is a profound idea, though it is usually scoffed at. It points, I believe, to the prior community of mind and being in question here. Monads are elemental "for-selves," marked by a certain absolute singularity; this is their idiocy. Yet in their deepest ontological intimacy, monads reflect the universe from a particular point of view. This reflection is the determination of their being by this prior relativity of community, and this they do not produce but rather it constitutes them. There is a reflection of the other in the self; the reflection of the other monads in each monad is the coimplication of the community of being. And though God is called the chief monad, in fact, as *Creator* He cannot be adequately described in monadical language. Creation demands the language of agapeic transcendence. The absolute original is the agapeic origin of metaxological community. Leibniz is much more profound than Descartes with respect to the community of mind and being. Descartes is entirely superficial, almost foolishly blind to the issues at stake. Why is Leibniz more profound? In his hermeneutical generosity for premodern philosophy, Leibniz remembered the Good.

7. Mind and the Erotics of Idealism

I want to take another approach to the question of mind beyond lack, but now in contrast to the ancient Platonic way, I consider a dominant stategy of post-Cartesian philosophy. I mean the view that underscores the self-activity of mind. Leibniz is a rich mixing of modern and premodern possibilities. Kant learned deeply from him. Here I am interested in doctrines that stress the a priori nature of knowing. Kant said in effect: All validated knowing may have a beginning in experience, but that does not mean that all of knowing comes from experience. Concerned with a source of necessity in knowing, reacting to Hume's treatment of causality, Kant saw that experience could not provide the requisite universality and necessity. Necessity must come from sources other than the deliverances of experience. I am not concerned with the question of necessity here, but with the prior source of knowing where Kant finds the rational necessity. The question is: How is mind an origin *other than* the beginning of knowing we derive from experience? Will this question help us think of mind as, from the outset, something other than lack, as something always already more? Let us pursue the point.

The scholastic adage, repeated by Locke was: nothing in the intellect that was not first in the senses. Leibniz added the crucial qualification: except the intellect itself. Part of what is at issue here is the way mind is marked by a distinctive self-relativity: the intellect can reflect on itself and its own power. Even the empiricist acknowledges "ideas of reflection," albeit while trying to derive them from primary sense impressions. Leibniz, and later Kant, saw that this will not at all do justice to mind's self-relativity, and self-reflexivity. Fichte, Schelling and Hegel further developed some of these insights. A congeries of sense impressions might explain some of the details of information a mind might possess, if the mind were a wax tablet, or an empty room, or a registering machine, or some such. But such congeries cannot account for the self-consciousness of this putative wax tablet, or empty room, or register of information. The same problem marks every mechanical and cybernetic model of mind.

The self-reflexivity of mind points to a self-relating that is dynamic. Mind is a dynamic source of activity, an activity that monitors itself, and knows itself as self-relating, even as it receives impressions from sources other to itself. If you like, the intellect, an "idea" of the intellect, is in the intellect itself, in a manner underivable from any external sense impression. This "idea" of the intellect in itself and of itself finds expression in its self-reflexive self-relativity. This "idea" is not like some passive picture; this "idea" of mind is an active self-mediating dynamism. Hegel saw this very clearly. It is explicitly reflected in his own idea of the Idea: the Idea is the self-generating, self-externalizing, and self-relating mind. Here also the Hegelian concept or *Begriff* carries the same active meaning of the dynamic power of minding.

Kant, too, saw that mind as dynamic, and as a source of categorial intelligibility, must be prior to experience, in order for experience itself to be synthesized into an intelligible whole or coherent order. Apart from what Kant himself might think, it seems to me that this "prior mind" can offer us some hints about agapeic mind. I cannot see how this prior synthesizing power could ever be adequately described as the lack that seems to initiate an erotic quest. There is something "powerful" about the mind prior to all quests. A quest of meaning, intelligibility, and truth could not be meaningfully and intelligibly undertaken were not this prior "power" presupposed.

Granted its presupposition, the difficult question is the philosophical interpretation of its significance. As should be evident from what has gone before, and as will become more clear, this "power" is not to be interpreted as "will to power." Empiricism helps us little. One need not deny the importance of experience, but the issue is the nature of mind in making intelligible sense of experience. Classical empiricism is captive to those metaphors of mind as like the blank sheet, or the wax tablet, or the empty room needing to be filled with furniture. Today the metaphors are more technologically sophisticated, as when mind is compared to the memory bank of a computer. All of these metaphors fail, in that mind is in itself really nothing and contributes of itself almost nothing; every source of knowing derives from some externality that imprints, or implants itself, or gets itself saved on the memory bank of the cybernetic machine. These metaphors and the conceptual counterparts that interpret them are incapable of making sense of the synthetic and differentiating power of mind, of its self-reflexive power, of the self-relativity that is there, even when mind relates to what is other to itself. The distinctive dynamic being of minding is simply covered over, to say nothing of its self-transcending *towards* what is other.

Kant is a double thinker, often an equivocal philosopher. He interprets in a transcendental direction this prior source of synthesis marking mind. Transcendental philosophy, as I understand it, privileges this dynamic power of mind in its enigmatic self-relativity. As such it is almost inevitably an idealism, when it treats this dynamic self-relativity as ultimate. There is a community between mind and being—after all this is the basic issue relative to agapeic mind—but now this community is defined in terms of this prior synthesizing power of self-relativity. The intelligibility of the community of mind and being is granted as something prior to the externality of sensible beings; but the primary priority lies in the transcendental ego. The latter becomes the focus of interpreting the community of being and mind, as the constitutive source of its very intelligibility. Instead of Leibniz' preestablished harmony, the immanent resources of the mind's own prior synthesizing power become the ground of harmony between mind and the world.

What happens then? The mind as prior becomes the privileged term that properly dominates the space of intermediacy between the self and what is other. Mind's prior power becomes such that what is other to mind becomes a means by which mind itself relates to itself. Hence the between constituting the community of mind and being becomes the medium in which mind mediates with itself. The community of mind and being gets ultimately determined as the mediating self-relativity of mind, not indeed the particular mind of a finite subject, but the absolute all encompassing mind. We here see the step from Kant to Hegel.

This is a step Kant himself will not take, though he made it first possible with the doctrine of the transcendental ego. Kant knew that the otherness of sensible reality could not be entirely subsumed into the self-mediation of mind. There is a more radical, and in some ways more important, bar to total subsumption of externality and otherness into self-mediating mind; that is the very nature of mind itself. Here we touch on Kant's doctrine of the unknowable, the noumenal self. Kant's view suggests that even in the privileged self-reflexive, self-relating power of mind, something escapes complete grasping, and explicit conceptual comprehension. His idealist successors will scoff at this idea of the unknowable as a logically incoherent notion, and as a mere residue of the allegedly redundant thing in itself. Their scoffing only makes sense if we share the desire to carry the movement Kant initiated through to absolute self-transparent conceptual comprehension. It makes sense only if we fully consent to their philosophical eros for absolute self-mediation.

Kant wanted this conceptual comprehension, but equivocally. He could not escape the nagging suspicion that the self-mediating mind put its root into a power of being that could not be entirely brought into the light of categorial comprehension in quite the same sense as could the entities within finite experience. We know the mind as it appears to us; but there is something about mind that also disappears, and that we know that we do not know. I grant that the idealist will claim a logical incoherence in being able to talk at all about what we cannot know. Of course, one can find many places where Kant seems to be involved in self-referential contradiction. But there is a deeper issue here; and there are depths of elusiveness in Kant that are easily flattened when we brusquely apply too stock standards of coherence. To know the unknowable is, no doubt, contradictory; to think the unthinkable, no question, is to be a logical fool. And yet—I know Kant will not forgive me for saying it out so straight—we have to run the risk of folly.

The point made previously about self-reference and Freud has an application here. There is no claim to avoid the demand of self-coherence; but in meeting this demand, we may need to acknowledge something that cannot be fitted into any purely self-coherent scheme. Kant's successors claimed lack of self-coherence in his views. But the real point might be: the more radically self or mind tries to be radically coherent with itself, the more it escapes total self-relation. The more it tries to grasp itself completely in a total system of conceptual categories, the more something about it—ungrasped, unconceptualized, uncategorized—eludes it. In the intimate idiocy of its own self-relativity, the self is other to itself. Any pure self-coherence is cleft by the being at work of otherness that is not of its own self-determination.

And is this folly? Namely, the acknowledgement that the language of univocal cognition has to be transcended at this point. We must yet think and seek to know an enigma of being that ultimately resists our power of knowing. But why should knowing and unknowing imply a simple "either/ or?" The latter is the demand of univocal mind. And what is often best in Kant is a philosophical honesty that dictates he skirt the edges of a more secure and consoling univocal logic. We have to acknowledge the recalcitrance of the given world of sense to complete conceptualization, as well as the mysterious root of mind itself: the source of mind as itself a source of meaning is finally enigmatic. Outerness and innerness, at their limits, offer recalcitrance to complete self-mediating conceptualization.

To this Hegel says no. He carries Kantian transcendentalism in the direction of a more radically erotic conception of mind. He does not deny complex dialectical relatedness to what is other, but the undoubtedly central role of the self-relating Subject becomes the center.[10] This center becomes the power that mediates the extremities of self and other, inner and outer, and so on. This ultimate Subject as center becomes the middle, the absolute mediating power that constitutes the between as the self-externalization and self-appropriation of itself. Why is this elevation of the self-relating Subject into the absolute a radical erotic conception? This: the means by which complete self-relativity is constituted is a dialectical process which moves from a lacking indefinite origin, through an increasingly determinate articulation of what is merely implicit in the origin, to the fully self-determining end. Absolute self-determination is the mind that thinks itself in its other: thought thinking itself, through the appropriation of the other, that is so overreached as to become thought's *own* other. Need I repeat that we recognize the outstanding features of erotic mind, such as I have outlined.

Of course, questions have always been put to the transcendental idealism of Kant and Husserl as to whether it must end in a closed circle of immanence. The erotic mind of idealism might be described as the immanent self-mediation of the transcendental ego. Where this is closed to transcendence, there is also closure against agapeic mind which is radically for the other. To all appearances Hegel's position exceeds transcendental immanence in exploring mind's dialectical interinvolvement with the other. But this involvement is always *penultimate* to mind's mediated return to itself. In a way, Hegel is the more consistent transcendental philosopher than Kant: he gives a dialectical account of the immanent eros of self-developing mind. But his consistency merely makes systematic a crucial ambiguity in the entire

---

10. Substance become Subject is one of Hegel's ways of putting this in the *Phenomenology*. And again remember that this Subject is not any finite subject.

presupposition of transcendentalism which seeks to absolutize the dunamis of mediated self-relativity. If Kant is a less consistent transcendental idealist, what looks like a defect redounds to his favor.

What I mean emerges from the double recalcitrance mentioned above. To acknowledge this double recalcitrance—I would say the abyss of the self's inner otherness, and the metaphysical enigma of the sheer being there of givenness—is more true to agapeic mind. The acknowledgement means we cannot finally absolutize any "for-itself," or self-relativity. The centrality of the self is not the same as the absolutization of self-mediation. And there is a regard in which the self is central, namely, because it is an active mediating power in the middle. There is a plurality of centers of mediation in a community of being. The central self is also a decentered self from the standpoint of this community of otherness. The centrality of the self is not to be absolutized into a systematically complete conception of erotic mind. And it is not to be so systematized, because the sense of origin, of the prior, of the *prius* needs to be thought differently.

How reconsider the transcendental self to release its promise of agapeic mind? First I do not think we should simply understand the self at origin as an epistemological principle. Or, if we insist on epistemology, we need an erotic and agapeic epistemology which recognizes mind's dynamism as an ecstasis of transcending. How think a source of synthesis that is not itself a synthesis derived from finite, delimited experiences? Kant and idealism generally recognize that knowing involves a synthesis of experience, held together by principles or categories, in the unity of the thinking mind. I say "unity" reservedly, since the category of unity cannot here be univocalized, as we might univocalize the unity of a finite rock in the hand. The unity is a uniting, hence a dynamic, not static unity, a unity that is a relating, a relating that is also capable of differentiating any givenness indiscriminately presented to it. The synthesis of experience is a differentiated synthesis, for mind is the power to hold together and to set apart, to identify and differentiate, to relate and also to separate. But the prior synthesis is other again. It is not any derived synthesis we find in coherent experience; it is not any finite determination marking any differentiated experience. It is something other.

And again we must be careful not to describe this prior other in simply lacking terms. It has been described as negativity by Hegel, and as nothingness by Sartre, for the good reason that it is not a finite determinate entity with the univocal identity we frequently ascribe to such entities. If it is no thing in that sense, it is so, not because it is less than any thing, but because it is in excess of every determinate thing. The prior "something other" is an excess, over and above the determinations ascribed to finite entities, precisely because it is a determining source, not a determined delimitation. It is an originative surplus. It is a source of transcendence. The "trans" here not only points to a subsequent surpassing of every finite limit—though this is true; the "trans" refers to the other origin itself as over and above, beyond the beings.

We might be reminded of the the Good of Plato—*epekeina tes ousias*, but this source here is not the Good. It is more like the sun-like eye that is an image of the Good, though again these are metaphors which distort as much as reveal. What if there is an "eye" that is itself like the light? We are reminded of Plotinus' question (*Ennead* VI, 7, 41): "But what would it serve for the eye to see what is, if it were itself the light?" Is mind as agapeic like such a light? Being mindful would be being becoming mind. If the "eye" were in itself a light, there would no longer be "vision"—vision as determinate perception of "objects" over against it. There would be participation in a community of the truth which, without determinate "vision," might even seem blind. There would be the giving of every "light," without thought for self as over against the other, a mingling in the middle without objectification, a middle where one finds it hard to say what is given and what is received, for the middle simply is the give and take of agapeic originals.

The self as agapeic is an excess of being that out of itself bring mindfulness to the excess of being that is given to it, and whose intelligibility it would mediate. There is a double excess here, of innerness and outerness. The excess of self, as originating source, cannot be completely encapsulated in self-transparent concepts; such concepts are its issue, but no concept as issued exhausts the issuing source; something about its dynamism ever remains unexhausted; there is something inexhaustible about it. It cannot be thought on the model of a finite material well, out of which all its resources could be drawn; there is never a point when we can say, "Now I have exhausted it." Why so? Because this originative surplus is a source of original freedom. This cannot be completely determined, either in advance, or in terms of its subsequent unfolding. Otherness is built into innerness as its own reserve of surprise. Innerness is an abyss, not as an empty hole, but as a cornucopia never entirely depleted. Is not this mind as agapeic: a foison of energy that in being used is not used up, but that augments itself in expending itself? And is not this also the paradoxical power of mind: that the more it is spent, the more it has to spend; that in spending itself, it becomes richer rather than poorer; that it is a power heightened in being used rather than depleted?

But there is also the excess of givenness in outerness. This has to be thought with reference to its own being for itself. Its otherness is not simply a function of the self-determination of the transcendental self. Kant ambiguously realized this point when he called himself an empirical realist, though a transcendental idealist. Kant's equivocity prepared the ground for Hegel's erotic conception: transcendental idealism swallows empirical realism. But just as mind is not absolutely self-mediating, neither is the givenness of creation a means by which mind or spirit mediates and comes back to itself. Creation has its own being for self, given its own otherness by the origin. Even if we do participate in the constitution of its meaning, creation opens itself to us, in a creative cooperation perhaps more akin to what Adamic naming might imply.

A metaphysics of creation involves a rupture with the terms of transcendentalism and idealism, but these terms can be seen to suggest something beyond themselves. Thus, the surplus of being that is the originative self is erotic, but more than erotic; it is implicitly agapeic. If we primarily develop its exigence of self-mediation, erotic mindfulness comes to the fore. If we remember the relativity to the other as other, the agapeic promise of mind becomes manifest. Self-mediation points to something prior to self-mediation; relativity to self is rooted in a relativity to what is other to the self, and that can never be completely captured in the circle of self-relativity. The reason why "self" is an excess of originative being, a surplus of creative freedom is because it is given to be by the original power of being as agapeic. The being of self is an agape—a gift given from out of an enigmatic origin that we can hardly name as self or other, as mine or thine, and that is both, and neither. This agapeic surplus of free being overflows every closed ego, even the dynamic self that dialectically mediates with itself in an erotic process of self-determination.

The overdetermined power to be of selfhood is agapeic in these two ways: as *given to itself to be* out of an origin other to itself; and as the power to *give itself over to being* beyond itself in its own self-transcendence. The "is" of "I" is not "mine." Thus, the "not" and the "mine" are now said in an essentially different way to the previous saying of them. We hesitate to say "mine," not because there is no "my self," but because its being points beyond itself, as given to itself by an other origin, origin in a more radical sense than ever a finite self could be. The surplus originality of self images an originality that surpasses all mastery, all expectation, that is utterly beyond and yet radically intimate to our being. In this intimacy of being we are not consoled with the pleasures of solipsistic home. We may, it is true, renew our community with being as agapeic; and renewing it in an agapeic way, there may spring forth in us the generosity of creation. Our being is itself the gift of the generosity of creation. To consent agapeically is to create beyond oneself out of this generosity of being.[11]

---

11. Some of the things Kant as transcendental philosopher says about *genius*, and of *nature* in relation to genius, bring his thought to the limit of the transcendental approach, and beyond—though Kant, as usual, equivocates. On this, see Desmond, "Kant and the Terror of Genius: Between Enlightenment and Romanticism," in *Kant's Aesthetics*, ed. Herman Parret (Berlin and New York: de Gruyter, 1995).

In sum: Transcendental idealism remains entangled in an apotheosis of the "for-self," and so seems to be an entirely erotic philosophy. Deeper reflection shows that idealism presupposes agapeic mind, even though it characteristically thinks of itself in terms of mind's self-activity, whether the more usual synthesis, or Hegel's dialectical self-mediation. The limitation of idealism, transcendental or Hegelian, is its failure to think erotic mind through to its agapeic source. The promise of mind as agapeic is a condition of the possibility of all modes of mindfulness.

8. Creation and Agapeic Mind

I begin to step with caution when I hear the word "creativity." For the word, as now used, can mean everything and nothing.[12] And yet agapeic mind cannot be understood without reference to creation. What are we to say of this? The standard opposition of idealism and realism does not help us. Moreover, all forms of constitutive idealism are questionable, in that agapeic mind is not constitutive of the other. I do not deny the idealistic recognition of mind's dynamic transcending. Mind is not somnolent before a scene of otherness which impresses itself as on blotting paper; it dynamizes itself, and in so doing opens itself to the manifestation of what is coming to it. The issue is the constitution of the relativity of minding and being, and how minding creatively transcends in the milieu between mind and other-being.

Constitutive idealism claims that the thinking I constitutes, perhaps not the being of the other—though some constitutive idealisms make this claim—but certainly at least its intelligibility. Constitutive idealism as creative of the other is obviously ridiculous when applied to the human mind, though with proper qualification we might think of the divine mind as agapeic as thus creative. We do not constitute either the relativity to, or the intelligibility of the other. We may cooperate in the constitution of the relativity, and in contributing to the possibilities for significant intelligibility of the other. And this, because we are in the between. Relative to the between, our understanding of this cooperation demands an uncompromising break with any idealism that interprets originative activity purely in terms of self-determination. Ultimate creativity is not self-activity. The relativity mediated by a plurality of centers of origination cannot be reduced to the dominating constitutive activity of one absolutized pole—understood on the model of the absolute subject or self.

---

12. On this, see *Philosophy and its Others*, 87ff.; also some remarks in "Creativity and the Dunamis" in *Paul Weiss: The Library of Living Philosophers*, ed. L. Hahn (La Salle, Illinois: Open Court, to appear).

The transcendental ego serves this function in idealism; the absolute serves this function in Hegel. What is wrong with this is its collapsing of the difference between erotic and agapeic mind, assimilating the second to the first, such that the relation to the other and from the other is absorbed into self-relation. Agapeic minding as in the between allows for the relativity of minding and being as plurally constituted, and denies that this plural constitution can be subsumed within one overarching process of constitution, one process of total self-constitution. Most historical forms of idealism have not always gone to such monistic extremes, but I think this is the logical outcome of the apotheosis of self-relativity, and the confusion of the dynamism of erotic with agapeic mind.

Let me put the point more positively. There is a *patience* that is creative; creativity is not self-assertion. Suppose we say that agapeic mind is creative in making a welcome for the other. What is it to "make a welcome?" Making a welcome is not a physical fabrication, though welcome may be embodied and fostered by appropriate physical arrangements. There can be an aesthetics of welcome. What is there when one makes a welcome? No thing really, and yet more than any thing. When one makes a welcome one creates the conditions that promise of home. One makes it possible for the other not any longer to feel outside or out of it, but to feel at home.[13]

For there is an aesthetics of home: we feel at home, sense home. We do not first argue our way home; logic does not make home. Making a welcome is a making, but it is the making of a milieu of mindfulness for the other. In welcome itself there is the greeting of the good; the wellbeing, the being well, the welfare of the other is the first concern of welcome. There is a benediction that transcends towards the other. Thus, to make a person feel at home in strange surroundings is extraordinary elusive in its intricacy. There are comings and goings of intimacy in this hospitable between. The intimacy of being is cocreated by the making of a welcome.

Again I emphasize: standard models of production or fabrication which speak of imposing form on matter do not get us anywhere in understanding the "making" involved in the making of a welcome. The creative mode appropriate to the intimacy of being is almost impossible to articulate and resists rendition in a metalanguage. This is what is elemental about it. The elemental can be named, and beyond that our words begin to stammer.[14]

---

13. In addition to "welcome" there are various other elemental words of "home" that could be usefully reflected on here, such as "hail," or "hospitality."

14. Consider also the "making" in the "making of love." What makes, what is making, what is being made? The more one thinks about it, the more elemental the happening itself appears. And, of course, I do not deny that one can give complex analytical or other accounts, but there is an intimate being of this "making" that is elemental, irreducible, and escapes all such accounts.

There is no metalanguage of being at home. In a way we are already home, though not always at home. Any position "outside" it is inside it, as a sleepiness, or neutering, or refusal, or blindness, or desecration.

Agapeic mind makes a welcome in the manner it *prepares the way* for the other to come to self-manifestation. Preparing a way is making a space in the middle, a space for the freedom of the other. How does one make that way? When I make way for you, I allow you to pass through, without violence. To make way for you does not mean I simply withdraw into autistic silence. If I withdraw into autistic silence, I turn away from you, not make way for you. To make way may mean to stand aside, yes, but standing aside in this welcoming mode may be an alert being-there. One does not stand aside in standing aside, one is there fully in standing aside. To make way for the other is to create an opening for freedom that is not for oneself, though in that opening one is fully there for whatever may eventuate along the way. One is fully there, but not there as filling the between, but as opening it for the other, such as to seem not to be there. One is fully there for the fullness of the other to come into the between. Come what may, agapeic mind makes a way. It is a way that is no way, in the sense of a completely determinate track. It is no way, since it is a space of openness: it is space of expectation; it is a space of faith and hope. These await what comes, come what may.

Against any form of constitutive idealism, making a way for the other to come to self-manifestation is not the work of transcendental subjectivity determining the relation of self and other, and so mediating the between. Transcendental subjectivity is said to constitute the way in which the other appears; hence the way of manifestation is always the *result* of the transcendental self's constitutive work. By contrast, with agapeic mind there is an ontological *readiness* of an entirely different sort. This is a readiness at the limit of self, where the self may have to find a way beyond its own utmost limit, learning that there may be no limit to its readiness in relation to the other.

Paradoxically, at this extreme, readiness brings us back to the middle. Readiness is an expectancy that dwells in a state of being between. For readiness is no simple passivity, and yet is no self-absorbed activity or self-assertion. It is an expectancy between passivity and activity, between tranquility and tenseness. It is not gaping, it is not imperialistic surveying: it is an undemanding waiting, awaiting the demand of transcendence as other. But transcendence itself makes no demand, only extends an agapeic promise and welcome. Though asking of us the fullest activation of attentiveness, such expectancy of the other originates a reversal of self. One might be turned inside out, or upside down, by what appears. One is not sure that the other will appear. If it does not, so be it.

Think of it this way. A younger self is erotic, is expectancy for a future it believes will be self-constituted. It boasts: I will make my future, make myself, make my future self. My younger I looks to the future as my way to make myself what I will to be. In that regard, constitutive idealism is the philosophy of the erotic romanticist. Time will provide the space, the stage for self-definition, self-determination. Others will enter this drama, but the self with them will be its own main protagonist, its own hero. The others will revolve around this central character, sometimes clashing, sometimes supports, sometimes mere props.

Time reverses the play of this erotic drama. The older self has had time, has touched, or been touched by certain limits. A reversal begins, and how to name it is hard. Beneath the bustle of itself, it is as if another story all along was taking shape, gnawing away the foundation on which the erotic self in its own apotheosis seemed to reign secure. Something other nags, and one suspects the drama as a fool's play. One does not utter this in contempt or revenge for the sorties of erotic selfhood. These have their time, their necessity. In fulfilling their line, they falter and fall. Time wears away the surge of the erotic self; time washes the silt from its muddied flow; time sieves its chaff. Something other is polished in this wear and erosion.

One is at the limit of self-activity. Perhaps one has done one's best, done one's utmost, but there is a point when there is nothing to be done. Nothing. What happens? A break, perhaps a breakdown, certainly a reassessment of erotic selving. There is a slowing down, a stilling, but this is an other energizing. What breaks through? A glimmer, a hope flickering in the dark night that is oneself: there now, gone now. What is coming towards one? One does not know for sure. One does know it is folly to continue as before. And yet one is energized, energized otherwise. Desire breeds its necessary illusions, which desire now gives over to death. And yet another selving is being resurrected in this dying of erotic expectation.

A fire is being kindled, but the wood is damp from a life soaked in mean-minded evasion. The soul is wet and not tinder, or resists taking fire, or smolders with the frailest flame. Or one smells the smoke and reek of self, as a blazing, not of one's own lighting, begins to burn off the soak of falseness. Something else is burning one. Through trial by fire, the older self may be burnt in time, burnished into a shine of manifestation. The shine is everything and nothing. It is the ecstasy of itself out of self, that gives beyond itself, in a radiance that it simply is, because that incandescence is what it was—always.

Strangely enough, exposure to *being at a loss* is absolutely significant now. The agapeic self is the I released in its passage through the time of mourning. Eros surges with anticipation of its completeness, in time future; but *that* completeness fails, and eros retreats, ebbs, falls into passing out. Is this just failure? No. After eros an elegy of being springs up, an elegy that surprisingly is highest expectation. This again is paradoxical, since elegy usually refers to the past. Am I talkng about an elegy that looks to the future? Not quite. I mean an elegy that I cannot conceive of except as a kind of prayer. What prayer? For the coming of the flash of transfiguration when, not quite believing it, one is inspired to murmur: "All will be well." The extraordinary words of Jesus come to mind: "Blessed are those who weep." There is a lamentation from which, impossibly, blessing comes. One has to undergo being at a loss to its extreme before coming into this comfort. The end of welcome is the coming of blessing, the unthinkable blessing: All is well.

There is lamentation of loss in the expectancy of death, but a different energy of creation can be set free, let loose in this losing of being. This energy is carefree about the instrumentalities; it cares about the finalities, and not just for the self as an end that uses other things as instrumentalities for itself. The Irish call death *slí na fírinne*, the way of truth. Expectancy of death makes way for the way of truth. Is radical generosity of being possible for us at this ultimate loss of being? Pure generosity, that would be for nothing but the goodness of being, affirmed for no reason, beyond its goodness as being. Who shows it? Who speaks the word of pure welcome? Rare, rare, rare. Perhaps impossible for us.

9. Agapeic Mind and the Passion of the Good

If agapeic mind takes us beyond the dualism of realism and idealism, it also surpasses the dualism of being and the good. Ontology and ethics do not have to be finally opposed to each other, as, for instance, Levinas opposes them. The dunamis of mind is a condition of being that always implicates, mediately, if not overtly, an orientation to the good. Nor does an appeal to objective mind contradict the point. The orientation of objective mind to the truth of the world is to that truth, as the good of the mind. Truth, in whatever guise, is what is worthy for mindful being, or that of which mindful being must make itself worthy. Agapeic mind transcends the dualism more explicitly than the implicit orientation of objective mind to the good as truth. We come to a point previously mentioned: knowing and love are not unrelated. The being of the good is at work in the origination and unfolding of agapeic mind. Knowing is a mode of love of being. It is a fidelity to being. Knowing is the good of mind in its love of the being of truth.

I suggest also that here the standard dualism of "voluntarism" and "intellectualism" does not really apply. What are normally called "intellect" and "will" cannot be entirely separated from each other but are two articulations of a basic orientation of the mindful human being towards the truth of being as good. Normally, again, "intellect" is said to know things that are; "will" is said to seek things that are not yet, but that will be. "Intellect" has thus been coupled with a voyeurism of passive being; "will" has been associated with an activism that glories in the becoming of the good beyond being. Relative to the first, we must reject the implied stasis of being; relative to the second, we must reject the apotheosis of futurity that often accompanies a voluntaristic privileging of becoming. Think here of Nietzsche's apotheosis of "will," as erotic being, as opposed to "intellect." Becoming, again as erotic will to power, is set against being, as dead stasis. There is no intimation of being as the gift of the agapeic origin. The apotheosis of "will" ends, at best, with an erotic absolute, at worst, with nihilism. Nietzsche wavers between these two poles.[15]

"Intellect" shows the dynamism of mind. "Will" shows the dynamism of self which can be more or less mindful. "Good will" is mindfully activated will. "Good will" as agapeically mindful is an energization of the ethical promise of human selfhood, relative to which the standard separation of will and mind, the good and being, seems sterilely abstract. A more richly concrete sense of knowing indicates that all being mindful is ethical.

Knowing is a delight in being. We see this clearly in the wonder of the child. Our mindful being is inherently a love of being and the light of truth. We quickly forget this, or tame it, or grow ashamed of it, or distract ourselves with technical twistings of the elemental delight. This is an *appreciation* of being. Appreciation says "yes" to the preciousness of this being, that being in itself, for itself. It is a movement towards the delight of the other, and hence a form of agapeic mind. A child says: "Oh! look at the rainbow!" "That is a birdy, look at it!" Looking, knowing, and naming are first of all forms of delight, love of being as other. Our self-insistence vanishes in the ecstasy of delight that goes beyond itself, mindfulness being itself just this way beyond self to the other as other. We live first in this light. This is why children are first absolutely trusting. They live in the expectation of truth, fresh to the opening of the middle. Their expectancy as lived is an unself-conscious transcending towards the openness of truth.

But being in the middle is a double condition, hence potentially duplicitous. So the expectation comes to be soured, for there is untruth in the middle. There is a closing of the opening, in lies and malice, even in well-meaning euphemisms. There is lack of patience for truthful minding by those already in the middle. Sometimes formulae are easier, quicker, and for my convenience, not for the good of the child as other. But the opening of the goodness of the origin—lived, not known explicitly, then as well as

---

15. See again Desmond, "Rethinking the Origin: Hegel and Nietzsche."

later—haunts the unfolding of human mindfulness. In a word, we mature into the chiaroscuro of the middle. Our adult darkness is shadowed by the delight of first opening our eyes in expectation of an ungrimed world, the first agape. The artist recovers the agape of the word, or the eye, or the ear, or the body. The saint recovers the agape of the holy. The ethical exemplar recovers the truth of the good, of life lived in light of being good. In the chiaroscuro of the middle all are individuals haunted.

These "recoveries" are not the product of "will" or "intellect," for there happens now to us a *suffering of otherness*, an undergoing which breaks up the closing. This is full of pain, since the closing has stabilized itself into "the self" or "the world," wherein we have taken up settled habitation. We think we have secured ourselves in such enclosures. They will be broken. They will be interrupted, and often in emergencies. What are emergencies? Emergencies are emergences of being-other, beyond the closures we construct in the face of our death. They break into our closure in moments of crisis, and return us to an original moment of elemental consent or refusal. Such emergencies offer the occasion for renewal of the opening, the chance of generosity towards being, even in all loss.[16] This is, as we say, the moment of truth. What is put to us is the question: Would we be the mindfulness that would affirm beyond our own "for-self," beyond the fear of our own death? Would we affirm life beyond our own life, beyond our own death? Would we, could we, say "yes" to being, beyond death? No defiant bravado or hubris is being asked. Rather is asked a condition of humility—the humility of generosity, born in the knowing of suffering. And this flows into the suffering of the other, as in the compassion of Buddha, or Jesus, or Francis of Assisi.

What is this compassion? It is a pluralized passion, or patience, or pathos. It is an undergoing, and a going out of self, and an inwardizing of the other's suffering. It is a community of passion, a community of suffering. I see another subjected to unbearable pain. I can do nothing about it. Suppose every physical remedy has been tried and none is further effective. Voluntaristic activism is helpless. We are at the limit of our ability to master or influence the situation through the control of our will alone. If I could will it, I would have the sick person cured. I cannot. The other is in pain. My power is nothing.

At the point of powerlessness I might withdraw into myself and say: Nothing can be done; it is beyond us. I might say: Since I can do nothing, what is it to me? I will retreat to myself and cushion myself against a horror I am powerless to effect through my will. This happens all the time. We see

---

16. On the emergencies of interruption, see *Philosophy and its Others*, chapter 6.

the picture of appeal—a starving child—and we cannot take it. I excuse myself with the shrug: What can I do? And though I give money, I find it futile to feel pain for the pain of the starving child. There is a return into the self which protects the self from being overwhelmed by the otherness of suffering beyond its influence. Stoicism will offer us the consoling philosophy: Some things are up to us, some things are not.

Reasonable people will uphold the self-protective return into self, as the properly intelligible response. The explanation will run: the primary motivations of humans are self-preservation and self-interest; these coalesce into a survival of the fittest. The law of self-being is to put the self first, and the other in terms of the first, as an extension of the first. The protective self-return will be seen as serving the first, in its self-preservation and self-interest. Since the pain of the other is here beyond both, no other movement but towards the self can make rational sense. To move otherwise towards the other is a kind of madness. And yet this compassionate movement happens, seemingly futile in its solidarity in powerlessness.

Notice that the above retreat to self is performed *against* the urge to go towards the other otherwise, in compassion. I see the starving child. My heart goes out to him or her. What does it mean to say that "the heart goes out" to the other? The heart is a word for the elemental self; the heart is the elemental self. It is a metaphor for the whole self that loves or hates, that praises or reviles, that is delighted or disgusted. The heart is the self living in being as good or worthless. The heart goes out to the suffering one. In a way, this elemental going out to the other defines our being. It is happening all the time, in situations without pain. We explicitly notice it in situations of suffering, for here we find a check, or shock to the immediacy of our being borne along in the elemental going out. In order to return protectively to self, we have to resist this elemental going out. As we say, we have to harden the heart. To harden the heart is to go against its spontaneous impulse which is just this immediate going out of self. We must stop ourselves.

Those who think in terms of self-interest and self-preservation may grant that, despite the stoppage of the hardened heart, the impulse of going out may still win, and that something like compassion occurs. But the occurrence will be linked to self-interest. The argument will be: self-interest is the basic law of life; though compassion seems to be for the other, this being for the other really serves the self; but now the "self" is not this or that self, but the self of the species, or of humanity as species-self. So my compassion for this other is not for this other, but is for myself as a member of species humanity, or for species humanity as myself writ large. Thus compassionate going out is assimilated to erotic self-relation, even if this self-relation is complexly mediated through humanity's species-being.[17] Not surprisingly, Schopenhauer has a view of compassion like this. Since his absolute, the Will, is erotic, this erotic self-relativity will reappear in human community, even at the limit where the self seems to give itself over to the other. Our compassion for the other is our pain for ourselves, as we are mirrored in the other; there is no sorrow for the other as other.

Whether we understand the going out in terms of individual self-interest or species self-interest, the primacy of self-relativity does not do justice to what is involved in compassion. I stress the genuineness of plurality implied by the "*cum*": compassion is a community of suffering. It is a community of suffering at the limit of the will to power. To return protectively to self is to retreat to a position where will to power still holds sway; and thus this going out serves return to self. But I think there is a *different willing* at the limit of will to power. It is a willingness even to be overwhelmed by what is beyond will to power: the otherness of unbearable suffering in the other. To be exposed to this is to be opened to what would wound the circle of selfhood irremediably. We cannot bear this, and yet we dare not close ourselves off from this overwhelming otherness. To be thus between—between this unbearable exposure and the impossibility of closing oneself off—this is a crushing burden.

Indeed, the will to power is crushed by the suffering of the other, and yet one goes with eyes open towards this crushing negativity. There is no reason for this, if we think in terms of self-interest and self-preservation. Quite the opposite, there is every reason why one ought not to expose oneself. Yet one is exposed, one does expose oneself. I can do nothing for the other. This is beyond my will. And still the pained going out of compassion solicits in me a different willingness. This is not will to power, but a willingness beyond power; a *willingness that renounces will*, that sacrifices its own self-insistence in breach of the rationality of self-preservation.

One might even say that this elemental sacrifice silently takes place all the time, when one goes out of self. We may take note of this in the pain of compassion, but it is at work in every act of self-surpassing. And there is no reason to suffer *with* the other, beyond the self-justifying community of suffering that binds humans together, beyond all will to power. The willingness of compassion is thus a will-lessness, in that the will as "mine" is in abeyance. Further, will-less willingness may prepare a way to alleviate the distress of being. For it is very striking that if this act of will-less willingness is commu-

---

17. We find this notion of species humanity in thinkers like Marx. But the idea has been given a biologistic, as well as sociological expression. Even the *genes* will be said to be *selfish*—the opposite end of the spectrum to the "self" of Hegel's absolute Subject or Spirit.

nicated to the suffering other, if the going out goes over and the pained other knows this, there can be a breach in the limit of power, and a different remedial power can come to appear in powerlessness, a different power in powerlessness, and beyond will to power. For there is nothing I can do for the other; yet I suffer with the other in compassion; in this going over of the heart, the afflicted one can be heartened by the simple solidarity, and the burden of its suffering lightened. To know that one's suffering is known is to be strangely released. To be known thus is to be granted a mysterious deliverance.

How to explain this strange happening: the embrace of suffering, the *widening of suffering* in the compassion of "suffering with," *lightens the suffering* of the afflicted one? The rationale of self-interest might seem the only rational response: diminish suffering by escaping *my* suffering before the suffering of the other I cannot diminish.[18] But here in compassion, I suffer in embracing the suffering of the afflicted, and in this *doubling* of suffering the suffering of the heart can be *diminished*. This flux and reflux, this heightening of suffering that is its lightening, is a great mystery of the heart. What kind of *burden* can suffering be, what kind of weight? What is it to bear a burden of spirit? What kind of weight can it be that is lifted by compassion? Our understanding of such things is crude, our words are coarse. Very coarse, it seems to me, is the assimilation of genuine compassion to any law of the survival of the fittest. Thus, we reduce the spiritual to the biological, and undercut what might be greatest, and most mysterious, about human solidarity and suffering.

Compassion cannot be made meaningful, I mean the fullness of compassion, if we do not grant the possibility of something like agapeic mindfulness. Like the latter, compassion is a going out of the self, and not for the sake of a return to self, but for the sake of the other as other. Of course, there *may* be a return to self: The other *may* give itself in return to the self, just as there may be a willingness beyond will, a power beyond will to power, a healing beyond

---

18. One thinks of persons like Hobbes for whom passions like "sympathy," and "compassion" reduce to pleasure in *our own exemption* from the suffering of the other, which we experience on beholding the suffering other. Even Rousseau, who makes so much of sympathy, is not immune from this way of thinking, as my friend Paul Bagley has pointed out to me. One thinks also how in Hume our sympathy with others is inseparable from our own "self-esteem." We hear the echo of Descartes' peculiar understanding of "generosity" which, too, is tied to "self-esteem." One also hears again the voice of Neitzsche whose "generosity" is inseparable from "self-aggrandizement." I think the crucial equivocity on "generosity" here is implied by the colloquial way we say: "Such and such a person is *full of himself*." All the above thinkers finally define "generosity" and its kin in terms of "being full of oneself." But while true agapeic generosity is a "being full," it is not just being full of *oneself*.

all healing, a lightening of the heart in the distressed other and then in the self that sacrifices itself, its time, its "Darwinian duty" to itself, or the species. (Of course, it is nonsense to speak of a "Darwinian duty" to those who are burdens on the species. Why then should we love those ruins—as we should?) Or there may be *no* return to the self: The distressed other may be so wrapped in its affliction that no gesture of reciprocal solidarity may escape its absorption in pain. It is lost in itself in its agony. Regardless of this silence of loss, the agapeic movement of compassion may still take place. It will still be the only thing to do.

In another sense, this is not a "doing," since one cannot simply will this willingness. The movement of the heart, and the flow of the full self must already be in stream, as it were, outside itself, outside its self-conscious self-mastery. And naturally, most of our doings and openings are *mixed*: between the harder heart of self-relating self-insistence and the flow of the heart in its being outside itself with the other. We are in between: between the first love of self-insistence, and the second love of agapeic relativity to the other. The movement of the second is always at play in the between, though its play can be severely constrained, to the extent that the first tries to completely dominate the middle, as it can try to do, as it almost inevitably tries to do. The hard heart, the stony heart is the self that has frozen *itself*, even in the stirring of this second movement.

To unfreeze this movement means to transform entirely the self of self-insistence. A willingness beyond self-will has to take root in the deepest sources of the self; one has to be refashioned utterly into an other self of agapeic good will. This latter is not just an act of will, or a sequence of acts of good will. It is a transfigured condition of being. This transfiguration of being we can never complete, since the partial closure of self-will will never be entirely overcome in the middle. We are torn in the middle between these two, being their conjunction and their fork. The transfigured willingness has to send its roots into its own self-will, must release the agapeic willingness already at work in it.

At the deeper level again, one finds that one's own will is not owned as absolute willingness. It is not that the words "my own" are to be disowned; rather "my own" is to be owned differently, by being dispossessed of ownership. "My own" is not "my own." "Ownness" is a gift. Only then is it "my own." No longer possessing myself, I am myself in a truer way, truer to the other, truer to "my own" self. I find myself in loss of self; in yielding I find the other; I am found when I no longer look. "Mine" is not now entwined with "no." The different owning here is twinned with a "yes," that is not my "no" to the other. "Yes," "no," "mine," "yours," "ours," all must receive transfigured expression.

10. Agapeic Mind, Transcendence and Transfiguration

How can we at all speak of mind as transfigurative? Would we not, at a minimum, have to rethink given being as other than any neutral thereness, that is, rethink the worth of being? Certainly any positivist obeisance to a neutral given would have to be rejected, for this obeisance makes mind a blank registration, lacking critical, indeed originative capacities. Obviously, such a "giving over" cannot be what is meant by agapeic mind. There is a giving over for the otherness of being, but it is not an abdication of mind's critical powers. Mind is not mind if it is not critical, where "critical" carries the connotation of *krinein*, to discriminate. Nor need being critical mean being suspicious or debunking; more deeply, it means to be discerning. All genuine mindfulness is thus critical in discerning the nuance of what is at play beyond it. To discern is to give oneself over to what is at play in all its nuance.

There is a discerning acceptance here. But what is acceptance, and of what kind here? Acceptance is not primarily a proposition, but a change in being towards the other, a change that issues in one's doing and speaking. Acceptance may be elemental in the end, but the process that releases it is complexly mediated. A self-transformation is asked, and this has an originative dimension. Origination need not be confined to work on an external material, such as we find with activities like sculpture or painting that overtly issue in production. This is not what I mean. There can be an original struggle with oneself that does not always and necessarily occur via the mediation of an external medium. "Internal" and "external" invariably are slippery words here, and do not capture the wealth of meaning of the field of intimacy, where the inwardness of the idiotic and the communicative being of the between are not counterposed. This struggle in question may be intimate, which is not to say that it does not occur in the between, and in mediated interplay with others to self. Let us say a poet tries to find the right word; he is wrestling with himself, and in one sense he is a source of the word; but his being an origin, his original self-transformation, is for purposes of releasing a passage of transcending in the middle; he struggles to be a source through which the source which is the word wells up.

If there is an origination which is self-transformation, the whole point is not at all concern with self, but just to be released from all self-absorption. Here one is open to being remade as a way wherein transcendence may come to manifestness. One is preparing oneself, not for oneself, but for the coming towards one into the middle of the other. Moreover, this self-transformation as making a way is a never ended process. One can never be sure that one is up to what may be coming; indeed the more a way is prepared, one is sure that one is not up to the transcendence of the other, purely through oneself alone. One is gripped by trepidation that one has prematurely closed oneself to what may come from the other. And there is a similar humility before the possible betrayal of the promise that is the self itself. This self-transformation is never ending because the self in process evidences, not lack simply, but a surplus of inexhaustibility that is intimately known as never completely spent, or objectified. To become a self of acceptance is to be drawn into, caught up in, and never freed completely from, the call of an original self-transformation.

This process is not the accumulation of additional skills or the amassing of further information. Nor is there any growth in selfhood, as we might think of biological growth. The development is primarily intensive. In being transformed one is being deepened, deepened towards one's own source, whose depth is never plumbed. One has to enter the abyss of self, like going into the grave, wherein all constructed selves die to their source, and this source to its ultimate origin. Acceptance is like dying and being born again.

This abyss might be likened to a well wherein the water can mix the polluted and the pure. The process of self-transformation towards consent means passage through a purification, a catharsis. Such an idea of a *purgatory of mind* is not at all congenial to modern epistemology, to say nothing of the tastes of the general culture. It means that our quandary is not mere ignorance as a lack of knowing, but, so to say, a kind of epistemic stain that threatens to infect mindfulness in its entirety. If this seems the opposite of the affirmative surplus of mind, remember we are finite and intermediate, hence the promise of agapeic being, rather than its ultimate realization. Something about mindfulness gives one to wonder if there is something at fault in our thinking, that even in the glory of the greatest thinking a fault is constitutive of our mode of mind. What would this be? The fault would be the invisible line running through the mind as intermediacy itself, where the extremities of good and evil, truth and error, consent and malice face each other and mingle.

Consider the religious story of the Fall, purely as a story, if you like. We denizens of post-modernity, after all, breathe the superior air of knowing that a story is only a story. The story suggests: Our mind darkens in the darkening that follows the Fall. Suppose: Once upon a time which was no time, before the Fall, the purity of agapeic mind was at work, realized and concrete; the harmony of humans with the Creator and the rest of creation was there; being there was the harmony of creation itself; this was the givenness of being, the gift of being. Nor was there any question of consent or acceptance, for one lived acceptance. One's being was mindfulness as consent. Hence, too, the originative dimension of being as consent: the Adamic naming was the creative naming, given as a power to the human being to cocreate and complete creation as an other to God. Our being was creative consent.

The Fall names refusal, the Fall was simply refusal. How refusal enters into the primal "It is good"—and the "It is good" was not only God's consent to creation; we, too, were partners in the "It is good," for our being was agapeic consent—remains as complete an enigma now, as it ever was. This is the ineradicable mystery of spiritual freedom.

After refusal, mind becomes a problem. We might say epistemology is one of the fruits of the Fall. Philosophy, too, is conceived in sin; though this need not mean philosophy is sin. The perplexity of mind itself looks different in this light. Every effort to know, subsequent to the dimming of the primary agapeic mindfulness, starts in the middle of a mixture, the differentiation of which into the worthy and the worthless is extremely hard. For the beings seeking to effect the differentiation, namely, we humans, are *ourselves mixtures* of pure and impure, refusal and consent. The mind is no pure means which sifts the mixture, and sets pure and impure apart. As intermediate *minding is itself mixture through and through.* Hence, in some respects, the most difficult sifting is the one performed by the mind on itself. The impure mind is sifting itself of its own impurity, hence seems to carry the stain of its mixture with its every effort to transcend mixture, and so regain a more pure condition of agapeic mind. To transcend impurity seems itself another impurity, hence to be agapeic mind seems a possibility always compromised by failure. It seems like a promise that must necessarily be betrayed, even in the sincere effort to fulfill it.

The conclusion then would seem to be: Either the desired purity is an impossibility, for every act performed by the mind on itself reenacts the impurity that was to be transcended entirely; or else, through our own power alone it is an impossibility, but not an impossibility with the aid of powers other than our own. The first solution seems to spin around in its own mixture, perhaps thereby seeking a self-separation of the pure and impure, the true and the false. This image of a self-spinning mind is not fanciful, since it corresponds almost exactly to the model of autonomous self-determining thinking, which we saw was a version of erotic mind. Agapeic mind seems to demand some version of the second resolution, since the other, the *heteros* must be allowed to come into the middle, and not on terms dictated by autonomous self-thinking thinking. For such terms contract the promise of what is to be allowed, and overestimate the capacity and completeness of mind's own self-purgation.

But even this second possible answer has the difficulty that we have to *consent* to the aid of powers other than ourselves; we have to give ourselves over to the other; hence we *already* have to have some measure of agapeic mind, which at this point it is not clear we can claim. If agapeic consent is to be possible at all, must we not, then, *somehow always be already within it,* even when we refuse it? Are we forced to conclude: We must be purified behind our own backs, as it were; that far from being a self-catharsis, the cleansing is the cruel agape of an other that rinses us in the teeth of our will, being cruel to be kind, offering suffering out of love? Given our perplexed understanding of our ultimate dilemmas, we cannot simply dismiss this possibility. God, or time, is washing us away; or God is washing us in the wearing struggle of time; in suffering time, we are offered a restoration even in our refusal; every refusal becomes the occasion of divine ingenuity, as if God were as sly as a fox, and as gentle as a dove, and yet as violent as a lion. For washing scrubs as well as soothes.

I know well that God is not to the tastes of epistemologists, but all honor to Descartes, the Ur-father of all epistemologists, he was not so fastidious. His thought of the evil genius is here very important. Why so? It raises the most horrifying possibility. Many commentators scoff at it as a hyperbolic excrescence of epistemological imagination. And perhaps Descartes, devotee of mathematical clarity and distinctness, was himself ashamed of the thought and quickly squashed it. For it opened up an abyss, and almost immediately he could not stand it. Potentially it is the most horrifying and extreme of all the suspicions of doubt. The supposition of the evil genius, we might say, is the true beginning of the honest critique of pure reason.

The supposition voices the terrifying possibility that pure reason is not the pathway to truth, but a lie or a swindle. There is a darkness in reason, reason is a darkness; and what is worse, reason has no way of knowing this about *itself*. The swindle performed by the evil genius is one that by its nature reason cannot detect through itself alone. For every one of its efforts falls under the same suspicion. Even the highest, most clear and distinct efforts by mathematical reason are themselves infected by the possibility of this taint. How really does Descartes solve it? By going outside the power of reason, relative to something not within its own power to effect or create: the thought of God. The thought of God is not an invented idea, is not an idea that mind itself can create purely through its own powers.

When Descartes treats the evil genius and God as opposite, the stress is on God's goodness, the undeceiving perfection of the infinite. We might say that the evil genius would be the epitome of the refusing mind, the anagapeic mind, so to say. Such a mind would be extraordinarily clever. For to be able to swindle reason, without reason even suspecting it, one would have to be extraordinarily intelligent. It would be brilliant, but cold and sinister, absolutely rational but also absolutely malignant.

And one must ask: From where does Descartes get this thought? On the basis of the thought alone, there is no way that pure reason would suggest it. For pure reason, after all, is being swindled into self-confidence. It is a question no commentator has asked: What is the source of this most horrifying and audacious thought of Descartes? Is it not a source other than the immanent resources of reason itself? Does it arise, not at all from pure reason, but from the chiaroscuro of mixture, and the threat of the sinister in the middle? How can epistemology deal with such sources? Must not epistemology's desire to have a doctrine of purely autonomous knowing always be threatened by the appearing of thoughts like these, which it cannot control in advance, and which it must dismiss quickly once they arrive? What if there are sources of knowing and unknowing, of consent and refusal, of seeing the truth and being defrauded, that escape entirely the self-mediations of the rational mind? And do not rationally console me with expert appeal to a psychology of the unconscious, or a sociology of historical crisis, or some such. None of these is adequate to the metaphysical audacity and horror implied by Descartes' thought.

Do not analogous considerations apply to the putative antidote to the evil genius, namely, the idea of God as infinite perfection? Is not this, too, an excess that is always surplus to rational mind? There is no determinate logical category true to the infinite; every effort to think the infinite ends up thinking finitude, hence not thinking the infinite; there is always a surplus to the idea of the infinite. This excess may always interrupt the coherent self-mediations of mind. Just as the evil genius may refuse to take its order from rational mind, even in seeming to take them, what guarantee have we that the infinite God will also take orders from our rational mind, in seeming to take them? None whatsoever. Does not the circle of self-mediating mind, when it tries to close on itself in pure self-determination, not seem like an idolatrous simulacrum of absoluteness? Is not its will to certainty a will to security, the securing of its own will to power from outside threat, or interference, or indeed welcome?

Well I know that commentators have dismissed the idea of God, as well as the evil genius. Why? Because knowing, it is claimed, must refuse any interference from what are deemed extraneous sources. To appeal to such sources is considered not to play the game of a purely immanent epistemology. True, but why should one play that game? Why should we take these particular orders from reason? Even Descartes himself was afraid of his two most extreme and audacious thoughts. He gave more attention to God, because over the millenia this idea has been categorially more domesticated. Descartes himself ends up perpetuating this domestication, for the eros of his mind was impatient to get on with the business at hand of perfecting his new mathematical science of nature. He did not dwell with the perplexity, much less make a way for the renewal of agapeic mind. God and the soul become the most easily known. And then one speaks of God, as if there were not something absolutely disrupting about the idea, as if it were known because it were familiar, as if the thought of absolute goodness were the carrier of a finite consolation, when, in fact, it also explodes all finite consolations, for we have no clear and distinct idea of absolute goodness. To the extent that we have any idea, we vaguely and uneasily sense that it calls us to account, that in the shadow of even a hint of its reality all our claims to be good are shabby. These two ideas are radically humbling to the mind, to its pride, to its pretension to complete self-mediation.

With the thought of the evil genius, there surges up the foreboding of a fault that runs through all of reason's efforts. Struggle as it may, reason will be apprehensive about this vestige of fault; in its claim to know, there will be the ever self-concealing misgiving of evil, always and ineradicably. This foreboding occurred to Descartes. He did not will it. It happened. One suspects it was given, horrifying and humbling. It struck him, a flash in a dream, and an abyss opened up. Descartes woke to close the abyss, and return to the dreamless sleep of self-satisfied reason.

What about the epistemological immunity of the *cogito*? This is to the point, but not always the point Descartes takes. There is a truth to the *cogito* argument—the self in being denied or deceived cannot be denied to be. I see this as the ineradicable intimacy of being, the idiocy of self-being. But this ineluctable idiocy has to be interpreted; its being given has to be probed. The self that cannot escape itself is not a neutral place-holder for anonymous epistemological necessity. Nor is this intimacy of being without tension with the public universality of the ideal intelligibility that Descartes the mathematician wants to ground. We are back with objective mind. The publicity of the neutral universal proves its value by its being susceptible to mathematization. But in this mathematization, the idiocy of selfhood is not given heed. Descartes does not embrace the philosophical purification of the intimate self as an infinite task. As a cognitive ground, it is used as a link in the chain of epistemological security. Once this ground is laid, the infinite task, if there is any at all, is the methodical and progressive accumulation of mathematicized knowledge about finite creation. The abyss of self and the abyss of God are both instrumentalized.

Even Descartes cannot avoid acknowledging this idiocy, because he knows that only *this I as this I* can do or perform the *cogito* argument. Strictly speaking, the *cogito* argument establishes only the fact that I cannot escape from myself; once I think, I cannot think myself away. Each intimate self in its singularity has to enact the argument for himself. No one else can do it. To be sure, the claim is that if *any* self performs the argument, then the conclusion will follow with inescapable necessity; there will be no escape from self, for any self. But the fact is that the primary inescapability is of *this* I from itself. We can escape the inescapability of the other self from their own selves. Any self is free not to perform the argument, and to distract itself from itself in diversions. Both the freedom and necessity revealed by the *cogito* argument cannot be adequately conceived outside of this intimate singularity.

It is ironical that this intimate singularity of the I performing the *cogito* is used to ground an ideal of knowledge in which all singularity will be severely restricted or abolished. Descartes' love of method is intended thus: there are no heroes, singular selves of method, except perhaps its originator; a method curbs and disciplines the singularity of the self using the method; and even the singularity of its originator is irrelevant, once the method is properly operative; method is a means of self-forgetfulness in the interests of the progressive and disciplined accumulation of determinate knowledge. Of course, the surplus of the singular self has been merely silenced, thus sharing in the fate of the evil genius and of God. The paradox is that the public universality of mathematicized intelligibility is ultimately grounded in a milieu of mindfulness marked by three ideas that cannot be contained within that ideal of intelligibility: the self as idiotic, the evil genius as the ontological lie, God as the ultimate agape of the truth.

Descartes believed, of course, that his idea of God served to transfigure the repulsive thought of the evil genius into a more benign face of universal intelligibility. Is this agapeic mind as transfigurative? No. God transfigures nothing in Descartes' scheme, except perhaps Descartes' metaphysical confidence in the transfigurative power of his own method. There is no suffering or patience, as there is no insomniac perplexity, before the abyss of self and God. There will be a mathematical "transfiguration" of the world, a technological one, neither a tragic, nor a comic one. Thought singing its other gives way to a universal geometry that neither sings, nor weeps, nor laughs.

Agapeic mind cannot escape these, the weeping of the mindful human being, the honesty of its laughter and its song. I write these words again at Inchydoney, West Cork. One day, not long ago, mulling on the evil genius, ruminating on God, finding it impossible to digest the thought, I passed an old man in the streets of Clonakilty, the neighboring town. The man was old, very old, and very ugly. He was stooped. He stopped and looked at me. His eyes were red, rheumy. I thought, these are hardly the eyes of a man, not even an animal. A ruin. My senses were taken from me by these senseless eyes on the edge of life. A decrepit human being, with the body decaying, supported sideways on a stick, a repulsive apparition. The dead eyes pierced me and I shuddered. Yet the thought immediately flashed in my mind: this, too, is the face of God. The eyes of self, the intimacy of self, the idiocy of being looked at me from the repulsive face. Later I thought of St. Francis and his transfiguring kiss of the leper. He must have felt the revulsion, and perhaps something like the flash of recognition I felt. I did not kiss the man.

Is there an agapeic mindfulness that transfigures the ugly? Heraclitus said: Here, too, be gods! How can a dying human being be the presence of God? How can one say this? I am asking this, knowing I have no complete resolution to the perplexity of the evil genius, or the equivocity of our mixed being, torn between refusal and consent. Yet, we look at being as good, and sometimes being looks to us as good. It is like the idiot wisdom of Don Quixote. One looks at an ugly being as worthy of acceptance, and the ugliness of the ugly begins to fall away. A way is made for the shine of the good.

A few days later, I was driving out beyond Clonakilty near Inchydoney, and coming around a corner an old man stepped out, stood before the car, stick raised high. It was half appeal, half admonition, and it brought us to a halt. It was the man. He asked for a ride to Ardfield. He was smelly, he reeked of whiskey and unwash. His speech was slurred, hard to comprehend. I opened the window for air, then quickly closed it, as if I risked insult to God, and I talked as best as I could to him. His eyes were on the fog ahead, not on me. I drove him into the fog, and left him out, an unsteady stranger, some miles up the hills near Ardfield. The we drove on to Red Strand, where in the fog one could hear, but not see, the lapping of the sea on the sand. Later we returned to our house, and there was no fog.

Does not the thought of an agapeic absolute ask that we dissolve the category of the ugly in our more usual, domesticated senses? Everything is to be loved, even the repulsive, even the ugliest man. Is this why the thought of God as agapeic is horrifying to us? Is there not a level where the idea of God loving what is hateful to us, is also hateful to us? Do we find repulsive the idea of God loving the repulsive? Do we find repulsive the solicitation that we, too, must love the repulsive? For everything in our self-being seems to cry out in protest at the love of the unlovely, at the embrace of the dying old man. Reason should know no repulsion, since it allegedly can look on things beautiful and ugly with eyes that are as stones. And yet we are attracted and repulsed. It is our whole self-being that is drawn into the movement of attraction or recoil. In the face of the unutterably ugly, the surge of erotic mind reverses itself into recoil. If there is a "yes" to that face, it seems only the movement of agapeic mind can do it.

So the question of the transfigurative power of agapeic mind concerns the transformation of self such that it can love the hateful. Can this be done or effected? What ordeals must we undergo to release it? Perhaps none. Maybe it is an unmerited gift. What if we cannot accept the gift, if we cannot consent to consent? Must we be laughed into consent, cajoled into consent, wounded into it? Must not the true goodwill to being, the amen to the other, be converted to something like this? And yet this seems impossible for a human being.

What purification would be necessary for us to be restored to ontological consent? Would we not have to die? Does posthumous mind arise here? In the face of death does the primal "It is good" dissolve like a phantom? Or was our refusal of the primal "It is good" the fault bringing on the dissolution of agapeic mind, placing us equivocally in the middle between yea and nay?

Does death invite the last consent which is the first consent? If we refuse, do we continue to refuse, for eternity? Is this hell?

Why this idiot wisdom? Why any desire still to speak of the goodness of creation? I came upon a dead small bird on the causeway near Inchydoney. Still whole. I picked it up. Blood in its eye. Delicate beauty. So perfect. Its life gone. Never again. Cold and perfect still. I looked at the estuary, tide ebbed. Other birds, so various, oyster catchers, herons, gannets, gulls. . . . The quiet stunning beauty of the world. The world is perfect. Yet there is death. Blood in the eye of beauty. I turned to the grey, darkening clouds over the hills. And the beauty of the world was menacing, menaced. How can one see this perfection, in death, beyond death? Does mindfulness itself have to go into death, to see if it can consent, beyond death? Agapeic love of posthumous mind? Philosophy as the practise of death? No science here. No geometry of death. No technē of transfiguration. Only the dream of a ridiculous man?

And does not death mock every "yes"? And yet we say "no," and recoil from death. Death written in the flesh as corruption. Death violator that sets upon the flesh. Death smotherer of vitality in age and impotence and rage. Death insinuator of incontinence and the body closing down. Death the assailant in motiveless cruelty. Death kneaded into the heart as failure to ask or give forgiveness. Death suffusing the tongue in sterile silence. Death scorching the tongue with curses. Death consuming memory with regret for the irrevocable insult. Death making rancid with ridicule the innocent who try. Death hollowing the will in malevolence. Sour death the envy of goodness. Death the hemorrhage of hope. Death the choking solitude that none can break. Death the mocker of prayer. Death the dry rasp of profanation. Death devouring the spirit as a gasp for air in a suffocating cell. Death assaulting the terror-filled soul that cannot consent to its now impending nothingness. Tormenting death that taunts all things and us all. Death the torturing deafness that hears but will not hear the plea for mercy. Death the mockery of being that will not let be.

Death is the cold word that undoes every word, the unmaking word making everything written as if it were not written at all. When I think of such things a wave of crushing hopelessness inundates my being. I am tempted to say: Let us sleep; it is better for us not to know, or to think such things. Dejection breaks my strength. I die in my tracks.

I am at a loss. Loss is all I have then. But it is hopelessness that makes me continue. It is either death or continuation. We must choose. Consent or refuse. But then we are back with the dilemma of how to break through into consent at all. Maybe we cannot make a breakthrough. Perhaps all we can do is try to make a way and await, await what comes, welcome what comes. We cannot consent simply through will, at least not consent in the sense at stake. We must be aided to the deeper willingness from some other source. We ask for that willingness, we would welcome it were it given.

Perplexity in the dilemma of consent must give way to a readying. Who can honestly say that she or he is ready? But if we choose to continue, even in hopelessness, are we already given the glimmer of agapeic mind, in hopelessness itself? For such continuation is consent to being, though it knows not why. But though it knows not its why, it knows it must refuse refusal. This is its why: there is no reason for this consent, beyond the goodness of consent to being itself. Is not this agapeic mind?

Chapter 5

Perplexity and Ultimacy

1. Perplexity and Ultimacy

One of the nobilities of philosophical thought is its willingness to risk questions it may not be able to answer definitively. Why should this be a nobility? Surely it shows an inability to live with the truth of things, which again and again returns us to our finite place. Better to ask only those questions that can be formulated determinately and answered definitely. Speculative philosophy is a wild goose chase, and not even a noble one at that. It is a folly of excess. The metaphysician who thinks he is homesick for eternity is a mere malingerer before finitude. Better to consent to that finitude and cease the torment of the unanswerable.

So speaks critical caution. And speculative weariness. Would that one could sleep the slumber of satisfied finitude. There are philosophers who suffer from insomnia here. They find themselves opportuned by questions which will not go away, all prudent rationalizations of finite thinking notwithstanding. These are questions which voice an essential perplexity: a perplexity we cannot suppress, a perplexity we cannot entirely answer, a perplexity to which we must return again and again. Such perplexity rises up relative to the engima of ultimacy.

To take the question seriously is not intellectually fashionable. Why? Among majors reasons are the following. The question has been sidelined by modern science in its rejection of all final causes from its explanatory schemes. There are no ultimates, because there are no ends of nature. There is simply the process of continuing being. Perhaps this is marked by certain laws or regularities or structures that might be said to have some provisional ultimacy. But this is no ultimacy of ends, but that of a merely given neutral thereness, beyond which reason merely strays if it thinks of anything more. Nor is there any ultimacy to the process as a whole, or processes within the process as a whole. Of course, such formulations are already equivocal. Properly speaking, we should not even talk of the process as a *whole*. For this would imply a standpoint that comprehended the process from a position not to be surpassed. The equivocation is significant: We seem unable to prevent the smuggling back of descriptions that surreptitiously imply some sense of ultimacy, all conceptual cautions to the contrary. Essential perplexity haunts the categorial schemes that would banish such speculative wonder.

Suppose one then says: Very well, there is no process as a "whole"; there are processes and things, and within process and the relations of things and processes, there are more or less determinate regularities that can be formulated intelligibly. Talk of the process as a "whole" is a slide towards unacceptable discourse, but with a little methodological self-policing, we can prevent this slide. No question we can do this. But ought we to do it? Do we not have to impose a harness on mind, clamp a bridle on thought, against which thinking's dynamic drift balks and chafes? Mind then orders itself not to ask questions that seem quite in order, were thinking allowed its own spontaneous drift.

One grants: there are processes and determinate regularities, and we seem to know them; there are determinate things in becoming, articulated in a complex web of interconnections; we ourselves inhabit this complex web. Surely it is inevitable that we ask: What is the energy of being that manifests itself in the process? What is the grounding energy that allows things to be? Things are there, to all appearances intelligibly in being, but why there at all, why in being at all? The *that* of beings is deeply perplexing. So also is the *what*. Can we speak of an origin that generates the being there of beings, and that allows the articulation of things into an intelligible community of interrelations? And what is it about us as thinking beings that allows for this astonishing community between mind and the community of beings in their finite givenness?

Let thought follow its own dynamism and such perplexities will emerge and recur. These perplexities already take us to the edge of finite entities, indeed take thinking to the edge of its own limits. They reveal the dunamis of mind as the wakefulness of a finite being marked by self-transcending thought, on which no univocal limit can be imposed a priori. I will not say there are no limits. But the limit, relative to such self-transcending, is not easy to articulate. "Limit," like ultimacy, is itself metaphysically perplexing.

Besides the rejection of final causes by modern science, I will name two more reasons why we order mind against perplexity about ultimacy: first, equivocity before religious transcendence; second, the modern rejection of Platonism. In fact, these are related to the scientific excision of final causes.

Relative to religious transcendence, we need only think about this equivocation in Descartes: his willingness to hand over the question of eternal salvation to the ecclesiastical authorities, while rational mind frees itself to pursue its own methodical self-perfection here and now, a self-perfection which will not be idly speculative, as with the ancients, but useful, producing powerful devices to aid the human being in becoming the "master and possessor of nature." The equivocity lies in this combination of factors: a putative *de jure* respect for the religious, which all the while, *de facto*, is being superannuated.

For Descartes rational mind cannot really make any intelligible sense of such matters, for faith is something entirely other to *ratio*. A declared diffidence about reason's competence in religious matters coexists with a declared confidence in reason's potential mastery of the things that matter in this world. The accentuation of the latter confidence leads to the withering away of the former diffidence, indeed its withering into an eventual indifference relative to religious transcendence. The last outcry against this indifference was uttered by Nietzsche's madman whose metaphysical insomnia made him shout the spine chilling words: God is dead. The words no longer chill, because the indifference has choked the outcry.

Pascal—mathematical genius like Descartes, but Descartes' religious twin—early saw the latent nihilism in Descartes' equivocation. The self-perfection of Cartesian reason produces a sleep of mind not in the least troubled by the enigma of transcendence. This sleeping mind takes itself as the epitome of wakefulness. It reacts with irritation to the suggestion that, relative to metaphysical perplexity, it slumbers deeply. This is what Pascal saw. This is also what Kierkegaard believed he saw relative to Hegelian logicism. This is what Nietzsche claimed to see relative to idealistic metaphysics. But there is a Nietzschean equivocity here that brings us to the modern rejection of Platonism.

Nietzsche was marked by a restless eros for eternity. But his eros for eternity was one that had grown suspicious of the eros for eternity—as Platonically articulated. In that regard Nietzsche was heir to Descartes' equivocation. However, this is not where we find his real spiritual seriousness. This lies in his being Pascal's blood brother, in his seeing the ultimate valuelessness, hence nihilism, of a completely Cartesianized world. I will have more to say about this devaluation. Within the milieu of Platonic philosophizing, mind's eros for ultimacy was not mutilated. Yet the stock picture prevailed that this very eros led to, or fed on, a mutilation of our eros for time. Nietzsche helped perpetuate this caricature of Platonism, and so furthered the slumber of modernity about ultimacy.

There is a difficulty here, but it is not that we must extirpate the eros for eternity. Rather eros has to be understood such that we do not fall into an excessively dualistic way of dealing with the perplexity. The danger with the dualistic way is this: the eros for eternity seems to function as a parasite on temporal eros; in the process of transcending time, such eros sucks the life blood from that temporal eros with a violent ingratitude. Eternity is then said to be what time is not; this "not" becomes the operation of a reiterated negation on all things temporal; this "not" erects and consolidates a dualistic opposition between time and eternity, the one relative becoming, the other unconditional being. In truth, the "not," and the dualism it produces both feed on the dunamis of being as it is manifest in becoming, even though the "not" turns against the very dynamism. Hence Nietzsche will imply: Platonic eros is the self-mutilation of the temporal dynamism, as manifested in human desire and external becoming.

The difficulty can be thus stated: If we seek the ground of temporal becoming, and if we determine that ground as the dualistic opposite of the temporal, the very ground is set in opposition to that which it is supposed to ground, hence instead of grounding it, it infects it with a deeper ontological insecurity than it previously had. I think that the real issue of ultimacy is not one of substituting stasis for dynamism.[1] For if the ground is a stasis, it seems to me that the ground then produces another kind of metaphysical slumber: eternity becomes a dead principle that is incommensurable in an invidious way with the dynamism of being as given in time. I say incommensurable in an invidious way, for there might also be a non-invidious incommensurability between the ground and time. The ultimate might be other than the grounded, it may in a certain sense unground the grounded. It may be an enigmatic abyss, relative to the mind in thrall to restricted categories of finitude. It may unsettle all self-satisfied finitude. But this would be an agapeic incommensurability, one that does not induce the slumber of mind, but energizes it into renewed restlessness.

A dualistic thinking of ultimacy, if pushed to the extreme, has the same effect as the Cartesian equivocation with respect to religion transcendence. In a word, the otherness of the ultimate becomes the basis of its own *redundancy*, in the long run. It seems to me that the Cartesianization of mind, with its consequent scientistic reduction of all intelligibility to immanence, conspires with this equivocity of Platonic dualism to produce a diffidence in modern metaphysicians with respect to even *raising* the question of ultimacy. Instead the restlessness driving Platonic eros is appropriated by Cartesian mind as a redirected will to power in immanence, a will to power that can be determinately and progressively perfected, under the guiding eyes of scientific method. By contrast I want to suggest: this very restlessness testifies to a

---

1. See *Desire, Dialectic and Otherness*, chapter 4.

deeper indeterminate, metaphysical perplexity, never to be satisfactorily answered by any determinate answer.

Thus, we can reformulate the customary way of putting the Platonic eternity: To this perplexing indeterminacy of restless eros, it seems to offer an excessively determinate idea of the ultimate, as the immutable, univocal *eidē*. The dualistic opposition of time and eternity might seem to suggest a *univocal* eternity as a complete determinate answer for the equivocations of time. In this respect, there is a kinship between Platonic and Cartesian dualism: neither adequately avoids a propensity to offer a univocal answer to a perplexity seen as equivocal. Instead of a Platonic flight to a univocal eternity, Descartes promises a univocal *mathēsis* of time to dispel the ambiguities and equivocations of being.

In both cases the univocalization of the ultimate as the complete determinate answer can produce just that sleep of mind against which I spoke above. To wake up again, we have to transcend this oscillation of univocity and equivocity, whether applied to time itself, or to the opposition of time and eternity. There may be no *univocal* answer to the ultimate metaphysical perplexity. In part, this is because the perplexity in question is not directed to a determinate problem with a univocally determinable answer. In the main, it is because our attempted answer to an essential perplexity is itself beyond the dualism of univocity and equivocity. Every univocal answer is not *the* answer, and this because of the very nature of perplexity about ultimacy.

The issue of the *devaluation* of being arises. Properly speaking, the Cartesian rejection of final causes means that being as such is valueless. There is no intrinsic worth ingredient in the nature of things. The result—if we are honest about the logic—is nihilism: nothing has any inherent value. If anything has any value—and we the metaphysical animal cannot help but value, seek the worth of being, despite all scientist prohibitions—it is a derivative of human desire and will, an instrumental outcome of our effort to master being. All value is merely an anthropocentric construct and projection, and ultimately there is no ground of value beyond human will.

However, in this Cartesian will to univocalize all being, we find equivocation once again: for the human will, indeed the Cartesian will, to univocalize all being, cannot serve as an ultimate ground of value either, since human beings are in the same position as all beings in nature—just there—neither good nor evil—just there. The Cartesian will to univocalize all being then hides its own ethical hollowness, indeed the hollowness of all human willing, despite it strutting about, having crowned itself in advance as "the master and possessor of nature."

If we univocalize being, all beings are just there—not good, not evil—just there. Nietzsche wanted to inherit Descartes' crown, but diagnosed the nihilism of this monarch of modern mind. Following this he would speak of the sheer being there of beings in terms of the "innocence of becoming." In my view the innocence of becoming hides yet another equivocation. At the ultimate level what Nietzsche really wanted to say, indeed to sing, is the goodness of being, the worth of becoming, the praiseworthy nature of being in itself, freed from the "moral order," as an allegedly vengeful human construction. But since Nietzsche is caught up in the slipstream of Cartesian nihilism, the innocence of becoming is hard to distinguish from the indifference of being there, the purposeless, valuelessness of being that ensues in all of modernity. Instead of the praiseworthy value of being, instead of the transvaluation of being, nihilism, infinitely chameleon, simply changes its camouflage. Instead of constructing mathematical equations, nihilism now sings Dionysian dithyrambs.

The human being alone cannot produce the projected transvaluation of values. For if the human being is part of the valueless "whole," his efforts ultimately are themselves valueless, on the terms of the stated view. "Transvaluation of values" is an effort to sing being as intrinsically praiseworthy. Unless, however, there is an ultimate hospitality for value in being itself, this singing is merely a whistling in the dark. Even the whistling itself is only another manifestation of the valueless darkness. The human being cannot give ultimate value to being, if being itself does not have ultimate value. I think this devaluation of being must inexorably follow if we excise from metaphysical consideration perplexity about the ultimate, in a sense more than the human being's projective power, and in a sense transcending the putative indifferent thereness of finite things and processes.

This brings us back to Plato who is certainly ambiguous to us, perhaps even equivocal. Nietzsche may accuse Plato of being the real originator of the devaluation of being as becoming. And above I mentioned some of the arguments relevant to certain equivocations in any dualistic opposition of time and eternity. Nevertheless, Plato as the Ur-nihilist is a caricature. Why? Plato absolutely refuses any such devaluation of being in so far as the privileged name he gives to the ultimate is the Good. Ultimacy is not exhausted by the human being, nor by the ensemble of finite entities: the value, the goodness, the worth of all that is, is "grounded" on the Good itself as the ultimate. Plato, far from being insensitive to what we now call the question of nihilism, was acutely aware that, short of eros opening to the ultimate in its otherness, there was no way of avoiding nihilism. His "answer" is the Good.

My interest now is not in giving an account of Plato's answer, but in the kind of question at stake. I venture: Plato's "answer" in terms of the Good is not a univocal solution to dispel all the equivocations of time; it is an answer full of enigma. There is a certain indeterminacy about it, an indeterminacy some commentators have branded an emptiness. Perhaps it is the commentators who are mistakenly anticipating a univocal answer. Plato, whose slipperiness so irritates them, is superior. Plato already knew that there is no univocal answer to perplexity about the ultimate. The ultimate ground of determinate being, intelligibility and value cannot be another determinate univocal thing.

The "Good" is what I call a "metaphysical metaphor."[2] As such an answer, the Good suggests an enigma which will not let us excuse ourselves from thinking. Quite to the contrary, this enigma renews perplexity and makes the mind sleepless. Beyond every determinate problem and every univocal answer, there is another, second perplexity, beyond all determinacy. When Socrates says: I know nothing, perhaps it was this *other* perplexity that was at work, perplexity about the enigma of the Good, and this perplexity despite the fact that he "knew" lots of determinate things, about this, that and the other.

We moderns know an enormous number of things, determinately formulated to satisfy scientific curiosity. What do we know of this other, indeterminate perplexity, beyond scientific curiosity? What "answers" do we have for it, if by chance it breaks through the admirably determinate articulations of our sciences? Having supped on a diet of Cartesian purposelessness and the ontologically thin fare of an indifferent cosmos—not even a cosmos, this is a misuse of a great Pythagorean word—supped on a world empty of ultimacy, except perhaps for the human surrogates dreamt up by our will to power, alternatively anxious and arrogant—after this metaphysical undernourishment, is there not something too much for us, something astonishing about Plato's answer, something hard to begin even to digest: the ultimate is the Good? So used are we to the indifferent view of the indifferent "cosmos," about which we know so much, we have to struggle, as if from an overpowering slumber, to waken for even a little moment to this metaphysical astonishment.

2. Perplexity, Being Truthful, and the Between

Does not this mean that perplexity about ultimacy makes peculiar demands on us? I think so. It demands of us a certain *being truthful* which is reflective of our condition of being between. I now want to explore this. Then subsequently I want to ask how perplexity relates to matters such as groundlessness, skepticism, contingency, absurdity, and the audacity of philosophical questioning that concerns itself with God.

---

2. See below chapter 6; also *Being and the Between*, chapter 5.

Being truthful seems to suggest a notion of truth not exhausted by the truth of propositions. Propositional truth is not inconsequential, but there is something about being truthful that exceeds propositional truth. To be truthful asks that we be honestly mindful of being. It is a *condition of being*, marking a way of being of mindful selves. A proposition may be true or false, but a proposition is not honest or dishonest. It can be said to be honest or dishonest, only when we take into account the selves that speak. Thus, a true proposition can be uttered mendaciously; a true proposition, relative to its dishonest communication, can foster untruth.

Being truthful points to an intimacy between the "what" of what is being said, and the self-being or "who" of the one saying or communicating. There is a being truthful of saying, not reducible to objectification in the truth of what is being said. There can be a lie of saying, other than the lie or truth of what is objectively said. In a word, there is an idiocy to being truthful that transcends complete determination in propositional form. Of course, I do not mean to deny that the truthful self will communicate with others with the utmost integrity, relative to propositional truth.

The ontological dimension of being truthful is suggested, for instance, by the way the Medievals, following Aristotle, spoke of the good in terms of honesty: there was *bonum delectabile, bonum utile* and *bonum honestum. Bonum honestum* was good inherently, the integral good. In line with this, we might say that honesty is a condition of the integrity of being. Integrity itself invocates the notion of "wholeness." There is an honesty of being about a truthful person; the being truthful of the person expresses an integrity of being, a certain wholeness. This is not a closed whole; how could it be, since truthfulness is *communicated* by this integrity of being. The truth is communicated out of this open wholeness. Such a being truthful reflects the agapeic mind which goes forth from itself, not out of indigence, but out of an enigmatic prior plenitude. In our being truthful, somehow the truth is already with us. The integrity of honest being, in communicating beyond self to the other, gives articulation to this prior enigmatic relatedness to truth.

If being honest is good for itself, this does not mean it is the good. On the contrary, the openness of its integral wholeness makes it to be a good in communication with the good of the other. Honest communication is energized by a fidelity to truth, to the truth as good, to the other as recipient of truth that knows no closure, of a good that is not for any one self. We might say that the generosity of truth as good is evident in being honest. An honest person or good does not dissimulate about truth or value, even when it is not absolute truth or the good. Taking to mind all the complexities of an occasion of communication, the honest self speaks in service to the truth. This is agapeic service, sometimes implicit, sometimes overt. The truthful self, in the intimacy of its being, is opened to the truth as other, as transcendence itself. There is an implicit orientation of honest self-transcendence towards the absolute truth as other to our own self-transcendence.

But this is to run ahead, so let us us return to the middle. There the skeptical taunt is not easily silenced: we know nothing, and all this talk is only a mask of vanity! Perplexity about the ultimate is a knot we cannot untie, a knot we had best let be, for our finite efforts invariably come to nothing. And yet can one renege on the question, even while nagged by the suspicion that one's efforts come to nothing? Must we fall into a willed dogmatism that squints at limits? And is there not a self-satisfied skepticism that is nicely complacent with its own comfortable confines? Do not our very limitations incite us to perplexity, impel mindfulness to self-transcendence? Are we not between these extremes: the extreme that simply claims for philosophy something it does not, and cannot deliver; the extreme that simply dismisses philosophy as an old fraud that wraps its fright before emptiness in the swaddle of noble ideals?

When we are honest, or at least willing to be honest, we let ourselves be open to the truth, let it be what it may. Does not this require our willing submission to what may be other to our heart's desire? Does it not ask of us a certain unconditional respect for truth? Indeed does not honesty *turn back* on itself, in our willingness to acknowledge truth as possibly beyond us? We may say we are willing to be honest, but the saying itself does not constitute the honesty. Abuse is quite possible, indeed very common. I say: "Let us be honest," and then immediately proceed to propound a series of falsehoods. Someone proclaims "Let us be honest," and we await the lie that immediately follows.

So there is an ambiguity of honesty which may be dishonestly used. This means also that being honest is a condition we must struggle to attain, against the tempting relapse into the old self-serving falsehoods. This struggle may involve an intense skepticism about the ways truth is ordinarily handled, or mishandled. This is the paradoxical situation: our commitment to truth must call *itself into question*, to purge itself of self-serving lies, and most especially those sincerely held.

Hence there is an *existential* dimension to all this. We may delight to interrogate others, but more intimately and more harshly we cannot evade self-interrogation. The philosopher, sometimes against his will, finds it hard to avoid being an agent of disenchantment. This is not all, but the hermeneutics of suspicion is this old skeptical exigence baptized with a new historicist name. What is more, it is also hazardous to direct one's suspicion outward at the other. Just this suspiciousness may be a flight from the darkness enfolding more the accuser than the accused. The stratagem is not unknown in post-Nietzschean thought: the other is from the start suspect, while the accuser, having plea-bargained with himself, secretly gives himself immunity. The tribunal of critique: debunking skepticism of the others; the dogmatism of skepticism for oneself. The exceptions who see through these ruses of reason are singular. Nietzsche's accusation of the other was often grounded in his own self-accusation. Nietzsche's devotees may seem merciless in their suspicion of others; one wonders if they are deficient in their master's pitiless self-suspicion. I am not saying Nietzsche always noted the beam in his own eye while removing the mote from Plato's eye. Nevertheless he knew that philosophical honesty exacted this existential necessity: the I must call itself as I to account.

I am between the promise of knowing the truth, and my repeated exposure to the temptation to be closed against the truth. Not possessing the truth is not to be closed to the truth. Rather being in the middle shows its own truth of being, which is not the truth, but a willingness to be truthful. The singular self can be truthful, and this even while it does not possess the truth. It may be necessary to attain this intermediate condition in order to open oneself to truth, in a sense that transcends oneself. To be between is to move between these extremes, of being truthful, and of truth as trancending us.

The question then is: Is being truthful merely a subjective condition, perhaps a means to an end, with the means left behind on attaining truth as other to us? And, of course, truth has most often been understood in a universalistic sense, binding on all human beings, or rational agents, binding even on God. Philosophers have tended to think that we are mere instruments of the truth; the final act is a self-negation; to get to the truth, our singularity must be extirpated. We find this in Hegel, for instance, when he refused to speak of *his* philosophy; one cannot say "my" philosophy. This is especially true of philosophers who look to a scientific model. The final embrace of the impersonal universal puts the singular self in a position of not finally counting in the truth of things.

As I said of agapeic mind, there is a kind of sacrifice of the "for-self" in self-transcendence towards the other. But agapeic mind is not the extirpation of singularity in a neutral universal. The matter itself is ambiguous within the philosophical tradition. Thus we find ancient idealists who did acknowledge the in-betweenness of the philosopher. Perhaps they were sometimes equivocal about this, nevertheless they did acknowledge it. Consider Socrates again. Socrates seems to epitomize the philosopher who sacrifices himself for the universal. After all what does Socrates as this person matter? What does the this as this matter? Is it not the *eidos*, the universal that matters? Hence his question to Euthyphro: Are you not just giving me an example matching your personal situation, and not giving me the logical universal of piety, rationally binding on all cases or instances? And yet Socrates comes down to us from the tradition as a singular hero of philosophical honesty—honesty not as an impersonal logical consistency, but as a courageous being true to his philosophical mission, a mission itself never grasped with Cartesian clarity and distinctness. Socrates is a hero of philosophical honesty because of the singularity of his being truthful, in face of death itself, and not just for the logical consistency of his arguments, as applying to all and to none.

Perhaps we should distinguish thinkers in relation to the following tendencies. On the one hand, thinkers like Pascal, Kierkegaard, Nietzsche are fierce critics of rationalism and scientism. They seem to privilege their own idiosyncratic vision, even in defiance of the impersonal deliverances of universal science. On the other hand, perhaps most philosophers veer in the opposite direction, for instance, Plotinus, Spinoza, Hegel, Husserl. They seem to want to lose just their singularity in a universal truth which assuages the burden of isolated selfhood. One side accentuates singularity, the other seeks alleviation from singularity. Of course, many philosophers show both sides, in some form: Pascal was a mathematician of genius; Hegel's writings are often saturated with existential pathos. Thus, too, with regard to philosophy itself, Plotinus indicated that impersonal universality and necessity are transcended by the quest of what he calls the "most worthy" (*to timiotaton*). One also thinks of Spinoza's taste of anguished despair concerning the true good in the *Emendatione*, in contrast to his putative geometry of the good in the *Ethics*.

The singularity of being truthful means that there is an *ethics to the truth*. The ancients knew this well. Philosophy was not first a science or a system; it was a way of being, a way of being mindful which might include scientific and systematic concerns, but which could not be exhausted by these concerns alone. This ethics of the truth takes us beyond any non-engaged submission to truth, truth as indifferently true in itself, one might even say, truth as dead in itself. It takes us beyond the truth of an impersonal *mathēsis* wherein the truthful human has no place, indeed cannot even be explained.

In fact, this ethics of the truth is presupposed by all our talk of impersonal truth. The passion that drives the mathematician to mathematical truth is not itself fully explicable on mathematical terms. It is something which is not included in the system of mathematical truth itself. Differently put, the truth of system is sustained by a passion for truth that itself cannot be absolutely systematized. Hence reflection on the nature of systematic truth brings us, and perhaps despite ourselves, to the edge of system, and back to the singularity of the thinker being truthful, the singularity that the system may claim to have transcended. This claim is a fugue state, a form of philosophical amnesia.

The true self-transcendence of agapeic mind includes memory of the singular as singular. The singular honesty of being truthful, and the truth as what is other to us—these are not opposed. What is suggested is a community of being between truth as other to us and the mindful self as singularly truthful. There must be a nonimpersonal form of the universal with a truth *higher and more ultimate* than systematic and mathematical universality. We move beyond the dualistic opposition of the singular self and the impersonal truth, existence and science. Being between moves us to a further mediation, other than any reduction of universal to particular, other than any absorption of the particular in the universal. Truth comes to appearance in a community of truthful singulars who are open to truth beyond their singularity, a beyond that does not impersonally negate, but grounds and supports their very singularity. The universal cannot be exhausted by the atemporal necessity of logical or mathematical necessity. It must be living truth itself, and not the singular human self as trying to be truthful either, but the truth itself as living ultimacy.

Must we not say that any search for God must be guided by this other sense of universality? For only this can do justice to the singularity of truthful selfhood, its perplexity about ultimacy, its idiotic intimacy of being, its community with being-other, as shaped by the self-transcendence of agapeic mind. Strangely enough, such a searching would open up our kinship with seekers who make no bones about their godlessness. Put it this way: The God-seeker sees the brother in the godless Nietzsche, just as he sees the trace of godlessness in kindreds like Kierkegaard or Dostoevski. Being in the middle, everyday labels and categorizations have to be used with circumspection, perhaps even suspended. And again, we need a hermeneutics of generosity to plumb the identities of other philosophers, like Plotinus or Spinoza or Hegel or Kant, and to fathom within the official mask of impersonal reason something other also at work, a different passion of transcendence. Any stark opposition in the above contrast of tendencies—the accentuation of singularity against the universal, the dissolution of singularity in the universal—loses some of its polarity.

3. Perplexity, Audacity, Being Ungrounded

I now want to consider a certain audacity that is connected with philosophical perplexity. I mean perplexity puts us into question in a way which takes mind to the limits of its own conceptual comfort. There is the provocation of philosophy to its own extremes. The audacity of questioning makes things harder for philosophy. It does not let the philosopher remain unvexed in the maelstrom. Perplexity will not let itself be immune from perplexity.

This, in fact, is one of the oldest and hardest concerns of philosophy. Philosophy questions what makes possible the very enterprise of philosophy itself. If it calls other modes of being and mind into question, it also calls itself to account. There can be a violence to self-certainty in this. Honest philosophizing is its own most severe antiphilosophical critic. Indeed, in its self-questioning it opens itself to being *ungrounded*. Paradoxically, this audacity of self–questioning can serve to refresh the philosophical quest. It can come alive again in its own self-disruption.

The audacity is manifest in the question: Not just what is reason, but what is the ground of reason itself? This is a question at the extreme: Is the ground of reason itself reasonable? Is thought not self-grounding? Is it thought that provokes itself to this extreme? Or is it something other than thought that, while necessary to shape thought, disturbs it at its very foundations? Is thinking willing to go to the edge of rationality when it ask the grounds of that rationality? In being ungrounded, does it continue to cast for the being of the ground? Is it then stretched between being ungrounded and the being of the ground?

Does reason ground itself? Hegel will say yes, followed in agreement by Husserl and many others. Truth is the measure of itself and falsity, said Spinoza, and thus expressed the widespread view that reason ultimately is self-validating: reason grounds itself. Hegel's *Science of Logic* is a long dialectical footnote to Spinoza's aperçu, itself an echo of the implicit ground in Descartes' *cogito me cogitare*, itself a modern subjectivization of the philosophical god adored since antiquity, Aristotle's *noēsis noēseōs*, thought thinking itself. Reason grounds itself; thought thinking itself is the absolute tribunal. The claim will be that there is nothing absolutely other to rational thought to which reason must submit. This will also be true of God, even when God is not explicitly redescribed as the pure thought that thinks itself.

Has not the audacity of questioning now turned around into the self-satisfaction of reason with itself? And the metaphysical perplexities of the between: Are not these now less threatening, since we are now confident that reason, simply by being true to itself, will dissolve every enigma that troubles it? Has not philosophical audacity now shifted from honesty in perplexity to a confidence that it can produce from itself all the categorial lucidity that is needed? This audacious trust in categorial intelligibility will extend to all being at a loss, including that of the tragic.

It seems to me that metaphysical perplexity is troubled by any such logicist audacity. Logicist audacity is less audacious than it appears to be. It lets the vector of transcending mind go towards the unknown, but there comes a turning point when the terror of the unknown as other makes it quail; it bends the vector of transcending mind back in a categorial circuit wherein mind finitizes its own metaphysical perplexity. I am not suggesting we repudiate reason, or exult in the irrational. Nor am I suggesting that this logicist divinization of reason reveals the full story about what is great in philosophy. It is not true that reason will always refuse to find against itself.

Philosophical perplexity will turn against reason's self-divinizing. The greatness of reason is just that, at a certain extreme, it can, and will find against itself, and hence be self-subverting.

The fact that reason wants to account for *itself* is the obverse side of its possible willingness to acknowledge that it may not be able to account entirely for itself, through itself. It is willing to find against its own idolization of self-thinking thought, self-validating reason. At its utmost limit, thinking countenances a divestment of all self-certainty, including reason's own self-certainty. There is a philosophical humility here, one of whose masks is the skepticism that disavows any idol erected in the name of self-thinking thought. Perplexity, we may say, exists on this edge between the false closure of reason on itself and reason's acknowledgment of what is other to itself. In the narrow pass of that between, reason becomes *other to itself* as self-validating reason. Nothing is unquestionably self-evident to it anymore. Honesty forces on it the other, second perplexity, beyond all determinate knowing. If there is an ultimate reason, it is other to our reason as self-validating.

One cannot insist in advance that rationality *must always be self-validating.* One must raise the possibility that the ultimate grounds of reason are not themselves reason, certainly reason as identified with human reason. The perplexity persists even if we say that the ground is divine reason. For such a ground is enigmatic to us. If one replies that divine reason is just like human reason, one risks attenuating the disproportion between the human and divine. While seeming to affirm God, one may have set in motion the idolization of human reason, and the ultimate logical consequence of this, namely, that there is no ultimate reason.

For if we say all reason is human reason, this reason—and again out of philosophical honesty—will soon begin the process of its own self-deconstruction, as happens in post-idealistic philosophy. We are tossed in the backwash of this self-deconstruction. Human reason will finally confess that it floats on an otherness it does not, cannot comprehensively master. Starting with divine mystery, we try to alleviate our perplexity by assimilating divine to human reason, only to end with the self-deconstruction of human reason in an incomprehensible dark ground. Darkness, enigma, perplexity seem to await us at both ends, both extremes.

In the everyday course of things, we make life intelligible in more or less determinate categories between these extremes of perplexity. Determinate knowing is thus bounded by two extremes of indeterminate perplexity. And yet these extremes do not remain at the limits, but fecundate in the middle itself, especially relative to the metaphysical enigma of its sheer being there at all. In this middle, perplexity precipitates a kind of sleepless thinking concerning what might be other to thought—be it the mystery of the divine, or the inward otherness of human selfhood, or again the sheer being there of beings, just in the contingent otherness of their being there. We may have to undergo a kind of Pascalian lostness. Yet there may a liberation in this. The release of extreme questioning can be the provocation of the human being into unwilled honesty at the limits. In consenting to the unwilled honesty, we again meet the audacity of philosophy.

We also meet a *counterthrust* to the apotheosis of thought thinking itself. This counterthrust means: what is other to thought thinking itself has to be rethought, in its resistance to the immanent categories of reason, purely at home with itself. Reason drives itself out of its domesticated security, makes itself own up to, be honest about, what lies at the edge of its most powerful rational mediations.

We discern this counterthrust in the self-deconstruction of idealism and transcendental philosophy after Hegel. Many thinkers participate in this counterthrust: Kierkegaard, the later Schelling, Schopenhauer, Nietzsche, and in the twentieth century, Heidegger, Marcel, Jaspers, Levinas and Derrida, to name only some. This countertrust is very differently articulated by each, but all seek to provoke seemingly all-powerful reason into the betrayal of its own impotence, at the end or edge of all system. The point here is not my detailed agreement or disagreement with their views. I think the counterthrust does not do justice to its own promise when it spends its energy in the hermeneutics of suspicion. The suspicion of reason, in all honesty, should also become suspicious of itself. I accept the question in the counterthrust, but any answer must come from sources beyond the hermeneutics of suspicion, and as I see it, in some form related to agapeic mind.

There is the fact, too, that the repercussions of this self-deconstruction of reason are not at all confined to rational knowing. A nihilism may be unloosed that extends to all the modes of human being, ethical, religious, aesthetic, philosophical, political. The self-deconstruction of idealistic reason leads, for instance, to Nietzsche's baiting of moralistic ideals and pieties, now imputed to the entirety of the Western tradition. There is philosophical audacity here too, but its effects are very equivocal. One can understand this audacity in relation to the taboos of Nietzsche's *own* time. We ought not, however, underplay the insidious effects of Nietzsche's own courtship of nihilism. After a century of Nietzschean impiety, the breaking of these old taboos has become a new pseudo-piety which wearies any honest thinker. There is nothing any longer provocative for thought in tilting at nineteenth century pieties, for no honest thinker now bends the knee here. We are the heirs of Nietzsche's godlessness, not his God-seeking. It is that heritage, not the pieties of idealism, that maybe now should be whipped.

Suppose, like Plato, we cannot forget the Good beyond beings? Who in all honesty can identify the Good for Plato with the Good of the humanitarian idealism of the last two centuries? Nietzsche, Dostoevski, sensed the insidious soft-center of a certain idealism, expressed in a view of the moral world order that lacked an honest suspicion about the human-all-too-human underpinnings of its sacred ideals. Hence, the hatred of Dostoevski's Underground Man for the true and the good and the beautiful. Hence, also Nietzsche's contempt for morality and for romanticism and idealism. But only historical parochialism or metaphysical small-mindedness could identify the Good with the "Good" as articulated in that humanitarian idealism. The "Good" is a simulacrum of the Good.

In any case, now a century after Nietzsche, we are no longer cloyed with a pervasive saccharine idealism. Nor do swarms of metaphysicians set out in systematic quest of universal and self-evident necessity. And this, despite the expectation created by the rhetoric of the "critique of ontotheology." I have looked long and far for contemporary "ontotheologians," but my search has so far found scant evidence of that nasty creature. "Ontotheologians" do not swarm. We are more likely to be assaulted by a rampant nihilism that impugns every claim of logical universality as a hidden play of power, or that denies any basis, except an ugly basis, to ethical ideals. Ethical honesty, when it loses spiritual seriousness about the Good, decomposes into a negativity that unlooses an orgy of debunking. Nor does this negativity open up the space, beyond logical necessity, for a new release of reverence for God. God, all gods, anything other than the human being—these are excoriated as only another evasion of the deep down ugly truth of humanity. Nietzsche again bears some responsibility for this.

Nor can we forget—now that experiment after experiement in totalitarianism has failed—the world-historical murder perpetrated in the name of some world-historical universal, be it the communist utopia, or the Third Reich. Honesty demands the utmost in memorial mindfulness concerning the infernal outcome of human will to power in revolt against God. Compared to the spiritual death of political Prometheanism, the hypocrisies of moralism, the platitudes of a comfortable idealism, and the festishes of epistemological self-evidence, are as mere dull pecadillos.

Perplexity about the ground cannot be extirpated, perplexity that undergoes the experience of being ungrounded. And in all fairness, philosophy at its best always displays what I call the "urgency of ultimacy." I use this phrase to characterize the vector of transcendence that marks being religious[3]; but it is at work in any venture of spiritual seriousness, be it in art, or ethics, or philosophy. Carried by the self-surpassing of the urgency of ultimacy, honesty may demand the very openness, even patient humility of thought before divine transcendence. There is to be no slandering of philosophy.

---

3. See *Philosophy and Its Others*, chapter 3.

There is to be no giving up on the task of thinking what the urgency of ultimacy means. Thinking may even come to a limit where it falls silent. Or it may come to say about its own grandiose systems, as Aquinas said at the end about his own *summa: videtur mihi ut palea*—it seems to me as straw. Mindfulness may increase rather than decrease the burden of perplexity. The thought of God may cause to fade the pretense of all human thought. It fades, not always into nothing, but sometimes into praise. Honesty then means a philosopher must say: my thought is *my* thought, not God's, and before the face of transcendence, it melts like the dream of a thinking reed.

4. Perplexity, Skepticism, God

If perplexity makes it impossible to avoid the question of God, this question is not like any other. It cannot be assimilated to a determinate problem expressing a specific curiousity, one that calls for as univocal a determinate answer as possible. There is no answer to the question of God in that sense, because the matter is not a question in that sense at all. The question rises from an essential and ineradicable perplexity about ultimate transcendence. And it makes demands on our truthfulness that call into question the integrity of our metaphysical honesty. No mere intellectual puzzle, it asks a mindfulness of the utmost discernment, rooted in a way of being that seeks, so far as a human being can, simply to be truthful. To be truthful means that our being must somehow become itself the very living mindfulness of truth, truth that is not simply mine or thine, and that yet shakes what is mine and thine to its very foundations, foundations that are other to everything that is mine and thine. God remains other to our thinking in our thinking of God.

The question of groundlessness comes before us again. Recall an idea previously suggested: That Descartes' *cogito me cogitare* subjectifies Aristotle's self-thinking thought; that this subjectification makes problematical for all modernity the question of what is other to self-thinking thought. Recall also Descartes' hypothesis of the evil genius. Why? The evil genius is the night terror of Cartesian reason, of all reason. It raises the question if perhaps the entire enterprise of rationality is a swindle. There is a horror for reason here, for this swindle might be such that reason could never expose it. Every effort to expose *rationally* the swindle will be itself another swindle. The evil genius is perhaps Descartes' most audacious and horrifying thought. It exposes us to the thought of complete groundlessness. Reason might turn out to be absolutely helpless. Dismay will follow.

To sound common sense, to already secure scientific method, this will seem the madness of hyperbole. One can see it, however, as the extremist impulse of *honest reason*, which calls its own faith in intelligibility into account. Honest reason puts the question to itself: Are reason's grand systematic constructions more than the windblown dreams of a thinking reed? Perplexity as to whether ultimately human knowledge is as nothing is something both epistemological and ontological. It not only taunts the impotence of reason, but also it casts a sinister shadow over our fundamental sense of being as such. The thought of the evil genius is the absolutely *opposing* other to the possibility of agapeic mind and being, and to the thought of the origin as agapeic. This is why we dwell on it.

The dismay that follows the mockery of reason is recurrent with philosophers. Even Hume skirts the edges here. Hume could not finally endure the thought of groundlessness. He had to exorcise the nightmare with a glass of claret and a game of backgammon. He escaped into what Pascal called diversions. His answer to philosophical dismay is to distract himself with entertainment. Reimmersion in the ordinary order of common sense will bring one sweet forgetfulness.

Hume's account of causality in terms of habitual and customary connection raises many questions, but I am interested in its implication relative to something at which Hume himself squints: the radical contingency of being in the world—the fact that beings and their connections are just so, but might well be otherwise. There is no sign of absolute necessity written into things; things might be otherwise. One might seek, of course, to canonize the existing order, and fasten thinking to the brute thereness of things. Alternatively, a different mindfulness might be released before the marvelous thereness of beings, just in the gratuitousness of their being there at all. There can a liberating power in skepticism. Skepticism, perplexity, audacity are kindred. We find no absolute necessity by means of empirical induction. Hence things might be otherwise, might yet be other. Given being need not be seen as just an unintelligible surd, mocking inclusion in a system of necessary categories. It might be seen as the excess of a gift of being, given to be in the finitude of the between. We just find it there, as given by an other we do not determinately comprehend. Beyond the frustration of categorial necessity, there can be the release of a mindfulness that assents to given being as an ontological enigma beyond the measure of all categories.

Whether it crushes or releases, skepticism can be an expression of philosophical truthfulness. One cannot be a philosopher without being a skeptic. Of course, skepticism can take significantly different forms. There is a merely debunking skepticism which would dissolve all positive claims to knowing, exhausting the promise of metaphysical perplexity in reiterated negation. Empiricist skepticism, in its epistemological intent, is hostile to claims concerning God as transcendent. But there is a skepticism that opens up a space for the sacred. Such a skepticism would deconstruct finite knowing to release the possibility of a movement of mind beyond finitude. The lack of absolute necessity in finite knowing generates an opening for the thinking of being as other than finite. Recall ancient skepticism, named by Hegel the noble skepticism. It reveals the nothingness of finitude but thereby opens up the space of relativity between finite and infinite. By contrast, Humean skepticism lacks audacity, since its commonsensical canonization of everyday habits, as well as habits shaped by Newtonian science, consigns the infinite to nothingness.

There is a metaxological skepticism which is tied with the mind's willingness to find against itself, and its efforts to live up to the demand of openness to the other. Honesty about self drives audacity about the possibility of what is beyond. Sometimes the honesty can be desperate. One despairs at finitude, its nothingness, and is provoked to the thought of God as the promise of being being-other. Descartes' thought of the evil genius, and the possible groundlessness of reason, might induce such despair. Such despair might generate a new audacity of thought, turn mind to the question of God as the question of the extreme, the *ne plus ultra* of thinking. This thought of God provides no anodyne but incites perplexity even further.

The desperation in skepticism can surface in proclamation of the ultimate *caprice* of all things. One finds this in Shestov who even says "God is 'caprice' incarnate, who rejects all guarantees."[4] Caprice, after all, will give the hopeless, the despairing, some chance of things being otherwise; implacable necessity will wither such hope. At other times, Shestov does suggest that beyond the eternal, necessary laws of mathematical reason, there is a different sense of the eternal and that providential love is the basis of all being. This may be set in opposition to reason, but it is our reason as instrumental, or impersonal, or self-serving that must feel the lash of skepticism, or the sting of hopelessness. But there is a world of a difference between "caprice" and "providential love." Both may be beyond us, but their mode of being beyond is radically different. "Caprice" can be as crushingly cruel as the implacable necessity that Shestov hates. And what of mindfulness as a love, mind as agapeic? What of the philosopher as a *philos* of truth? Beyond the despair of truth, friends enter a community of trust beyond skepticism. How can we describe the friendship of truth as a "caprice," even though friends do not demand guarantees?

---

4. *In Job's Balances*, trans. C. Coventry and C. A. Macartney, intro. B. Martin (Athens: Ohio University Press, 1975), 82. I admire Shestov greatly, and have been greatly provoked to thought by him. Some of the ideas in the present chapter will appear in a somewhat different context in "Philosophical Audacity—Shestov's Piety," *Lev Shestov: Reason and Volition*, H. Durfee and D. Rodier, eds.

5. Contingency, Absurdity, God

We must further interpret the contingency of finite being. For we can move in quite opposed directions, in reflection of the different skepticisms. Thus, one direction moves towards existential absurdism, epitomized perhaps by Sartre. Contingency is irremediably absurd—beings evidence no inherent reason why they are this rather than that. This existential absurdism is also an atheism, since Sartre's idea of God is of a necessary being who would absolutely determine the structures of finite being, in a manner analogous to Spinoza's God. Hence to affirm contingency and its corollary, human freedom, means to reject necessary and eternal truths, and God as the necessary being.

Like Nietzsche before him, Sartre rebaptizes despair before God as exultant, anthropocentric creativity. Though Sartre is shadowed by Spinoza, there is a world of difference in their ultimate metaphysical commitment. Spinoza evidences Stoic calm and *acquiescentia mentis* in rational necessity—though perhaps the invulnerable calm is itself a vulnerable conquering of despair, as we often suspect with Stoic philosophers. By contrast, Sartre's despair before absurd being seeks alleviation in action rather than in calm contemplation. The "will-lessness" of Stoicism becomes the willfulness of defiant revolt against the given conditions of being. It is no accident that freedom is inseparable from negativity, and that nausea before the given is considered the primordial revelation of being. It is no accident that the later Sartre sought a more than individual alleviation of despair in Marxist revolution of the masses. Flight to the world-historical universal wins out.

In fact, the flight to the world-historical universal is a secular salvation from the contingency. The world-historical universal is made God, idolized. Sartre is only one of many in modernity who have worshipped this idol. I find it ironical that the idolatry accuses the genuine search for God as guilty of its own sin: God is the flight of the metaphysical coward from this absurdity of contingency. I would say: One turns towards God, one does not run away from contingency.

There is another direction of response to contingency. The surd thereness of contingency makes us think less of the absurd than of the marvel of creation. One grants the radical contingency of finite being. Finite being is there; it is given; and the givenness of its being shows no inherence in creation of absolute rational necessity.[5] It is so, but it might have been otherwise, if one were simply to look at the constitutive contingency of its

---

5. A similar consideration, properly qualified, is true of human history, but this is not at issue here.

being. But it is contingent because its origin is other than itself. It is created, not self-created. As created it may exhibit intrinsic structure and intelligibility, but such structure and intelligibility itself is not absolutely necessary, but is itself a creation of the absolute origin. God is the absolute origin, and the being of finite entities is the givenness of a free creation.

As such a contingent creation finite being exhibits its own constitutive intelligibility. Intelligibility is not simply the production of the human mind, or the transcendental ego, or one of its historicist surrogates, or its deconstructing night terrors. This order of intelligibility is not just the neutral atemporal order of the Platonic *eidē*, but a created order that, though it inheres essentially in the intelligibility of the finite world, is not itself absolute or absolutely neccessary. In other words, our choice is not between absurd contingency, the inherent intelligibility of the cosmos, and the radical creation of God. Intelligibility does not have to be identified with dead rational necessity, those "eternal truths" of the philosophers who, like Spinoza, place the God of creation in a subordinate position, a subordination which, in effect, is the denial of God. When Shestov questioned the rational "self-evidences" of these "eternal truths" from the standpoint of the recalcitrance of the absurd contingencies, he sought to reaffirm the God of creation. I am saying that each of these three, contingency, essential intelligibility and God's creative power can be rethought, thought differently. While granting the primacy of the creativity of God, this can be seen as the ultimate source of the inherent intelligibility of creation as itself an originated order, and of the contingency of finite being as the free gift of the origin.[6]

Pascal is one thinker who offers us a religious skepticism concerning inherent intelligibility, understood as the "eternal truths" of the philosophers. He suggests the following: We think of habit as a second nature; but perhaps we ought to think of nature as simply a *first habit*. This might be said to anticipate Hume, but Pascal is much more radical as a skeptic. He has more of the extreme audacity of thought that we later find in Nietzsche. We must break this first habit which might really be a set of chains. Breaking the first habit will serve the release of thought about the ultimate, God. I think we here risk shortchanging the given constitutive intelligibility of creation in our efforts to liberate the thought of God, because of excessive anxiety lest we fall in with those philosophers, Spinoza for instance, who would elevate the inherent intelligibility of nature into a position of ontological superiority relative to God as Creator.

The world is God's creation, not ours; we do not create, we cooperate in creation, and create after our kind by that cooperation. Pascal is an oppo-

---

6. I offer fuller discussion of intelligibilities in chapter 9 of *Being and the Between*.

nent of Descartes but he is also his twin.[7] He does not escape influence from the modern privileging of the human mind as a source of determinate intelligibility. The void infinite spaces of the cosmos are given intelligibility through our habitual categories which, like all habits, are not eternal but merely provisional ways of dealing with things. But these void spaces poignantly named by Pascal are already a *degraded creation*. God's creation is not a void infinity of empty space. We do not have to think of either God or nature in terms of such a vacant infinity. The creative infinite might be seen as an agapeic plenitude, not an indigence of indefinite being. Do we not risk the slander of God if we think of his creation in such degraded terms?

I am not denying some truth to the view that our categories as *our* categories are our habitual modes of thinking that might be altered by different habituations. The question is—Is this all? Are there patterns of intelligibility that are constitutive of the nature of things themselves, regardless of our subjectivistic categories? I think so. Let me invoke Aquinas and by implication Aristotle. Aquinas' third way to God can be interpreted as a meditation of the contingency of the finite creation. As radically contingent, the world of finite beings is not self-explanatory. Hence to remain at the level of contingency is always to lack any ultimate "explanation." Sartre is right so far—contingent being is absurd. But if being is not exhausted by contingency, and if thought is moved to think being as plenitude in excess of finite beings, then perhaps the being-there of beings has its ground in something other than the contingent.

My point is not to subscribe to all the details of Aquinas' way. I do not think we need take God as an "explanation," if we mean some determinate univocal reason why things are thus and thus. God as a merely univocal explanation would be a ruse by which reason uses the idea of God to shirk the deeper ontological perplexity about God. Reason then uses God to allow itself to go back to sleep again. If God is an "explanation," there is a sense in which this answer is darker than the question it answers, because the answer involves a certain extraordinarily complex *acknowledgement* of the mystery of the ultimate. This mystery is the answer, but this answer is no answer in the more normal sense of a relatively self-transparent, rational demonstration. God deepens our perplexity about being, makes mind sleepless, with the sleeplessness that Shestov finds in Pascal, and into which Pascal was wounded by the thought of Gethsemane night. This deepening of perplexity, this

---

7. On Pascal, skepticism and the between more fully, see Desmond, "Between Finitude and Infinity: Hegelian Reason and the Pascalian Heart," in *Hegel on the Modern World*, ed. Ardis Collins (Albany: SUNY Press, 1995), 1–28.

sleeplessness, is closer to the "answer" than all the determinate transparencies of a univocal *ratio*.

I take the ways as ways: *viae* for *homo viator*. They demand a wandering, venturing nomadic thinking that has left the domestic houses of commonplace behind, a thinking that has gone out like Abraham into the desert, not knowing where he is going. The "answer" that makes us wayfarers is a blinding, like the eruption of Plato's *exaiphnēs*. Is this why Aquinas liked to echo Aristotle's homely metaphor for the metaphysician overwhelmed by the truth of the ultimate: bats in sunlight?

There is an excess about God as an "answer" for the groundlessness of contingent beings. In the obscure divination of this excess, contingency becomes a pointer to transcendence, through its own need of the beyond. Aquinas will name this transcendence as necessary, but also will name it as God and identify it with the absolute origin that creates *ex nihilo*. In this regard, resort to God does not have to be interpreted as a running away from contingency at all, but as a way of thinking through its meaning and the truth of its very being: its givenness as there, as open to the possibility of being other than it is, yet as ineradicably being there. Thus, to affirm the radical contingency of being in the world is not to deny the possibility of God. Quite the opposite: it raises questions about the nature of the ground of being, and its contingency and necessity.

If God is beyond our rational necessity, God's unmastered otherness still remains perplexing. Certainly God's "freedom" cannot be assimilated to some putatively arational capriciousness, or to the contingency of created being. Such an assimilation would reduce God to the level of created entities, and hence not preserve the difference of God at all. It would be idolatry. And idolatry, philosophically subtle or fetishistically crude, is what is to be avoided. If God is free, if in this sense of freedom there is a "contingency" in God, this must makes us wonder if some of our cherished presuppositions about freedom and necessity must be shattered. The most genuine of speculative metaphysicians were always threading the "ground" of this groundless enigma, or rather threading water on the surface of this creative abyss. They were not simply concerned to hush up the scandal of divine incomprehensibility by means of an abstract categorial schema, that now becomes the new God of reason, to replace the unmastered transcendence of the true origin.

A radical act of origination, which may also promise a radical recreation, may seem hard to distinguish from arbitrary fiat. In defending God's transcendence, a break is asked with every idolatry of reason that sets up its own categories in the place of living transcendence. Must we not exercise extreme caution, indeed reticence relative to God as the groundless ground? Terms like freedom and necessity cannot be used in any ordinary sense, since the very issue that is at stake is precisely the extraordinary. An idolatry of reason is to be rejected when it tries to make the extraordinary ordinary, domesticate the divine by means of the logic of its categorial system.

Aquinas is just one example who grants the radical contingency of created being, a sense of the divine as the absolutely creative origin of all that it. This last point is so stressed that the word "creation" is reserved exclusively for divine action. Compare this to the modern conceit of dubbing any human making an instance of "creativity," and the debasement of the term "creativity" that follows. Nor is this debasement unrelated to the ambiguous elevation of human "creativity" by modern Prometheanism, and not least by Nietzsche. This audacity of "creativity" debases the meaning of creation.

If in Aquinas, following Aristotle, there is a commitment to the basic intelligibility of being, is God constrained by any necessity? Aquinas would say yes, but add that any such necessity is identical with the divine nature itself. We need here a rethinking of the meaning of freedom and necessity. It is not clear we know what we are talking about. Certainly for Aquinas there is no external constraint on God; in the radical nature of creation *ex nihilo*, God is not a Platonic Demiurge that has to look elsewhere to necessity and shape his making act in accordance with it.

This might seem like a criticism of Plato, but it is very interesting that in Plato's *Timaeus* (48a, 56c) *Nous* does manage to *persuade Anankē*. Plato does not bow the neck in adoration of indifferent necessity. He distinguishes two causes, the necessary and the divine, and says that we seek the necessary for the sake of the divine (*Timaeus*, 68e–69a). The implication I take is that the divine is more ultimate than the necessary. There is an ultimacy beyond the ultimacy of necessity. As we so often find, Plato is an exception that stops us in our tracks, and offers us unexpected food for thought.

6. Will to Power, Creative Possibility, Agapeic Transcendence

Perplexity about being between, about being grounded and groundlessness, cannot avoid the dangerous ambiguity of human freedom. Let me conclude with some reflections on this. This ambiguity can determine how we think of transcendence, not only relative to human transcendence, but to ultimate transcendence.

Freedom is one of the glories and catchphrases of modernity. Modernity is saturated with the rhetoric of freedom. Yet the meaning of freedom remains open. The dominant answer is in terms of the ideal of autonomy as self-determination. This coheres with the erotic conception of being, where being is ultimately made intelligible in terms of self-mediation, self-determination. Erotic freedom is "for-self"; it is autonomy, *auto-nomos*, law of the same. I think this must be qualified by the promise of freedom as agapeic. There is a release of self beyond itself that is not simply for itself. This is free transcendence for the other. There is agapeic freedom beyond autonomy which releases the self into the goodness of the between as the metaxological community of being.

Of course there have been rumblings of disquiet with modernity's dominant understanding of the autonomous self as a rational sovereign that legislates for itself. The rumblings have grown to howls with singular thinkers, like Kierkegaard, Dostoevski, and Nietzsche. Each hated the self-congratulating autonomy that modern Enlightenment man made for himself. Each claimed that this "autonomy" was a lie, a lie that paraded under the high-flying banner of ethical superiority. The idol of false autonomy has to be smashed to release openness to the other. The equivocity of our asserted autonomy is that it is our closure to what is other to ourself, including God.

Nevertheless, the idol can be smashed differently. We can debunk in a way that merely furthers nihilism. While at the end of the twentieth century almost everyone sings hymns to freedom, we find it extraordinarily hard to conceive of the promise that agapeic freedom is. Nietzsche qua atheistic nihilist has overshadowed Kierkegaard qua religious reformer. The destruction of idealistic autonomy has served the return of the human being to the anonymous, sometimes demonic power of the impersonal, call it will, will to power, the necessity of history. We have not been recalled, as Dostoevski and Kierkegaard would recall us, to our freedom as creations of God. And there is a sense in which the choice between Nietzsche and Kierkegaard runs deeper than the choice between Hegel and Kierkegaard. I mean that the hermeneutics of suspicion can make us so intent on attacking classical reason in the figure of someone like Hegel, that we do not always see the worm of *another nihilism* creeping into the human soul out of something like the unredeemed disgust of Dostoevski's Underground Man, or the exaltation of Nietzschean self-deification.

The promise and peril of freedom emerges from the fact that it cannot be reduced to any determinate structure, hence to any determinate intelligibility as defined by a definite structure. There is an indeterminacy to freedom as beyond determinate intelligibility. This is why freedom will always be perplexing: it is always beyond univocal determination. This is the openness of self-transcendence which is a source of determination and is expressed in different determinations, but is not itself a determination. How do we think of this free indeterminacy, beyond fixation in any one determinate condition of being, or aggregate of such determinations?

I propose that this indeterminacy can be interpreted erotically and agapeically. Even though Nietzsche criticizes Enlightenment autonomy, his own will to power is understood in light of an erotic conception of transcendence. By contrast, I am struggling with the thought of agapeic transcendence. In the between, this is always mixed with self-transcending in erotic form. This mixture can mean that erotic self-transcending can itself be sucked into the vortex of nihilism, when it cannot surpass itself towards the other condition of agapeic being. Our efforts to see the difference is also tied to how we conceive of the ground as other, of the origin as agapeic.

The connection of freedom and possibility is here important. Free being shows an opening to being as being otherwise, hence shows being as marked by what we might call "creative possibility." I do not mean possibility in any logicist sense, understood as noncontradictory conceivability with respect to human reason. Possibility as creative is ontological. It refers to the promise of being as concretely offered in the between, a promise that is given, but that is not completely actualized in its givenness. Promise may be a gift that has to be actualized, or actualize itself in freedom. Ontological promise is especially evident with the human being as free. Creative possibility reveals the transcending energy of being itself; in the promise of human freedom, the original power of being becomes freely self-transcending

Suppose we look at Kierkegaard's reiteration that "All things are possible for God." What can "possibility" here mean? We find it hard not to mingle our understanding of human freedom with that of the divine. How we think of one influences how we think of the other, and sometimes with questionable results. Suppose we grant absolute freedom to God. This seems to imply a certain indeterminacy in God. It also seems to imply that we do not quite know what we mean by "possibility," since it is by an act of faith that we must say: "All things are possible for God." What "possibility" here means remains dark. The question is: What kind of possibility is here at issue? Can we think of possibility relative to agapeic mind and being, relative to transcendence itself as an agape of original being?

What is the difference between creative possibility and "mere" possibility? Possibility does refer to what is not yet, and that yet might be; being might yet be otherwise, even though being is not yet other. "Mere" possibility refers to what might conceivably be other, and what is not logically contradictory. Creative possibility, by contrast, refers to the power to originate or effect a movement of transcendence from being as it is to being as it might be as other. It is the originative power to other, in a manner that is not completely determined by being as it now is. But—and this is the crucial point—we can think of this original power to other either in terms of erotic becoming or agapeic self-transcendence.

If we think of it in terms of erotic becoming, possibility will signify a present lack which will be subsequently overcome. Possibility will be other to being as something that is nothing from the standpoint of present being.

But that "nothing" will not be absolutely void; for to be possible it must somehow be; possibility must be somehow creative. Through itself the lack will overcome itself; possibility will possibilize *itself*, so to say. The release of this possibility to make itself possible, and hence to mediate its own self-actualization, I will call "erotic freedom."

By contrast, if we think of this power to other in terms of agapeic self-transcendence, possibility as creative will refer to the promise of a present plenitude that is not now exhausted in its present determination. Out of this plenitude it will give rise to being as other to its present determination. Possibility will be other to present being, but other as inherent in it, as the promise of a fullness that is never exhausted, and that yet is always at work. Creative possibility refers us now, we might say, to the promise of the goodness of being. The language of lack or "nothing" may serve indeed to jolt us out of our sleep in habitual determinations of being, but it is not fully adequate to express the fullness of this promise at work. Possibility does not so much possibilize itself, but offers the promise of the good of being to the other. Its being other than itself creates beyond itself. The release of creative possibility, thus understood, I will call "agapeic freedom."

The above account of erotic and agapeic freedom is compact. It is no easy matter to grasp the difference and what is at stake in it. My aim is not at all to reject the erotic conception but to call attention to crucial ambiguities in freedom when we fail to think possibility in the light of agapeic freedom. Let me illustrate with some less arcane repercussions.

The future-oriented metaphysics of modernity tends to place immense confidence in the power of the possible. This is understandable, if we believe that the future holds the promise of perfection. Often this perfection is identified with the complete autonomy or self-determination of humanity. Our infatuations with various progressivisms, evolutionisms, historicisms, revolutionary utopianisms testify to the bewitching work of the erotic conception. Time is a thrust of becoming towards the not yet, which now is the possible, but which then, when attained, will complete the hopes of the present and the past. Our confidence in the possible allows us to believe we are on our way to the absolute. This will be true even when any mention of the absolute is loudly protested.

But there is the peril of a toxic sting to this confidence in possibility. What is possibility after all? Almost nothing, it seems. . . . And yet. . . . It all depends on how we begin to fill the blank spaces. When we put our hopes in possibility that remains equivocal, perhaps empty, there arises again the danger of nihilism. Without appropriate qualifications, this also applies to the view that for God all things are possible. If God is seen in terms of a privileging of possibility, what guards the indefiniteness from emptiness? What meaning can we give here to possibility? Possibility is either empty, or grounded on the character of being, or revealed through the promise of being as given. The meaning of possibility is determinable with respect to being as already determined, or with respect to the promise of being as an open dynamic process which partially anticipates, hence hints at, its own future form. In a word, there is a privileging of possibility that can easily court an eschatological utopianism, in a bad sense. Utopia is a no-place; but a no-place that can be given no content whatever easily becomes merely an empty hope, that is to say, metaphysical, theological folly. Without some further determination possibility dissolves into the merely nebulous, thence into vacant nothing.

How do we think of the indeterminacy in more than negative terms? There's the rub. One might say "perhaps" or "maybe" to almost any possibility. But if this is the case, can we escape the nihilism of "everything is permitted?" It was Dostoevski, after all, who implied that if God does *not* exist, everything is permitted. By contrast, Kierkegaard and Shestov imply that if God exists, everything is possible. But if everything is possible, there is the risk that the ethical and religious dimensions of the possible are destroyed. Put with maximum conciseness: If possibility is so privileged, then no possibility is actually privileged. The privileging of possibility then deconstructs itself.

Though Kierkegaard repeats that for God all things are possible, he also saw the self-deconstruction of possibility with respect to the aesthetic, as an endless play with possibility. Possibility in itself can be inherently equivocal. The pure play of possibility in the aesthetic seems the promise of limitless satisfaction, but it actually degenerates into despair, if it does not open beyond possibility to the further demands of ethical and religious actualities.

One is reminded of the ambiguous Heideggerian dictum that possibility stands higher than actuality. This dictum is intended as a break with Aristotle, considered as a substance metaphysician. But it is incoherent without a deeper sense of being than actuality reduced to static substance. And the question of God has to be pitched at the level of our deepest conception of being. I think here of Cusanus' view of God as *posse*. If the possible is to have creative power, how then is it determinable apart from what must be the original power of being? Being is not static substance; but if possibility cannot be described apart from some reference to the original power of being (which it cannot if you invoke its creative power), then we are back with the old question of being. Differently stated, if you cannot give an account of possibility in terms that go beyond mere possibility, then possibility becomes a vanishing not-yet, or even a not-ever, or worse, a never-never. The God for whom all things are possible becomes a God for whom nothing is possible. The eschatological utopia of unfettered, boundless possibility is empty. It is not the kingdom of God, but the void apotheosis of man's will to power.

This void apotheosis is, I think, the outcome of an absolutization of erotic possibility, coupled to an occlusion of agapeic transcendence. Think of the equivocality of Nietzsche's condition "beyond good and evil." Can this be identified with freedom? Would we be in a condition like Eden, before the fall into the knowing of good and evil, as if marked by a god's boundless freedom of possibility? But as creatures of the between, we can never be in the Nietzschean innocence of becoming. We are never univocally beyond good and evil. Even in Eden, possibility is constrained by God's command: Do not eat of this tree, for you will die! Even in Eden, a divine command is voiced; we are not "beyond good and evil," but in good before evil. There is a major difference.

Being "beyond good and evil" might easily lead to the idolization of a crushing, amoral fate, all Nietzsche's rhapsodies to *amor fati* notwithstanding. Being "beyond good and evil," one will have nothing to do with the choice of this or that fate, as better or worse, more worthy of the promise of being or dishonorable to creation. By contrast, one might say that agapeic freedom has to do with a condition of being, wherein the good is simply our being. Our being is to be agapeic. The good does not constrain us then, since it is what we are. Through ourselves we will never be thus free, for only God is the free identity of being and the good. Only God *is* agapeic transcendence.

We are in a situation more complex than is initially evident. Once we think, once struck into perplexity, once outside the immediacy of the good, we must move on the momentum of being stricken, and the thinking going with it, to open ourselves to the good, both as other to ourselves, and yet as that in virtue of which we have our being. We can here be aided by individuals like Pascal, Kierkegaard, Nietzsche, Shestov. Their perplexity made them ill at ease with stock views; they are tormented thinkers, awakened to a dislocated condition. They arouse metaphysical insomnia, against the torpor of self-forgetfulness that is satisfied with its own putative powers of autonomy. This is the autonomy that is a lie. If there is a true freedom, it has to be awakened. Sometimes it is more awakened outside of philosophy. But we will not be awakened simply by *any* audacity at all. Indeed our condition of sleep is partly the result of an audacity that, far from agapeic freedom, is an assault on its release.

On that score, in our time the hegemony of instrumental mind seems to be completing itself inexorably. All of being is more and more instrumentalized. Our erotic self-transcending has reached out to being-other and progressively appropriated its difference as other; we have made it to be for the self, for ourselves alone. Having constructed a prodigous cocoon of technological self-mediation, we live in the materialized mathematics of our own production, as the blank screen of the cybernetic age fills with the traces of our own

face. Where are the traces of the divine other? The blurring, perhaps excision of those traces is partly the result of this form of audacity—scientistic,
technicist audacity.

Moreover, our enlightened slumber is deepened, if all we do is applaud the
"success" of the debunking of ethical ideals by Marx, Nietzsche, Freud. This
debunking has helped irritate the pathology of spirit, their suspiciousness of
ethical ideals obscuring the freedom of spirit that is the pathology's cure. The
freedom of spirit of the kind sought by Kierkegaard is jeered at with an intensity,
even more unrelenting than any post-idealistic provocation of the ideals of the
true, the good, the beautiful. At least the latter ideals keep alive the guilty
memory of a condition of spirit at odds with nihilism. Nor does one hasten any
opening up of a space for divine disclosure by accelerating the attack on the
goodness of creation. Not trusting God, lacking trust in nature, one might also
expect us to be wary of ourselves, that is, suspicious of ourselves as suspicious. But
in the place of trust, our aggression on creation has added to the horrors of
existence. This, too, is an audacity, but an audacity that is faithless.

There is then no agapeic release. If there is to be release, the promise of
freedom must be distinguished from any self-glorifying will to power, à la
Nietzsche, or the hubris of instrumental mind. How do we tell the idolatrous
simulacrum from the true original? We must think again about the origin as
agapeic transcendence. We must find and follow the traces of this agape in
being as given to us in the between. By contrast, the self-glorifying will to
power is erotic rather than agapeic: it concretizes its possibilities for-itself. It
short circuits the movement of radical transcendence by always circling back
to itself, even when it passes through the other. The track it follows always
leads back to itself, and ultimately there is no genuine transcendence.

Agapeic transcendence goes forth, pours its creative power abroad for
the other, for the otherness of creation. Nor need eternity be interpreted in
terms of mathematical intelligibility as a kind of dead neccessity. Creation
may be marked by its inherent intelligibility that is not the production of
humans. Creation need not be the degraded world of the gnostic vision, or
indeed the degraded creation that Pascal sensed the post-Cartesian mechanism to be. Creation may be the gift of the agapeic origin, good for itself.
The agapeic origin might be called the "universal God," but this universal
would not at all be what Shestov calls "omnitude." It would embrace the
singular as an ontological marvel, not as an instance of a neutral universal.

We are not "beyond good and evil" but are in the good of creation, good
because a creation of the agapeic origin. Even then the agapeic other can be
the companion that consoles in the evil, the suffering God, the one whose
watch outlasts every other sleepless watch in the world's Gethsemane night.
Even though we sleep, even when we are sleepless, we, too, are watched, or

watched over. There is a metaphysical audacity that seeks a way to such an affirmation of creation as good. But this affirmation would be ultimately meaningless without the agape of the origin. It is the good that is the last enigma, the agape of the good.

In agapeic release there can break through an opening of the good. There is a song of mindfulness that is not simply of Athens, or of Jerusalem, it is not of paganism, or of Judaism, or of Christianity.[8] A soul has been tested to the edge of despair; its perplexity is a weight of enigma that often crushes it; and yet it seeks the good, seeks to be good, and seeks to think of being as good. In the travail of the between, it is pressed into itself, it is torn from itself and stretched between extremes that all but sunder it. And yet it seeks. In its seeking, something is given to it, unexpectedly, suddenly, inexplicably. It seeks because obscurely in its seeking it is being found. It has waited for this. A soul is overcome and sings. It sings it knows not why; but an elemental agapeic mindfulness, a motiveless willingness, leaps in the enigmatic goodness of creation. This is an idiot wisdom. And is not this—this its unpremeditated yes to the goodness of being, and not the self-deification of will to power, nor the harsh cruelty of revolt—is not this yes the last audacity?

---

8. The standard contrast of Athens and Jerusalem is not final here. I am not denying that there are things said in Jerusalem that must make the citizen of Athens wonder. But the minute we talk in justification of either Athens or Jerusalem we are all philosophers and so fallen into the perplexity of the between. Religion is as much a sign of our fall into perplexity, as is philosophy. The faith of unfallen man, or restored man, would be neither of Athens or Jerusalem, neither of religion or philosophy. I do not say it would be between them. It would be other to them, certainly considered as antithetical opposites. There is a way of being between which seems closer to this other way than either Athens and Jerusalem, so far as these are reduced to dualistic opposites.

Chapter 6

Agapeic Being

1. Back to the Between!

We go back to the between once more, to ask again about the ultimate, this time in terms of our understanding of agapeic being.

Who are we? We are not the ultimate. Where are we? We find ourselves in the middle of things. What kind of middle is this? "Being in the midst of things"—Is this locution a mere metaphor without realistic purchase? I think it states where we are. I also think metaphor is inescapable. What about the ultimate, if we in the midst of things? Are we not in a middle whose boundaries cannot be plotted with any absolutely determinate definition? Is not this a paradoxical middle, if its defining extremes cannot be univocally fixed? How do we make intelligible sense of this?

If we take a middle in a *finitely bounded* sense, we can call it a middle, without bad intellectual conscience, precisely because we can stand outside of the middle, and survey the defining limits constituting it as a middle. Let us say that B is a determinate middle between A and C. Because A and C as limits are available for determinate fixation, B is a middle that can be specified and located. But the middle wherein we find ourselves cannot be thus defined or fixed, for we seem unable to stand outside its englobing "in the midst of . . ." This seems to constitute our finitude: we lack a determinate Archimedean point outside the middle that would let us survey its determinate limits. It follows that if all intelligible thinking is determinate, or defined in terms of univocal determination, we must give up talking about being in the middle, as if our talk meant anything of significance. Since we cannot fix the boundaries, there would be no middle.

I reject this rejection, and still say we are in the middle. The fact that we cannot determinately pin down the limits, does not mean there is no middle. It means we inhabit a middle that is open, and with respect to limits that themselves may be open. I know this runs the edge of any definition of intelligibility in terms of specifiable determinacy. What is an open limit? What is an open middle? What is an indeterminate boundary? If there are such paradoxical "realities," do not the limit and unlimit shade into each other? Does not the middle pass over into its extremes, and the extremes pass over into the middle? Does not the bounded pass into the unbounded, and the unbounded into the bounded? Does not the determinate give itself up into an indeterminacy that paradoxically makes possible its definition as determinate? Does the indeterminate provide the ground or background relative to which the determinate comes to definite manifestation?

If the middle we inhabit is not static, we must take these suggestions seriously. The supposition of a static middle seems to require the ideal of a completely determinate specifications of its defining limits. We cannot live up to this ideal, less because of impotence, as because of the way the dynamic middle subverts every such univocal fixation. The idea of an open whole goes hand in hand with this dynamic middle, and below I will turn to two major ways of trying to think of it, beyond univocity and equivocity, namely, the dialectical and metaxological ways. But let me first comment on three major examples of an inveterate tendency to fixate the open middle.

The first example is *one* strategy of Plato (Plato has more than one strategy). The openness of the middle is explained in terms of the indeterminacy of becoming; becoming is equivocal, neither being nor nothing, but something between, neither one nor the other; such equivocal becoming as between is to be ontologically stabilized by the univocal eternity of the Ideas. The Ideas are beyond equivocity, not betwixt or between, not becoming, always the same. They offer the fixed determinate boundaries of intelligibility that make possible the intelligibility, indeed the being of those things, in whose midst we find ourselves.

A second strategy to stabilize the middle follows from a confluence of metaphysics and theology: God as the ultimate is the univocal *Ens Realissimum* outside the openness of the dynamic middle. Here we find the idea of an eternal God who stands aloof from time, absolutely fixed, outside time, never in the midst of what is in process here and now. Such a God contemplates the eternal truths in Itself, entirely other to any putative truth of temporality. Perhaps we might not even want univocally to fix the ultimate itself; we might want to include dynamism in the ultimate. Nevertheless, the manner of this inclusion will be one which closes the open middle. The ultimate becomes a circular self-mediating absolute. As with Aristotle, the ultimate becomes defined as thought thinking itself. Ultimately from the standpoint of such ultimacy, there is no open middle. There is the absolute self-en-closed, self sufficient "middle," in the sense of the self-mediating divinity, thought thinking itself. Variations of this strategy are numerous throughout the metaphysical tradition, from Greek thought to German Idealism.

A third strategy to determine the open middle consists in a turn to the Cartesian *cogito* as an *immanent* determining limit. (The point is relevant, with some qualifications, to appeals to the transcendental ego, whether Kantian or Husserlian.) The *cogito* is not a transcendent Archimedean point, in the sense of the previous two strategies. But it is the privileged point within the middle that in itself is said to yield us a pure self-transparency. As such it is said to be capable of determining the relative determinate transpar-ency of other things in whose midst we are. The *cogito* is not an Archimedean point transcendent *to* the world, but an Archimedean point transcendent *in* the world: an immanent transcendence that will make determinate the intel-ligibility of everything transcendent to itself in the immanent middle that it dominates.

These three strategies are obviously different, yet they share something fundamental: in each the privileged point of reference seems to allows us to master the open indeterminacy of the middle by relation to an ultimate principle of intelligibility. The three principles may be different but each, in its determination of the indeterminate middle, raises the same difficulty: namely, the question of the possible openness of this ultimate to what is *other* to itself.

First, how does the Platonic *eidos* open to its temporal other, if its purely univocal eternity is defined precisely by its self-sufficiency and lack of con-tamination with anything other to itself? Second, how does the God who is the *Ens Realissimum*, or alternatively thought thinking itself, condescend to think what is other than itself? How does it not merely think, but indeed originate and love, bring into being and have the providential care of what is other to itself? For its very definition as the ultimate is in terms of just that retraction from the open indeterminacy of the middle itself, and the other-ness of finite being marking the middle. Third, how does the Cartesian *cogito* escape the circle of its own conceptual solipsism, how is the circle of idealis-tic immanence breached, and an opening to the world of nature or being as other made possible?

These are fairly traditional questions, but all testify to what was not always traditionally recognized, namely, a certain *duplex* requirement con-cerning the ultimate: within itself it must be genuinely unconditional or of absolute nature; yet this cannot be closed in on itself in opposition to the conditioned and the relative: it must contain within itself the possibility, indeed the creative power to institute and constitute its relativity to what is other to itself.

Thus, the Platonic *eidos* is a redundant eternity, if temporal instances cannot participate in it. The doctrine of participation is already an acknowledgment of the second requirement, namely, the relativity of time and eternity. The issue is not only one of defining the nature of participation, but of the being of the unconditional that makes possible a participation of the conditioned in the unconditioned. We are asking not only about a double requirement in the ultimate, but about a *two-way mediation* between the ultimate and what is other to it.

If this double requirement cannot be avoided, we must move beyond the ideal of intelligibility as determinacy. For an ultimate that would be open to what is other to itself, would be an open absolute, hence on a purely univocal logic not an absolute at all. An open absolute would break beyond its own self-determination and not only be open to the relative, but be implicated in community with what is other to itself. But any such thought of a double requirement must inevitably seem paradoxical, if not contradictory, to a pure univocal logic.

Consider the idea of God as self-thinking thought, an idea in some respects the metaphysical and theological apotheosis of univocal logic. In God as self-thinking thought there would be no contradiction, only the absolutely pure self-consistency of mind at one with itself. But what can be the *relation* of such a God to finite struggling beings for whom thought is an intermittent possibility? How could such a God become other to itself, while yet remaining itself? How could it think the other, create the other, and yet not renege on its own inherent absoluteness? How could it be beyond the world, yet be at work within it, in solidarity with the good and the suffering of the creature? There is no way to answer such questions if our thinking is dominated by the ideal of univocal intelligibility. Such questions already initiate a rupture with this ideal. Philosophers have always been drawn to thought thinking itself, precisely because of their will to reduce all indeterminacy of being to intelligibility, considered as determinate univocity. But the above questions asks for a thinking which will allow for the creative power of the indeterminate. They ask about a certain creative openness in the ultimate itself that grounds the promise of a double mediation between itself and what is other to itself.

What about the *cogito* and this double requirement? This, too, proves to be an ultimate that cannot sustain itself in the self-sufficiency of its own circle of selfness. It cannot sustain itself, since a deeper exploration of *itself* dispels the illusion that the thinking self is the complete self-mastering principle of conceptual lucidity. The deeper we explore the self, the less we can hold, as Descartes held, that the self is the thing we know with greatest clarity and distinctiveness. We do know that selfness has an ontological intimacy over which we cannot leap. But this very intimacy is marked by a certain inward otherness that dispels the illusion that we here possess the determinate boundary of all intelligibility.

Of course, we may seek to avoid this insight by ceaselessly generating structures of intelligibility, constructs of mathematicized order to quell the ambiguity of the open middle. But all of this springs from rationalistic horror of the possible vacuum, the abyss that may be the "ground" of all mathematicized intelligibility. Such wearying unweary production of intelligibility is in mathematical fugue from the possibly deeper unintelligibility of subjectivity's own proud productions, its castles of conceptual sand. The more we know determinately thus, the more we have to suppress the open indeterminacy that precedes, sustains and exceeds every determinate intelligibility that we produce.

Of course, there is the even deeper difficulty signaled by Descartes' realization that the idea of God as infinite nests in the *cogito*. This points to an even more incalculable otherness in the idiocy of selfness, more incalculable than the intimate abyssal otherness of inwardness itself. Cartesian and idealistic claims to reduce the ultimate to a single principle, in the sense of merely univocal epistemological or transcendental principle, inevitably fail, because in that single univocal principle the demand of otherness, the plural demand of an intermediation between selfness and otherness inevitably makes itself felt, in a variety of ways. The middle remains open in spite of the single univocal principle, because the univocal principle itself demands a double to make possible its intermediation with what it other; and hence this doubleness is necessary to the constitution of the middle itself. If there is a singular ultimate it cannot be univocal but must be within itself the original ground of really creative pluralization. It must be originally creative of the openness of the middle, its openness in its genuine otherness.

2. Middles, Metaphysics and Metaphors

Finding ourselves in the middle, we think about where we find ourselves. Nor must we think that the middle is an objectified, static space "out there." We, too, have to be thought about, as ourselves a kind of thinking middle. Our very thinking is itself a reflective mediation: it mindfully mediates the initially perplexing givenness of being between. Further, our mediating is itself double: it is a self-mediating in which we ponder our own being; it is also an intermediating with what is other, whereby we seek to come to terms with, metaphysically and existentially, the meaning of being in its otherness. Reflecting on our being as an open, dynamic, intermediating power is crucial to how we think about the ultimate in a sense that passes beyond our power. For within the middle as englobing us, the mediating power we exhibit as living, thinking, loving beings, breaks forth as a desire for ultimacy. Our self-transcending helps define our place within the middle, as does the englobing field of beings in whose midst we are.

Is this an endorsement of the Cartesian effort to find a way to truth through the self? I would prefer to endorse a modified "Platonic" or "Augustinian" way, since the Cartesian way flattens the ontological power constitutive of the self's mediating capacity, and in the long run produces that amnesia about ultimacy discussed on a previous occasion. Why "Augustinian" or "Platonic," since I seem to have rejected Platonism, albeit equivocally, and thrown cold water on the self-sufficient God, said to be uncontaminated by the fevers of time? Plato, however, does offer more approaches than the dualistic opposition of time and eternity. I mean especially the idea of the *metaxu* as related to philosophical eros. One's view of the *metaxu* need impose no static fixation on the middle. The between is rather the field of being in which and through which we have our being, but just there our transcending being is unfolded as the quest of ultimacy. The field of being and our being in that field, both point beyond themselves.

What would one venture about the ultimate, given this pointing beyond? Think again of Augustine's description of the double nature of his own quest: *ab exterioribus ad interiora, ab inferioribus ad superiora.* I understand this to mean that in the midst of things—the exteriors—we come to know the dunamis of our own being as an interior middle. If this is the first movement, the second movement is: in this interior middle, within the self-transcending urgency of desire, we find an opening to the ultimate other. We are the interior urgency of ultimacy, this other is ultimacy as the superior. This superior ultimate cannot be identified with our own erotic self-mediation; it is irreducible to us and mediates with us—the inferior—through the agapeic excess of its own plenitude. This second movement also allows the possibility of a double mediation: our own erotic quest of the ultimate; the ingression of the ultimate as a superior other that intermediates with the middle out of its own transcendence.

The point is not to appropriate the ultimate in its transcendence to human self-transcendence, nor yet to depreciate the energy of human self-transcendence. A complexly balanced togetherness of these two is sought. Hegel's answer can be seen as foil to the view I want to recommend. His answer is: the middle is dialectical. It offers a powerful articulation of the interplay of the two sides, but in the end I think it undercuts the difference between the ultimate in its transcendence and our own self-transcendence. Against this, and to preserve the double mediation, and thus to think the ultimate differently to Hegel, the answer I suggest is: the middle is metaxological. Even in the interplay of the two, there is an excess to the ultimate, and a disproportion between its transcendence and human self-transcendence.

Hegel's criticism of Kant is not without some force: any imposition of a limit on reason is self-canceling, self-refuting; to plot any such limit is already to have surpassed it. Apart altogether from Hegel, I believe philosophical thinking can be defined by this activity of surpassing, this mediating mindfulness of transcendence. Nor is a merely irrational leap into the void implied, as a variety of critics have claimed. Nor yet does an unlimited reach imply an unlimited grasp, as Hegel has been taken to claim.[1] The otherness of the ultimate may entail another sense of limit—a paradoxical limit that cannot be fixed, hence a limit that is an unlimit. Like a horizon that retreats when we near it, this limit/unlimit is never there, there where we claim to master it, and always there, there where we must let it be.

On the one hand, being in the between reveals a certain inexhaustibility relative to the mastery of all our categories. On the other hand, our infinite restlessness reveals the self-transcending of our outreaching in the middle, between finitude and what is other to finitude. This restlessness flowers into that other, second perplexity, beyond determinate curiosity and its correlative univocal answers. So it unfolds and is stressed at the very juncture of tension between these two exigences: to be appropriately self-mediating and hence as whole as possible, *and* yet to be ineradicably open to the other, and hence always to find any closure of selfhood unsettled by the deeper indeterminate dynamism, at work in us, at work in what is other to us. How then do we take this double stand in the middle, avoiding closure of the gap between reach and grasp, and yet not reneging on the intentional infinitude of that reach, in favor of a self-satisfied antimetaphysical finitude?

We seem caught in an aporia: We cannot determinately specify the limits of such a double middle; yet we cannot avoid trying to think the limits. Does this aporia tell us something about how we might speak of the ultimate? It does tell us this, I think: We cannot offer "proof" vis-à-vis ultimacy. Why? Proof tries to articulate a relation of logical necessity be-

---

1. Since I have denied that the "between" be entirely characterized as a dialectical middle, I reject the Hegelian claim to close the gap between the mind's reach and grasp. I say the indeterminate restlessness of mind is best characterized as an intentional infinitude, never as actual infinitude: the difference keeps the gap open; an intentional infinitude marks our finite mindful being as a self-mediating but essentially open dunamis. On intentional infinitude, see *Desire, Dialectic and Otherness*. I distinguish between *intentional infinitude* as marking the mediating power of human selfhood, the *infinite succession* marking the becoming of nature, and the *actual infinitude* of the absolute original that is the ultimate ground of self and world. I argue that the relation of these three infinites constitutes a metaxological community; we do not have just the Hegelian totality, defined as the one infinitude that dialectically mediates with its own finitude.

tween one determinate proposition and another; but what is at stake with the ultimate cannot be a determinate proposition; since we are talking about the very grounds of determinacy, all proof as determinate logos presupposes the question of such a ground, a question generated by a perplexity which is itself beyond proof. Perplexity is aroused, or incited, or precipitated; it is not proved. One might be struck into perplexity. One cannot be "proved" into perplexity. The life of proof itself lives from a perplexity that itself cannot be proved, or awakened by a proof.

Part of what we need is an ontological hermeneutic: to think through, as deeply as possible, the meaning of being, the grounds of its intelligibility, the grounds of our truthfulness to being. A kind of metaphysical *groping* may be far more honest here, than a proof preening itself on its pert precision. In the dark we may confidently articulate our syllogisms, but syllogisms light no candles, and still the darkness enshrouds us. More genuine thought may be incited in this darkness than in the garish syllogistic light of systematic logic.

I agree with Aristotle when he says it betrays a lack of philosophical education to demand proof in everything. I accept this not to hide slyly behind irrationality, but because the matter at issue demands it, and with cognizance of the risks of dishonesty. To refuse proof can be a ruse of mindlessness; but to insist on proof can also be a ruse, indeed an aggression of mindlessness. There is a philosophical mindfulness whose perplexity extends to such a limit that it becomes quite clear that the call for proof is not a sign of our loyalty to reason and logic, but a sign of *not understanding* what the matter at issue is. To insist on a proof might be just to display philosophical mindlessness of the matter at stake. And if we were to talk of "proof," it would have to be as a "proving" in a more extended sense of a "probing," a sense suggested by the Latin root of "proof," namely, *probere*.

It cannot ever do to offer a determinate category of the ultimate, since every such determinate category would be untrue, not only to the indeterminacy of the middle, but to the possibility of a certain constitutive indeterminacy in the ultimate itself. This also follows from the double requirement concerning the ultimate: that it be absolute in itself, yet capable of relatedness to what is other to itself. If we think the first requirement as exhausting the ultimate, we might think of it as completely determinate in itself; but given the second, there must be an openness to otherness ingredient in its absoluteness. This openness cannot be completely determinate. For the completely determinate is just itself and nothing but itself. And while a finite determinate thing might be related to another fixed determinate thing, the relation would be purely external, if both terms of the relation were absolutely determinate. And such a merely external relation is not the kind of relation demanded by proper opening to the other. The opening of the ultimate to the finite other must be indeterminate but in no merely lacking sense.

This implies, I think, an affirmative sense of indeterminacy, and not a mere indefiniteness to be made progressively more definite. It might be better called an "overdeterminacy," with stress on the "more" than determinate nature of the "reality," rather than on the "less" than definiteness of the indefinite. It refers us to the inexhaustibility of a dynamic plenitude, not the static completion of a totally determinate being. Such a plenitude would be ultimate, not by being constituted in the end, but by already being an origin that is full, overfull in itself. Such an ultimate is what I call the agapeic origin.

I will come to this more fully, but how can we speak at all of such an origin? Our "categories" here must have a peculiar character. I prefer to call them "metaphysical metaphors."[2] The agapeic origin is a metaphysical metaphor of ultimacy. Metaphysical metaphors are responsive to what Jaspers calls "boundary questions." Within the boundary, we make intelligible sense of things by means of determinate finite categories. But at the boundary, and relative to the boundary, no such finite determinate category will do. Here we ask about the ground of determinate categories that exceeds complete categorial determination. The very movement of mind in its infinite restlessness to the boundary is itself in excess of finite categorization, precisely as a dynamic movement. Mind as dynamically thinking is in excess of its every determinate thought. Univocal categories crystalize something of this excess into specifiable determinations. But our ability to speak about the movement and the boundary already presupposes the possibility of a discourse that is *not determinable* in completely univocal categories. Metaphysical metaphor is one name for this other kind of discourse.

The question with respect to this excess is: Does the failure of univocity result in a complete equivocity of saying? Is metaphysical perplexity and its groping mindfulness merely equivocal thinking? Is that about which we are perplexed a merely equivocal chimera that univocal logic must exorcise? And is our choice between determinate univocity and indeterminate, in the sense of indefinite equivocity? Not necessarily, and especially if there is an affirmative kind of indeterminacy. If we conceive of metaphysical discourse as metaphorical in an extended sense, we are already beyond this opposition. Nor are we confined to dialectical categories in Hegel's sense.

The following relevant points must be made. A metaphor is not univocal: it does not have one determinate sense, is not reducible to one clear and

---

2. On metaphysics and metaphors more fully, see *Being and the Between*, chapter 5. One needs to speak also, as I do there, of analogies, symbols, and hyperboles. My use of "metaphor," in the present instance, tends to telescope these different needs.

single sense. And while some metaphors are not devoid of equivocity, they can also reveal a richer sense of ambiguity. This richer sense is also a mediation; indeed since it cannot be reduced to one single, univocal sense, it is a pluralized mediation. Metaphor is determining, hence articulating, hence also openly mediating beyond univocity. It is the carrier of a constitutive indeterminacy, which is not any indefiniteness of articulation, but a certain opening of freedom, whether of being or mind. The metaphor carries us beyond univocity and equivocity, fixed determinacy, and inarticulate indefiniteness. The sense of determinacy is opened to what is other than rigid univocity; the sense of indeterminacy is guarded from a merely privative indefiniteness.

In this regard, metaphor is indispensible to speculative philosophy. Metaphysical metaphor is the carrier of our perplexed mindfulness in the middle which does not merely analyze the surface distinctions carried by the categories of ordinary usage, but seeks the very articulating source of these categories and distinctions, an origin which is other to them. A narrowly technicist sense of reason has to be surpassed.

Nor can we remain with the dialectical category in Hegel's sense. This resolves the tension of determinacy and indeterminacy in the following way. The indeterminate is said to be the merely indefinite which must be completely determined; and not externally either, but through its own *self-determination*. The tension is resolved, finally dissolved, by the absolutizing of self-mediation, and the redefinition of the indeterminate as merely privative indefiniteness. The affirmative otherness and transcendence of ultimacy, as an indeterminate *plenitude*, never to be made absolutely determinate by our categories, is not addressed.

To acknowledge this plenitude, without reduction to univocal or dialectical determinacy, inevitably puts a strain on our language. Hence the otherness to everyday usage of the language of speculative philosophy. This does not have to be attributed to emptiness and mystification. Rather the very dynamism of thinking and the matter to be thought, in that these both take us to the boundary, force philosophical language into new ingenuities. To try to say something at the limit inevitably taxes thought and language with an almost intolerable burden. Bearing the burden will make no sense unless mindfulness has already been awakened to the deeper perplexities, made unquiet by a questioning that will not rest short of the extreme, even if it must bruise and wear itself out in its search.

In truth, when such metaphysical insomnia takes hold, it becomes the case that mind sees nothing "ordinary" any more. The "ordinary" as a manipulable region of being, or a familiar aggregate of determinate happenings, ceases to function as absolute. It becomes a pragmatic abstraction, needful to muddle through the twilight of the daily middle. By contrast, it is the metaphysical metaphor that carries the promise of a more ultimate truth. A light has flashed momentarily across the middle, and now the day looks dark, and the things one saw in the flash, make one turn to the dark everyday with a new astonishment, with a troubled groping unfamiliarity. Things, too, were briefly other, are still the promise of being other, though sunk again into the invisibility of everyday visibility.

In the language of the fourfold sense of being, a metaphysical metaphor is metaxological. It involves a complex mindful intermediation between us and what is other, offering no direct possession of the ultimate, but an indirection that is respectful of its enigma. As a carrying across, metaphor is a also a carrying between. Thus the word "*meta*" can mean both "beyond," but also "in the midst." The conjunction of the two meanings points to a sense of the "beyond," the "more" as also moving in, and through, and between the middle. The metaphor carries us through the middle to a beyond that is not the mere beyond of a dualistic opposition. It is a "more," a plenitude as other to the middle, but with an otherness that marks a community, not an antithesis, with the middle. Our indirect or periphrastic approach to the ultimate mirrors the otherness to be acknowledged as other. The metaphor may bespeak some sense of the beyond in the between. It is an image that mediates an open sense of the "more."

Since we are not the "more," nor is our saying, it follows we must not claim *too much* for our discourse. It is well to remember that the etymology of "*metapherein*" also carries meanings of "to alter" or "to change," indeed "to pervert." Every mediation we try risks a deformation. The very communication of the metaphor also risks its perversion into a dissimulation. In the deliverance of the communication, something may have been lost or missed or misinterpreted. Then the promise of rich ambiguity becomes instead deceptive equivocity. Nor is this deception to be chalked up to a transgression of the ideal of truth as univocity. The metaphor enables communication, but if we are devoid of mindfulness, or disseminate our thinking on endless equivocation, metaphor disables communication.

Despite this, metaphor may still allow the original advance of thought. Something new is being said, something other than the already given categories. Metaphor tries to stay with the dynamic intermediation of thought in its encounter and communication with the other and strange. Its "staying true" seeks to be a fidelity to the saying of this otherness without domestication. A metaphysical metaphor (like the "agapeic origin," or the "Good" in Plato), as a "category" beyond finite thought-determination, is a concretion and saying of speculative perplexity. It never just articulates the mediating mastery of our categories, whether univocal or dialectical. For it is open to being *struck* into perplexity by the otherness of the ultimate. And so it also asks for a speculative *suspicion* about its own ultimacy. In other words, it may be the best we have, but the best we have in naming the ultimate is not itself the ultimate. The image images the original, it is not the original. No name is the name, and the best names name themselves as other than *the* name. The best name names its own necessary failure, even in its best success.

Metaphysical metaphor must dissolve the pretension finally to have uttered the final word, for every word of ours is in the middle, and hence carries the trace of an inevitable untruth. This subverts every claim to have the categories to master the ultimate. Yet this very subversion is affirmative in its own way, for it opens the space of otherness once again. To try to say what is ultimately other, there must be opened up some mediation with it, or it must open up some mediation with us. But such continuity, indeed community, as is then opened up, cannot be categorized as a sameness. Metaphor, under the skeptical shadow of this speculative suspicion, rejects the seduction whereby a likeness is turned into an identity. Thus, it rejects the consolation of univocity, without losing all articulacy in nameless equivocity.

We might say that while univocity creates idols of definite names, equivocity matches it with an indefinite fetishization of not-naming. The metaphysical metaphor rejects all idolatry, including the fetishization of equivocity. So also it rejects the speculative idolatry of dialectic when it absolutizes self-thinking thought. We need the image, but every image that takes itself for the absolute original becomes an idol and must be smashed. But there is no need for violence. Of itself every idol will wither into its own hollowness.

It seems to me that every genuine metaphysical speech about the ultimate must be open to the judgment of this withering. It must try to accept the inexorability of its own death. It springs up in the morning, sings its brief middle day, and withers like the grass. A philosopher knows the straw of his own speech. And yet one tries to speak. For though the metaphysical metaphor tries to name the ultimate, or in common language "picture the whole," there is a regard in which there is no picture, nor any determinate whole. We are beyond any framed picture or bounded whole. There is no determinate whole which we can encompass. If we are trying to "picture the whole," this is a paradoxical picturing, since it immediately confesses that every pictured whole must be broken open, every frame unframed.

How can one picture an overdetermined whole, how frame an inexhaustible plenitude, how image an overflowing infinite? Every image, frame, or picture closes the open. Let then our speech be double: an image said, an iconoclasm in the saying; every framing a tentative opening, every success a naming of its own failure. The ultimate other that thought tries to think cannot be reduced to thought thinking itself. Hence, all honest thought must call itself into question, lest it substitute its own thought for the ultimate other that calls for ceaseless thought. Every saying is straw. Some sayings are song. But no saying sings, if not born in the night, that perhaps is the light, of ontological perplexity.

3. Erotic and Agapeic Being as Metaphysical Metaphors

I now turn to two key metaphors of ultimacy in the middle. I do not mean merely linguistic devices but concretions of the power of being at its ontologically richest. A metaphysical metaphor is an ontological image, in the sense of an immanent manifestness of transcendence. Ontological richness refers to the double requirement: a certain internal wholeness or self-determination; a self-transcending power of openness that may even surpass itself towards the other in an unlimited way. Perplexity about ultimacy hovers on the edge of agapeic being. Here we find the promise of the requisite ontological richness: on the one hand, the original power and promise of freedom as internally self-determining; on the other hand, this free whole need not be closed in on itself, though it may be tempted to become so. On the one hand, the promise of agapeic openness to the other surpasses all closed wholes. On the other hand, this openness is relative to the mediation of the other from its otherness; it is not pure self-creation; its creative power may be for the other as other. These two sides must be kept clearly in mind. Because a certain mixture of the two occurs, a blurring of the second can happen with significant repercussions in how we image the ultimate.

Relative to the twofold requirement, erotic and agapeic being are the two metaphysical metaphors I offer for reflection. The first coheres with the emphasis of dialectical self-mediation; the second is consistent with metaxological intermediation, its stronger sense of otherness, hence also its different sense of selfhood.

Erotic being marks desire that reaches out from itself as lacking to the other as meeting and requiting this lack. In the process of reaching out and appropriating the needed other, erotic being come to complete itself, makes itself whole. Speculative philosophers have often been tempted to image the ultimate whole in terms of such a self-completing dunamis. Such a dunamis in itself is initially lacking determination or full realization; it produces itself and produces finite being as other to bring itself to determinate realization. It is nothing apart from the process of self-production, which is also the production of the finite world, or the middle. Its production of the finite middle is its own self-production, such that the finite middle as other is not ultimately other; its being is finally not for itself as other, but for the ultimate and its self-completion.

With agapeic being, by contrast, there is a movement of transcendence that is a going out of self; but it is a going out from being that is not initially lacking, but already full, overfull. It is not a movement from lack through self-mediation to self-perfection, but from perfection to perfection, from pluperfection to an other perfection, not from imperfection to perfection. The pluperfect in itself is overdetermined in an affirmative sense, not in the privative sense of erotic transcendence. As in itself positively overdetermined, the being of agapeic transcendence is open to the origination of the other, which is let be as other. So the giving out of the other is not for the sake of the origin in itself, but for the other itself, as being constituted with its own ontological perfection and freedom. The reaching towards the other of the agapeic being is not the appropriation of the other for the purposes of the self-completion of the origin, but for the support of a community of plurality wherein otherness is not dualistic opposition.

Note that in *both* these views we are beyond the univocalization of being that marks the Parmenidean static eternity and also the Platonic *eidos*. The dunamis of being is preserved in both. But in the first, the double requirement of ultimacy is reduced to a totalized process of self-mediation and self-completion. In the second, the double requirement persists as grounding the community of plurality; the agapeic ground in itself does not ground *itself*, in grounding the community of originated others; rather the agapeic ground as overfull grounds the community of finite others, in the sense of letting the community of others be as free. Without this overfull, freely originating ground there would be no community of plurality. As originated from agapeic excess, the community of plurality does not collapse into the ground as into an absorbing god.

By agapeic being I do not mean the infinitely self-satisfied smile of the Chesire Cat that hides its full richness in invisibility, behind the dangling smirk of condescension. The term "condescension" is traditionally used in connection with the divine agape. We do not have to subscribe to any supercilious self-satisfaction. Agape is not the condescending smile that doles out a little to finite things, creatures of the day. It is not this at all. Note the word *descend*: there is a way down. This is a reversing of the directionality of our own upwardly directed eros. The ultimate other comes to meet us in our search, meeting us somewhere in the middle, assuming even the burden of the middle, its mystery, joy and grief, life there but also death. Such a way down, such a descending would be kenotic, in the sense of an emptying out of any superimposed superiority. We might say the majesty of God does not lord over the creature, as does a tyrant. Majesty is not imposed power, but embrace of the powerless, consent to the powerless and the broken in the middle. Superiority is patience and humility.

Hence, the other word that qualifies the descent: *con*-descend: "*con*" as *cum*, as "with": the descent into the middle is the word of community, of being with the other, even in brokenness and powerlessness. Condescension is a descent into solidarity with the finite other, the community of the agapeic origin with the sorrowing, wasted, evil others, in the midst of things. They, too, are creatures of the agapeic origin, and though blasted or deformed, their very being as a gift constitutes a certain ontological perfection. That they are at all is a certain value, a certain good. They are because they are loved. Even the vile are loved, and are because they are loved. There is a certain horror in this thought for humans. We calculate value on a different scale, not on this ontological scale. But I have moved ahead too quickly and will say more on this below.

Erotic and agapeic being both image "being full," but do so differently. Hence, they differently image the ultimate in its excess to the finite. Since all our talk about the ultimate is from the middle, we cannot avoid this way of speaking. In the history of human efforts to speak of the ultimate, one of the most religiously influential and metaphysically fruitful has been associated with the saying: In his image and likeness God made man. This religious saying already is spoken in the religious middle: imagistic likeness of the ultimate is ontologically constitutive of the being of the middle; imaging is not a mere subjectivistic linguistic projection on being that in itself is neutral to metaphor and to imaginative articulation. *The middle itself as being* is an ontological image of the ultimate. The human self is the mindfulness of the being of the middle, instantiating the same ontological constitution, though freely knowing it, and opening freely to otherness, through this mindful inhabitation of the middle. Man is a thinking image; his being is itself a thinking metaphysical metaphor.

Resort to this image, of course, risks anthropomorphism. The ambiguity of "image" can be turned this way and that, turned up and down, turned upside down or rightside up. This ambiguity goes with freedom of being as an irrevocably given gift. Every saying, in fact, runs this risk. However, the risk has a positive and negative side.

Negatively, we want to avoid an anthropocentrism which reduces the being of the ultimate to human being. Our antireduction comes out in the metaphysical attention we give to what is excess about the being of the human. This excess is the enigma of transcendence in self-transcendence. If self-transcendence is an image, as excess it is an image that does not reduce, but points beyond itself to an even more radical excess of being or transcendence. This image of excess does not pull down the superior to the inferior; rather it carries the inferior beyond itself; it shows the finite self as already beyond itself, beyond itself in a manner demanding metaphysical rumination, not objectifying reduction. It shows human self-transcendence as already drawn upward to transcendence as other.

Positively, the unavoidability of anthropomorphic language may serve to refocus us on the devaluation of being that follows in the train of any objectifying reduction. If the human being is a concretion of ontological richness, being itself may be revealed mediately through the image of the human as not void of worth, as not reducible to an indifferent, neutral thereness.

In fact, this is the double-edge of anthropomorphism. *Anthropocentrism* is a major source of idolatry, false imaging of the ultimate, and also a major source of the historical debunking of questions of the ultimate. Anthropocentrism breeds illusory gods, projected out of human lack, rather than out of ontological richness. "The masters of modern suspicion," Marx, Nietzsche, Freud, will say: gods are made in our image, not we in theirs; in lack, in impotence we project our power on the heavens; but there is nothing there; debunking the other, the power of our being will be retracted to the ontologically valueless middle. Then, and only then, can the human being truly begin to be anthropocentric in a way that is religiously and metaphysically disillusioned. Notice that there is an erotic conception of being here, be it implicit or overt. I mean transcendence is understood as the projection of human power out of its own lack. The belief that transcendence is other to human transcendence is rejected in favor of the *return* of the erotic energy back to the human self, as its origin, middle, and proper end. Transcendence as other is refused, for it shortcircuits or shatters the circle of erotic self-completion.

The ensuing atheism, parasitical on the debunking of religious anthropocentrism, inaugurates a new anthropocentrism: the human being must revalue the inherent valuelessness of things through its own power of being. It is not that there is no ultimate; rather the power of the ultimate is retracted into the power of the human being, and the value of being other is redefined as a function of the power of *our own self-mediation*. The human being is beginning, middle and end, in an ontologically middle that, as other to human being, is completely devoid of intrinsic value. Human self-transcendence is erotic self-surpassing and self-returning; there is no transcendence as other, and no ultimate agape of being, whether in human being or in other-being.

Of course, if the ontological middle is ultimately valueless apart from human erotic surpassing, so also the value of our values is ultimately valueless. For we ourselves, our valuing, our erotic self-transcendence are creatures of the worthless middle. One may twist and turn in the circle of human self-mediation, but if this is the ultimate, then inexorably the ultimate in being is the worthlessness of being.

But anthropomorphism, understood *differently*, can issue in a severe debunking of all anthropocentrisms, whether of the atheistic or religiously idolatrous sort. I mean that in thinking on the image of ontological richness in the human, we discover a *reversal* between the self and the other that breaks open the impotent hubris of all such anthropocentrisms. Such a possibility is granted with agapeic being. Freud clearly could not comprehend what this means. Marx had great difficulty also, since his view of history is grounded on the privileging of conflict, class war, though, in fact, an ethical community of solidarity is only intelligible on the grounds of the promise of agapeic being. Of the three masters of modern suspicion, Nietzsche was the closest to thinking the agapeic origin, though this thinking is equivocal, due to a toxic residue of idealistic self-mediation of which he never purified his thought.

To think through the promise of agapeic being means unequivocal refusal of anthropocentrism, whether tied to the idolatries of religion or atheism. In mindfulness of the middle, a reversal can occur in the human and through the human in which both these idolatrous anthropocentrisms are shattered. The paradox is that through agapeic anthropomorphism the possibility of a non-anthropocentric sense of the worth of being in its otherness is made thinkable. In mindfulness of the human as the promise of agapeic being, the human discovers this reversal of the ground of value from its own supposedly projective subjectivity to an ultimate source that grounds not only the value of the human, regardless of what it does, but of all being simply as being.

4. Agapeic Being and Ultimacy

An understanding of the ultimate as erotic is more widespread than one might think, especially in post-Kantian philosophy. An erotic absolute offers a sense of eternity in process of striving to become itself, in process of determining itself fully in the productions of time which are its own self-production. I would include Hegel, Schelling, Whitehead and process philosophy as proponents of such an erotic absolute. I think Schopenhauer's Will, Nietzsche's Will to Power articulated in the eternal recurrence of the same, Solovyov's sense of the ultimate, the later Scheler's notion of the self-becoming of God, all are variations on the erotic absolute.

Some of this reflects the emphasis on evolutionary dynamism so dominant in recent centuries, and a reaction to the Parmenidean tradition of static eternity which has had a long and deep influence on Platonism and Christian theology. It also reflects a rejection of definitions of the ultimate in terms of the logicist eternity of necessary, atemporal truth. Moreover, any view stressing the impassibility of the ultimate makes problematic the ultimate's ingression and involvement in time. This coimplication was proclaimed by the entire Judeo-Christian tradition, albeit complicated by mixture with the ideal of absolute self-sufficiency, say, of Aristotle's thought thinking thought. In this respect, any erotic absolute, which asserts the ultimate's becoming or evolution or progress in history, recognizes the need to acknowledge some coimplication of the ultimate with the world of the middle. The erotic absolute also, as it were, does an end run around the dualism of time and eternity bedeviling thought about the ultimate since Plato. I suggest that the agapeic absolute also offers a basis for response to these concerns by meeting the double requirement: absoluteness in itself, yet relatedness to finitude. The dilemma seems to be that if we affirm the first, we make impossible the second; while if we affirm the second, we compromise the first.

The erotic conception tries to avoid the dilemma by locating the first—true absoluteness—actually at the end: the absoluteness of the absolute only comes at the end of a process of self-realization; and to get to this end, the dunamis of the absolute has to realize *itself* in and through the finite and conditional. The relatedness of the finite and the ultimate are *necessary* for the absolute to be absolute in itself. Without the world God is not God, as Hegel said. The double requirement is said to be preserved by making the ultimate whole dependent on its own passage, on its own *self-realization*, in and through the finite world.

If the real absolute will only be at the end of this entire process, the beginning is then the indeterminate origin—indeterminate in an indigent sense. We affirm the absoluteness of the whole in the end, but it seems we compromise the true absoluteness of the beginning, since this is almost nothing, without its necessary self-development through the finite and the conditional. Hence the appropriateness of the term "erotic absolute"—eros serves as metaphor for this dynamism of being that moves from indigent indeterminacy or lack of being, through its own self-development, through its progressive appropriation of otherness, to a final wholeness, that is a complete self-appropriation. Nowhere is this more evident than in Hegel for whom the ultimate is this singular process of total self-mediation. Hegel is more consistent that many more thinkers who often think of the ultimate, when they think about it at all, on erotic terms (even Heidegger), without seeing, or being willing to see, as Hegel does, the consequences of this conception.

The notion of an agapeic absolute also tries to meet the double requirement, but in terms of metaxological intermediation rather than total dialectical self-mediation. Thus, it claims to preserve the absoluteness of the beginning by interpreting indeterminacy in a nonindigent sense: the origin is full in itself, overdetermined in itself, inexhaustible. The origin does not constitute *its own* wholeness by a detour through the conditional. Its origination of the conditional and finite is from the agape of its surplus, its pluperfection. The otherness of the finite is not a fall from original unity but a gift of ontological freedom which is let be as other, as good for itself, and not merely as a means whereby the absolute lifts itself up from original indigency to final self-completion. Hence, there is an *otherness* between the ultimate and the finite that is irreducible, but again not in any negative sense. This otherness is not to be described as a dualistic opposition, as in the standard Platonic scheme, a dualism the Hegelian scheme claims to sublate into the self-completing whole.

No doubt, if the otherness of the ground is to be defended, we have to recognize the problem with dualism. The danger with any defense of eternity as time's other, which wants to preserve the real pluralism of the ultimate and finitude, is that it becomes entrenched in a dualistic opposition. This, in turn, tends to produce an equivocal difference between time and eternity without the possibility of mediation. This equivocity itself springs from thinking of eternity in univocal terms. Eternity is the unsurpassable stasis of univocal being, beyond the equivocal mutability of time.

Hegel can be seen to have criticized, correctly in the main, this wavering between equivocal becoming and static univocal eternity. If the view is endemic in traditional metaphysics, even the deconstructers of metaphysics are parasitical on it. Crudely, it is reflected in an oscillation between Nietzsche (equivocal becoming) and Parmenides or perhaps a bowdlerized Plato (univocal eternity). Of course, one cannot have the deconstruction of metaphysics by the first without the rigidification of ultimacy attributed to a standardized version of the second.

The erotic absolute of Hegel is dialectically beyond this wavering. The agapeic absolute is also beyond it, but beyond it in a metaxological way that gives a different accentuation to the affirmative otherness of the ultimate. The metaxological between points beyond finitude, through the intermediacy of becoming, towards the absolute origin as an agapeic other. The agapeic origin, even in mediating the between, lets the other be as other. There is no reduction of plural intermediation to any one singular process of self-mediation. While Hegel also avoids the dualistic equivocity between time as equivocal becoming and eternity as univocal stasis, he dialectically produces his own speculative univocity in rendering the ultimate as the absolute self-mediating whole. Hegel's erotic absolute, initially marked by a certain lacking indeterminacy, must articulate itself in time to complete itself concretely and overcome its initial lack. Time itself is the necessary process of articulate self-development by which the absolute mediates with itself and brings itself to completion.

Thus, ultimacy in itself becomes a mere abstraction, as does any transcendent otherness. Without history, Hegel implies, the absolute would be a lifeless solitary (*leblose Einsame*), as he puts it at the end of his *Phenomenology*. But how can an absolute that in itself is merely abstract and empty, a lifeless monad, be absolute at all? Whence comes the energy of being in the indeterminate lack that necessitates the drive of the absolute into time? This lack in the origin offers no basis for saying that the development of the origin will overcome the initial lack. This must mean that the so-called lack of the origin is not so lacking after all: if self-development shows us the conversion of lack into self-completion, *already* at work in the initial lack must be presupposed the original energy of being, and in no merely lacking sense. In other words, the erotic absolute presupposes the prior energeia of agapeic being. Without this it could never get "off the ground" in its nisus towards self-completion.

Hegel is obsessed with the problem of beginning because of his will to completion, and I think because he is nagged by the suspicion that he has not at all accounted for a true beginning. If the origin is merely indeterminate lacking being, how has he accounted for the true origin? Does not Hegelian dialectic then becomes obtuse to the truth of being as there and the marvel of the agapeic origin? Is not the freedom of the latter replaced with a logical necessity that constrains the erotic absolute to become in time, to become itself in time? But the crucial fact cannot be blinked: the emptiness of the origin haunts the entire process of self-completion with the suspicion of its own final nothingness. The agapeic origin represents a different approach to the problem of dualism, to the preservation of the otherness of the ultimate, to the inexhaustibility of the beginning. The very lack driving erotic articulation is itself only possible on the basis of the prior original energy of being which in itself is plenitude rather than lack. Other than the negative self-determination of an erotic absolute through time, we are pointed to the original energy of being as agapeic creation. Against Hegel's understanding of being as the emptiest of categories, what is at stake relative to the plenitude of the original energy of being is not a category at all. There is, in fact, no category of the creative being of the ultimate origin.

The agapeic origin in itself is not lacking indeterminacy. Its transcendence is more than every determinate being; it is excessive as overdetermined and infinite. Time is not originated to concretize the necessary determination needed to fill up its own lack as origin. As origin it is not the indeterminacy of lack, but the affirmative indeterminacy of inexhaustibility, the overdetermination of plenitude in itself. The agapeic origin defines the absolute as absolute in itself, such that in allowing it to be other to finitude, there is also allowance for finitude to be other in itself.

Agapeic creation would be the giving of being to the other that lets that other-being be as other. Finite being is let be as irreducibly other. For the agapeic origin, to be *itself*, does not have to recover finite being for itself. The middle between origin and finite creation can never be entirely mediated in terms of self-mediation alone, whether from the side of origin, or of creation. In agapeic creation, the freedom of the other as finite cannot be reduced to the self-mediation of the origin. The being of the finite creation is given its irreducible otherness in agapeic creation. This ontological freedom undermines any monistic claims concerning ultimacy as an absorbing totality, relative to which plurality is depreciated.[3]

The ancient problem of the one and the many receives a particular interpretation here. At one level, the erotic absolute, in its difference to the stasis of univocal eternity, seems to signal an embrace of the many, of time, of heterogeneity. At another deeper level—and precisely because erotic being finally privileges the same over the other—it seems to me that every version of the erotic absolute finally remains enclosed in the embrace of the one. The ghost of Parmenides continues to walk. This is so with Hegel, as I have tried to indicate. Parmenides' ghost, albeit in Dionysian dress, even haunts Nietzsche, especially the younger Nietzsche, still shadowed by Schopenhauer's monism of the dark origin, Will as the metaphor of the ultimate.

The older Nietzsche, I also believe, provides his own variation on monism. Thus, he describes will to power as a monster of energy, without increase or decrease, eternally circulating within itself, wherein plurality and difference and the multiple configurations of heterogeneity are concretized.[4]

---

3. See *Being and the Between*, chapter 6, "Origin," and chapter 7, "Creation—The Universal Impermanence" for a more systematic account in terms of the fourfold sense of being.

4. *The Will to Power*, trans. W. Kaufmann and R. J. Hollingdale, ed. W. Kaufmann (New York: Random House, 1967), 549–550. The passage is worth citing: "And do you know what the 'world' is to me? Shall I show it to you in my mirror? This world: a monster of energy, without beginning, without end; a firm, iron magnitude of force that does not grow bigger or smaller, that does not expend itself but only transforms itself; as a whole, of unalterable size, a household without expenses or losses, but likewise without increase or income; enclosed by 'nothingness' as by a boundary; . . . as force throughout, as a play of forces flowing and rushing together, eternally changing, eternally flooding back, with tremendous years of recurrence, with an ebb and a flood of its forms; out of the simplest forms striving toward the most complex, out of the stillest, most rigid, coldest forms towards the hottest, most turbulent, most self-contradictory, and then again returning home to the simplest out of this abundance, out of the play of contradictions back to the joy of concord, still affirming itself in this uniformity of its courses and its years, blessing itself as that which must return eternally, as a becoming that knows no satiety, no disgust, no weariness: this, my *Dionysian* world of the eternally self-creating, eternally self-destroying . . . my 'beyond good and evil,' without goal, unless the joy of the circle is itself a goal; without will, unless a ring feels good will towards itself—do you want a *name* for this world? A *solution* for all its riddles? . . . This world is will to power—and nothing besides! And you yourselves are also this will to power—and nothing besides!"

For further discussion, see my "Rethinking the Origin: Hegel and Nietzsche."

The monster of energy pulses with a immanent rhythm not unreminiscent of the flow of dialectical unfolding. Nietzsche reminds us of a kind of lyrical, intoxicated Parmenides in such descriptions. He is, if you like, an heir of the poetizing Parmenides, not of the logicizing Parmenides. He even countenances the "teleology" of the whole. In no sense is this a determinate teleology of any finite end. It is simply the inalienability of the process of the whole from itself. The goal of the monster of energy, if one can call it a goal since it is not a finite objective, is the love of the ring of eternity *for itself*. This circuit of eternity which unfolds as the heterogeneity of the will to power in time itself, and *always seeks itself* in this circular unfolding, is the very rhapsody of an erotic absolute.

Aristotle says pithily that "the least number, strictly speaking, is two" (*Physics*, 220a27). How do we get from a one to a real two? Can Hegel, for instance, with his glorification of the number three, even count to two? Is not Hegel, when he dialectically counts to three, finally counting back to one. The third turns out to be the first, for the second, in dialectically turning into the third, also turns out to be the first. Three turns out to be one, two turns out to be one, Hegel does not finally count beyond one at all. Everything "beyond" one is finally for the sake of the one, and is dialectically bound to return to the embrace of the one. There is no real transcendence of the one for the second as irreducibly other. There is erotic transcendence for, to put it briefly, *the one itself in the one as othering itself*.

If this is Hegel's dialectical monism, Nietzsche's rhapsody of Dionysian eros does not get us much further, in its ability to account finally for *more than the one*. In many ways, Nietzsche leaves us less well off than Hegel, relative to the clarity with which we can see the problem. Nietzsche's inability to account for more than the one is fuzzied because, on the surface, there is an excess of rhetoric about plurality. But if the whole as ultimate is will to power, and if the will to power is as Nietzsche describes it, there is *nothing but* will to power, as Nietszche himself joyfully sings, and there is no ultimate basis for real plurality, otherness and transcendence.

To allow counting to two, counting for two, the second has to be given, beyond self-mediation, by a genuinely self-transcending one, given its genuine secondness by the first. What kind of first would that be, that lets the second be as a second, as really other? The agapeic origin would be such a first. It would not merely give the second as *its own* double, but would give the second its secondness as *for itself*, and for itself *in its otherness* to the first itself. Such a doubling cannot be reduced to self-doubling, whether of Hegel's Idea or Nietzsche's will to power. It is the basis of a metaxological community between the origin and created being. The doubling is not absorbed back into the one, but redoubled, first through the one, and then through the originated other, and then again by the original one for the originated other.

This redoubling of doubleness, without return to closure in the first, would be the openness of actual infinitude. Plurality itself becomes the generosity of creation, the irreducible gift of the agapeic origin. The gift is not given for the one, or for a return to the one, but for itself, for the *very goodness* of finite being, and this apart from any return it might make. The goodness of finite being in just this givenness. The agapeic origin is thus the ground of a between that is genuinely nonreductive of plurality, even while it allows the intermediation between the one and the other.

For us humans this is a hard, well nigh impossible thought. To make sense of it we must have some inking of the transfiguration of being demanded by agapeic mind. We humans make a gift and secretly expect some return. We cast our bread upon the waters. . . . and we think joy comes in getting more back. We find it almost impossible to give for nothing, expecting nothing in return. The agapeic origin casts its bread but asks for nothing in return, constrains nothing, but lets it be, lets it be in its promise, loves it to be in its real otherness. Its cast of being is from its joy, flows forth from its agape. This is a freedom of being that we find all but incomprehensible and unbearable, since its why cannot be fitted into any finite teleology we construct: the giving of being has no purpose beyond the goodness of giving, and of the being given. We might say: God's generosity is horrifying to our rational prudence; relative to our prudence it seems purposeless; there is no determinate purpose to being. If being were reduced to finite determinate purposes, being would be ultimately purposeless, absurd. Ultimate generosity is "purposeful" beyond every finite purpose.

Being is given. It is good as given. Strange to say, this goodness of creation is not altogether unlike Nietzsche's innocence of becoming, though Nietzsche could not see this. This means that God's generosity is horrifying, since it seems to suggest: All is permitted. Freedom means all is permitted. It also means that not all that we do is good; for little of what we do lives up to the promise of freedom, which is the originative being of agapeic generosity. The metaphysical difficulty of thinking the agapeic origin stems from our disability of being, our own being as the living lack of agapeic generosity. We fail to understand an unconstrained gift. For us its excess is too much, something for nothing, purposive in its purposelessness beyond all our finite purposes.

5. "It Is Good"

In regard to the devaluation of being, may I be permitted to say something about the astonishing saying: "And God saw that it was very good?"

The saying calls to mind the issue of what sometimes is referred to as the "integrity of creation." This is an issue made all the more urgent by concern with the ethics of nature in a time of pervasive ecological menace. A term like "integrity" implies that we can speak of nature as in some sense a "whole." A term like "creation" suggests an originative source that grounds the world as a whole. We often use the terms thoughtlessly, but any properly mindful use of them takes us to a limit. When the value of nature is at issue, the extreme question is: Does the "integrity of creation" imply an inherent value to being as a whole? Is being in itself valueless? Do we have any ground for affirming that being, hence finite beings, in some sense, manifest a certain ontological perfection that is the prior basis of ascribing a more usual sense of value to them, the value we give to them? Does the value we give to things presuppose a prior sense of value that inherently marks the creation as an integrity that is for itself, before it is something that is for us?

This way of talking has not been dominant in Western thought for centuries. Leibniz is an evident exception in his refusal to discard final causality, and his desire to link finality to the question of the origin. This hearkens back to premodern modes of thinking about the being there of beings. The fact of being, considered purely as a contingent fact, carries no special weight, unless we also manage to see that fact of being in relation to the possible goodness of being. Modern science dismisses teleology from its explanatory scheme of things and confines itself to determinate forms of process, regularity, correlation and so on. But if we do want to talk about the "integrity of creation," we have to raise not only the issue of ends, but also that of origins. We require an archeology of value as much as a teleology. I am not talking about the value of things for the human being. I am talking about the goodness of being or beings *simpliciter*.

The spectre of nihilism arises again, nihilism in its widest and deepest extent. It might seem odd to cite Nietzsche, Nietzsche notorious for his hatred of any hint of a metaphysical, or theological resonance. Yet Nietzsche did see what was in jeopardy. He saw that modern science and culture effectively lead to a neutralization of all being. They lead to a deadening of the earth. The resulting nihilism means that nothing really matters in any ultimate sense. Hence too the values necessary for us pragmatically to survive, even prosper, themselves have no ultimate ground at all. The "integrity of creation" raises just this extreme issue of the ground or groundlessness of all value.

Nietzsche himself, having granted the ontological groundlessness of value, claimed to reground value in the transformed will to power of the "creative" human being. Nihilism is tied to the banishment of inherent ends by scientific reason. Nietzsche accepted this banishment—there is no ontologically constitutive value in being as a whole. But his further rejoinder to nihilism cannot avoid a new nihilism. If the integral character of being is devoid of inherent value, Nietzsche's claim that human beings, even the coming supermen, are the only source of value, ultimately also leads to the nihilism. We protect ourselves against nihilism by claiming the human being to be the source of value. Then we remember that human beings, albeit originative, are themselves participant in the larger process, hence also devoid of any inherent value. The house of cards collapses.

Otherwise put, if we are participants in the "whole" as inherently value-less, ultimately we are ourselves valueless parts of the valueless whole. Our projection of values on the void cosmos is mere metaphysical whistling in the dark. Our constructions will eventually be engulfed by the valueless, purposeless whole. Our constructions turn out to be self-serving, perhaps self-deceiving ruses that incoherently claim to give value to being. In sum: if being itself has no value, we can give it no value, for our own being itself, and everything we do, including our giving of value to being, ultimately has no value. The human giving of value to being is finally without value. Nietzsche sought a transfiguration of being by a transvaluation of values. He wanted to recharge the world with a sense of deeper worth. But we cannot do this, if the world itself is not marked by, or inherently hospitable to value. The "integrity of creation" must itself provide the basis of this transformed evaluation.

Again metaphysics and ethics are inseparable. Without proper meta-physical ground, ethics is groundless. You will object that we need to be less ambitious: that within our limited sphere we can construct relatively coher-ent systems of value that pragmatically get the job done. This is all very true in its own prudent way. But the philosopher is an extremist who will not desist until he has pushed the question to the ultimate. Sometimes the ex-tremism leads to bad folly. Now and then it leads to a touch of wisdom, divine beyond the domestic prudence of sound common sense, or science. Pragmatic truth is necessary for day to day survival and flourishing. But some pragmatic truths may be metaphysical lies. They may be necessary meta-physical lies, but a lie is still a lie. We may need lies to live, but philosophers should at least try to be honest about this. Philosophers should not force us ("reason demands that. . . . ") to sing hymns to metaphysical lies, method-ologically canonized as pragmatic truths. The capricious Nietzsche was supe-rior in his honesty here, that is, in his divine folly, to many a more prudently cautious thinker, including his host of followers.

I am not singing a hymn to Nietzsche. Yet his extremism is superior to the modest analyst of concepts. Let the latter sharpen his analytical tools, this will have minor effect. Lockean underlaborers and their contemporary kin can labor under the grandest delusions of banal modesty. The earth is on fire and the philosopher sharpens his analytical tools. There can be some-thing monstrous about having an intellectual good conscience about this. The sharpening adds a few meager sparks to the fire.

Nor am I singing a hymn to the extremism of *rational hubris*. Consider again how the idea of "integrity" calls to mind a certain wholeness. Question: If creation has an integrity, who is on a par with this "whole?" Again do we not find ourselves in the middle of things wherein none of our efforts can completely overreach the extremes? If we are driven to think the extremes, this thrust to the limits is from the middle. Hence, we must take due care in how we move from the middle towards the extremes.

One important source of our impasse is precisely in certain rational efforts to totalize nature. On a previous occasion I mentioned the Cartesian project of making ourselves "the masters and possessors of nature." Descartes looked for the Archimedean point from which the "whole" could be surveyed, perhaps subject to a quasi-mathematical method. Creation will be *made* an "integer" by being subjected to human *ratio*. As in the middle of things, the thinking thing claims for itself the rational power to mediate the meaning of the whole. Descartes proves to be Nietzsche's twin: he mathematicizes the will to power where Nietzsche rhapsodizes it. The "integrity of creation" is dissolved in this project of hubristic *ratio*—the subjection of the world's ambiguity to the univocity of mathematical determination. "Integrity" as a certain ontological wholeness marked by its own perfection becomes reduced to rational univocity, with no place whatever for ontologically constitutive value. Again this conquering of nature by mathematical univocity is only possible by the exclusion of ends from nature. The human being of *ratio* makes himself the beginning, middle, and end. The otherness of nature is homogenized into a neutral *res extensa*. And we recur again to the problem of nihilism.

Have contemporary philosophers of science, while dissatisfied with the Cartesian outcome, done better? I do not know of any contemporary philosopher of science who has adequately addressed the issue at its proper ontological level. The majority of philosophers of science seem blissfully unaware that there is a problem at all, even when they sing new rhapsodies to the post-Einsteinian cosmos. I do not find the precise question asked: How does the cosmos, as described within the current science, offer the ontological basis for such cosmological hymns? Does the account offered of the science help us make sense of this basis? The ground of value in being, the ontological basis of the value of being itself, is not addressed at all. (There was more serious debate of this issue in the nineteenth century, when the tension of science and religion was more explicitly to the fore; something has been attenuated by the indifference to this tension in standard philosophical discourse today.)

It should be clear that we find little help from deconstructionists. They do help us be wary of totalizing claims. But "integrity" need not be totalizing. Our thinking of the middle must allow the "integrity of creation" as an open community of plurality that cannot be reduced to univocal manipulation. Moreover, such integrity makes us ask about an ultimate other that in some way "integrates" the community of being. The human being cannot do this in the sense required, since it is always in the middle. The other that "integrates" the community must be an originative source of being in excess of the community that comprises the integral creation. The openness of the finite creation suggests its own ground in an absolute origin that is the creative source of all that is.

How seriously do we take the word "creation?" On a previous occasion I said that we now use "creativity" almost indiscriminately, so banalizing it as almost to empty it of meaning. Nevertheless, the word has powerful implications. In any proper sense, creation must entail reference to an originative source that is creative in a more ultimate way than the product of its own creative activity. Even in Romantic and post-Romantic notions of *self-creativity*, we find reference to a source of creativity in the self that is other to its created products, even the richest. Self-creativity implies reference to the inward otherness of the source of creation in the self itself. What of the world as a creation? Traditionally the world was seen as the outcome of an act of radical origination, itself bound by nothing. Whether we can give a rational account of such radical origination is a major question.[5] Yet any talk of creation puts us in a horizon that is more metaphysically charged than the neutral "cosmos" of modern science. Finite beings are defined by reference to something beyond themselves; the finite whole is not self-explanatory; its being, its intelligibility, its value, its ultimate truth are by reference to an ultimate other. There is no such thing ultimately as a neutral metaphysical framework. Even the putative value-neutralism of science is itself a value and fuels the construction of a series of evaluations, which on the premises of the stated view are ultimately unintelligible. Value is unavoidable.

The question come back again: How can we speak of such value as intrinsic to being? The language of "creation" points in a direction which cannot stop short of metaphysics, indeed a certain theology. Creation is good because to be is to be a value; to be a value is to be so because one is valued; but who is the one that values the creation? The most radical answer is that the origin does. Do not now close your ears, as if this were some childish piety that we adult philosophers have outgrown. The view that a being has both its being and value because it is valued in some ultimate sense is an astonishing conception.

I recall again Plato's belief that no proper accounting of things is really possible outside of some invocation of the absolute Good. I know this

---

5. See *Being and the Between*, chapter 7.

invocation gives no determinate explanation of a determinate happening. But that is not its point. What is at stake is a sense of being as a whole, not the determinate intelligibility, or indeed determinate value, that marks this aspect of being, or that specific entity. Outside of some unsurpassable sense of the worth of the whole, the human passion to make sense of things remains unanswered. The invocation of the absolute Good names a kind of positively indeterminate horizon within which we begin to look at things differently.

Consider now the saying: "It is good, it is very good." God does not say: I am good. He does not say: It is good for this or that purpose. He does not say: It is good for this thing or that being, say, the human being. A primal original "yes" is spoken: It is good. *It* is good, good for itself. It is as if the Creator, in giving being to the creation also gave it its value for itself. Anything we humans do subsequently follows in the train of this first absolute amen to the goodness of being. To comprehend the meaning of this amen is almost impossible for us.

"It is good." This not to deny the pragmatic fact that we often exist in hostile relations to other things. These things, like the mosquito that brings malaria, are not evidently good *for us*. This is the thought here: the good for us presupposes a more primordial sense of the goodness of being; this we must acknowledge and take into account in the ethical mediations we devise with others beings. Being other does not need the justification of our evaluation for it to be good. To take to heart this prior "It is good," demands an interpretation of the derived good for us that is significantly different to any view deriving from an ontologically neutral basis.

I am not denying the mystery of iniquity. The good for us, even in relation to the prior "It is good," does not preclude the possibility of tragic loss and metaphysically enigmatic evil, or suffering, or moral vileness. In fact the disjunction, even hostility between the "for us," and the "It is good," creates the space of freedom wherein the human being "for itself" can assert its "for itself" in refusal of the prior "It is good." This space offers the sinister opening of evil. A granting of the prior "It is good" may also offer the basis for a different benevolence to being, in our determination of the good for us.

It is extraordinarily difficult even to approach the mindfulness needed for this. Being has been so thoroughly instrumentalized in modernity that the mind-set we inhabit is sometimes a prison-house of assumption. Neutralized of any intrinsic value, being is made a means to an end, namely, to serve our desire, flattened into something that only is for us. The ontological yes of the "It is good" is silenced. The limits of this instrumentalization have now become evident—even for us. True, much discussion of, say, the ecological crisis seeks a new, more effective instrumentalizing. We would devise a new instrumentalizing to hold in check, or avoid, some of the worst consequences of our old instrumentalizing. And yet everything remains instrumentalized, everything a means to an end—for us.

This total instrumentalizing again means nihilism. And it does no good to say that the human being is the only end in itself, if there is not a deeper sense of goodness on which the human being is grounded. All such well-meaning efforts to preserve our special place within the valueless whole ultimately fail. I might be laughed at for invoking God. But why not laugh at the claim that the human being is an end in itself? Kant, for example, sweated with anxiety lest God be introduced as a *Deus ex machina*. He did not sweat as much as he should have, when he introduced man as an end in himself. The *homo ex machina* slips in too easily. I repeat: If the whole is valueless, then the human being as part of the whole partakes of this basic ontological valuelessness; and every assertion of his special place really carries no ultimate weight. The human being becomes a this-worldly *deus ex machina*. The value of being, and indirectly the value of the human being, has to be thought in relation to an other origin of value.

The confluence of ethics and metaphysics requires a metamorphosis in our thinking. Possibilities of such thinking were less repressed in premodern thought than in modern, where this instrumentalizing is carried forward with an almost unstoppable momentum. This thinking otherwise is more often carried by the images of religion than by the concepts of the philosophers, or the theories of the scientist. These concepts and theories purport to give rational enlightenment, but relative to the value of being they can produce the muting of the voices of the earth. We need a new sense of the sacramental earth.

What I mean, in part, is that the "integrity of creation" suggests the "wholenesss" traditionally ascribed to the work of art. We need not accept the deconstructionist debunking of "wholeness," while granting the suspicion of totalism. Consider how, relative to the work of art, "wholeness" and "integrity" resist being identified with totalism. The great art work is an open whole that may be inexhaustible relative to complete analysis. It creates its own rich world, but this world concretizes the suggestion of what is other, and hence is not a closed whole. It communicates reference to its origin, and hence to an other that is not completely enclosed within the work. Such creative integrity is an intimation of transcendence as other. Creativity itself can be seen as the expression of the generosity of being. Creative work issues from a plenitude of originative power that would give the work for another.[6]

---

6. See *Philosophy and its Others*, chapter 2, on the fact that this is not the negative debunking of the other, the kind of "creativity" that we find in post-modern parody—post-modern "creativity" as parodic is parasitical on the creativity of another. Also see *Art and the Absolute*, chapter 6.

Can we think creation as like a "work of art" in this double sense: a whole unto itself that yet is open to its own origin, as other to itself? We cannot "prove" it is so. We have no determinate, univocal proof. We do have images, and metaphysical metaphors. These give articulation to our prereflective and nonobjective sense of transcendence, and the "whole." They also are suggestive for the question of ultimate value. Aesthetic value is a form of metaphysical value: the value of a work of art is not merely instrumental. The majesty of the great work is that it is the concretion of its own intrinsic value. It is good for itself, which does not mean that it is closed in on itself. Nor is its value a projection of a controlling subjectivity; *it* is good. Perhaps we should say that the work creates a space of free value that emerges for contemplation in the creative interplay of the artist and work, and then of the beholder and the given work.

The sensuous being there of the world can evoke a metaphysical astonishment that is akin to the complex delight, not devoid of troubled thought, aroused by a great work of art. The world, the work is appreciated. It is valued for itself, and in itself, as we experience a liberation of mindfulness towards its worthy otherness. Premodern philosophers and theologians often were mindful of the being of creation as like to such an art work, and less closed to modes of metaphysical admiration.[7] Their basis in being is emptied out in the Cartesian *res extensa* and its heirs, like the primary qualities, devoid of the so-called subjective value of secondary qualities. Certain contemporary scientists want to reaffirm this metaphysical astonishment before the intelligibility and order, and indeed beautiful design, in the cosmos.[8] They seek a wholism that repudiates merely mechanist explanation. For one cannot love a clockwork cosmos; we neither live nor think in such a cosmos. Astonishment before the cosmos points to a ground of ethical, metaphysical, and aesthetical value that no clockwork mind, not even a cybernetic mind, can comprehend.

This astonishment demands a rethinking of the community of aesthetical, ethical, and metaphysical value. Philosophers have the responsibility to pursue the large questions, the extreme questions. We are now so *in extremis* relative to nature that we need radical and extreme thinking: radical as going to the roots or origins; extreme as going to the ultimate ends. Such thinking is not closed to possibilities that have been taboo to most post-Enlightenment intellectuals. We have drawn a chalk line on the earth, and we have cast some holy spells on this chalk line, and henceforth find it impossible to

---

7. I mention the Pythagorean sense of "cosmos," and the Stoic *"sumpatheia ton holon,"* where the aesthetic, the ethical, and the metaphysical resonate with each other.

8. See, for instance, A. Zee, *Fearful Symmetry: The Search for Beauty in Modern Physics* (New York: Macmillan, 1986).

walk past this line. Our Enlightenment and post-Enlightenment taboo on the thinking of God is one such chalk line.

We must now break the taboo and regain the passion of ultimacy, the last outcry of which was perhaps uttered by Nietzsche's Madman. We have not done very well this century. Idolatry stalks thought: the idolatry of the instrumental mind; the idolatry of the mind of reductive analysis; the idolatry of itself of the mind that supposes itself superior to all idolatry; the idolatry of totalizing mind we find in Marxism and Hegelianism; the idolatry of the fragment we find in deconstructive thought; the idolatry of no mind that marks various irrationalisms exasperated by the burden of thought. And each idolatry asleep to the perplexing enigma in those words that will smash every idol: "It is good, it is very good."

6. Agapeic Giving and the Good

I am sometimes visited by the mockery of Dostoevski's Underground Man when he sneered: If man is not stupid, then certainly he is monstrously ungrateful! Agapeic being? Come, come! Lear learned about ingratitude from his daughters and paid for his folly with madness. Agapeic being? Come now!

I did say before that being agapeic is almost an impossibility for us. We are spiteful, grasping, thankless. And if there is something monstrous about the Underground Man, there is also, it seems, a monstrous audacity in the thought of agapeic being. That audacity drives us to think of agapeic being in relation God. How then might the matter look?

We would have to break with any dualism of being and the good, and any divorce of ethics and metaphysics. Consider how Levinas, for instance, claims that the concern of traditional ontology with being ends in a philosophy of power and a subordination of the other to the same. He does grant that what he calls "metaphysics" allows for the other as other. Plato's Good beyond being is invoked by him, and the claim is made that metaphysics in his sense must become an ethics of the other.[9] What I call erotic mind and the ontological outlook going with it might be correlated with what Levinas calls "ontology." By contrast, agapeic mind is related to metaphysics. But agapeic metaphysics is a philosophy of being, agapeic being. Contra Levinas we do not need to dualize being and the good. It is crucially important not to do so. If the ultimate is agapeic, it is the good. To be is to be good. Absolute being is the agapeic good.

---

9. See my article on Levinas in *Routledge History of Philosophy Volume VIII: Continental Philosophy in the 20th Century*, ed. Richard Kearney (London and New York: Routledge, 1994), 156–168; also "In Reply," *CLIO* 20: 4, 1991, 393ff.

If we think of God as agapeic being, God could not be defined just as thought thinking itself. The latter suggests the closed circle of absolute self-mediation. Ultimately it stems from an understanding of the good primarily in relation to erotic being. By contrast, agapeic mind makes way for the thought and the being of the other, beyond the circle of thought thinking itself. Every closed circle is broken open. Moreover, the model of exit and return, *exitus* and *reditus*, *monas*, *prohodos*, and *epistrophē*, so dominant in the tradition of speculative theology and metaphysics, must be qualified. What I mean is the following.

The erotic absolute might be said to mirror this movement: origin as the indefinite abstraction or lack; self-exit into otherness; return to self through and from the otherness; now in the end explicit self-constitution, finally determined as fully real. By contrast, the metaphor of the agapeic absolute would run: origin as excess plenitude, transcendence itself as other; creation as finite concreteness, but not for the return of the origin to itself; the "exitus," if we call it such at all, is for what is given as other in the middle; and while there may be a different "return" in the metaxological middle, this is not dictated by the logic of a circular erotic self-becoming; it is gratuitously emergent in the created other as itself trying to be agapeic being; "return" is the cocreation of community by the finite other. In other words, the teleology of erotic being is finally closed, or looks forward to a closure in a completely self-determined whole. By comparison, the teleology of agapeic being is there at work as the opening of being as free community. It is also more rupturing, more anarchic relative to finite ends.

Were the origin conceived in terms of agapeic being, the origin would be creative in a more radical way than could be ascribed to any finite being or process. In this absolutely singular instance, agapeic mind would be creative of the finite other. Would this finite other be simply the externalization of the agapeic original? If that were the case, the origin would not be agapeic at all but erotic, and the created finite other would be the mirror in which the self-relativity of the origin was effected. Instead the agapeic creation of the finite other is for the finite other as other. Finite creation is given its true otherness; and this is irreducibly given, given as irreducible.

This, in fact, suggests the primal meaning of gift. This is the original meaning of the givenness of being: a generosity of being that gives for no reason beyond the goodness of giving being. This, I believe, is the ultimate basis on which also we must think the value of finite being. The worth of being is its being agapeically given. We might say that the "yes" to the being of the gift is ontologically inscribed in the being of that gift. The very giving of the being is itself an ultimate "yes" that is for the being that is given. This is why, as we saw before, when God says "It is good," He does not say simply "I am good," or that it is good for me, or for humans, or for some extrinsic purpose. It is good. It, the being there of the being, is good in itself. This is the primal "yes." This is something different to the elemental "no" and "mine" shaping the psychogenesis of the human self. These are themselves given by the primal "yes," which they ambiguously reveal, and inevitably can come to disfigure. The power of freedom is the power to let the "no" shut out the primal "yes," closing itself in, by closing transcendence as other out.

Here we come across the generosity of freedom as a gift. The absolute origin as agapeic, as it were, sacrifices its own for-itself. It gives, and supports, and preserves the other as other. It lets it go as other. Freedom is not originally given in the expectation of a return on the gift. One gives for nothing. God gives for nothing. This is why in one respect being is for nothing. Being is without a why. There is a kind of agapeic nihilism implied by this, but the nihil is not any negating or destructive nihil. God does nothing for Himself; everything is done for the other. There is a sense in which nothing is *for* God. God lets be, since everything given by God is for that thing, given for that thing itself.

Since our minds and being are so insistently erotic, such absolute agapeic being seems hardly conceiveable, much less believable. Should this surprise us? The whole thing is something exceedingly perplexing. The agapeic origin is infinite transcendence, hence always beyond dialectical self-mediation. As overdetermined plenitude it is more than any definite whole. "Mystery" is constitutive of its excessive being. No determinate intelligible structure could capture its "essence." Its "essence" as plenitude is beyond every determinate why.

This gives us an inkling of why God's justice or mercy can so appall thought. We suspect a radical *disproportion* to our definition of what is a true measure. Our understanding of measure is generally defined in terms of a determinate calculable standard—an eye for an eye, say. Our measure is generally the measure of equivalence. But there is no equivalent measure in the case of the agapeic origin. The origin as an indeterminate plenitude is beyond measure, beyond all our measures. The measure of the absolute original is beyond every equivalence. There is a divine disproportion in this measure that can cut across and subvert every finite standard we erect.

The inequality of the agapeic origin is its unequalizable plenitude. This is why we can never really think it, since all our thinking tends to reduce the other to the measure of our own thought, or make its otherness intelligible in terms that, more or less, are equivalent to ourselves. The plenitude of the absolute original overflows determinate wholeness. It is transcendence, a surplus, an excess, an overwholeness. It is not perfect but pluperfect: pluperfect not in a past, or present being achieved and having being achieved; not pluperfect in terms of the promise of the about to be achieved; its pluperfection is impossible to measure in terms of the dimensions of past, present, or future; it is pluperfect beyond the measures of time; it is pluperfect in the immeasureability of eternity.

The pluperfect excess is for the finite other, as already having been given being as other. The greatest gift is independent being in which one would not ask for anything back. The absolute origin gives and demands nothing back. Again this is beyond measure, for our giving and return are subject to determinable measure. A giving without the expectancy of return is beyond our measuring. This is pure gift. God demands nothing. This is agapeic expectancy: nothing determinate is expected in return, which is not to deny a solicitude for the other. Solicitude is expectancy that the gift will be not only well received but well *lived*.

Does this mean that we must give nothing back? If nothing is demanded of us, must we turn from the giving source without any expectation on our part? The situation is more complex, if expectancy is solicitude for the other. One can give for nothing, but that giving for nothing is informed by good-will to the other; so its expectancy is such as to want no malice or violence to befall the recipient of the gift. This gift given for nothing is in the light of its *goodness* to the beneficiary.

So it is not that we must give nothing back, like ontological ingrates. Nothing is asked of us, yet in that non-demand there opens up the mystery of free generosity. That is, the non-demand of the source solicits freely the giving of agapeic mind *from our side*. "It is good;" and we humans taste the "It is good" knowingly. The mindful taste of the "It is good" arouses in us a call to *live beyond ourselves* the "It is good." *We* become the expectancy of nothing. *We* are asked by the expectancy of nothing that we try to give for nothing, beyond the goodness of the giving itself. The gift of agapeic being solicits in us the gift of agapeic being. We, too, must be the release of the divine freedom of generosity. Is this "the glorious liberty of the children of God?"

As finite others we are free; but our freedom is a gift of generosity. There is no univocal reason for it. The reason for it is that it is good. This freedom becomes itself creative in generosity. We give back because this is the onto-logical *anankē* of freedom. The deepest character of being, human and di-vine, is agapeic freedom. We give back because nothing is demanded of us. There is no external coercion. We give, demanding nothing for ourselves. We give ourselves to and for the other.

7. Agapeic Imaging

I am talking about what might be called an "agapeic imaging" between our being and the origin. What do I mean? First, to be "like" is not to be identical. So also to be an image can be to image, where "imaging" is not an inert likeness inscribed on the structural features of a picture. Frequently we think of imaging as a mirroring structure of relations: for example, the image in the mirror reflects, in the structure of its internal relations, the original face that has similar structural relations. But what can it mean to image in freedom, in free creation? It must be a likening in dunamis, a likening of possible doing and undergoing. "Mirroring" here means something more elusive. Example: we catch a taste of another in the inflection of a speaker's voice; he speaks just so, though we cannot quite pin it down; it is not univocal; it is ambiguous and shifting; we indicate the "just so" by imitating the voice. Now my point is that this mimesis is at least partly agapeic. For it goes beyond self towards the other as other, and creates beyond self a likening of the elusive singularity of that other. What I mean by agapeic imaging is like this likening. Agapeic imaging is a being like, both a mimetic undergoing and creative activity in the difference between one and the other, that yet is in community with the other across the difference.

There is an indeterminacy in freedom, and in the plenitude of giving. This indeterminacy is very difficult to image, precisely because it is so much easier to picture an already definite reality. We then can see the comparison point for point, determination for determination. For how can an indeterminacy image an indeterminacy? Is not imaging a relatively determinate relation? How then image a determinate relation between two indeterminacies? Must not the imaging itself have the character of indeterminacy? Must it not be a non-fixed imaging? Must not the image be in some respect indeterminate? But how so, since to give an image is already to make determinate, at least to some extent? Are we not talking about an image that is a determinate indeterminacy? If so, must it have no rigid boundaries, must it be no closed whole? Must it not be an open whole?

Not incidentally, this notion of an open whole is how above I described a creation or an art work, as the issue of creative generosity. It seems we must think of our own created being also as an open whole. We might say that "indeterminate imaging" calls attention to the freedom of the two sides of an agapeic relation that, as a relation, absolves itself from constraining the two sides. But again what can such an open relation be, since a relation seems to be a determination of two determinate terms? An open relation must be an open relating. The activity of freedom, the activity of freeing, must enter into this opening of relativity, this open imaging between free indeterminacies. In other words, the relativity of two centers of freedom is very different to the relativity of two terms that are more or less univocally determined. This freeing of relativity, this free opening of relating, I think, marks the middle as metaxological. The middle itself is the space of free opening and relating. It is a community of different centers of self-transcendence.

And the following questions prove unavoidable. What gives the middle? What gives the middle as a space of open being? What opens the middle? What keeps the middle open? What opens and keeps the middle for good? These questions ask us to think about the origin, not only in light of the relativity of mind and being, or of self and other, or of man/world and God, but of the ultimate grounding of relativity. What ultimately gives relativity? Moreover, what ultimately gives relativity as marked by the opening of real freedom?

These questions do not concern just the origin of differentiation, but the origin of relativity and free difference. For one might conceive of differentiation as the necessary articulation of an origin that by necessity is self-differentiating. But if we have to take into account free difference, as we must, and the form of relativity appropriate to free difference, as we do, then the differentiation cannot be simply the necessary self-differentiation of an origin that must explicate itself. The latter necessity might be conceivable within the terms of an erotic absolute. But the givenness of free difference and the relativity that opens community with it, the opening of open community, cannot be adequately conceived in terms of an erotic absolute, a self-differentiating unity.

This is why, I believe, we must think the agapeic origin: giver of the middle in its being; giver of the middle as the space of open being, keeping its openness open, and keeping its openness for good; keeping it open for the good of the other, as it dissolves its own "dominance" of the beings within the relativity. This self-dissolving keeping is the agapeic renunciation of the origin's "for-itself," in order to let the "for-itself" of the finite creation come into its own. Then the finite creature out of its own being might turn again with agapeic generosity towards the other, and the origin as other. Agapeic creation is for the good of the creature. When something is "for good," we imply a certain irrevocability—perhaps not quite "for ever," but certainly a promise beyond the immediate present, a fidelity. What does it mean: "being kept for good?" In what is our being in safe keeping? Keeping is a kind of minding, as when we say a child keeper minds a child. To be a keeper or minder is to take care; to be kept or minded is to be cared for. This is solicitude again. We cannot address what is at stake outside of an affirmation of the ontological good of the middle.

Agapeic imaging asks of us a mindfulness that does not compromise the transcendence of the ultimate. Dwelling in the middle and articulated in metaphysical metaphors, such mindfulness opens in itself to otherness. There is no appropriation, hence surmounting of the excess of transcendence. Agapeic minding, in us, is a readiness for the advent (to use Augustinian terms) of the superior within the interior, its advent in its inward excess to interiority itself, which breaks open any pretension on the part of interiority to be the measure of the superior. Interiority itself cannot be completely self-mediating, for into its most profound self-mediation an other otherness, even beyond its own inward otherness, breaks through.

Thus, we can relate agapeic imaging to the double mediation: there is the erotic movement of philosophical perpexity from the inferior to the superior, from human lack to divine plenitude; there is readiness for the agapeic movement from the superior to the inferior that is the metaxological intermediation of the other out of the excess of its own transcendence. This is the overflow of the surplus of transcendence towards the finite being and for the finite being as other. This second movement is the agapeic advent of transcendence as other, an advent that comes to the self from the other, resisting every closure on itself of erotic self-mediation. It is the agapeic rupture of all self-mediation that claims self-sufficiency or completeness.

There is a manifest disproportion in this advent of transcendence. The agapeic absolute is the "more," the Unequal Itself: it cannot be equalized with any finite determinate counterpart or substitute. As the Unequal Itself it has no equivalent with which it could be interchanged. And yet interchange is given by it. No directionality of our giving out of finitude would be the proper equal of the directionality of its giving of being out of excess. This divine disproportion is beyond all equalization, undertaken from the side of, or for the sake of immanence. Any "equalization," out of transcendence, is the agapeic gift of the Unequal Itself.

Thus, agapeic imaging is related to the doubleness of metaphysical metaphor as it imaginatively enacts a self-transcending opening to this otherness. Agapeic imaging is an ontological acknowledgment that the being of the divine other always exceeds our comprehension. It asks for a redoubled salutation of the excess of transcendence. This redoubled "yes" is beyond erotic transcendence. Its very power is, paradoxically, the granting of a powerlessness of the human being in the face of the ultimate excess, the Unequal Itself. There is agapeic patience in this powerlessness. There is the grateful acknowledgment that all being and power is given from the other, the agapeic origin. Beyond univocal reduction, beyond dualistic opposition, beyond lost equivocation, beyond dialectical subsumption or erotic possession, there is a metaphysical praise and thanks for this other, and all that is given from it.

8. The Agapeic Origin, Perfection and Compassion

If we think of the origin as agapeic, do we have some basis for thinking of God as "compassionate." Do we put ourselves at odds with traditional doctrines that would place God beyond all suffering? Is the view more consonant with process theology, and reformed theistic views seeking to bring their idea of God into closer harmony with the Biblical image?

If I am not mistaken, the process view thinks of God more erotically than agapeically, resulting in difficulties about the genuineness of God's aboluteness and transcendence. We might well criticize transcendence reduced to a dualism, but the agapeic view reformulates otherness and transcendence in a nondualistic way. Clearly, when Whitehead speaks of God as the companion in suffering, he is approaching an agapeic conception. But otherwise his God seems to be erotic: God's primordial nature seems to be lacking without the actuality of finite creation; God's subsequent nature is more intensively fulfilled and concrete, having taken up into the primordial nature what is of essential worth in the finite creation. This is not as far from Hegel's self-mediating absolute as it might seem. By contrast, the agapeic view offers a different understanding of the origin, of the primordial God other than an erotic or process conception. If we do want to say God is process, we must say the process is agapeic. From this we can grant, first the plenitude of God in Himself, second His transcendence to finite creation, third the gift of creation as the issue of agapeic generosity, fourth the being-for-itself of the finite creation which is given to be itself as other to God, and finally the promise of agapeic community between creation and the origin out of the agapeic promise of creation, as well as out of the agapeic actuality of the origin.

And of course, if God as agapeic is "compassionate," we must look differently at the attribute of *impassivity*, traditionally ascribed to God by all doctrines stemming from Aristotle's thought thinking itself. The influence of Greek metaphysics is undeniable with regard to the traditional privilege accorded to impassive self-relativity, self-sufficient self-relation. Aristotle's view is only one of the the most explicit. One finds expressions of it in all views influenced by Parmenidean ideas: the magnificent solitude of the circle; the well-shaped sphere of being; the absolute beauty in Plato's *Symposium*; Stoic self-sufficiency, *autarkeia, ataraxia, apatheia*. To be divine is to be a self-sufficient completeness, beyond lack, beyond need of the other, entirely free of relativity to the finite other.

This traditional conception of perfection or completeness claims to be free of the lack of eros. Nevertheless, on this view dynamism is implicitly conceived in terms of the movement from lack to completion. The completion tends to be seen as beyond all dynamism, as other than dynamic, to the extent that dynamism is tied to lack. I, too, think of the absolute origin as marked by an internal wholeness beyond lack. But it is beyond lack, not as stasis devoid of dynamism, but as wholeness beyond finite wholeness, as overwholeness, as power beyond will to power, as dynamism that does not move from lack to completeness, but from wholeness to the "more," or from more than wholeness to the real other as given its otherness for good, irrevocably. Creation calls forth the other into being, for good, irrevocably for itself; and yet its truth for itself as an other, is not simply for itself.

This overwholeness cannot be adequately described in terms of impassivity. On the contrary, the transcendence beyond itself of the agape of being recalls (see chapter 4 above) the going out of compassion towards the other, and in the interests of release of the other from affliction. It recalls compassion's suffering with the other, the share in suffering as the basis of a community of solidarity. It recalls solidarity in suffering as the way to alleviate suffering, of the heightened suffering which lightens suffering and releases the heart, loosing it from its own self-created closure and the agony of its death.

If the absolute origin is agapeic, our thinking cannot be easily confined by Pascal's contrast of the God of Abraham, Isaac, and Jacob and the God of the philosophers. For that matter, I find far greater richness in the tradition of speculative philosophy than recent reiterations of Pascal's contrast would have one believe. How so? In the tradition of metaphysics, the idea of God was inseparable from the idea of the Good. Properly speaking, we are already beyond the stock contrast with this. Perhaps the Good was too often conceived in erotic terms: whether as the perfection and self-sufficiency at the end of all lack; or in terms of absolute mind as self-thinking thought beyond all otherness, rather than as agapeic mind as thought both at home with itself, yet also in community with what is other to itself; or in terms of the absolute univocalization of being by the so-called metaphysics of presence. But if God is the Good, the good as agapeic origin was always there as promising the rupture of the divine closure of impassive self-thinking.

Today we must pay explicit attention to this ambiguity. The tradition must be purified of the unacceptable consequences of the ambiguity. To this end, the present reflections hope to contribute. The tradition must also be defended from the caricatures, now ingrained as "truths," of post-Nietzscean and post-Heideggerian polemics. When these polemics do not close the question, they often cast a shadow of superiority which implies—we have left *those* questions behind us in the despised tradition. But perplexity about ultimacy is never behind us. Perplexity about ultimacy solicits a more radical opening of the question.

9. Agapeic Being and Givenness of the Between

The agapeic view does have implications for how we understand the givenness of the between. What are some of these implications? And how do they ask us to rethink the middle? First, being in the between is given, in the richest sense of "gift." Creation is the free giving of being to the finite other by the agapeic origin, and given for the finite other. This means there is no logical deduction of the many from the one. There is no Spinozistic geometry of *natura naturans*. There is no dialectical logic of God as self-created in the world. The agapeic origin demands a sense of transcendence between the origin and created being that we cannot find in Spinozism or Hegelianism, or idealism generally. Instead of the self-creation of the absolute relative to the finite other, we must speak of the generous giving of the plural.

Moreover, the pluralism of finite being is ontologically positive. It is not a fall from the One. Nor is this affirmative otherness to be interpreted as dualistic opposition; the latter is the offshoot of a contracted sense of the other. The agapeic origin supports plurality in its otherness. This is what its letting be means, the freeing of finite being into its own being "for-itself." This free "for-itself" is never a closed self-mediation, but may in turn become an originating openness for-the-other. The finite entity becomes itself the promise of being an agapeic source, a finite original in itself, capable of opening to the other for the other.

Further, this affirmative sense of ontological otherness implies that there is no univocal or dialectical monism of the whole. This does not imply an equivocal dualism that would infect something like Hegel's unhappy consciousness, or impel a Parmenidean nostalgia for an original undifferentiated whole. These latter are common responses in the philosophical tradition. The agapeic origin implies that the creation of the finite being is good in itself. But this, too, is traditional: to be is to be good. Not that the view has always been understood. Monistic and dualistic views, whether interpreted univocally, equivocally or dialectically, might seem to exhaust the possibilities, but this is not so. The plurality of finite entities comprise a metaxological community of being. The ground of that community as agapeic gives the other its irreducible otherness, but the metaxological interplay of self and other is ultimately grounded in the agapeic origin. The agapeic excess of ultimacy alone makes ontological room for the irreducibility of the affirmative otherness of finitude, that is, its "integrity" of being as other to the origin.

Nor must we think in terms of an absorbing god either. The agapeic origin and the metaxological community are not reductive of the singularity of beings. This is one of the most difficult points: to hold in balance such singularity such as we find in the idiocy of being and the ontological community of being. Most often any stress on singularity breeds a nominalistic or atomistic vision, relative to which plurality become a mere collection or aggregation. Contrariwise, stress on community breeds a social totalism, wherein the singular becomes a function of the larger whole and its network of internal relations. Neither of these views is adequate to the metaxological community, nor the agapeic grounding of otherness, nor the singularity of each being as a "this."

It is hard to conceive of such singularity, and this, not because the singular as singular always escapes our universals, but because the required knowing stems from an unconditional love of the "this" as a "this." We have an intimation of this when we relate to the singularity of a specially beloved this. We love some singular beings in a singularly unconditional way, say, a child, or a spouse, or a parent. The hard thought here is the universalization—in no abstract sense, and in no dialectical sense either—of that kind of knowing love. This universalization of singular knowing is called for by agapeic mind. This is not the knowledge of essential structures, but of the "this" as a "this" in its ontological worth, as a uniquely singular being. The human being flickers with the odd trace of such an agapeic mindfulness. Only a God could love the singular with this kind of creatively supportive knowing.

I think of the words of Jesus: Are not five sparrows sold for two farthings, and not one of them is forgotten before God? There is not a hair of your head that is not numbered (Luke 12, 6-7). I take it Jesus meant absolutely what he said. There is no logical or epistemological qualification: like "for the most part" God knows of the sparrows or their concept. He does not say: "For the most part, there is hardly a hair on your head . . ." or "In general, or by and large, or all other things being equal, these flocks of sparrows . . . and so on and on." Our ontologically ungenerous minds are minds of "for the most part," thinking of the "by and large," of the "in general" of things. Our minds are by and large *always* blinkered to the being of singularity in its truth. God does not take surveys of general probability or statistical averages. Agapeic mindfulness is not a calculation of statistical averages, but is absolutely attentive to the singularity of even those singulars that to us are insignificant, singulars that to us indeed are fundamentally repugnant.

This is an unsettling conception. It cannot be fitted without remainder into the Aristotelian concept of science with its emphasis on the universal and necessary. It is very different to the ethical neutralism of modern scientific views. Here, too, and not unlike Aristotelian science, any sense of singularity is immediately suspended, or subordinated to a neutral generality, or regularity, or uniformity. Even the human being becomes an instance of a more general process or law. Obviously such a view is antithetical to any personalistic view. By contrast, the idea of the agapeic origin suggests the ontological ground of genuine selfhood as singular and personal.

Of course, as I indicated before, the scientific view has always been afraid of so-called animism, anthropomorphism. For scientistic mind being is not even erotic; there would be too much of the "for-the-self" in this erotic conception; being is neutrally, indifferently there. Scientific universality shuns every personalization of being, and often does so from the genuine motive, even generous motive, to understand nature as it is, without subjectivistic superimpositions from us. The irony again is: This search for neutral disinterestedness springs remotely from a kind of agapeic mindfuless, one that is willing to grant nature's otherness, in all those aspects recalcitrant to our domineering desires.

In other words, the desire for scientific neutrality which deprives being of its agape presupposes the energy of that agape in the open mindfulness of the scientist himself. The scientist cannot explain himself, explain his own scientific openness, explain his own desire to be open to nature as other, if all of being is as neutral as he describes it. In claiming to be open to an indifferently there nature, he becomes closed to the being of the one, the scientist himself, who must exemplify something of the power of agapeic mindfulness to know nature in its otherness. Let the scientist think about himself as a singular concretion of the original energy of being. He may still try to describe himself neutrally, but this very neutrality just squints at the promise of agapeic mind he actually displays, in trying to transcend himself and his own closed "for-self."

If the agapeic view has truth, this scientistic view must be seen as an abstraction from the originary abundance of being in the between. It is an abstraction that is not devoid of truth, but it is one that is not the absolute metaphysical truth of being. It remains at the level of the univocal conception of being, where univocity here means the reduction of the inexhaustibility of thereness to clear and distinct hypotheses, indeed mathematicized conceptions.[10] Ironically again, in this univocal reduction the very singularity of a being vanishes, as does its worth. At most, singulars function as instances, or counterexamples, but this is just the loss of singularity in the sense at issue. There is no univocal concept of the worth of a being.

In this regard art is closer than science to the metaphysical truth of being as metaxological. It is truer to the charged thereness of being and beings. It sometimes tries to name the singular thisness of a "this," just so in the very givenness of its ontological texture. If aesthetic value, properly understood, points to metaphysical value, it is also relevant to the agapeic origin, for the origin of the art work is itself an act of generosity, an agapeic and festive celebration of being. Art concretizes the power of origination, but originative power is not "ours." We do not create; we participate in creation. We create because it is given to us to be originative. Artistic origination is here metaphorical in a metaphysical way. Creation is the generosity of being. Again the work of art is double: created for itself, and hence marked by a certain immanent perfection; but it is also a "for-itself" that is an opening to the otherness of being as inexhaustible enigma. It is an answer that is again a question. It is an imagistic concretion of the indeterminate astonishment and perplexity that fuels our metaphysical quest for the ultimate.

There also follows from the agapeic view a qualified exoneration of the truth of existentialism. I mean its critique of logicism. I am not subscribing to

---

10. See *Being and the Between*, especially chapter 2 for fuller discussion of univocity.

an absurdist existentialism, though there is an absurdism that is infinitesimally close to a ringing affirmation of being as meaningful. A vehement assertion of existence will not do, as if all that was needed was a kind of tantrum of irrationality. Rather, the truth of the existential is a certain affirmation of singularity that cannot be completely validated in logical terms alone. But this truth is betrayed if one cannot find some way to seeing the placement of the singular within the community of being. The metaphysical tantrum of irrational self-assertion has its basis in the freedom that gifts the self. But the absolute singularity of selfhood has its ground in the agapeic origin as the giver of freedom. Devoid of this relativity to the ultimate other, narcissism and nihilistic subjectivism are the lot of this self.

The point made above about scientistic neutralism also applies here, namely, scientism's forgotten origin in a more agapeic view of thinking mind. What I mean is that there is a logicism which, as rational openness to the universal as other, is superior to a perverse subjectivity which curves back on itself, seeking self-closure. The freedom of such self-closed subjectivism has its ground in the giving of the agapeic origin; but the assertion of this freedom turns against this ground, indeed against any free other that might curb its pretension to absolute self-sufficiency or self-mediation. Such self-retracted singularity is the perversion of agapeic being, a perversion itself let be as free by the agapeic origin. By contrast, the much reviled logicism presupposes a certain agape of mind that enables logical mind itself to think the universal. A logicism that is not closed on itself in the immanent rational idolatry of its own concepts is itself a manifestation of agapeic mind. Hugging one's own precious subjectivity may be a perverse form of erotic desire, certainly not agapeic. It fails to reach even the openness to the other that is present in self-driven eros. Finally it is not even a circle of self but a self-contracted point of lack. It expresses freedom in the distracted form of merely equivocal desire. It is neither dialectical nor metaxological.

10. Agapeic Being and Evil

The agapeic view has consequence for evil deserving special mention.[11] Consider the saying: God lets his sun shine equally on the wicked and the righteous. What does this mean? Is there not something unbearable in this? Does one have to draw away to survive intact? For it means that God does not hate the hateful; God loves the evil, the hateful, the enemy. From our moralistic standpoint the idea of God as agapeic is monstrous. Nothing is to be hated, not even the hateful. All being is good, even the evil. The lost are

---

11. For further discussion of evil, see *Beyond Hegel and Dialectic*, chapter 4.

to be loved, the damned are to be loved. God's agape seems to be an insult to our justice, a reckless generosity exceeding the measure of our rational self-mediating morality, such as the noble Kant loved.

On this point I find a surprising companionship between Jesus and Nietzsche. Both point "beyond good and evil," defined relative to such a rational self-mediating morality. Life gives rise to the repulsive, the monstrous. We harbor in ourselves the seeds, some sprouting, some dormant, some rampant, of the monstrous. But this, too, was created, given as a possibility of being by the agapeic origin. The ugly vile being is loved as being; it is in being because loved. There is here a horror to our consciousness that would always see God on the side of the good, meaning our good, our reason, our morality. But it is obvious from the way the sun shines on saints and monsters that God's agape is the absolute final freedom that is dissident to all our justified moralistic bleatings. This is a letting be that allows the monstrous, that makes allowance for the monstrous, that makes a way even for the hateful.

We see another side to a previous suggestion concerning the peculiar proximity of Nietzsche's "innocence of becoming" and God's "It is good." Good here is not good for us, or good for a particular purpose; good here is the goodness of being *simpliciter*; it is a ontological goodness that exceeds and escapes every finite teleology. The creation in its ontological integrity is not there in being just for a specific purpose, molded to the usefulness of a particular entity, like the human being. Before all finite teleologies, all use, all proximity or distance to human happiness, creation is good *simpliciter*. The innocence that Nietzsche craved was just this ontological transfiguration of being there, its purification from its encrustation by finite human teleologies, and their soiling effect on the goodness of creation.

I know Nietzsche would shun the latter way of talking, because he assimilated it to another soiling finite teleology. But good, in the prior sense indicated, points to a kind of ontological innocence, creation fresh issued from the agapeic origin, beyond our good and evil, before our good and evil. God's "It is very good" names the superlative worth of being, the issue of perfection from the pluperfect. There will come the evil, the repulsive, the monstrous, yet there remains the memory of the first "yes": a kind of idiotic amen to the whole, that Nietzsche tried to sing, and towards which the agapeic origin draws and urges us.

What will our idiotic amen be? It will be rinsed of complaint. It would sing without accusation. One would not judge and condemn creation. Not that evil is to be blinked. There is evil in finite being that sets itself up as superior to the origin and wills to redo the creation. It insinuates: God botched it; we will teach Him a thing or two; we will be one up on God. Here begins ontological revolt and usurpation. This usurpation, too, is allowed, and the darkness of our presumptuous improvement on the original goodness.

Will the idiotic amen be a letting be that either incites to evil, or endorses evil as ineradicably ingredient of the whole? How can the idiotic amen let evil be, let it be, and sing the goodness of creation? I cannot think of any other reason than this: the radical "let be" must be because of the supreme value of freedom. Without freedom there is no community of otherness, no community of finite others, no community between finite being and its origin as transcendent. Without freedom we end up, in the end, in a monistic absorbing god. But within the assimilating whole of any absorbing god, God's "It is very good" makes no ultimate sense. When God says this He is not congratulating Himself. It is the finite other as free, as other that is very good. Once again: Not I am good, but it is very good.

I hear the understandable objection that if we sing this "It is good," we end up as quietists. Quietism is one of those words we easily bandy about. The usual implication is that "being quiet" amounts to being tranquilized into slumber. Quietism is then the wretched sleep of mindless contentment. Who would endorse this? After all, it is the supremacy of agapeic *mindfulness* that is the point. Yet it is good to be quiet: to listen, to hear, to recuperate. There must surely be a quietness in "It is good," a quietness so radical it startles the soul into a different kind of hearing. To hear this "It is good," perhaps the human being would have to give itself over to a new quietness, one that would shatter false faith in the endless chatter that presumes to speak sense into the enigma of being. One asks again: Are we capable of hearing this "It is good" without a radical breaking and remaking of our being, a breakdown of the hubris of our categories, a breakthrough of the voice of an other beyond all our categorial mastery?

But even if there is this quietness, it awakens an unexpected inquietude of spirit. "It is good," and yet why does the face of things sometimes look to us so foul? Whence the ugly, the vile, the violence of being? A quiet quieter than any quiet requites its gift with a sleepless inquietude, with another restlessness that is, once again, inexplicable in terms of any finite teleology. The inquietude springs up as the charge that one *work for the good*, not simply for this good or that good, this or that human project, but for the good *simpliciter*, and for this or that project in terms of the good. This is a charge, a recharging of our being that would issue in a new way of being. And the charge is indeterminate but in an affirmative sense: overdetermined, inexhaustible, the issue of a plenitude. It is not an indefinite vague longing, nor is it antithetical to commitment to determinate goods and projects. Indeed it asks commitment to the realization of singular goods within one's world. But it comes from a source in excess and surpassing all such finite goods. Somehow the restless energy of our own being is a charge of the agapeic being, and the charge is that we *be* agapeic.

The inquietude of quiet asks us to "strive" to be agapeic. Admittedly, in this context to speak of "striving" is unavoidably ambiguous, since "striving" evokes an erotic movement of self-surpassing. From this ambiguity can follow the misunderstanding that agapeic being could result from some autonomous act of willpower. "Striving," if agapeic, must always keeps itself open to a possible reversal of directionality, a communication from the other from beyond the claimed autonomy of will to power. Agapeic "striving" is not erotic desire, but a different goodwill. There is a letting be of evil which is a "no" to evil in the very "yes" to being as good. This complex condition is very hard to articulate. Wise people traditionally have spoken of returning loved for hatred, good for evil. But love and the good cannot be forced. Must one then be willing to die in the face of the malignant? In the face of the malignant, goodwill is without any guarantees. This is a trust in being exceeding human power. Forgiveness itself is a recreation from nothing. We cannot create from nothing; neither can we recreate. In a sense, only God is capable of forgiveness.

Lear in his idiot wisdom came to say: None does offend; none, I say. . . . Tragic loss and suffering, tragic madness issue in the new attitude: No "justice"—no revenge. Surely only a God could be such as to condemn no one, nothing? To condemn nothing; not merely to forgive; but to love. Who can take upon himself evil and violence, guilt and punishment and death? There are evils and forgivings, and no human being is on a par with them. One must confess that for philosophy such ideas are at the outer edges of comprehensibility. Yet we must not disarm such possibilities by conveniently placing them in the category of anthropomorphic projections, such that when later we "demythologize" them, we extract from them some reasonable, innocuous platitude. We think we have moved reason to the edge of the comprehensible. Instead we have blunted the sharp terror of that edge. Instead of expanding the comprehended, we have camouflaged our flight from the incomprehensible, in a chatter of psycho-babble, or perhaps demythologizing hermeneutics.

What am I talking about? I am talking about the elemental truth of the heart. I am asking the simple question: Who can forgive? Who can really forgive? Does any honest person step forward and without fear and trembling claim: Yes I have forgiven; I am forgiving. A truthful person hesitates here with an infinite hesitation. Who can absorb the infinitely crushing burden of evil, and yet not be crushed? Who would allow themselves to be absolutely reviled, allow an other to revile them, though good, and yet love, love *simpliciter*?

Suppose I am insulted, yet I restrain the revenging fist of violence. I might be tempted to congratulate myself, but is not my restraint witness enough to the violence already at work in my forbearance? Who can absolutely forgive, free of any grinding of the teeth? Who can? Who can bear the unbearable burden of evil? Who can carry the absolutely crushing burden of evil? What power of good would not be crushed by evil? Not a human power; no human being can bear it without being crushed. Only a God. The agapeic origin means: bearing the infinitely crushing burden of evil, and yet not being crushed. How could *we* think this? How *dare* we think this?

11. Agapeic Being Beyond Reason?

What of the truth of the agapeic view? Can I prove it is true? I cannot. There is no foolproof proof in this matter. Proof moves mind along a sequence of determinations or categories and their definite connections. Determinate relations of intelligibility and evidence are understood to obtain between determinate grounds, however simple or complex, and the determinate conclusion that is to be established on the basis of such rational and evidential grounds. But relative to the agapeic origin we are talking about the ground, not only of categorial or intelligible determination, and indeed of evidential determination as given, but also of being as being. In brief, we are at the limit of the principle of sufficient reason.

Sufficient reason has the ontological and epistemic faith that for every determinate happening there is a proportionate reason or cause. Ultimately there are no causeless happenings or determinations without reason. What is the validation of this principle of sufficient reason? What is the reason for holding this principle? Is the principle self-validating? If, in the application of the principle, one determinate reason serves as explanatory cause for another determinate happening, is there any *determinate* reason why this principle itself should be held as universal? Must we not raise the possibility that sufficient reason is not sufficient to explain itself? Sufficient reason is not sufficient reason to explain our faith in reason. There is something other to sufficient reason, understood as the determination of reason to ground its claims in intelligible and evidential determinations of beings, and this "something other" is prior to determinate happenings and connection, and is not itself a determinate being or intelligibility.

In other words, the ultimate ground of reason cannot be reasonable in quite the same fashion as the determinate reasons obtaining within a system of reason. Our consent to the principle comes from a reason beyond sufficient reason. Hence, I would say that in our ontological and epistemic commitment to the principle, there is always an element of venture, or faith, or consent. Our trust in the principle, and the trust in rational intelligibility evident in the principle, are themselves initially *nonreflective concretions of agapeic mind*. For in consent to the principle, mind gives itself over in trust of the intelligibility of being and beings as other. But before giving itself over thus, it has *not first secured* this trust in the intelligibility of being-other. It goes towards the other with the prior expectancy that being-other will present itself to mind as rationally intelligible. The principle of sufficient reason is a *later* logical and reflective formalization of what, in the prior acting of thinking, is the self-transcending movement of agapeic mind towards other-being and its intelligibility.

Determinate reason is thus a determination of the agapeic power of mind that easily can forget its own origin and ground as coming from beyond itself. The power of mind to be open to an other is a given. Indeed it is potentially the freedom to think all possibility, and hence is a freedom beyond the principle of sufficient reason. Freedom is also the freedom to think what has no determinate reason or why. The principle of sufficient reason is not self-sufficient. Determinate reason cannot be completely self-mediating but points beyond itself to a ground of reason that is not determinate. This ground is just what I am calling the agapeic origin.[12]

Let me illustrate the point with reference to some other significant views. Consider Schopenhauer's Will which he claims is beyond that principle. Will is the ultimate ground of all being, and intelligibility. Schopenhauer's Will is, like Hegel's absolute, an erotic absolute. The erotic language he uses is very evident. Will is described as a striving of blind energy that manifests itself diversely in the world, and most concentratedly in the human being. The genitals themselves are the metaphysical organs of the Will, Schopenhauer says explicitly. Our knowledge of our own will, contra Kant, is our access to the thing itself. Schopenhauer's Will is not a generous will that creates an other out of agapeic excess. It is certainly not neutral; it is dark and sinister, not a good will, and not at all a reasonable will. As an erotic source it is also a futile absolute, since there is no final self-completion. Unlike Platonic eros, Will here is endless striving, ultimately fruitless. Schopenhauer, we might say, reinterprets Kant's purposiveness without any definite purpose as a *purposelessness* beyond all our definite purposes. But the transcendence of determinate purpose is a futile transcendence, not the agape of the good.

Hegel, by contrast, identifies the ultimate origin with reason. Further reason itself determines itself through the erotic negativity of dialectically self-determining thinking. All reason is dialectically self-determining, and there is no ultimate transcendence in the autonomous circle of thought

---

12. The grounding trust and the nature of intelligibilities is more fully explicated in *Being and the Between*, chapter 9.

thinking itself. Hegelian *Vernunft* shows the erotic absolutizing of self-deter-mining reason. If Schopenhauer's erotic origin is imaged on will as beyond all reason, reason is always merely instrumental, as are all our purposes. There is an excess to Schopenhauer's origin which is its excess to reason. There is no excess to reason of Hegel's absolute.

I have sympathy with the view that the origin is dark, but not in the sense Schopenhauer intends. The darkness of the agapeic origin is not this blind Will from whose ultimate futility we must escape. The agapeic origin may be on the other side of sufficient reason, but why should this imply malignancy in the origin? We need not exclude the possibility of an ultimate mindfulness that in itself is agapeic and beyond what we call the principle of sufficient reason. Mind is a manifestation of the agapeic original energy of being; that energy itself as agapeic is mindful of the other as other. Hence mindfulness need not be always instrumental. There is a sense of mindfulness beyond instrumental reason, the recognition of which makes the usual con-trast of reason and will, Hegel and Schopenhauer, less than ultimate. The ultimate mindfulness is agapeic; the ultimate agape is a mindfulness of the other. If we grant some sense of excess, such as Schopenhauer indicates, the excessive will must be thought agapeically, not only erotically.

It is helpful to listen to Hegel when it comes to mindfulness *beyond* instrumental reason. But Hegel's understanding of mind, just like Schopenhauer's sense of will, must also be rethought agapeically, and not just erotically. Perhaps Schopenhauer was trying to get at something like this other meaning, when he speaks of a rupture and reversal of will into will-lessness. But he does not characterize this will-lessness in terms of an agapeic amen to the marvel of being. Being for Schopenhauer is always erotic, and eros is eros *turranos*, not eros *uranos*—a tyranny that leads to nothing in the end. Hence, Schopenhauer's will-lessness is an *extirpation* of the very root of being as futile tyrannical will. Must the root of being, the ultimate origin, be dark in this malign sense? Might it not be a surd to instrumental reason just because it is an excess of plenitude, and not the malign futility Schopenhauer wants to escape?

Schopenhauer's Will strikes one as a degenerated Platonic eros. Nietzsche's diagnosis of nihilism in Schopenhauer is here to the point, though he is wrong to assimilate Plato to Schopenhauer. Beyond sufficient reason, Nietzsche himself offers a sense of the origin as Dionysian. His statements are always ambiguous, but this Dionysian origin is often described in explicitly erotic terms, especially in earlier work, and in less guarded moments later. For Nietzsche to be true to his deepest insights, I believe he would have to rethink the Dionysian origin in more agapeic terms. He never managed entirely to purge from his thinking the toxic residue of nihilism and Schopenhauerian Will. There does break forth in his thinking a song of plenitude. I say a song of plenitude, since Nietzsche clearly recognizes that true creativity was the issue of overflowing excess, and not just compensation for a lack. His greatest inspiration came to him in this overflow of excess. But this, too, is equivocal, since Nietzsche describes this in the language of self-aggrandizement.

Yet again, in tandem with the toxin of nihilism, Nietzsche, too, was wary of the anthropomorphism rejected by science. Indeed he was more suspicious of the seemingly self-glorifying anthropomorphisms than of the self-deprecating ones. I mean those anthropomorphisms that imaged the world as manifesting the ultimate good. Not for a moment would I deny that the metaphor of the agapeic origin can be abused as a cover for moralistic humbug. We falsely place our smug self-congratulation at the apex of the moral world order. This, of course, is an abuse of the metaphysical metaphor, a failure of thought, a dishonesty.

Nietzsche's hermeneutics of suspicion was often lacking in the openness to the other required of agapeic mindfulness. Suspicion can mediately serve agapeic mind, in the sense of clearing the way for our acknowledgment of repressed forms of otherness. Because of a failure to think through the ambiguities of agapeic creation, Nietzsche exhibits a deep tension, if not impossible contradiction, between his consent to a valueless universe and his will to transfigure all being in *amor fati*. If the universe at bottom is valueless, if there is no agape inherent in being itself at its most ultimate, no such transfiguration can be effected by any human self—this transfiguration is metaphysical folly, and not in any benign sense. To make the human self the only source of agapeic being, while all being is valueless, is ultimately to make the human self valueless, and hence not a genuine source of agape. At some point there has to be an elemental confession: I alone cannot effect this transfiguration. Nietzsche could not utter this final confession: I cannot do it; I am nothing; the transfiguration is beyond me, always in excess. If he could have said "I am nothing" differently, a different release might have been communicated . . . towards the other. Because of his horror of pity, and compassion, Nietzsche choked on the possibility of this agapeic release.

And yet this is how he was struck in his breakdown—breakthrough of the stifled compassion, compassion for the thrashed horse in the street in Milan; the wretched, degraded other, the worthless other that the mad Nietzsche rushed to embrace as worthy of embrace for itself. This is metaphysical pathology in the literal sense: a pathos, a suffering of breakdown at the extreme, before the other, this wretched animal that only a God could love so singularly. Then there is the astonishing letter, written to Peter Gast, and signed by the Crucified: "To my maestro Pietro. Sing me a new song: the world is transfigured and all the heavens are full of joy." This is usually dismissed as the ravings of a madman. I pause and ponder. Is such dismissal a protective prudence by the scholar against what might be at stake at the extremities? But what protection can there be, if we think beyond the principle of sufficient reason? These are the ravings of a madman, but there might yet be a wisdom in this idiocy. The new song of the transfigured world might sing the breakthrough of the agapeic origin: simply seeing the heavens as they are. Yeats said of an inspiration: "Black out; Heaven blazing into the head." And afterwards, when determinate mind returns? The excess of the agape destroys the frail light and a night of unknowing descends? The ultimate truth of agape may be a death that is life, a life that is on the other side of death. At least let us hesitate and confess we are no longer sure.

Have we moved to embrace a nihilistic irrationalism? Once again the issue is much more complex than any simple either/or between reason and unreason. "All is permitted": This is a formula for nihilism. Dostoevski thought that if God does not exist, all is permitted. Thus, he pitted faith against nihilism. I would say "All is permitted" is also a name for the promise of the agapeic origin, the majestic and horrifying promise of a freedom given to us and that will be let be, even unto the most demonic evil. I repeat, it is not: If God does not exist, all is permitted. It is: Because God exists, all is permitted. There is an unnerving silence of God in forbearance before the horrors we have inflicted on creation.

This patience is perplexing and horrifying. That is, the freedom of finitude given by the agapeic origin lets be even demonic possibility. The extremity of spiritual nihilism as a free possibility is allowed by the agapeic origin. This freedom at the extreme of nihilism forbears to let one assert as truth the view that nothing in being is intrinsically praiseworthy. One is allowed to shout the false as the true, to peddle the malign as the good, to pass off the pseudo as the integral. This, in truth, is not the truth of being, but the agapeic truth is forced on no one, since there is an absolute freedom of consent or refusal here.

This truth is not like mathematical truth or scientific truth. At the extremity of nihilism the "yes" to being can also be uttered, and one will commit oneself to this truth: the truth of being as good and praiseworthy. This metaphysical truth is not an impersonal necessity or universality but a singular decision between the above "no" and this "yes." Everything else follows from this. Nihilism as freely chosen is the extreme face of refusing freedom. The free self, as given its otherness, faces itself away from the agapeic origin. This facing away is granted by the agapeic origin as a possibility of freedom; the origin lets the other let be for itself. The ultimate truth is agapeic freedom. There is no compulsion. There may be an appeal to the free self that it freely face back towards the origin. In the open space between our freedom and the origin, we see that the middle world, too, is good. But this metaphysical consent is beyond the bounds of logical necessity.

12. Agapeic Being and Being True

There is no logicist "proof" of the agapeic origin, for there is no "proof" of that sort of the truth of a metaphysical metaphor. Nor is there any univocal criterion by which to judge. I know this offers no help to a more methodically or logically oriented thinking. This is not my fault. It is not anybody's fault. It is simply a recognition that the issue is not the kind that will yield to a univocal logicism.

And yet there is, in all of this, an entirely relevant way of "being true." The matter calls for ceaseless thought, for thinking does not come to a dead halt with what seems a convenient dispensation of "proof." If metaphysical thinking is not exhausted by a univocal logic, it is capable of a truthfulness, a kind of elemental honesty. And this, even in all the categorial camouflage sometimes so daunting to the uninitiated. This elemental honesty is the hardest of all, demanding a severity of mind that is beyond all logical rigor, a severity that seeks truthful generosity of mind. The truth of the agapeic view is to be measured relative to the profundity of one's hermeneutics of being. Profundity? Yes. One is compelled to speak *de profundis*. Our participation in being, our living mindfully, life minded philosophically, these are the experiment, the metaphysical experiment. One wants to know what is, what is ultimate, as best as one can know, as best as human thought can even formulate its own metaphysical perplexity and astonishment before being. There is no answer to the question of truth except that one thinks, and thinks, and thinks about the essential perplexities of being. And then one thinks again about the paltriness of one's last thought, without respite.[13]

Agapeic mindfulness is the self-transcending of thinking that will not rest in itself before it has opened itself ultimately to the other as transcendence. There is no method even to raise its perplexities, for they cannot be forced. To be open to such thinking about the ultimate is itself an issue of freedom. There is no guarantee that one will even get to the point of discerning the grip these perplexities have on thought. One may prefer to sleep the quiet of everyday certitude. One may prefer to sleep the metaphysical quietude of scientistic self-assurance. One may sleep the quietude of moralistic confidence. One may sleep the quietude of pragmatic accommodation, or of nihilistic indifference. One may force oneself into the anxious torpor of aggressive rejection of the ultimate questions. One may even construct a variety of imposing philosophical justifications for each of these forms of metaphysical slumber.

---

13. See *Being and the Between*, chapter 12, on the different meanings of truth and being true. See chapter 1 on astonishment and perplexity. The distinction between these is important, even though it is recessive in the present work.

The question of truth, the charge of truthfulness, awakens in us a meta-physical insomnia. Any "answer" that comes in that insomnia is often coupled with the troubling thought that one's insomnia is itself in the chains of only another slumber. One cannot force wakefulness. Mindfulness keeps alive its truthfulness in the hope that something of the truth may break through its struggle with sleepiness, break beyond the dread that its thoughts are dreams of nothing.

Simply to be is the metaphysical test, to be as mindfully as possible. One's encounter with being in its otherness, in suffering, in sublimity, in ethical sacrifice, in joy, in sickness, greed for life, disgust with life, self-hatred, serenity, the refusal to be beaten, the willingness to try to lay aside one's egotism, all these as entering the life of our being between constitute the elemental metaphysical experiment. Since the middle remains a middle for us, the metaphysical venture does not freeze into a finalized form. I reiterate: there is no univocal answer to an essential perplexity; such a perplexity is not a determinate problem; not the Ideas, not the One, not the *Ens Realissimum*, not the *cogito*, or the transcendental ego will serve as the deter-minate answer. Not even the agapeic origin is intended as a determinate answer to a determinate problem. It is heard and thought as a different answering—from out of the otherness of being—to the second, overdetermined perplexity of our being in the middle.

There are moments of breakthrough in the middle when this sense of being as agape is manifested. Such moments can give rise to the philosophi-cal mindfulness that I call "thought singing its other." A significance, impos-sible to exhaust determinately, is given in such manifestation. It might take a lifetime of thinking to plumb the significance of such manifestation. And yet in the interim one consents to the enigma of what is enigmatically mani-fested. Where is the "proof" of the praiseworthy goodness of being, the "proof" of the truth of such a song? Where is the determinate logic of the truth of a song of being? You cannot prove a song. You cannot prove a metaphysical "yes." Both are idiotic from the standpoint of determinate in-telligibility. They are not unintelligible, but their idiocy implies a intimacy of being that resist complete objectification in neutral categories. It is not that we must give up on logic, but philosophical logos must expand, or be ex-ploded, to try to think the significance that is borne by such song.

So if we cannot have proof beyond question, there is a being truthful in the between. Philosophical honesty is required as itself a middle mindfulness between the truthful perplexity about the ultimate and ultimacy as itself the truth of transcendence. This involves wager and hazard in the between, where there is no possession of the truth of the ultimate. There is a being truthful, as fidelity to the self-transcending of mind in its perplexed ecstasy towards ultimacy.

What I say demands no invidious *sacrificium intellectus*. I am only too aware of our final inability to control the appearances of things. If the agape of being has any truth, that truth must not be the mere projection of wishful thinking. The thoughts proffered here are entirely compatible with the unsettling fact that the otherness of being inevitably subverts all merely wishful thinking. Since the process of becoming mindful of being is never univocally finalized, there are moments of breakdown, as well as breakthrough, moments when the middle loses for us the radiance of agapeic festivity.

What then? The middle may revert to the insipid neutralism of scientistic nihilism. Or worse, the shadow of the sinister may hover ominously over our best efforts to be truthful. The face of being becomes dark, it becomes a burden, it becomes a vale of tears, it becomes a prison, we experience our own selves as dungeons. We cannot snap the chains of illusion that keep us in thrall. We suspect we are being helplessly sucked into a gurge of metaphysical stupor. It is as if the otherness which the origin makes possible now mocks us with the taunt: the origin has hurled finite creation out into a cold void, and would have no more to do with it. There is a horror when we experience this abandonment, especially if we have any memory of the moments of breakthrough when being offers itself as festive agape.

Some exposure to this horror of abandonment is inescapable in the middle. A standard philosophical response to the above denial of "proof" is a skepticism that shakes its head in dismay. But standard philosophical skepticism is only a pale shadow of the shaking of foundations of which I speak, a merely conceptual play acting with ultimate groundlessness, often not even that, but an inconsequential game of clever negation. The banality of cleverness becomes clear to us. The real exposure to groundlessness, to abandonment, to ontological shaking, causes a trembling of being deeper than any earthquake in the neutral cosmos of science. Let the academic skeptic shake his head all he may, but when this other shaking is felt, the silliness of mere cleverness will find nowhere to hide, and no category will offer it shelter.

Our exposure to groundlessness, our thinking of ground and groundlessness, makes us more than all categories, more indeed than the cosmos, within which we would be as nothing, were we not entities marked by the privilege of thought which can honestly go to the extremes. We may flee from this trembling into the consoling neutral universality of logic, or mathematics, or science. We may settle for a pragmatic nihilism that works as long as we stay away from the thought of ultimate groundlessness. This pragmatic diffidence about the ultimate may even be necessary, simply to continue to live. For the truthful thinking of groundlessness may literally break one, destroy one, become an intolerable truth. The consolation of science, or everydayness here is bought by a necessary blinding before the dread of horror. Surely we should not canonize the results of such a blinding with the privilege of the truth?

Such truth is one species of lie: a necessary lie may be a pragmatic truth, but for all its necessity it may still be a lie.

When we refuse this lie, and undergo the darkening that comes with this honesty, instead of the song of being, there can come from one's lips a choked outcry of despair. A howl of desperation, or tragedy, or madness breaks from our lips, like Lear's Howl, Howl, Howl. I think the cry of desperation is deeper in its truthfulness than the well-validated truth of mathematical, or scientistic neutralism, or the pragmatic truth of customary everydayness. In the dry desert of abandonment, in this skepticism beyond all logical skepticism—for it is a skepticism of being, not of logic—the cry of despair springs from the antithesis of creation from nothing. It springs from retraction into nothing. Instead of the song that emerges into being from nothing, the song destructures itself into a Lear-like Howl.

Instead of the "It is good," the Howl cries out "It is nothing, it comes to nothing." This is ontological skepticism because it is the destruction of every claim to ultimacy that we attribute to any and every finite form of being. Everything less than the ultimate comes to nothing. The universal devouring of false ultimacy threatens to issue in the final negation: nothing is ultimate, there is nothing ultimate. Such a thought can shatter one's very being. Such shattering happens.

Sometimes the cry of despair is spoken aloud, but it need not be even uttered, for it to be at work insidiously. Can we think the possibility of absolute emptiness here? As long as we continue to be, is not that continuation itself a gesture of faith against complete retraction into nothing? Is not the Howl itself a choking outcry of the energy of being that would otherwise be a song? Does not erotic being itself powerfully testify to the impossibility of sustaining such complete retraction, when the lack of eros seeks to invert itself into its opposite self-affirmation?

Even more, is there not a level at which the cry of ontological despair hides in itself an *appeal*? It is nothing, I am nothing; but in the extremity of groundlessness, my outcry is an appeal, perhaps involuntary, for the agape of the other. I cannot create through myself the oasis of water that would alleviate me, heal me in this desert of groundlessness. I cry out to the other, for the agape of the other. The happening of appeal affirms what the outcry of despair ostensibly denies. Despair at being is itself let be as a possibility of freedom by the agape of being. But the happening of its outcry may secretly attest to the longing for, hence implicit love of, that agape which the words of its outcry seem to negate.

13. Agapeic Being, the Last Yes

The truth of these views is only evident from the life of the between itself, our living of it, its living of us, and from the deepest thought we bring to bear on its ambiguous enigma. In the desert our sense of agapeic being can be destroyed, never to be recuperated. Everything said here will then appear as pious illusion. I think a philosopher has to risk the possibility that his own words will mock him. There are no guarantees. Yet one must try to think as best one can. The truth of agapeic being may be very often dark to us in the middle, yet it calls us in the darkness to the service of its truth.

Honesty dictates that I confess this much. I have not been immune from savage derision of everything I say. In searing uncertainty of the ultimate truth of what I say, perhaps of all philosophical saying, I have said to myself: "It is nothing." The night descends on one's best logic. The voice chokes and one cannot sing. One is like Macbeth who murdered sleep, and yet lives to ask: "But wherefore can I not pronounce 'Amen?' I had most need of blessing, and 'Amen' stuck in my throat."[14] Let us say that Descartes' thought of the malign genius seems never to be completely exorcised, Descartes' brilliant ruses notwithstanding. The *cogito* cannot do it. God may do it, but if He does it or has done it, while we are in the between we cannot know this with univocal certitude. In some measure we remain shadowed by the evil genius in the unsettling thought that behind our backs our best reasons are bewitchments.

One may undergo the breakdown of one's best effort to make sense of things, the breakdown of one's best logos. One may confront the failure of one's saying to connect with being. This failure may be ontological too: breakdown of one's life as itself the living embodiment of a lie. One then is engulfed by the "It is nothing." This is a kind of negative indeterminacy that counterparts the affirmative indeterminacy of agapeic being. "It is nothing" seems in part pathological, since it is not anything in particular that worries one. It is not something determinate and definite about which one says: "It is nothing." The "It" is itself "nothing." This is the breaking, retracting, subverting side of the enigmatic, indeterminate perplexity that exceeds all determinate problems and answers. From the standpoint of the various regions of determinate intelligibility—moral, commonsense, mathematical, scientific, psychological and so on—this "It is nothing" is pathological.

I will agree to say yes, it is pathological; but I cannot agree that this pathology is always a mere sickness. It may be pathological as inciting us to metaphysical openness to being beyond all manipulable determinacies. It may be pathological in revealing the ultimate pathos of our groundlessness before the ultimate. Philosophy itself is a pathology. It is a logos of our

---

14. *Macbeth*, II, ii, 31–32. Macbeth is paralyzed by the exchange between the servants guarding Duncan, one of whom says "God bless us!" and the other replies "Amen." " . . . I could not say "Amen," / When they did say "God bless us!" " "

pathos: an attempt to speak the truth of our undergoing of being; an attempt to speak honestly about our suffering outcry for the ultimate truth. We count for nothing, and yet we are; and we are because we are not nothing, but are willed to be by the agapeic origin. This metaphysical pathology opens the extremity of philosophical honesty because here we suffer a truth we would not otherwise will. We are made to suffer into a truthfulness that knows that no human thought is the measure of the truth. The edge of all human truth is pathological in this sense. There is no cure from metaphysical pathology by retreating from the edge and trying to convince oneself that everything on this side of the edge is health.

Wittgenstein was simply wrong when he said that the bumps we get on the head from running against limits are signs that philosophy is a sickness. We do get bumps, but it is the interpretation of the bumps that is the rub. Contra Wittgenstein, they may be signs that philosophy can be honest about the sickness that calls itself health, or well-being. Philosophy is the pathology that comes from honesty about our pathology. The cure cannot be to say that the sickness is not a sickness, but a category mistake, or whatever. This is analytical whistling in the dark, or witch doctoring.

The failures of honest philosophy are the wounds of its greatness. The greatness of philosophical mind is revealed in its allowing itself to risk destruction by its own negation. There is humility in this greatness, patience beyond arrogant self-assertion. This can be a Golgotha of mind as erotic, that is, as seeking to define the otherness of being in terms of the self-mediating categories of mind itself. The Golgotha of erotic mind is its breakdown before what is other to its self-mediating categories. The rupture opens a space wherein we suffer the other, wherein mind finds breaking through its own agapeic possibility.

What is asked is a complete step beyond instrumental mind, even instrumental mind that has been eroticized.[15] Is not the philosopher, after all, a *philos*, a friend? Is this friend capable of love of truth as other, willing to consent to its ultimate otherness as truth? Can this friend not give herself or himself over, in community with this other, beyond an economy of scarcity; for the friend is not exhausted or depleted by the giving, but augmented. We

---

15. Think of Luther's metaphor of reason as a "whore" whose eyes are to be torn out. How does this compare with the tragic blinding of Oedipus, or the gouging of Gloucester's eyes? Is there not a face of mindfulness which is not the mask of a "whore," a face whose eyes seem sightless, if we judge by the "seeing" of instrumental mind? Is not reason the "whore," reason the *ancilla*, reason instrumentalized into the "handmaiden" available for indiscriminate use? The "whore" is available with an empty eros; there is no real giving to the other at all; there is no gift. Instrumental reason, thus eroticized, tries to put out the eyes of metaphysical mindfulness, but there are eyes beyond eyes it cannot touch.

might say that metaphysics is a service of the truth, but there is instrumental service, eroticized or not, and there is agapeic service. The servant of truth tries to live fidelity to truth. To serve he must consent to embody agapeic mind, though he be haunted by the shadow of death.[16]

Before this death, logos trembles at the possible nothingness under all saying, the nothingness of all saying. There is a savage doubt at the opposite extreme to that singing astonishment before the sublime mystery of the being there of beings. In the metaxological middle, savage doubt and singing astonishment coexist in radical tension, struggle against each other. There can never be for us a complete reduction of one side to the other. The tension defines our being in the middle.

Let loose, the rasping voice of doubt may want to destroy, may reach a pitch of desperation that it wills only to destroy. It may try to exhaust itself in unbridled negation. I know this. I know this too: in the moment of exhausted negation, a stray note from the song may suddenly sing out, as if from nowhere. In the abyss of despair, *de profundis*, the cry wants to sing. I look at the dying sun in sunset, glorious in the last burst of its going under, and the mockery goes quiet. I hear the lonesome call of a bird flying home and the mockery quietens. The agape of being cannot be killed completely. The grateful memory of such breakthroughs, the moments of singing astonishment, make it impossible to hug the savage negation. The violence of the latter now seems to be the void twisting of the very generous energy of being itself. Every destruction is seen as parasitical on the original power of creation. It would be a radical betrayal of being not to let the memory of the singing astonishment speak again to one. It seems to me that the ineradicable memory of this astonishment makes it impossible to break finally with being as agapeic excess.

In response to the latent appeal in our outcry of despair, there arises another appeal from nowhere, from the indeterminate. The void seems to be transfigured into the plenitude. The wind buffets the grasses on the shore, and the mocking voice subsides. Quietness, emptiness, startled astonishment,

---

16. Recall Socrates' obsessive reiteration of his own "service to the god" (*tēn tou theou latreian*, *Apology*, 23b). It would be a desertion, a betrayal if he reneged on the station in life the god has given (28e). We find also a paradoxical interchange of plenitude and poverty: he endures a great poverty because of this service of the god, for which he was never paid (31c). The service of the philosopher is noninstrumental, for this *philos* philosophizes for nothing, in service of the truth, and in the case of the teacher, in the service of truth as the good of the other. Philosophizing is an agapeic giving of mind. Socrates' poverty ensued from the giving. There also is gift in his being simply what he is, a kind of gift of the gods (31b). His death will transfigure him into a sacrificial victim—witness beyond death to the truth of thought.

a gentle going out purged of mockery. I am passing, I am a passage way, and a song for nothing, given from pure generosity, passes through. I am wrapped in a sudden peace, for an interim, I am blessed and could bless, how long? I do not know, expanse of time seemed not to count. I am roused from the bewitchment stopping me saying—it is good. There comes over one a breaking through of an impossible trust, an idiotic inability to shake off the promise of being as good. The grateful memory shames one vis à vis one's present truculence. The desperation that thrashes around in itself, as its own thrall, is penultimate to breakthrough into this ultimate trust.

For there is no ultimate answer in the sense of a packaged foundationalism. There is the ever renewed thinking of the ultimate, nurtured on memory of those moments of breakthrough, and on struggle with the periodic devastation of the darkening of being. The doubleness persists. Thus again our need of metaphysical metaphors: They do not dissimulate the failure of logos before the ultimate, yet they help articulate the original energy of mind as agapeic. They are a venture and a risk, mind at the edge of its control of the determinate, mind at the edge of its own self-thinking and self-mediation, mind launching into the open space between itself and the unmastered ultimate. Thought is in the void beyond self-mediation, the void of that space between us and the ultimate other beyond the void, the agapeic plenitude beyond the void. This void is a space of possible destruction, but it is also the space of freedom, and the only place for us of new creation.

In that void of freedom, there may arise the slow radiance of a new consent. This is an amen to being that is idiotic to prudent rationalism, folly to secular atheism, nonsense to positivism, affrontery to the moral earnestness of social activism, pious to an all too-knowing Nietzscheanism or hermeneutics of suspicion. Death, our last suffering act and greatest pathos of being, will offer the ultimate occasion for us to strip the masks. This idiot wisdom is elementally honest. There comes a point of renunciation of all doctrines, or theories, or systems, or ideologies, all those conceptual shelters we erect against the ultimate. Beyond the last buffer of any master category, even a "category" like the metaxological, idiot wisdom has nowhere else to go. It must say its "yes" or go under. The last saying is not reducible to any categorial system. It is a simple, elemental "yes" or "no" to the worth of being.

We cannot retreat into any of the reductions of being that make the middle a medium of our own self-mediation. We may know nothing, and yet we must say "yes" or "no." One might die shouting, expiring in a Howl of "no." There is every reason to say "yes," and still we refuse, for we are the only beings marked with metaphysical ingratitude. Ingratitude is a refusal of pathos, a refusal of the worthy other as beyond our self-mediation, as marked by a perfection that is for itself, and that does not have to ask our permission to be. Ingratitude cannot let be. It secretly hates the worthy other for being worthy in its own right, without the permission of the one who would have all other-being bow to its autonomy.

Metaphysical gratitude is not only a thanks for this or that, but in the this and the that its consent overflows the boundaries of determinate things. It is our share in agapeic festivity, a share that issues in a salutation of the generous excess of the origin. Ingratitude is hiddenly a hatred of this festivity without a why, of being good for itself, being good simply because to be is good. Instead of salutation, ingratitude lays a blight on being. Its offspring is like the cuckoo's egg: a parasite that heedlessly battens on the life of its host. We humans are sometimes the metaphysical cuckoos that talk to rationalize our battening. There are philosophies that lay cuckoo's eggs.

As there is an ultimate thanks, there is a last ingratitude which retracts beyond all theories, and systems, and categorial saying. This is the retraction of freedom into a stubborn knot of inward otherness which cannot be entered, cannot be forced, and which must be let be, in its complete curvature back on itself. The agapeic "yes" can only offer its festivity to this retracted self, and let the void be the space of proffered welcome—an allowance that also allows the response of a malign hostility.

Being is astonishing, being is appalling. It stuns, it troubles, it delights. We are in it, found and lost in it. In the end we want to say, it is good, but we can never know until the end, in the void beyond all categories, if we have the elemental greatness of spirit, or humility, needed to say honestly: It is good.

Index

Absolute Original, 21, 135, 137, 205, 210, 231

Absorbing God, 84, 212, 238, 243

Adorno, T., 14

Aesthetic and poetry, 6, 22; and the tragic, 36, 39; and presencing, 66, 67, 109, 110, 112; and mindfulness, 77, 99, 100; and theodicy, 136; and Kierkegaard, 194; and value, 228, 240

Aesthetic self, 66, 100

Agapeic being, chapter 6 *passim*; 54, 110, 157, 192

Agapeic origin, 131, 133, 135, 137, 150, 196, 207, 209, 213, 215, 217, 218, 220, 221, 231, 234, 235, 237, 238–242, 245–251, 255. See origin

Agapeic self, 70, 73, 112, 128, 148, 192, 193

Alexander, 74

Alienation, 16, 18, 104, 130

Analytical Philosophy, 8, 112

Anaxagoras, 28

Anthropomorphism, 213–215, 239, 248

Aquinas, St. Thomas, 4, 8, 35, 37, 126, 183, 188–190

Aristotle, 1, 12, 16, 27, 34, 37, 53, 106, 116, 119, 174, 179, 183, 188–190, 194, 200, 206, 215, 220, 236

Artist, 30, 43, 94, 151, 228

Astonishment, x, xi, 3; metaphysical, 25, 34, 39, 45, 47, 54, 173, 228; and desire to know, 106; and metaphor, 209; and art,

240; and breakthrough, 256. See perplexity, wonder

Atheism, 21, 186, 214, 215, 257

Atomism, 61

Augustine, St., 11, 204

Autonomy, 78, 121, 190, 191, 193, 195, 244, 258

Bacon, F., 88

Barden, Garret, 8

Beauty, 2, 21, 31, 164, 228, 236

Body, and death, 42, 44, 164; and "myness," 66, 68, 69; and torture, 89, 90; and aesthetic, 109, 110; and suffering, 151

Breakdown, and loss, 29; and logos, 33, 35, 254, 255; and Nietzsche, 43, 248; and erotic selving, 148; and categorical hubris, 243

Breakthrough, and skepticism, 35, and Nietzsche, 116, 248, 249; and death, 164; and evil, 243; and agape of being, 251, 252, 257

Buddha, 151

Caesar, Julius, 74

Capitalism, 86

Categories, and otherness, 16; and perplexity, 25–26; and loss, 27–28; and tragic, 39; and singularity, 58, 60; and Kant, 140, 142; and God, 188, 189; and ultimacy, 205, 207–210;

259

and origin, 218; and proof, 245; and good of being, 251, 252, 255, 258

Causality, 78, 79, 138, 184, 222

Child, 46, 47, 51, 54, 68, 69, 95, 96, 114, 120, 126, 150, 152, 234, 239

Christianity, 197

City, 85

Closure, 15, 16, 56, 57, 65, 66, 141, 151, 155, 174, 180, 191, 205, 221, 230, 235, 237, 241

Coherence, 15, 140

Collingwood, R. G., 8

Comedy, 24

Communism, 85

Community, and being, 12–16; and home, 19, 94; and singularity, 57–70 *passim*, 81–86; and love, 90; and likening, 95, 97–100; and agapeic mind, chapter 4 *passim*; and agapeic being, chapter 6 *passim*

Contemplation, 52, 186, 228

Continental philosophy, 17, 229

Contingency, 173, 184, 186–190

Contradiction, 14, 33, 34, 62, 140, 202, 248

Cusanus, N., 194

Dante, 2

Death, and exile, 17, 19; and tragic loss, 28, 30, 31, 37, 38, 40–46, 49, 51–54; and idiocy of being, 59–61, 69, 74, 75, 82, 83, 93; and torture, 89–91; and Hamlet, 95–97; and God, 101; and "view from nowhere," 111; and eros, 121; and agapeic being, 126, 128, 249, 256, 257; and erotic selving, 148, 149; and consent and mockery, 151, 163, 164

Deconstruction, 13, 14, 20, 24, 35, 62, 63, 71, 72, 117, 126, 180, 181, 194, 217

Derrida, J., 14, 20, 82, 181

Descartes, R., 1, 16, 52, 55, 64, 79, 137, 154, 159–162, 169, 171, 179, 183, 185, 188, 202, 203, 224, 254

Desert, 69, 121, 189, 253, 254

Despair, 3, 36, 38, 100, 177, 185, 186, 194, 197, 253, 256

Dialectic, 6, 8–10, 14, 21, 24, 34, 48, 50, 82, 113, 134, 170, 205, 210, 218

Dialogue, 24, 33, 34, 44, 59, 98, 100, 136

Dignity, 87, 90

Diogenes, 27

Dogmatism, 175, 176

Dostoevski, F., 28, 52–54, 178, 181, 182, 191, 194, 229

Doubleness, 14, 20, 63, 94, 110, 203, 221, 235, 257

Doubt, 18, 32, 98, 100, 111, 134, 140, 159, 217, 256

Dualism, 14, 65, 68, 73, 94, 103, 104, 110, 149, 170, 171, 216–218, 229, 236, 238

Earth, 3, 5, 28, 44, 74, 87, 110, 128, 222, 223, 227, 228

Eden, 132, 195

Einstein, A., 103

Empiricism, 56, 72, 73, 109, 139

Equivocity, 13, 14, 33, 67, 73, 79, 105, 117, 125, 143, 154, 162, 168–171, 191, 200, 207–210, 217

Eros, 9, 11, 32, 55, 87, 104, 107, 109, 114–118, 121, 128, 130, 131, 135, 137, 140, 141, 148, 160, 169–172, 204, 212, 216, 220, 236, 241, 246, 247, 253, 255

Erotic origin, 134, 247. See agapeic origin

Erotic Self, 11, 70, 132, 148, 152, 153, 192, 195, 204, 214, 230, 235

Eternity, 14, 24, 48, 95, 96, 133, 134, 136, 137, 164, 167, 169–172, 196, 200, 202, 204, 212, 215–217, 219, 220, 232

Ethics, and the ethical, 22, 25, 39, 40, 41, 86, 108–109, 136, 149, 177, 182, 222, 223, 227, 229

Evil, 21, 24, 79, 82, 157, 159–162, 171, 183–185, 195, 196, 213, 219, 226, 241–245, 249, 254

Exile, 17, 20, 82

Existentialism, 241

Extremes, 3, 14, 18, 29, 43, 55, 100, 104, 130, 146, 175, 176, 178, 180, 197, 199, 200, 224, 252

Failure, 33, 35, 85, 105, 119, 133, 145, 148, 158, 164, 207, 210, 248, 254, 257

Faith, 4–6, 30, 32, 34, 37, 41, 43, 44, 52, 72, 147, 169, 184, 192, 197, 243, 245, 249

Fall, 3, 68, 124, 135, 148, 157, 158, 163, 169, 175, 187, 195, 197, 216, 238

Family, 2, 17

Fear, 6, 14, 23, 42, 111, 127, 151, 244

Fichte, J. G., 76, 77, 138

Finitude, 45, 84, 119, 137, 160, 167, 170, 184, 185, 188, 199, 205, 216–218, 235, 238, 249

Flesh, 43, 60, 66–68, 70, 89, 90, 110, 164

Folly, 28, 140, 141, 148, 167, 194, 223, 229, 248, 257

Forgiveness, 164, 244

Francis of Assisi, St., 151

Freud, S., 128, 132, 140, 196, 214, 215

Genius, 43, 79, 94, 107, 144, 159–162, 169, 177, 183–185, 254

Gift of being, 45, 51–54, 133, 144, 150; and eros, 131; and contingency, 187; and possibility, 192; and agapeic transcendence, 196; and being as good, 221, 230–232

God, xiii, 2–5; and philosophy, 35, 37; and Lear, 41, 60; and loss, 50–53; and Fichte, 77; and finite self, 80, 84; and idiocy of being, 100, 101; and "God's eye view," 111; and Adamic naming, 124; and Leibniz, 137; and after the Fall, 157–163; and Nietzsche, 169; and perplexity, 173, 178–196; and truth, 176; and Ens Realissimum, 200; and thought thinking itself, 202–204; and agapeic being, 212, 213, 215; and Hegel, 216; God's generosity, 221; and "It is good," 226, 227, 229–232; as agapeic, 234–239; and evil, 241–245; and nihilism, 248, 249; and Socrates' service, 256

Gratitude, 117, 258

Grounds, 178–180, 202, 206, 212, 215, 222, 245

Hamlet, 3, 7, 31, 35, 45, 95, 96

Hegel, G. W. F., 1, 2, 8, 11, 12, 14, 15, 18, 20, 21, 24, 27, 29, 33, 36, 37, 40, 41, 43, 47, 48, 50, 51, 54, 58–60, 82, 113, 116, 120, 126, 134, 138, 140–143, 145, 146, 150, 153, 176–179, 181, 185, 188, 191, 204, 205, 207, 208, 215–220, 236, 238, 246, 247

Heidegger, M., 8, 20, 42, 82, 130–135, 181, 216

Heraclitus, 106, 162

Heteronomy, 8, 79

Hobbes, T., 132, 154

Holism, 12, 56, 59, 61

Holy, 37, 83, 151, 228, 237, 256

Homer, 98

Hume, D., 8, 56, 62, 70, 72, 77, 138, 154, 184, 187

Husserl, E., 29, 34, 104, 109, 141, 177, 179

Hyperbole, 19, 83, 183

Idealism, 6, 8, 9, 62, 63, 65, 112, 132, 137, 139, 141–149, 181, 182, 201, 238

Idiot self, 65, 73–75, 79, 85

Idiot wisdom, 49, 101, 163, 164, 197, 244, 257; idiocy of being, chapter 3 passim

Idolatry, 86, 186, 189, 190, 210, 214, 229, 241

Immediacy, 48, 59, 67, 132, 133, 152, 195

Incommensurability, 170

Infinitude, 72, 205, 221

Innocence, 172, 195, 221, 242

Inspiration, 248, 249

Instrumental mind, 64, 195, 196, 229, 255

Integrity of creation, 221–224, 227

Intuition, 73, 76, 77

Inward otherness, 48, 60, 86, 88, 89, 92, 180, 203, 225, 235, 258

Irony, 40, 239

Jaspers, K., 181, 207

Judiasm, 197

Kant, I., 1, 9, 14, 25, 27, 73, 76, 112, 138–144, 178, 205, 227, 242, 246

Keats, J., 120

Kierkegaard, S., 51, 61, 64, 169, 177, 178, 181, 191, 192, 194–196

Lear, 27–30, 32, 36, 41–43, 45–47, 49–54, 60, 61, 74, 229, 244, 253

Leibniz, G., 137–139, 222

Levinas, E., 42, 135, 136, 149, 181, 229

Locke, J., 56, 138

Love of being, 121, 149, 150

Luther, M., 255

Macbeth, 254

Madness, 28, 31, 32, 43, 49–51, 100, 152, 183, 229, 244, 253

Marcel, G., 42, 181

Marx, K., 20, 153, 196, 214, 215

Memory, and death, 44, 45; and being shaken, 74; and Plato, 133, 135, 136; and

metaphysical torpor, 252; and break-
through, 256, 257
Metaphor, and metaphysics, 207–211, 213;
and erotic being, 2
Misology, 44, 55
Moloch, 84
Myth and mythic, 34, 37, 44, 52, 59, 100,
106, 116, 124, 134, 135

Naming, 83, 94, 99, 124, 144, 150, 157, 210
Narcissism, 241
Natura naturans, 237
Negation, 48, 50, 51, 89, 127, 170, 176, 184,
252, 253, 255, 256
Nietzsche, F., 1, 6–8, 22, 24, 29, 30, 33, 36–
39, 43, 48, 98, 99, 106–108, 116, 134–136,
150, 154, 169–172, 176, 177, 178, 181, 182,
186, 187, 190, 191, 195, 196, 214, 215, 217,
219–224, 229, 242, 247, 248
Nihilism, 5, 6, 21, 22, 39, 150, 169, 171, 172,
181, 182, 191–194, 196, 222–224, 227, 231,
247–249, 252
Nostalgia, 13, 17, 238
Nothingness, 48, 50, 72, 93, 127, 132, 142,
164, 185, 218, 219, 256

Objectification of being, 64
Objectivism, 103
Objectivity, 105–110, 112, 116
Oedipus, 31, 43, 255
Ontological Revolt, 242
Origin, and Nietzsche, 37, 38; and self, 68;
and eros, 130–135; and Leibniz, 137; and
transcendental philosophy, 141–144; and
transfiguring self, 156, 157; and God, 189,
190; and agapeic transcendence 197; and
metaphor, 207–209; and erotic and agapeic
being, chapter 6 *passim*. See agapeic origin
Original self, 71, 75, 156, 157
Originality, 24, 133, 136, 144

Parmenides, 12, 30, 31, 35, 54, 103, 217, 219,
220
Participation, 85, 108, 109, 143, 202, 250
Particularity, 2, 3, 22, 32, 41–43, 47, 50, 52,
58, 59, 62, 63, 82, 86, 96, 98, 123, 124
Pascal, B., 18, 128, 169, 177, 184, 187, 188,
195, 196, 237

Patience, 17, 51, 52, 69, 74, 122, 123, 128,
146, 150, 151, 162, 212, 235, 249, 255
Perplexity, ix–xiii, 3; and speculative
philosophy 15–16; second indeterminate
perplexity, 25, 26; and tragedy, 31, 33–35;
and self, 69; and prayer, 101; and mind,
103, 105, 106, 108; and evil genius, 160,
162; and consent, 165; and ultimacy,
chapter 5 *passim*, 237; and metaphysics,
209, 211; and truth, 250, 251; and "It is
nothing," 254. See astonishment, wonder
Phenomenology, 21, 47, 58, 141, 217
Piety, 2, 58, 176, 181, 185, 225
Plato, 8, 9, 12, 22, 24, 29–31, 33–44, 54, 59,
98, 99, 118, 126, 130–136, 143, 172, 173,
176, 181, 189, 190, 200, 204, 209, 216, 217,
225, 229, 236, 247
Platonism, 168, 169, 204, 215
Plotinus, 143, 177, 178
Poet, 5–7, 18, 22, 36, 39, 42, 120, 156
Politics, 41, 49, 52, 82, 86
Positivism, 12, 26, 257
Posthumous mind, 44, 53, 111, 163, 164
Prayer, 84, 101, 149, 164
Presence, presencing, 3, 13, 17, 24, 30, 34, 35,
44, 53, 61–63, 66, 67, 69, 76, 81, 83–85, 87,
91–94, 109, 110, 112, 121, 123, 124, 126,
133, 162, 237
Property, 66
Putnam, H., 112

Rationalism, 26, 64, 177, 257
Realism, 112, 113, 143, 145, 149
Religion, 4–7, 21, 24, 32, 82, 100, 170, 197,
215, 224, 227
Romanticism, 6, 144, 182
Rousseau, J. J., 154

Sacred, 37, 38, 80, 83, 84, 90, 101, 182, 184
Sacrifice, 40, 43, 51, 60, 63, 80, 121, 153, 176,
251
Saint, 128, 151
Sartre, J. P., 8, 43, 125, 132, 142, 186, 188
Scheler, M., 215
Schelling, F. W. J. von, 138, 181, 215
Schopenhauer, A., 37–39, 90, 153, 181, 215,
219, 246, 247
Scientism, 5, 39, 177, 241
Service, 126, 174, 254, 256

Shame, 5, 68, 89

Shestov, L., 185, 187, 188, 194–196

Singularity, 3, 42, 46, 47; and idiocy of being,
55–63, 66–68, 73, 77, 79, 83–86, 93–99;
and Cartesian *cogito*, 161, 162; and being
truthful, 176, 177, 178; and God, 238–241

Skepticism, 9, 18, 35, 173, 175, 176, 180,
183–185, 187, 188, 252, 253

Socrates, 2, 11, 17, 23, 25, 27, 31, 33, 37–44,
48, 54, 58, 59, 134, 136, 173, 176, 177, 256

Solovyov, V., 215

Spinoza, B., 1, 12, 28, 36, 40, 48, 177–179,
186, 187

Stalin, J., 74

Stoicism, 96, 152, 186

Subjectivity, 40, 53, 64–66, 72, 82, 108, 110,
111, 128, 147, 203, 215, 228, 241

Theodicy, 36, 50, 136

Thisness, 47, 51, 55, 58, 60, 61, 68, 97, 100,
240

Thomism, 8

Transcendental philosophy, 9, 139, 181

Transcendental self, 73, 142, 143, 147

Trust, 32, 69, 79, 83, 91, 92, 101, 105, 137,
179, 185, 196, 244–246, 257

Ultimacy, and perplexity, xi-xiii; chapter 5
passim; and fourfold sense of being, 11–14;
and origin, 100; traditional approaches,
200–201; and Hegel, 204; and metaphysical
metaphors, 205, 207–211; and erotic and
agapeic being, 212, 215, 217, 219, 229, 237,
238; and truth of transcendence, 251, 253

Urgency of Ultimacy, 11, 22, 182, 183, 204

Utilitarianism, 132

Utopia, 182, 194

Value, of particulars, 3; and nature, 5, 6; and
tragic loss, 32, 39, 45, 49, 53; and
instrumentalization of being, 83, 85, 87;
and objectivity, 109; and devaluation of
being, 171–174, 213–215, 222–228; as gift,
230 and univocity, 240; and freedom, 243

Vaught, Carl, 8

Weiss, Paul, 145

Whitehead, A. N., 215, 236

Wholeness, 9, 57, 80, 131, 174, 211, 216, 224,
227, 231, 236

Wittgenstein, L., 35, 255

Wonder, 5, 34, 82, 85, 106, 137, 150, 157,
168, 189, 197. See astonishment, perplexity

Wordsworth, W., 2, 5

Worth of being, 32, 39, 136, 156, 171, 215,
230, 242, 257

Yeats, W. B., vi, 49, 249

Zeus, 27, 131